Algebra Test Prep and Review

Algebra I & II Concepts and Skills

Written by

Meizhong Wang

Edited by

Joe Walker

Chip Dombrowski

Graphic Design by

Chip Dombrowski

© 2014

THE CRITICAL THINKING CO.™

www.CriticalThinking.com

Phone: 800-458-4849 • Fax: 541-756-1758

1991 Sherman Ave., Suite 200 • North Bend • OR 97459

ISBN 978-1-60144-651-0

Printed in the United States of America by Sheridan Books, Inc., Ann Arbor, MI (March 2014)

Contents

Preface

If you are looking for a quick exam, homework guide, and review book in algebra, "*Algebra Test Prep and Review: Algebra I & II Concepts and Skills*" is an excellent source. Skip the lengthy and distracting books and instead use this concise book as a guideline for your studies, quick reviewing, tutoring, or helping children with homework.

This unique and well-structured book is an excellent supplement and convenient reference book for algebra textbooks. It provides a concise, understandable, and effective guide on basic algebra plus the following topics: factoring, radicals, exponents, graphing, linear equations, quadratic equations, inequalities, functions, conics, logarithms, determinants, matrices, and more.

Lecture notes that built the foundation of this book have been class-tested for many years, and received very good response from students. The following are some sample evaluation comments from students:

- "Excellent ability to make difficult material understandable."
- "I feel Mei is an excellent teacher. She makes everything seem black and white and straight to the point."
- "The material is presented in a manner that is readily understood."

Key Features

As an aid to readers, the book provides some noteworthy features:

- An excellent supplemental and convenient reference book for any algebra textbook. Each topic, concept, term, and phrase has a clear definition followed by examples on each page.
- A concise study guide, quickly getting to the heart of each particular topic, helping students with a quick review before doing mathematics homework as well as preparation for tests.
- Key terms, definitions, properties, phrases, concepts, formulas, rules, equations, etc. are easily located. Clear step-by-step procedures for applying theorems.
- Clear and easy-to-understand written format and style. Materials presented in visual and color format with less text and more outlines, tables, boxes, charts, etc.
- Tables that organize and summarize procedures, methods, and equations; clearly presenting information and making studying more effective.
- Procedures and strategies for solving word problems, using realistic real-world application examples.
- Summary at the end of each unit to emphasize the key points and formulas in the chapter, which is convenient for students reviewing before exams.
- Quizzes at the end of each unit test students' understanding of the material. Students can take the quiz before beginning the unit to determine how much they know about the topic. Those who do well may decide to move on to the next unit.
- "Reviewing and Test Taking Tips" to help students improve their test score.

Suitable Readers

This book can be used for:

- Adult Basic Education programs at colleges.
- Students in community colleges, high schools, tutoring, or resource rooms.
- Self-study readers, including new teachers to brush up on their mathematics.
- Professionals as a quick review of some mathematic formulas and concepts, or parents to help their children with homework.

There are many algebra books on the market, but this unique *Algebra Test Prep and Review: Algebra I & II Concepts and Skills* provides a concise, understandable, and effective guide to algebra.

Acknowledgements

I want to thank Michael O. Baker, the president of The Critical Thinking Co.™, for his support in publishing this book.

Special thanks to Patricia Gray, the editorial coordinator of The Critical Thinking Co.™, for her hard work in helping and supporting me throughout the entire process.

I would also like to express my sincere gratitude for the math editors of The Critical Thinking Co.™, Joe Walker and Chip Dombrowski, for their accuracy in reviewing the book and checking all the answers. Their thoughtful and invaluable corrections and suggestions have helped to refine the writing of this book.

I also appreciate my daughter Alice Wang, who deserves an acknowledgment for proofreading this book.

Reviewing and Test-Taking Tips

Test Taking Tips

- **Scan the entire test as soon as you receive it.**
  - Mark the easy questions you know that you can answer quickly.
  - Mark the hard questions and do those later.
  - Mark the questions that you don't know.
- **Skip the questions you don't know.**

  Don't waste time on tough questions that you're not sure about. You can always go back if there is time.
- **Keep an eye on the time.**

  Make sure you are sticking to some kind of time schedule, so you can finish the entire test within the time limit. Allow a few minutes to check your work at the end of the testing time.
- **Read each question carefully.**

  Don't make some silly errors by misreading the information in the question.
- **Ask questions.**

  If you're confused about the wording or meaning of a question, ask your teacher. Don't risk getting a question wrong because you misunderstood it.
- **Write each step of the answer neatly.**

  It will make it easier to check, and you may get partial credit for correct steps, even if your final answer is wrong.
- **Check your answers.**

  Always check your work after you've finished the test. Make sure you didn't make any careless mistakes.

Reviewing Tips

- **Make a review schedule.**

  Make a review schedule and make sure you have enough time to review all contents before the test.

- **Go over materials and make notes.**

  Go over lecture notes, homework, practice tests, review material, the textbook, and exams of a previous class if available, etc. and make key notes.

- **Make a summary sheet.**

  Write the key concepts/principles/rules/formulas etc. on a sheet of paper and do a quick review before the test.

- **Form a study group.**

  A study group is a good way for students to help each other, review material quickly, and benefit from other's strengths.

- **Go to review sessions.**

  Ask your teacher about concepts and problems that you are not sure about. Also ask which topics will be included on the test.

- **Get a good night's sleep.**

  Try to study earlier (a little bit each night) before the test, do a quick review on the last night, and get a good night's sleep before the exam.

About the Author

Meizhong Wang (Mei) has been an instructor at the College of New Caledonia (CNC) in Canada for more than 23 years. She teaches algebra I and II for students of Adult Basic Education. She has also taught probability and statistics, finite math, calculus, technology math, electronics math, fundamental math, and other mathematical courses in different programs at CNC.

In addition to being an instructor of math, Mei teaches computer studies at CNC, and has taught physics, electronics, and Mandarin at colleges and universities in Canada and China.

The Higher Education Press, one of the largest and most prominent publishers of educational books in China, published the Chinese version of Mei's book "简明电路基础" (*Understandable Electric Circuits)* in 2005, and reprinted it in 2009.

Michael Faraday House of the Institution of Engineering and Technology (IET), one of the world's leading professional societies for the engineering and technology community, published the English version of Mei's book *Understandable Electric Circuits* in 2010.

CNC Press published *Math Made Easy – Essential Math Concepts Review* in Canada in July 2011, and issued the second edition in April 2013.

Lily Chow and Meizhong Wang published the English and Chinese versions of the book *Legends of Four Chinese Sages* in 2007.

UNIT 1 FUNDAMENTAL CONCEPTS

1-1 THE REAL NUMBERS

The Real Number System

- **Natural numbers** are the numbers used for counting. $\{1,2,3,4,5,6, \ldots\}$
- **Whole numbers** are the natural numbers including 0. $\{\mathbf{0},1,2,3,4,5,6, \ldots\}$
- **Integers** are all the whole numbers and their negatives. $\{\ldots \mathbf{-3, -2, -1}, 0, 1, 2, 3, \ldots\}$
- **A number line** is a straight line on which every point corresponds to an integer.

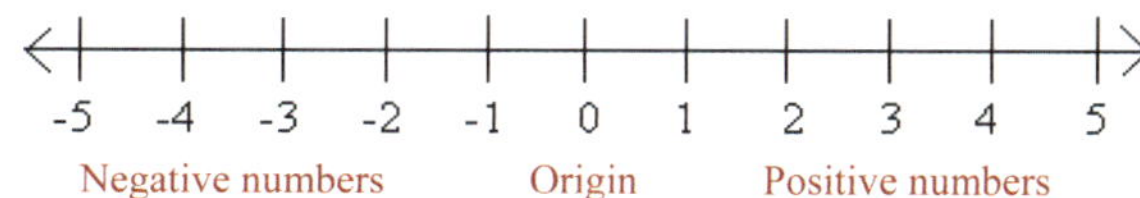

- **Rational numbers** are numbers that can be expressed as a fraction $\frac{a}{b}$, where a and b are integers and $b \neq 0$.

  Rational numbers can be expressed as decimal terminates or repeats.

  Example: $\frac{3}{4} = 0.75$ ← Terminating

  $\frac{2}{3} = 0.66666\ldots = 0.\overline{6}$ ← Repeating

  Example of rational numbers: $0.52 = \frac{52}{100}$, $-4.5 = \frac{-9}{2}$, $\frac{0}{7}$, $-11 = \frac{-11}{1}$

- **Irrational numbers** are real numbers that cannot be represented by a fraction (or the ratio of two integers).

  Irrational numbers can be expressed as non-terminating, non-repeating decimals.

  Example: $\pi = 3.1415926 \ldots$ ← Non-terminating & Non-repeating

  $\sqrt{2} = 1.1414213562$ ←

  Example of irrational numbers: $\sqrt{7}$, 2π, $-\sqrt{19}$, $5\sqrt{13}$

- **Real numbers** are the rational numbers plus irrational numbers.
- **The real number system**

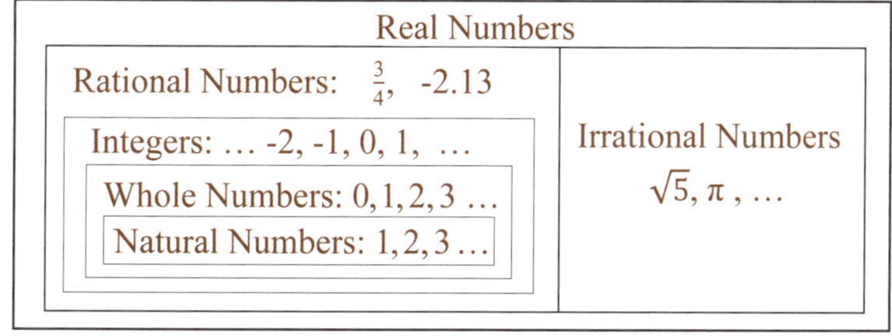

Sets

- **A set** is a group of elements or numbers (in mathematics).

Example: "the set of things in an emergency box" can be written as:

{A bottle of water, cookies, flash light, bandages, blanket, …}

The curly braces { } represent a set.

- **Roster Notation { }**

Roster Notation { }	Example
List all the elements or numbers of the set.	The set of odd numbers *between* 3 and 17: { 5, 7, 9, 11, 13, 15} Note: "between" — not including 3 and 17.

- **Set-builder notation**: a mathematic form $\{x \mid x \ldots\}$ used to represent a set of numbers.

Set-Builder Notation	Example
$\{ x \mid x \ldots \}$	$\{ x \mid x > 3 \}$
The set of x such as condition of x	The set of x such as x greater than 3

Example: Write in roster notation.

1. The set of all letters in the word "hope."

   { h, o, p, e}

2. $A = \{ x \mid x$ is a number between -4 and 6 $\}$

   $A =$ **{-3, -2, -1, 0, 1, 2, 3, 4, 5}** "Between" — not including -4 and 6.

Example: Write the following in **a.** set- builder notation and **b.** roster notation.

"The set of numbers between -3 and 4."

1. $A = \{ x \mid x$ is a number between -3 and 4$\}$ Set-builder notation

2. $A =$ **{-2, -1, 0, 1, 2, 3}** Roster notation

- **Elements of a set**: In set notation, $x \in Z$ means x belongs to the set Z.

Real Numbers and Sets

- **Real numbers summary**

Name	Set of Numbers	Example
natural numbers	{1,2,3,4,5,6, …}	2, 7, 11, 35, 167
whole numbers	{**0**,1,2,3,4,5,6, …}	0, 4, 8, 23, 2009
integers	{… **-4, -3, -2, -1,** 0, 1, 2, 3, -4 …}	-215, -31, -6, 0, 8, 24, 190
rational numbers (or fractions)	$\{\frac{a}{b} \mid a$ and b are integers, $b \neq 0\}$	terminating: $\frac{4}{5} = 0.8$ repeating: $-\frac{8}{9} = -0.8888\ldots = 0.\overline{8}$
irrational numbers	$\{x \mid x$ cannot be expressed as a fraction for any integers$\}$	nonterminating, nonrepeating $\sqrt{5} \approx 2.236$ $\pi \approx 3.1416$

- **A real number line** is a straight line on which every point corresponds to a real number.

Example: Put the following numbers in order from least to greatest on the real number line.

$\frac{3}{4}$, $-2\frac{1}{3}$, -0.67 , $\sqrt{3} \approx 1.73$, $\pi \approx 3.1416$

$-2\frac{1}{3}$ -0.67 $\frac{3}{4}$ $\sqrt{3} \approx 1.73$ $\pi \approx 3.1416$

-5 -4 -3 -2 -1 0 1 2 3 4 5

- **A prime number** is a whole number that only has two factors, 1 and itself.

Example: 2, 3, 5, and 7 are prime numbers. They all have two factors: 1 and itself.

- **A composite number** is a whole number that has more than two factors.

Example: 4, 6, 8, 9, and 10 are composite numbers.

Example: **Set-Builder Notation** **Roster Notation**

$\{x \mid x$ is a natural number greater than 2 and less than 7$\}$. **{3, 4, 5, 6}**

$\{y \mid y$ is a prime number between 2 and 9$\}$. **{3, 5, 7}**

$\{a \mid a$ is an integer greater than -2 and less than 4$\}$. **{-1, 0, 1, 2, 3}**

Example: Given $A = \{-2, \pi, \sqrt{7}, \frac{4}{5}\}$. Specify the following sets.

$\{x \mid x$ is a negative number$\}$. **{-2}**

$\{b \mid b$ is an irrational number$\}$. $\{\pi, \sqrt{7}\}$

Example: If I = irrational numbers, Z = integers, and N = natural numbers, then list the numbers in the following sets.

1. $A = \{x \mid x \in Z,\ x$ is less than or equal to -4 and greater than -7$\}$. $\{-7 < x \leq -4\}$

2. $A = \{a \mid a \in N,\ a$ is a prime number between 15 and 25$\}$. **{17, 19, 23}**

3. $A = \{y \mid y \in I,\ y$ is greater than $\frac{7}{8}$ and less than $\frac{3}{8}\}$. $\emptyset$

$\emptyset$ is an empty set that has no numbers.

Basic Mathematic Symbols

- **Basic mathematic symbols**

Symbol	Meaning	Example
$=$	equal	$a = b$, $2 + 1 = -1 + 4$
$\neq$	not equal	$a \neq b$, $2 + 7 \neq 6$
$\approx$	approximately	$a \approx b$, $3.667 \approx 4$
$>$	is greater than	$a > b$, $4 > -2$
$<$	is less than	$a < b$, $-3 < 0$
$\geq$	is greater than or equal to	$a \geq b$, $4 \geq 3$
$\leq$	is less than or equal to	$a \leq b$, $8 \leq 9$
$\pm$	plus or minus	$a \pm b$, 3 ± 2 $= 5$ and 1
$\mp$	minus or plus	$a \mp b$, 2 ∓ 7 $= -5$ and 9
( ) or ○	open (empty) circle: the point is not included	$x < 3$ (3) or $x < 3$ (3)
[ ] or ●	closed (filled) circle: the point is included	-5 $x \geq -5$ or -5 $x \geq -5$

Example: Sketch the graphs of the following inequalities.

1. $x < -4$ — -4 or -4

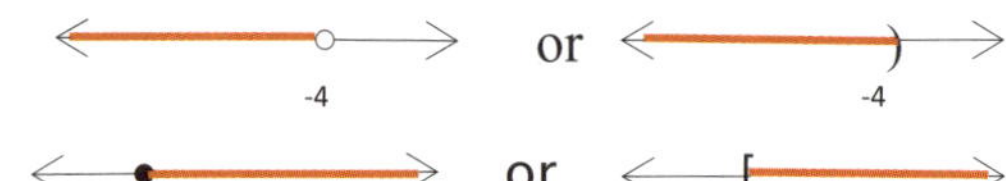

2. $-2.3 \leq x$ — -2.3 or -2.3

3. $\{ y \mid -4 \leq y < 8 \}$ — -4 0 8

- **A positive real number > 0, and a negative real number < 0.**

Example: $3 > 0$ $-2 < 0$

- **Memory aid for $>$ and $<$**

bigger $>$ smaller smaller $<$ bigger

- **$x > y$ also means $y < x$**

Example: Write an equivalent inequality. **Answer**

$-3 < y$ **$y > -3$**

$x \geq 2\frac{5}{7}$ **$2\frac{5}{7} \leq x$**

Example: Insert an appropriate symbol for the following numbers. **Answer**

-2.3 and -9.6 **$-2.3 > -9.6$ or $-9.6 < -2.3$**

$\frac{5}{4}$ and $\frac{3}{4}$ **$\frac{5}{4} > \frac{3}{4}$ or $\frac{3}{4} < \frac{5}{4}$**

Absolute Value

- **Absolute value:** geometrically, it is the distance (how far) of a number x from zero on the number line. It is symbolized by "$|x|$".

  Example: $|5|$ is 5 units away from 0.

- **No negatives for absolute value:** Distance is always positive, and absolute value is distance, so the absolute value is never negative.

  Example: $|2|$ is 2 units away from 0.

  $|-2|$ is also 2 units away from 0.

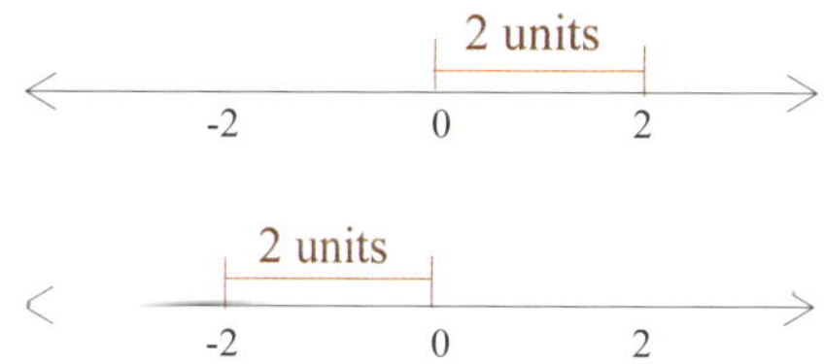

Example: Evaluate the following.

$|-18| = \mathbf{18}$

$|0 - 11| = |-11| = \mathbf{11}$

$\left|-\frac{5}{7}\right| = \mathbf{\frac{5}{7}}$

$-|-5| = -(5) = \mathbf{-5}$

$|-2 \cdot 7| = |-14| = \mathbf{14}$

$|7 - 5| - |3 - 8| = 2 - 5 = \mathbf{-3}$

1-2 OPERATIONS WITH REAL NUMBERS

Operations With Signed Numbers

- **Terms of operations**

Operations		
addition	addend + addend	= sum
subtraction	subtrahend – minuend	= difference
multiplication	multiplicand × multiplier (factor) (factor)	= product
division	dividend ÷ divisor	= quotient

- **Examples** of positive and negative numbers (signed numbers)

	Meaning	Example
temperature	+ °C: above 0 degree – °C: below 0 degree	+20°C -5°C
money	+ $: gain or own – $: loss or owe	own +$10,000 owe -$500
sports	+ points : gain – points: loss	gain 3 points: +3 lost 2 points: -2

- **Adding signed numbers**
  - To add two numbers with the same sign: add their values, and keep their common sign.
  - To add two numbers with different signs: subtract their values, and keep the sign of the larger absolute value.

Example

3 + 4 = **7**

(-2) + (-3) = **-5**

2 + (-5) = **-3**

(-3) + 7 = **4**

- **Subtracting signed numbers**

Subtract a number by adding its opposite.

Example

3 – (-4) = 3 + (4) = **7**

-5 – 3 = -5 + (-3) = **-8**

- **Multiplying signed numbers**

Signs	Multiplication	Example
(+)(+) = (+)	$(a)(b) = ab$	5 · 6 = 30
(–)(+) = (–)	$(-a)(b) = -ab$	(-5)(6) = -30
(+)(–) = (–)	$(a)(-b) = -ab$	(5)(-6) = -30
(–)(–) = (+)	$(-a)(-b) = ab$	(-5)(-6) = 30

		Example
the same sign	→ +	(-2) (-5) = **10**
different signs	→ –	(-3) (2) = **-6**
even number of negative numbers	→ +	(-2)(-3)(-1)(-4) = **24**
odd number of negative numbers	→ –	(-3)(-1)(-5) = **-15**

Dividing Signed Numbers

- **Dividing signed numbers**

Signs	Division	Example
$\frac{+}{+} = +$	$\frac{a}{b} = c$	$\frac{9}{3} = 3$
$\frac{-}{-} = +$	$\frac{-a}{-b} = c$	$\frac{-9}{-3} = 3$
$\frac{+}{-} = -$	$\frac{a}{-b} = -c$	$\frac{9}{-3} = -3$
$\frac{-}{+} = -$	$\frac{-a}{b} = -c$	$\frac{-9}{3} = -3$

Note: $-\frac{a}{b} = \frac{-a}{b} = \frac{a}{-b}$

- **Properties of zero in division**
  - The number 0 divided by any nonzero number is 0. $\frac{0}{A} = 0$ $(A \neq 0)$

    Example: $\frac{0}{9} = 0$ 0 apples divided by 9 kids, each kid gets 0 apples.
  - A number divided by 0 is undefined (not allowed). $\frac{A}{0}$ **is undefined**

    Example: $\frac{9}{0} = ?$ 9 apples shared by zero kids has no meaning.

dividing fractions	- Change the divisor to its reciprocal (switch the numerator and denominator). - Multiply the resulting fractions.	$\frac{2}{7} \div \frac{3}{5} = \frac{2}{7} \times \frac{5}{3} = \frac{2 \times 5}{7 \times 3} = \frac{10}{21}$

- **Signed numbers summary**

Operation	Method
adding signed numbers	- Add two numbers with the same sign: add their values, and keep their common sign. - Add two numbers with different signs: subtract their values, and keep the sign of the larger number.
subtracting signed numbers	Subtract a number by adding its opposite.
multiplying signed numbers	$(+)(+) = (+)$, $(-)(-) = (+)$, $(-)(+) = (-)$, $(+)(-) = (-)$
dividing signed numbers	$\frac{+}{+} = +$, $\frac{-}{-} = +$, $\frac{+}{-} = -$, $\frac{-}{+} = -$ Note: $\frac{0}{A} = 0$, $\frac{A}{0}$ is undefined

- **Opposite (or additive or negative inverse):** the opposite of a number (two numbers whose sum is 0).

Example:
1. The additive inverse of 5 is **-5**. $5 + (-5) = 0$
2. The additive inverse of $-\frac{3}{4}$ is $\mathbf{\frac{3}{4}}$. $-\frac{3}{4} + \frac{3}{4} = 0$
3. The additive inverse of 0 is **0**. $0 + 0 = 0$

1-3 EXPONENTS & ORDER OF OPERATIONS

Exponential Notation

- **Exponent (power)** is a number repeatedly multiplied by itself.
- **Exponent review**

Exponential Notation	Example
Exponent or power; Base: $a^n = a \cdot a \cdot a \cdot a \ldots a$ Read "*a* to the nth" or "the nth power of *a*."	$2^4 = 2 \cdot 2 \cdot 2 \cdot 2 = 16$ Read "2 to the 4th."

- **Basic properties**

Name	Property		Example
zero exponent a^0	$a^0 = 1$	$(a \neq 0,\ 0^0$ is undefined)	$15^0 = 1$
one exponent a^1	$a^1 = a$	(But $1^n = 1$)	$7^1 = 7,\quad 1^{13} = 1$
negative exponent a^{-n}	$a^{-n} = \frac{1}{a^n}$	$(a \neq 0)$	$4^{-2} = \frac{1}{4^2} = \frac{1}{16}$
	$\frac{1}{a^{-n}} = a^n$	or $a^{-n} \cdot a^n = 1$	$\frac{1}{4^{-2}} = 4^2 = 16$

a^n and a^{-n} are reciprocals: *since* $a^{-n} \cdot a^n = \frac{1}{a^n} \cdot a^n = \frac{a^n}{a^n} = 1$

Examples: Evaluate the following.

$(-3)^2 = (-3)(-3) = \mathbf{9}$ $\qquad a^n = a \cdot a \cdot a \ \ldots\ a$

$(-0.3)^3 = \mathbf{-0.027}$

$-5^2 = -(5^2) = \mathbf{-25}$

$n \cdot n \cdot n \cdot n \cdot n = \boldsymbol{n^5}$

$\left(\frac{-1}{3}\right)^3 = \left(\frac{-1}{3}\right)\left(\frac{-1}{3}\right)\left(\frac{-1}{3}\right) = \mathbf{\frac{-1}{27}}$

$\left(\frac{-1}{3}\right)^1 = \mathbf{\frac{-1}{3}}$ $\qquad a^1 = a$

$(-111)^0 = \mathbf{1}$ $\qquad a^0 = 1$

$\left(\frac{3}{2}\right)^{-2} = \frac{1}{\left(\frac{3}{2}\right)^2} = \frac{1}{\left(\frac{9}{4}\right)} = 1 \div \frac{9}{4} = 1 \times \frac{4}{9} = \mathbf{\frac{4}{9}}$ $\qquad a^{-n} = \frac{1}{a^n}$

$\frac{1}{3^{-2}} = 3^2 = \mathbf{9}$ $\qquad \frac{1}{a^{-n}} = a^n$

Order of Operations

- **Order of operations**

Order of Operations	
1. brackets or parentheses and absolute values (innermost first)	( ), [ ], { }, | |
2. exponent	a^n
3. multiplication or division (from left-to-right)	× and ÷
4. addition or subtraction (from left-to-right)	+ and -

- **Memory aid - BEDMAS**

B	E	D M	A S
Brackets	Exponents	Divide or Multiply	Add or Subtract

- **Grouping symbols:** If parentheses are inside one another, calculate the inside set first.
  - **Parentheses ( )** are used in the inner most grouping.
  - **Square brackets [ ]** are used in the second higher level grouping.
  - **Braces { }** are used in the most outer grouping.

Example: Evaluate the following.

1. $4 \times 3^2 + \{[5 + (2+1)] - 3\} = 4 \times 3^2 + \{[5 + 3] - 3\}$ ( ), [ ]

$= 4 \times 3^2 + \{8 - 3\}$ { }

$= 4 \times 3^2 + 5$ a^n

$= 4 \times 9 + 5$ ×

$= 36 + 5$ +

$= \mathbf{41}$

2. $\frac{|4-6|+3\cdot2}{2^2+6} = \frac{2+3\cdot2}{4+6}$ | | and a^n

$= \frac{2+6}{4+6}$ ×

$= \frac{8}{10} = \frac{4}{5}$ ÷ and simplify

3. $\frac{2^3+4^2-3\cdot5}{2|3-5|\div(-4)} = \frac{2^3+4^2-3\cdot5}{2\cdot2\div(-4)} = \frac{8+16-3\cdot5}{2\cdot2\div(-4)}$ | | and a^n

$= \frac{8+16-15}{-1} = \frac{9}{-1} = \mathbf{-9}$ × and ÷

1-4 ALGEBRAIC EXPRESSIONS

Evaluating Expressions

- **Review of basic algebraic terms**

Algebraic Term	Description	Example
algebraic expression	A mathematical phrase that contains numbers, variables, and arithmetic operations.	$5x+2$, $3a-4b+6$, $\frac{2y}{3}+4$
constant	A number.	$x+2$ constant: 2
variable	A letter that can be assigned different values.	$3-x$ variable: x
coefficient	The number that is in front of a variable.	$-6x$ coefficient: -6 xz^3 coefficient: 1
term	A term can be a constant, variable, or the product of a number and variable(s).	$3x-\frac{2}{5}+13y^2+73x$ Terms: $3x$, $-\frac{2}{5}$, $13y^2$, $73x$
like terms	The terms that have the same variables and exponents.	$2x-y^2-\frac{2}{5}+5x-7+13y^2$ Like terms: $2x$ and $5x$ $-y^2$ and $13y^2$, $-\frac{2}{5}$ and -7

Note: - In algebra we usually do not write the multiplication sign "×" (to avoid confusing it with the letter x).

- If there is no symbol or sign between a number and letter, it means multiplication, such as $5x = 5 \cdot x$.

- **To evaluate an expression:**
  - Replace the variable(s) with number(s).
  - Calculate.

Example: Evaluate the following.

1. $\frac{x}{y}$, given $x = -3$ and $y = 5$. Substitute x for -3 and y for 5.

$\frac{x}{y} = \frac{-3}{5}$

2. $3a - 4 + 2$, given $a = 5$.

$3a-4+2 = 3\cdot5-4+2$ Substitute a for 5.

$= 15-4+2$ Calculate.

$= 13$

3. $\frac{6x^2}{y-3}+7x-2$, given $x = 1$ and $y = 9$.

$\frac{6x^2}{y-3}+7x-2 = \frac{6\cdot1^2}{9-3}+7\cdot1-2$ Substitute x for 1 and y for 9.

$= \frac{6}{6}+7-2 = 6$ Calculate.

Translating Words Into Algebraic Expressions

- **Key or clue words in word problems**

Addition (+)	Subtraction (-)	Multiplication (×)	Division (÷)	Equals to (=)
add	subtract	times	divided by	equals
sum (of)	difference	product	quotient	is
plus	take away	multiplied by	over	was
total (of)	minus	double	split up	are
altogether	less (than)	twice	fit into	were
increased by	decreased by	triple	per	amounts to
gain (of)	loss (of)	of	each	totals
combined	balance	how much (total)	goes into	results in
entire	(amount) left	how many	as much as	the same as
in all	savings		out of	gives
greater than	withdraw		ratio (of)	yields
complete	reduced by		percent	
together	fewer (than)		share	
more (than)	how much more		distribute	
and	how many extra		average	
additional	how far			
	exceed			

- **Translate words into an algebraic expression**

Algebraic Expression	Word Phrases
$7+y$	the sum of 7 and y
	7 more than y
	y increased by 7
	7 plus y

Algebraic Expression	Word Phrases
$t-8$	8 less than t
	t decreased (or reduced) by 8
	subtract 8 from t
	the difference between t and 8

Algebraic Expression	Word Phrases
$2x$ or $2 \cdot x$	the product of 2 and x
	2 multiplied by x
	double (or twice) of x

Algebraic Expression	Word Phrases
$z \div 3$ or $\frac{z}{3}$	the quotient of z and 3
	z divided by 3
	one third of z

Algebraic Expression	Word Phrases
y^3	the third power of y
	y cubed
	y raised to the third power

Algebraic Expression	Word Phrases
$4y-9$	9 less than 4 times y
$2(t-5)$	twice the difference of t and 5
$6+\frac{2x}{3}$	6 more than the quotient of $2x$ by 3

Properties of Addition and Multiplication

- **Review properties of addition**

Additive Properties		Example	
commutative property	$a + b = b + a$	$4 + 7 = 7 + 4$	(Switch the order.)
associative property	$(a + b) + c = a + (b + c)$	$(7 + 2) + 9 = 7 + (2 + 9)$	(Switch the parentheses.)
identity property	$a + 0 = a$	$12.7 + 0 = 12.7$	
closure property	If a and b are real numbers, then $a + b$ is a real number.	If 9 and 11 are real numbers, then $9 + 11 = 20$ is a real number.	
inverse property	$-a + a = 0$	$-100 + 100 = 0$	

Example: Name the properties. **Answer**

1. $7x + 0 = 7x$ — identity property of addition
2. $(3 + x) + 11 = 3 + (x + 11)$ — associative property of addition
3. $11y + 7 = 7 + 11y$ — commutative property of addition
4. $(4y + 3) + [-(4y + 3)] = 0$ — inverse property of addition

- **Review properties of multiplication**

Multiplicative Properties		Example	
commutative property	$a\,b = b\,a$	$9 \cdot 5 = 5 \cdot 9$	(Switch the order)
associative property	$(a\,b)\,c = a\,(b\,c)$	$(3 \cdot 7)\,5 = 3\,(7 \cdot 5)$	(Switch the parentheses)
identity property of 1	$a \cdot 1 = a$	$100{,}000 \cdot 1 = 100{,}000$	
closure property	If a and b are real numbers, then ab is a real number.	If 3 and 5 are real numbers, then $(3)(5) = 15$ is a real number.	
distributive property	$a\,(b + c) = ab + ac$	$2\,(3 - 4) = 2 \cdot 3 - 2 \cdot 4$	
zero product property	$a \cdot 0 = 0$	$-76 \cdot 0 = 0$	
inverse property	$a \cdot \frac{1}{a} = 1$ (number, its reciprocal)	$(-97) \cdot \frac{1}{(-97)} = 1$	

Example: Name the property which the given statement illustrates.

Answer

1. $3(5x - 2) = 3 \cdot 5x - 3 \cdot 2 = 15x - 6$ — distributive property of multiplication
2. $xy = yx$ — commutative property of multiplication
3. $1 \cdot \frac{-1}{(25+6a)} = \frac{-1}{(25+6a)}$ — identity property of multiplication
4. $(y\,x)\,4z = y\,(x \cdot 4z)$ — associative property of multiplication
5. $-(7 + 3x) \cdot \frac{1}{-(7+3x)} = 1$ — inverse property of multiplication
6. $5a(2b - 3c) = 10ab - 15ac$ — distributive property of multiplication
7. $\frac{1}{4xy} \cdot 0 = 0$ — zero product property of multiplication

1-5 SIMPLIFYING ALGEBRAIC EXPRESSIONS

Equivalent Expressions

Equivalent expressions: Two expressions are equivalent if they have the same value for all allowable replacements.

Example: Complete the table by evaluating the expression for the given values. Then determine whether the expressions are equivalent.

	$3x - x$	$2x$
$x = 1$	**2**	**2**
$x = 2$	**4**	**4**
$x = 0$	**0**	**0**

Yes, $3x - x$ and $2x$ are equivalent.

Examples

Answer

1. Multiply by 1 to find an equivalent expression with a given denominator of $3x$.
   $\frac{2}{3} =$ $\qquad$ $\frac{2}{3} \cdot 1 = \frac{2}{3} \cdot \frac{x}{x} = \mathbf{\frac{2x}{3x}}$
2. Simplify: $-\frac{8t}{12t}$ $\qquad$ $-\frac{8t}{12t} = -\frac{2}{3}$
3. Factor: $4xyz - 2yz + 6z$ $\qquad$ $4xyz - 2yz + 6z = \mathbf{2z(2xy - y + 3)}$
4. Multiply: $-3p(2q - r)$ $\qquad$ $-3p(2q - r) = \mathbf{-6pq + 3pr}$
5. List the terms: $3a - 2bc + d$ $\qquad$ $\mathbf{3a,\ -2bc,\ d}$

Example: Use properties of addition and multiplication to find an equivalent expression.

Answer

1. ac : $\qquad$ $\mathbf{ca}$ $\qquad$ commutative property of multiplication
2. $wt + 6$: $\qquad$ $\mathbf{6 + wt}$, $\mathbf{6 + tw}$, or $\mathbf{tw + 6}$ $\qquad$ commutative property of addition/ multiplication
3. $(a + 6) - b$: $\qquad$ $\mathbf{a + (6 - b)}$ $\qquad$ associative property of addition

Example: Use properties of addition and multiplication to find three equivalent expressions.

Answer

1. $(t + u) + 3$: $\mathbf{(t + 3) + u,\ (3 + t) + u,\ t + (u + 3), \ldots}$
   commutative/associative property of addition
2. $(3 \cdot y) \cdot z$: $\mathbf{(y \cdot z) \cdot 3,\ (3 \cdot z) \cdot y,\ 3 \cdot (y \cdot z), \ldots}$
   commutative/associative property of multiplication

Combining Like Terms

- **Like terms:** terms that have the same variables and exponents (the numerical coefficients can be different.)

Example	Like or Unlike Terms
$3x$ and $-14x$	like terms
$-2x^2$, $43x^2$, and $-x^2$	like terms
$\frac{2}{5}a^2b$ and $\frac{-2}{7}a^2b$	like terms
$-7t^2w^3$ and $4t^2w^3$	like terms
$4x$ and $-35y$	unlike terms
$6x^3$ and $-9x^2$	unlike terms
$-7a^2b^3$ and $4a^3b^2$	unlike terms

- **To combine (or collect) like terms,** add or subtract their numerical coefficients and keep the same variables and exponents.

Note: Unlike terms cannot be combined.

Example: Simplify the following expressions.

1. $7x + 2y - 3x + 11y = (7x - 3x) + (2y + 11y)$ Regroup like terms.

   $= \mathbf{4x + 13y}$ Combine like terms.

2. $2y^2 - 0.9x + 1.4x - 5y^2 = (2y^2 - 5y^2) + (-0.9x + 1.4x)$ Regroup like terms.

   $= \mathbf{-3y^2 + 0.5x}$ Combine like terms.

3. $2a^2b + ab^2 - 7a^2b - 8ab^2$

   $= \underline{2a^2b} + ab^2 \underline{- 7a^2b} - 8ab^2$ Mark or underline like terms and regroup.

   $= \mathbf{-5a^2b - 7ab^2}$ Combine like terms.

4. $\frac{1}{3}x + \frac{5}{2}y - \frac{3}{4}x - \frac{1}{3}y = \left(\frac{1}{3}x - \frac{3}{4}x\right) + \left(\frac{5}{2}y - \frac{1}{3}y\right)$ Regroup like terms.

   $= \left(\frac{4}{12}x - \frac{9}{12}x\right) + \left(\frac{15}{6}y - \frac{2}{6}y\right)$ Combine like terms.

   $= \mathbf{\frac{-5}{12}x + \frac{13}{6}y}$

Removing Parentheses

- **If the sign preceding the parentheses is positive (+),** do not change the sign of terms inside the parentheses, just remove the parentheses. **Example**: $(a-2)=a-2$
- **If the sign preceding the parentheses is negative (-),** remove the parentheses, omit the negative (-) sign, and change the sign of terms inside the parentheses.
  Example: $-(a-2)=-a+2$
- **Remove parentheses**

Algebraic Expression	Remove Parentheses	Example
$(Ax+B)$	$Ax+B$	$(3x+4)=3x+4$
$(Ax-B)$	$Ax-B$	$\left(\frac{5}{6}x-3\right)=\frac{5}{6}x-3$
$-(Ax+B)$	$-Ax-B$	$-(2x+7)=-2x-7$
$-(Ax-B)$	$-Ax+B$	$-\left(\frac{1}{3}x-\frac{2}{5}\right)=\frac{-1}{3}x+\frac{2}{5}$

Example: Simplify the following expressions.

1. $2x^2+3-(x^2-2)=\underline{2x^2}+3-\underline{x^2}+2$ Remove parentheses.
   $=x^2+5$ Combine like terms.
2. $-(x^2+3x-0.5)+2(2x^2-7x+\frac{3}{8})$
   $=-x^2\underline{-3x}+0.5+4x^2\underline{-14x}+\frac{3}{4}$ Remove parentheses.
   $=3x^2-17x+\frac{5}{4}$ Combine like terms.
3. $-2(t^2-4t)+3(t-4)-(6+2t-3t^2)$
   $=-2t^2+\underline{8t}+\underline{3t}-12-6\underline{-2t}+3t^2$ Remove parentheses.
   $=t^2+9t-18$ Combine like terms.
4. $\frac{1}{3}(a+3)-\frac{1}{2}(a+2)=\frac{1}{3}a+1-\frac{1}{2}a-1$ Remove parentheses.
   $=\left(\frac{1}{3}a-\frac{1}{2}a\right)+(1-1)$ Combine like terms.
   $=\frac{-1}{6}a$

1-6 EXPONENTS & SCIENTIFIC NOTATION

Rules of Exponents

Name	Rule	Example
product of like bases	$a^m a^n = a^{m+n}$ $(a \neq 0)$	$2^3\, 2^2 = 2^{3+2} = 2^5 = 32$
quotient of like bases (the same base)	$\frac{a^m}{a^n} = a^{m-n}$ $(a \neq 0)$	$\frac{y^3}{y^2} = y^{3-2} = y^1 = y$
power of a power	$(a^m)^n = a^{mn}$	$(x^3)^2 = x^{3\cdot 2} = x^6$
power of a product (different bases)	$(a \cdot b)^n = a^n b^n$ $(a,\ b \neq 0)$	$(2 \cdot 3)^2 = 2^2\, 3^2 = 4 \cdot 9 = 36$
	$(a^m \cdot b^n)^p = a^{mp} b^{np}$	$(t^3 \cdot s^4)^2 = t^{3\cdot 2} s^{4\cdot 2} = t^6 s^8$
power of a quotient (different bases)	$\left(\frac{a}{b}\right)^n = \frac{a^n}{b^n}$ $(b \neq 0)$	$\left(\frac{2}{3}\right)^2 = \frac{2^2}{3^2} = \frac{4}{9}$
	$\left(\frac{a^m}{b^n}\right)^p = \frac{a^{mp}}{b^{np}}$	$\left(\frac{q^2}{p^4}\right)^3 = \frac{q^{2\cdot 3}}{p^{4\cdot 3}} = \frac{q^6}{p^{12}}$

Example: Simplify the following.

1. $\mathbf{10^2\, 10^{-3}} = 10^{2-3} = 10^{-1} = \mathbf{\frac{1}{10}}$ — $a^m a^n = a^{m+n}$, $a^{-n} = \frac{1}{a^n}$

2. $\frac{w^{-5}}{w^2} = w^{-5-2} = w^{-7} = \frac{1}{w^7}$ — $\frac{a^m}{a^n} = a^{m-n}$, $a^{-n} = \frac{1}{a^n}$

3. $(y^{-3})^{-2} = y^{-3(-2)} = y^6$ — $(a^n)^m = a^{n\,m}$

4. $[(-3) \cdot (0.4)]^2 = (-3)^2 \cdot 0.4^2 = (9)(0.16) = \mathbf{1.44}$ — $(a \cdot b)^n = a^n b^n$

5. $(3x^2 \cdot y^{-3})^3 = 3^3 \cdot x^{2\cdot 3} \cdot y^{-3\cdot 3} = 27x^6 y^{-9} = \frac{27x^6}{y^9}$ — $(a^m \cdot b^n)^p = a^{mp} b^{np}$, $a^{-n} = \frac{1}{a^n}$

6. $\left(\frac{x}{y}\right)^{-3} = \frac{x^{-3}}{y^{-3}} = \frac{y^3}{x^3}$ — $\left(\frac{a}{b}\right)^n = \frac{a^n}{b^n}$, $a^{-n} = \frac{1}{a^n}$, $\frac{1}{a^{-n}} = a^n$

7. $\left(\frac{t^5}{u^{-2}}\right)^2 = \frac{t^{5\cdot 2}}{u^{(-2)(2)}} = \frac{t^{10}}{u^{-4}} = t^{10}u^4$ — $\left(\frac{a^m}{b^n}\right)^p = \frac{a^{mp}}{b^{np}}$, $\frac{1}{a^{-n}} = a^n$

Example: Simplify the following.

1. $(-4u^3)^2(3w^4)^{-3}(-127v^{-15})^0$

$= (-4)^2(u^{3\cdot 2})(3^{-3}w^{4(-3)})(1)$ — $(a^m \cdot b^n)^p = a^{mp} b^{np}$, $a^0 = 1$

$= 16(u^6)(3^{-3}w^{-12})$

$= \frac{16(u^6)}{3^3 w^{12}} = \frac{16u^6}{27w^{12}}$ — $a^{-n} = \frac{1}{a^n}$

2. $\left(\frac{(4a^3)(b^5)}{2a^2b^4}\right)^2 = \frac{(4a^3)^2(b^5)^2}{(2a^2b^4)^2} = \frac{(4^2a^{3\cdot 2})(b^{5\cdot 2})}{2^2a^{2\cdot 2}b^{4\cdot 2}}$ — $\left(\frac{a^m}{b^n}\right)^p = \frac{a^{mp}}{b^{np}}$, $(a \cdot b)^n = a^n b^n$

$= \frac{(16a^6)(b^{10})}{4a^4b^8} = \mathbf{4a^2b^2}$ — $\frac{a^m}{a^n} = a^{m-n}$

Scientific Notation

- Scientific notation is a special way of concisely expressing very **large** and **small** numbers.

Example: $300{,}000{,}000 = 3 \times 10^8$ m/sec — the speed of light

$0.00000000000000000016 = 1.6 \times 10^{-19}$ C — an electron

- **Scientific notation:** a product of a number between 1 and 10 and power of 10. → $N \times 10^{\pm n}$

Scientific Notation	Example
$N \times 10^{\pm n}$ $1 \le N < 10$, n - integer	$34{,}005.9 = 3.40059 \times 10^4$ (standard form = scientific notation)

- **Scientific vs. non-scientific notation**

Scientific Notation	Not Scientific Notation		
3.5×10^3	35×10^2	$35 > 10$,	35 is not between 1 and 10
4.3×10^{-2}	0.043	$0 < 1$,	0 is not between 1 and 10
5.3×10^{22}	0.53×10^{23}	$0 < 1$,	0 is not between 1 and 10
1.03×10^8	10.3×10^7	N should be < 10	

- **Writing a number in scientific notation**

Step	Example
- Move the decimal point **after** the **first nonzero digit**.	0.0035 43270000.
- Determine n (the power of 10) by counting the number of places you moved the decimal.	$n = 3$ $n = 7$
- If the decimal point is moved to the **right**: $\times 10^{-n}$	$0.0035 = \mathbf{3.5 \times 10^{-3}}$ 3 places to the right
- If the decimal point is moved to the **left**: $\times 10^{n}$	$43270000 = \mathbf{4.327 \times 10^7}$ 7 places to the left

Example: Write in scientific notation.

1. $135{,}000 = 135{,}000. = \mathbf{1.35 \times 10^5}$ — 5 places to the left, $\times 10^n$
2. $0.0000000548 = \mathbf{5.48 \times 10^{-8}}$ — 8 places to the right, $\times 10^{-n}$

Example: Simplify and write in scientific notation.

1. $(3.4 \times 10^{-4})(4.79 \times 10^7) = (3.4 \times 4.79)(10^{-4+7})$ — Multiply coefficients of $10^{\pm n}$, $a^m a^n = a^{m+n}$

$= (16.286 \times 10^3)$ — $16.286 > 10$, this is not in scientific notation.

$= (\mathbf{1.6286 \times 10^4})$ — $1.6.286 < 10$, this is in scientific notation.

2. $\frac{(4\times10^{-4})(1.5\times10^3)}{5.2\times10^6} = \frac{4\times1.5}{5.2} \times \frac{(10^{-4}\times10^3)}{10^6}$ — Regroup coefficients of $10^{\pm n}$

$\approx \mathbf{1.15 \times 10^{-7}}$ — $a^m a^n = a^{m+n}$, $\frac{a^m}{a^n} = a^{m-n}$

Unit 1 Summary

- **Roster Notation { }**

Roster Notation { }	Example
List all the elements or numbers of the set.	The set of odd numbers *between* 3 and 17: { 5, 7, 9, 11, 13, 15}

- **Set-builder notation**

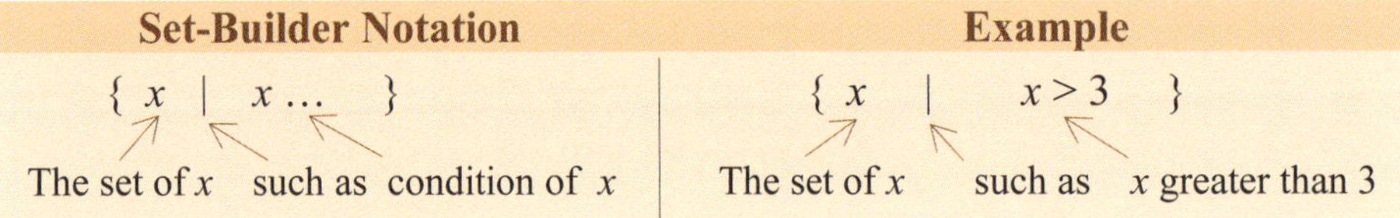

- **The real number system**

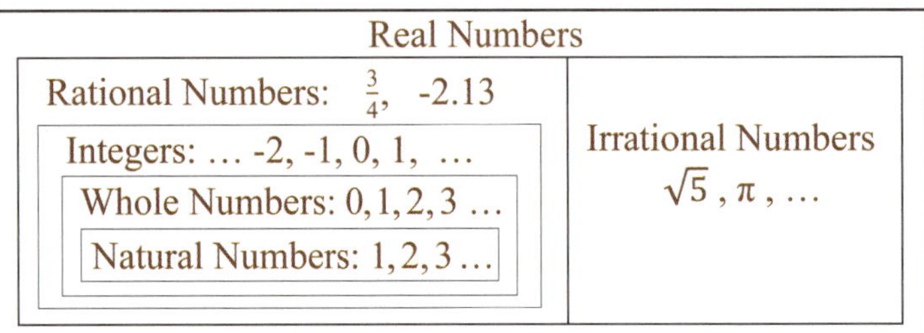

- **Basic mathematic symbols**

Symbol	Meaning	Example
$=$	equal	$a = b$, $2+1 = -1+4$
$\neq$	not equal	$a \neq b$, $2+7 \neq 6$
$\approx$	approximately	$a \approx b$, $3.667 \approx 4$
$>$	is greater than	$a > b$, $4 > -2$
$<$	is less than	$a < b$, $-3 < 0$
$\geq$	is greater than or equal to	$a \geq b$, $4 \geq 3$
$\leq$	is less than or equal to	$a \leq b$, $8 \leq 9$
$\pm$	plus or minus	$a \pm b$, 3 ± 2 = 5 and 1
$\mp$	minus or plus	$a \mp b$, 2 ∓ 7 = -5 and 9
( ) or ○	open (empty) circle: the point is not included	$x < 3$ (number line, open at 3) or $x < 3$ (number line, open circle at 3)
[ ] or ●	closed (filled) circle: the point is included	$x \geq -5$ (number line, bracket at -5) or $x \geq -5$ (number line, filled circle at -5)

- **Order of operations**

Order of Operations	
1. brackets or parentheses and absolute values (innermost first)	( ) , [ ] , { } , | |
2. exponent	a^n
3. multiplication or division (from left to right)	× and ÷
4. addition or subtraction (from left to right)	+ and −

- **Signed numbers summary**

Operation	Method
adding signed numbers	- Add two numbers with the same sign: add their values, and keep their common sign. - Add two numbers with different signs: subtract their values, and keep the sign of the larger absolute value.
subtracting signed numbers	Subtract a number by adding its opposite.
multiplying signed numbers	(+)(+) = (+), (–)(–) = (+), (–)(+) = (–), (+)(–) = (–)
dividing signed numbers	$\frac{+}{+} = +$, $\frac{-}{-} = +$, $\frac{+}{-} = -$, $\frac{-}{+} = -$ Note: $\frac{0}{A} = 0$, $\frac{A}{0}$ is undefined

- **Review basic algebraic terms**

Algebraic Term	Description	Example
algebraic expression	A mathematical phrase that contains numbers, variables, and arithmetic operations.	$5x + 2$, $3a - 4b + 6$, $\frac{2y}{3} + 4$
constant	A number.	$x + \mathbf{2}$ constant: 2
variable	A letter that can be assigned different values.	$3 - \boldsymbol{x}$ variable: x
coefficient	The number that is in front of a variable.	$\mathbf{-6}\,x$ coefficient: -6 xz^3 coefficient: 1
term	A term can be a constant, variable, or the product of a number and variable(s).	$3x - \frac{2}{5} + 13y^2 + 73x$ Terms: $3x$, $-\frac{2}{5}$, $13y^2$, $73x$
like terms	The terms that have the same variables and exponents.	$2x - y^2 - \frac{2}{5} + 5x - 7 + 13y^2$ Like terms: $2x$ and $5x$ $-y^2$ and $13y^2$, $-\frac{2}{5}$ and -7

- **Properties of addition**

Additive Properties		Example
commutative property	$a + b = b + a$	$4 + 7 = 7 + 4$ (Switch the order)
associative property	$(a + b) + c = a + (b + c)$	$(7 + 2) + 9 = 7 + (2 + 9)$ (Switch the parentheses)
identity property	$a + 0 = a$	$12.7 + 0 = 12.7$
closure property	If a and b are real numbers, then $a + b$ is a real number.	If 9 and 11 are real numbers, then $9 + 11 = 20$ is a real number.
inverse property	$-a + a = 0$	$-100 + 100 = 0$

- **Properties of multiplication**

Multiplicative Properties		Example
commutative property	$a\,b = b\,a$	$9 \cdot 5 = 5 \cdot 9$ (Switch the order)
associative property	$(a\,b)\,c = a\,(b\,c)$	$(3 \cdot 7)\,5 = 3\,(7 \cdot 5)$ (Switch the parentheses)
identity property of 1	$a \cdot 1 = a$	$100{,}000 \cdot 1 = 100{,}000$
closure property	If a and b are real numbers, then ab is a real number.	If 3 and 5 are real numbers, then $(3)(5) = 15$ is a real number.
distributive property	$a\,(b + c) = ab + ac$	$2\,(3 - 4) = 2 \cdot 3 - 2 \cdot 4$
zero product property	$a \cdot 0 = 0$	$-76 \cdot 0 = 0$
inverse property	$a \cdot \frac{1}{a} = 1$ (number: a; its reciprocal: $\frac{1}{a}$)	$(-97) \cdot \frac{1}{(-97)} = 1$

- **Terms of operations**

Operations	
addition	addend + addend = sum
subtraction	subtrahend – minuend = difference
multiplication	multiplicand × multiplier = product (factor) (factor)
division	dividend ÷ divisor = quotient

- **Remove parentheses**

Algebraic Expression	Remove Parentheses	Example
$(Ax + B)$	$Ax + B$	$(3x + 4) = 3x + 4$
$(Ax - B)$	$Ax - B$	$\left(\frac{5}{6}x - 3\right) = \frac{5}{6}x - 3$
$-(Ax + B)$	$-Ax - B$	$-(2x + 7) = -2x - 7$
$-(Ax - B)$	$-Ax + B$	$-\left(\frac{1}{3}x - \frac{2}{5}\right) = \frac{-1}{3}x + \frac{2}{5}$

- **Rules of exponents**

Name	Property	Example
zero exponent a^0	$a^0 = 1$ ($a \neq 0$, 0^0 is undefined)	$15^0 = 1$
one exponent a^1	$a^1 = a$ (But $1^n = 1$)	$7^1 = 7$, $1^{13} = 1$
negative exponent a^{-n}	$a^{-n} = \frac{1}{a^n}$ ($a \neq 0$)	$4^{-2} = \frac{1}{4^2} = \frac{1}{16}$
	$\frac{1}{a^{-n}} = a^n$ or $a^{-n} \cdot a^n = 1$	$\frac{1}{4^{-2}} = 4^2 = 16$
product of like bases	$a^m a^n = a^{m+n}$ ($a \neq 0$)	$2^3 2^2 = 2^{3+2} = 2^5 = 32$
quotient of like bases (the same base)	$\frac{a^m}{a^n} = a^{m-n}$ ($a \neq 0$)	$\frac{y^3}{y^2} = y^{3-2} = y^1 = y$
power of a power	$(a^m)^n = a^{mn}$	$(x^3)^2 = x^{3 \cdot 2} = x^6$
power of a product (different bases)	$(a \cdot b)^n = a^n b^n$ ($a, b \neq 0$)	$(2 \cdot 3)^2 = 2^2 3^2 = 4 \cdot 9 = 36$
	$(a^m \cdot b^n)^p = a^{mp} b^{np}$	$(t^3 \cdot s^4)^2 = t^{3 \cdot 2} s^{4 \cdot 2} = t^6 s^8$
power of a quotient (different bases)	$\left(\frac{a}{b}\right)^n = \frac{a^n}{b^n}$ ($b \neq 0$)	$\left(\frac{2}{3}\right)^2 = \frac{2^2}{3^2} = \frac{4}{9}$
	$\left(\frac{a^m}{b^n}\right)^p = \frac{a^{mp}}{b^{np}}$	$\left(\frac{q^2}{p^4}\right)^3 = \frac{q^{2 \cdot 3}}{p^{4 \cdot 3}} = \frac{q^6}{p^{12}}$

- **Absolute value $|x|$:** the distance of a number x from zero on the number line
  No negatives for absolute value: $|-b| = |b|$
- **Opposite (or additive or negative inverse):** the opposite of a number (two numbers whose sum is 0).
- **Equivalent expressions:** two expressions are equivalent if they have the same value for all allowable replacements.
- **Combine (or collect) like terms:** add or subtract their numerical coefficients and keep the same variables and exponents.
- **Scientific notation**

Scientific Notation	Example
$N \times 10^{\pm n}$ $1 \leq N < 10$, n - integer	$34{,}005.9 = 3.40059 \times 10^4$ (standard form = scientific notation)

PRACTICE QUIZ

Unit 1 Fundamental Concepts

1. Write in set-builder notation and roster notation:

   "The set of numbers between -5 and 2."

2. Given $A = \{-9, 7\pi, \sqrt{5}, \frac{2}{3}\}$. Specify the following sets.

   a. $\{x \mid x \text{ is a negative number}\}$

   b. $\{b \mid b \text{ is an irrational number}\}$

3. Sketch the graphs of the following inequalities.

   a. $x < -2$

   b. $-1.5 \leq x < 7$

4. Perform the indicated operations.

   a. $(-1.3) + (-2)$

   b. $12 - (-7)$

   c. $(-3)(-0.1)(-5)$

   d. $\left(-\frac{3}{5}\right) \div \frac{1}{5}$

5. Evaluate the following.

   a. $(-0.2)^3$

   b. $m \cdot m \cdot m$

   c. $(-10855)^0$

   d. $\frac{3^2 + 5^2 - 2 \cdot 2}{3|2-7| \div (-3)}$

6. Evaluate $\frac{3y^2}{x-2} + 7y - 4$, given $x = -1$ and $y = 3$.

7. Translate words into algebraic expression.

a. 3 less than the product of 7 and y.

b. Twice the sum of t and 9.

8. Name the property.

a. $(2x + 5) + [-(2x + 5)] = 0$

b. $(b\ a)\ 7c = b\ (a \cdot 7c)$

9. **a.** Factor: $5abc - 25bc + 35c$

b. Multiply: $-3p(2q - r)$

c. Combine like terms: $4x^2 - 0.5y + 1.5y - 2x^2$

d. Simplify: $-3(x^2 - 2x) + 5(x - 3) - (4 + 3x - 2x^2)$

10. Simplify the following.

a. $(-2x^2)^3(y^3)^{-4}(-2.357z^{-178})^0$

b. $\left(\frac{(2x^2)\ y^4}{4x^3y^2}\right)^3$

11. Simplify and write in scientific notation.

a. $(4.3 \times 10^{-5})(3.25 \times 10^9)$

b. $\frac{(3\times10^{-5})(2.3\times10^4)}{1.2\times10^7}$

UNIT 2 EQUATIONS AND INEQUALITIES

2-1 SOLVING EQUATIONS

Equations

- **Equation:** A mathematical statement that contains two expressions separated by an equal sign (both sides of the equation have the same value).

  Example: $3x + 2 = 5$

- **To solve an equation** is the process of finding a particular value for the variable in the equation that makes the equation true.

  Example: For the equation $3x + 2 = 5$, only $x = 1$ can make it true, since $3 \cdot 1 + 2 = 5$.

- **Solution, root, or zero of an equation:** the particular value of the variable in the equation that makes the equation true. This value is also called "root" or "zero" of the equation.

  Example: For the equation $3x + 2 = 5$, $x = \mathbf{1}$ is the solution.

  More examples: Indicate whether each of the given number is a solution.

a.	5:	$2x - 3 = 7$	$2 \cdot 5 - 3 \overset{?}{=} 7$	$7 \overset{\surd}{=} 7$	**Yes**
b.	-3:	$10 + \frac{4}{12}y = 9$	$10 + \frac{4}{12}(-3) \overset{?}{=} 9$	$9 \overset{\surd}{=} 9$	**Yes**
c.	1:	$3t + 2(t - 4) = 5t - 6$	$3 \cdot 1 + 2(1 - 4) \overset{?}{=} 5 \cdot 1 - 6$		
			$3 - 6 \overset{?}{=} -1$	$-3 \neq -1$	**No**

- **Solution Set { }:** the set of all values that makes the equation true.

  Example: The solution set to $x^2 - 4 = 0$ is **{-2, 2}.**

  Since $(-2)^2 - 4 \overset{\surd}{=} 0$ and $2^2 - 4 \overset{\surd}{=} 0$

Linear Equations

- **Linear equation (or first-degree equation) in one variable:** an equation in which the highest **power** (exponent) of the **variable** is **one**. (An equation whose graph is a straight line.)
- **Standard form** of a linear equation in one variable: $Ax + B = 0$ $\quad x = x^1$

  $A \neq 0$, A and B are constants.

  Examples of linear equations:

  $3x + 2 = 0$

  $7y - 5 = 3 + 2y$

  $9 + \frac{5x}{11} = 4 - 3x$

- **Second-degree equation:** an equation in which the highest power of the variable is two.

  Example: $5x^2 + 6x + 7 = 0$

  In general, a first-degree equation contains an "x" term (or any variable), a second-degree equation contains an "x^2" term, and a third-degree equation contains an "x^3" term, etc.

- **Equations of different degrees**

Equation	Standard Form	Example	Comments
first-degree equation (linear equation)	$Ax + B = 0$ $(x = x^1)$	$5x + 4 = 0$	The highest power of x is 1.
second-degree equation (quadratic equation)	$Ax^2 + Bx + C = 0$	$2x^2 + 7x - 3 = 0$	The highest power of x is 2.
third-degree equation (cubic equation)	$Ax^3 + Bx^2 + Cx + D = 0$	$3x^3 + 4x^2 - 8x + 1 = 0$	The highest power of x is 3.
fourth-degree equation	$Ax^4 + Bx^3 + Cx^2 + Dx + E = 0$	$x^4 - 9x^3 + 3x^2 + 2x - 5 = 0$	The highest power of x is 4.

- **Higher-degree equations are nonlinear equations.**
- **A linear equation in two variables:** an equation with two variables in which the highest power (exponent) of two **variables** is one.

  Standard form: $Ax + By = C$ $\quad A$, B, and C are constants.

  Example: $2x + y = 3$

Properties of Equality

Properties for solving equations

Properties	Equality	Example
property of addition	$A = B,\ A + C = B + C$	Solve $y - 7 = 2$ $y - 7 + 7 = 2 + 7,\quad y = \mathbf{9}$
property of subtraction	$A = B,\ A - C = B - C$	Solve $x + 3 = -8$ $x + 3 - 3 = -8 - 3,\quad x = \mathbf{-11}$
property of multiplication	$A = B,\quad A \cdot C = B \cdot C$ $(C \neq 0)$	Solve $\frac{-t}{6} = 7$ $\frac{-t}{6}(-6) = 7(-6),\quad t = \mathbf{-42}$
property of division	$A = B,\quad \frac{A}{C} = \frac{B}{C}$ $(C \neq 0)$	Solve $4a = -16$ $\frac{4a}{4} = \frac{-16}{4},\quad a = \mathbf{-4}$

Example: Solve the following equations.

Solution

1. $-7 + x = 3$

$-7 + x + 7 = 3 + 7$ — Property of addition

$x = \mathbf{10}$

Check: $-7 + 10 \overset{?}{=} 3 \qquad 3 \overset{\surd}{=} 3$ — Replace x with 10.

2. $y + \frac{1}{3} = -1$

$y + \frac{1}{3} - \frac{1}{3} = -1 - \frac{1}{3}$ — Property of subtraction

$y = -\frac{4}{3}$

3. $\frac{-1}{4}x = 5$

$-4 \cdot \frac{-1}{4}x = 5(-4)$ — Property of multiplication

$x = \mathbf{-20}$

4. $-2x = 14$

$\frac{-2x}{-2} = \frac{14}{-2}$ — Property of division

$x = \mathbf{-7}$

5. $0.3y = -0.96$

$\frac{0.3y}{0.3} = \frac{-0.96}{0.3}$ — Property of division

$y = \mathbf{-3.2}$

6. $-2x - 3 = 5$

$-2x - 3 + 3 = 5 + 3$ — Property of addition

$-2x = 8,\quad \frac{-2x}{-2} = \frac{8}{-2}$ — Property of division

$x = \mathbf{-4}$

Procedure for Solving Equations

Equation-Solving Strategy

- Clear the fractions or decimal if necessary.
- Remove parentheses.
- Combine like terms on each side of the equation if necessary.
- Collect the variable terms on one side of the equation and the numerical terms on the other side.
- Isolate the variable.
- Check the solution with the original equation.

Procedure for solving linear equations

Steps

- Eliminate the denominators if the equation has fractions.
- Remove parentheses.
- Combine like terms.
- Collect variable terms on one side and the constants on the other side.
- Isolate the variable.
- Check.

Example: Solve $\frac{1}{2}(x+1) = 3x - 2x$.

$2 \cdot \frac{1}{2}(x+1) = 2(3x) - 2(2x)$ Multiply each term by 2.

$x + 1 = 6x - 4x$

$x + 1 = 2x$

$x + 1 - 2x - 1 = 2x - 2x - 1$ Subtract $2x$ and 1 from both sides.

$-x = -1$ Divide both sides by -1.

$x = 1$

$\frac{1}{2}(1+1) \stackrel{?}{=} 3 \cdot 1 - 2 \cdot 1$

$1 \stackrel{\surd}{=} 1$ Correct!

Example: Solve $4(y-3) + 3y + 2 = 2(4-y)$.

$4y - 12 + 3y + 2 = 8 - 2y$ Remove parentheses.

$7y - 10 = 8 - 2y$ Combine like terms.

$7y - 10 + 2y + 10 = 8 - 2y + 2y + 10$ Add 2y & 10 to both sides.

$9y = 18$ Isolate the variable.

$y = 2$

Check: $4(2-3) + 3 \cdot 2 + 2 \stackrel{?}{=} 2(4-2)$

$4 \stackrel{\surd}{=} 4$ Correct!

Equations Involving Decimals/Fractions

- **Equations involving decimals**

Steps	Example: Solve $0.25x - 0.20 = -3.15x$.
- Multiply each term by 100 to clear the decimal.	$100(0.25x) - 100(0.20) = 100(-3.15x)$
- Collect the variable terms on one side of the equation and the constants on the other side.	$25x - 20 = -315x$ $25x + 315x = 20$ $340x = 20$
- Isolate the variable.	$x \approx 0.06$

Example: Solve $0.3y + 0.06 = 0.009$. — Multiply each term by 1,000.

$1{,}000(0.3y) + 1{,}000(0.06) = 1{,}000(0.009)$

$300y + 60 = 9$ — Combine like terms.

$300y = -51$ — Divide both sides by 300.

$y = -0.17$

Tip: Multiply every term of both sides of the equation by a power of 10 (10, 100, 1000, etc.) to clear the decimals.

- **Equations involving fractions**

Steps	Example: Solve $\frac{2x}{3} + \frac{1}{4} = -\frac{x}{2} - \frac{2}{3}$.
- Multiply each term by the LCD.	$12 \cdot \frac{2x}{3} + 12 \cdot \frac{1}{4} = 12\left(-\frac{x}{2}\right) - 12 \cdot \frac{2}{3}$
- Collect the variable terms on one side of the equation and the constants on the other side.	$8x + 3 = -6x - 8$ $14x = -11$
- Isolate the variable.	$x = \frac{-11}{14}$

2-2 LINEAR EQUATIONS AND MODELING

Geometry Formulas

- **Formula:** an equation that contains more than one variable and is used to solve practical problems in everyday life.
- **Recall some geometry formulas**

  P – perimeter, C – circumference, A – area, V – volume

Name of the Figure	Formula	Figure
rectangle	$P = 2l + 2w$ $A = lw$	w l
parallelogram	$P = 2a + 2b$ $A = bh$	h a b
circle	$C = \pi d = 2\pi r$ $A = \pi r^2$	r d
triangle	$\angle X + \angle Y + \angle Z = 180^0$ $A = \frac{1}{2}bh$	X h Y b Z
trapezoid	$A = \frac{1}{2}h(b + B)$	b h B
cube	$V = s^3$	s
rectangular solid	$V = lwh$	h l w
cylinder	$V = \pi r^2 h$	r h
sphere	$V = \frac{4}{3}\pi r^3$	r
cone	$V = \frac{1}{3}\pi r^2 h$	h r
pyramid	$V = \frac{1}{3}lwh$	h l w

Solving Formulas

Example: Solve the formula for the given letter.

Solution

1. $d = rt$, for t — $\frac{d}{r} = \frac{rt}{r}$ $t = \frac{d}{r}$

2. $I = Prt$, for r — $\frac{I}{Pt} = \frac{Prt}{Pt}$ $r = \frac{I}{Pt}$

3. $P = 2l + 2w$, for w — $P - 2l = 2l + 2w - 2l$

   $P - 2l = 2w$, $\frac{P-2l}{2} = \frac{2w}{2}$

   $\frac{p-2l}{2} = w$

4. $F = \frac{9}{5}C + 32$, for C — $F - 32 = \frac{9}{5}C + 32 - 32$

   $F - 32 = \frac{9}{5}C$

   $(F - 32)\frac{5}{9} = \frac{9}{5} \cdot \frac{5}{9}C$

   $C = \frac{5}{9}(F - 32)$

Tip: Solve a formula for a given letter by isolating the given letter on one side of the equation.

- **More formulas**

Application	Formula	Component
distance	$d = rt,\ r = \frac{d}{t},\ t = \frac{d}{r}$	d – distance r – speed t – time
simple interest	$I = Prt,\ P = \frac{I}{rt},\ t = \frac{I}{Pr}$	I – interest P – principle r – interest rate (%) t – time (years)
compound interest	$B = P(100\% + r)^t$	B – balance P – principle r – interest rate (%) t – time (years)
percent increase	$\frac{N - O}{O}$	N – new value O – original value
percent decrease	$\frac{O - N}{O}$	N – new value O – original value
sale price	$S = L - rL,\ L = \frac{S}{1-r}$	S – sale price L – list price r – discount rate
intelligence quotient (I.Q.)	$I = \frac{100m}{c}$	I – I.Q. m – mental age c – chronological age
temperature	$C = \frac{5}{9}(F - 32),\ F = \frac{9}{5}C + 32$	C – Celsius F – Fahrenheit

PROBLEM SOLVING

Steps for solving word problems

Steps for Solving Word Problems

- Organize the ***facts*** given from the problem.
- Identify and label the unknown quantity (***let x = unknown***).
- Draw a ***diagram*** if it will make the problem clearer.
- Convert words into a mathematical ***equation***.
- ***Solve*** the equation and find the solution(s).
- ***Check*** and state the ***answer***.

Number Problems

English Phrase	Algebraic Expression/ Equation
3 more than the difference of a number and 9.	$(x-9)+3$
The quotient of 3 and the product of 7 and a number.	$\frac{3}{7x}$
The product of seven and a number, decreased by five.	$7x-5$
9 less than 4 times two numbers is 2 more than their sum.	$4xy-9=2+x+y$
The sum of the squares of two numbers is 4 less than their product.	$x^2+y^2=xy-4$
6 more than the quotient of $2x$ by 3 is 5 times that number.	$6+\frac{2x}{3}=5x$

(Let x = a number ; y = a number)

Example: Three more than two times a number is fifteen less than the number divided by five. Find the number.

- Organize the facts. $+3$ $2x$ $=$ -15 $+$ $\frac{x}{5}$ Let x = number.
- Equation: $\mathbf{2x+3=\frac{x}{5}-15}$ Multiply each term by 5.

$5(2x)+5\cdot 3=5\left(\frac{x}{5}\right)-5\cdot 15$ Remove parentheses.

$10x+15=x-75$ Combine like terms.

$9x=-90$ Divide both sides by 9.

- Solution: $\mathbf{x=-10}$

- Check: $2(-10) + 3 \stackrel{?}{=} \frac{-10}{5} - 15$

  $-20 + 3 \stackrel{?}{=} -2 - 15$

  $-17 \stackrel{\surd}{=} -17$ Correct!

- State the answer: the number is -10.

Example: There are **three** numbers; the **first** is **two less** than **four times** the **second**, and the **third** is **five more** than **one-half** of the **first**. The **sum** of these **three** numbers **is sixteen**.

Find the second number.

- Organize the facts:

Number	Wording	Algebraic Expression
2nd number	let 2nd number = x	x
1st number	2 less than 4 times the 2nd number	$4x - 2$
3rd number	5 more than $\frac{1}{2}$ of the 1st number	$\frac{1}{2}(4x-2)+5$
sum	the sum of three numbers is 16	$1^{st}\# + 2^{nd}\# + 3^{rd}\# = 16$

- Equation: $\mathbf{(4x - 2) + x + \left[\frac{1}{2}(4x-2)+5\right] = 16}$ Remove parentheses.

  $4x - 2 + x + 2x - 1 + 5 = 16$ Combine like terms.

  $7x + 2 = 16$

  $7x = 14$ Divide both sides by 7.

- Solution: $\mathbf{x = 2}$

1st Number	$4x - 2 = 4 \cdot 2 - 2 = \mathbf{6}$
2nd Number	$x = \mathbf{2}$
3rd Number	$\frac{1}{2}(4x-2)+5 = \frac{1}{2}(4 \cdot 2 - 2) + 5 = \mathbf{8}$

Consecutive Integers

English Phrase	Algebraic Expression	Example
two consecutive integers	$x, \ x+1$	If $x = \mathbf{1}$, $x + 1 = \mathbf{2}$
two consecutive **odd** integers	$x, \ x+2$	If $x = \mathbf{1}$, $x + 2 = \mathbf{3}$
two consecutive **even** integers	$x, \ x+2$ or $2x, \ 2x+2$	If $x = \mathbf{2}$, $x + 2 = \mathbf{4}$ If $x = \mathbf{1}$, $2x = \mathbf{2}$, $2x + 2 = \mathbf{4}$
three consecutive **odd** integers	$x, \ x+2, \ x+4$	If $x = \mathbf{1}$, $x + 2 = \mathbf{3}$, $x + 4 = \mathbf{5}$
three consecutive **even** integers	$x, \ x+2, \ x+4$	If $x = \mathbf{2}$, $x + 2 = \mathbf{4}$, $x + 4 = \mathbf{6}$
The product of two consecutive odd integers is 10	$x(x+2) = 10$	
Three consecutive even integers whose sum is 35.	$x + (x+2) + (x+4) = 35$	

Example: The **sum** of **four consecutive even** integers is **20**; find each number.

- Organize the facts.

1st consecutive even number	x
2nd consecutive even number	$x + 2$
3rd consecutive even number	$x + 4$
4th consecutive even number	$x + 6$

- Equation: $\mathbf{x + (x + 2) + (x + 4) + (x + 6) = 20}$ Combine like terms.
- Solution: $4x + 12 = 20$ Solve for x.

  $\mathbf{x = 2}$
- State the answer.

1st consecutive even number	$x = \mathbf{2}$
2nd consecutive even number	$x + 2 = 2 + 2 = \mathbf{4}$
3rd consecutive even number	$x + 4 = 2 + 4 = \mathbf{6}$
4th consecutive even number	$x + 6 = 2 + 6 = \mathbf{8}$

- Check: $2, 4, 6, 8 \stackrel{?}{=}$ consecutive even integers Yes!

  $2 + (2 + 2) + (2 + 4) + (2 + 6) \stackrel{?}{=} 20$

  $20 \stackrel{\surd}{=} 20$ Correct!

Example: Find **three consecutive odd integers** such that **three times** the **first** integer **is one less than** the **sum** of the **second and third** integers.

- Organize the facts.

Integer	Consecutive Odd Integer
1st integer	x
2nd integer	$x + 2$
3rd integer	$x + 4$

- Equation: $\mathbf{3x = (x + 2) + (x + 4) - 1}$
- Solution: $3x = x + 2 + x + 4 - 1$

  $\mathbf{x = 5}$
- State the answer.

1st consecutive odd number	$x = \mathbf{5}$
2nd consecutive odd number	$x + 2 = 5 + 2 = \mathbf{7}$
3rd consecutive odd number	$x + 4 = 5 + 4 = \mathbf{9}$

Business Problems

Application	Formula
Percent Increase	Percent increase $= \dfrac{\text{New value} - \text{Original value}}{\text{Original value}}$, $x = \dfrac{N-O}{O}$
Percent Decrease	Percent decrease $= \dfrac{\text{Original value} - \text{New value}}{\text{Original value}}$, $x = \dfrac{O-N}{O}$
Sales Tax	sales tax = sales × tax rate
Commission	commission = sales × commission rate
Discount	discount = original price × discount rate sale price = original price – discount
Markup	markup = original price × markup rate original price = selling price – markup
Simple Interest	interest = principle × interest rate × time, $I = P\,r\,t$ balance = principle + interest
Compound Interest	balance = principle (100% + interest rate)^t balance $= P(100\% + r)^t$

Example: A product increased production from **1,500 last month** to **1,650 this month**. Find the **percent increase.**

New value (N): 1,650 — this month

Original value (O): 1,500 — last month

Percent increase: $x = \dfrac{N-O}{O} = \dfrac{1{,}650 - 1{,}500}{1{,}500} = 0.1 = \mathbf{10\%}$ — 10% increase

Example: A product was **reduced** from **$33** to **$29.** What percent **reduction** is this?

Percent decrease: $x = \dfrac{O-N}{O} = \dfrac{33-29}{33} \approx 0.12 = \mathbf{12\%}$ — 12% decrease

Example: The **tax rate** is **7%**, find the **sales tax** for a **$1,050** laptop.

Sales tax = Sales × Tax rate

= ($1,050)(7%) = ($1,050)(0.07) = **$73.50**

Example: The **commission rate** is **5%**, find **commission** for a **$550,000** house.

Commission = Sales × Commission rate

= ($550,000)(5%) = ($550,000)(0.05) = **$27,500**

Example: A women's jacket **originally** priced at **$47** is on sale at a **35% discount**. Find the **discount** and **sale price**.

Discount = Original price × Discount rate

= ($47)(35%) = ($47)(0.35) = **$16.45**

Sale price = Original price – Discount

= $47 – $16.45 = **$30.55**

Example: A condo **originally** sold at **$258,000**, and the **markup rate** is **10%.** What is the **markup** and the new **selling price**?

Markup = Original price × Markup rate

= ($258,000)(10%) = ($258,000)(0.10) = **$25,800**

Selling price = Original price + Markup

= $258,000 + $25,800 = **$283,800**

Example: Tom borrowed **$200,000** mortgage from a bank. Find the interest at **2.8%** per year for $5\frac{1}{2}$ **years**, and the **total** amount that he paid the bank.

Interest = Principle × Interest rate × Time

$$I = Prt = (\$200{,}000)(2.8\%)\left(5\frac{1}{2}\right)$$

= ($200,000)(0.028)(5.5) = **$30,800**

Balance = Principle + Interest

= $ 200,000 + $ 30,800 = **$230,800**

Example: Allan deposited **$5,000** in an account at **3.5% interest compounded annually** for **5 years**. How much was in the account at the end of **5 years**?

Balance = Principle (100% + Interest rate) ^{t}

$= P(100\% + r)^{t} = \$5{,}000\ (100\% + 3.5\%)^{5}$

$= \$5{,}000\ (1 + 0.035)^{5} \approx$ **$ 5,938**

Application	Formula
Sales	**Discount:** Original price – Discount rate × Original price = New price $x - \% \, x =$ New price
	Purchase: Original price + Tax rate × Original price = New price $x + \% \, x =$ New price
Commission	Commission on the 1st \$100,000 + Commission on the amount > \$100,000 = Total commission $\% \cdot 100{,}000 + \% \, (S - 100{,}000) =$ Total commission ↑ selling price

Example: Bob pays \$1,050 for a laptop. The price includes a 12% sales tax. What is the price of the laptop itself?

original price (the price of the laptop itself)	x
tax rate	12%
new price (price + tax)	\$1,050

- Equation: $\mathbf{x + 12\% \, x = \$1{,}050}$ — $x + \% \, x =$ New price
- Solution: $x\,(1 + 0.12) = \$1{,}050$

$$x = \frac{1{,}050}{1.12} = \mathbf{\$937.50}$$

The price of the laptop itself is \$937.50.

Example: The following is a real estate commission on the selling price of a house:

- 7% for the first \$100,000
- 5% for the amount > \$100,000

A realtor receives a commission of \$20,000, what was the selling price?

- Formula: $\% \cdot 100{,}000 + \% \, (S - 100{,}000) =$ Total commission
- Solution: $7\% \cdot 100{,}000 + 5\% \, (S - 100{,}000) = \$20{,}000$

$$0.07(100{,}000) + 0.05\,S - 0.05(100{,}000) = 20{,}000$$

$$7000 + 0.05\,S - 5{,}000 = 20{,}000$$

$$0.05\,S = 18{,}000$$

$$\mathbf{S = \$\,360{,}000}$$

Selling price

Motion Problems

- **Formula**

Distance = Speed · Time $d = r\,t$ $t = \frac{d}{r}$ $r = \frac{d}{t}$

Condition	Speed (r)	Time (t)	Distance (d)
A	r	t	$d = rt$
B	r	t	$d = rt$
Total			

Example: Two cyclists are **18 km apart** and are travelling towards each other. Their **speeds differ** by **2 km** per hour. What is the **speed** of **each** cyclist if they meet after **3 hours**?

Condition	Speed (r)	Time (t)	Distance ($d = rt$)
bike A	r (km/h)	$t = 3$ h	$3r$
bike B	$r - 2$ (km/h)	$t = 3$ h	$3(r - 2)$
Total			18 km

Equation: $\mathbf{3r + 3\,(r - 2) = 18}$ Distance of A + distance of B = 18km.

bike A: $\mathbf{r = 4}$ **km/h**

bike B: $\mathbf{r - 2} = 4 - 2 = \mathbf{2}$ **km/h**

Example: John **boats** at a **speed** of **30** km per hour in still water. The **river** flows at a **speed** of **10** km per hour. How long will it take John to boat **2 km downstream**? **2 km upstream**?

Condition	Speed (r)	Distance (d)	Time ($t = \frac{d}{r}$)
downstream	$r = 30 + 10 = 40$ km/h	$d = 2$ km	$t = \frac{d}{r} = \frac{2km}{40km/h}$
upstream	$r = 30 - 10 = 20$ km/h	$d = 2$ km	$t = \frac{d}{r} = \frac{2km}{20km/h}$

downstream (fast): speed of boat + speed of river
upstream (slower): speed of boat - speed of river

downstream: $t = \frac{d}{r} = \frac{2km}{40km/h} = \mathbf{0.05\ h}$

upstream: $t = \frac{d}{r} = \frac{2km}{20km/h} = \mathbf{0.1\ h}$

Value Mixture Problems

Item	Value of the Item	Number of Items	Total Value
A	value of A	# of item A	(value of A)(# of item A)
B	value of B	# of item B	(value of B)(# of item B)
C	value of C	# of item C	(value of C)(# of item C)
total or mixture			total value

Let x = unknown.

Value of item A + Value of item B + Value of item C = Total value of the mixture

Example: Jack has **$5.35** in nickels, dimes and quarters. If he has **five less** than **two times quarters of dimes**, and **seven more nickels than quarters**. How many of each coin does he have?

Coin	Value of the Coin	Number of Coins	Total Value (in cents)
quarter	25 ¢	x	$25x$
dime	10 ¢	$2x - 5$	$10(2x - 5)$
nickel	5 ¢	$x + 7$	$5(x + 7)$
Total			$5.35 = 535 ¢

Let x = numbers of quarters.

- Equation: $\mathbf{25x + 10(2x - 5) + 5(x + 7) = 535}$ value of quarters + value of dimes + value of nickels = 535 ¢
- Solution: $25x + 20x - 50 + 5x + 35 = 535$ Remove parentheses.

  $50x - 15 = 535$ Combine like terms.

  $x = \mathbf{11}$ Solve for x.
- State the answer:

number of quarters	$\mathbf{x = 11}$
number of dimes	$\mathbf{2x - 5 = 2(11) - 5 = 17}$
number of nickels	$\mathbf{x + 7 = 11 + 7 = 18}$

Example: Evan purchased 46-cent, 66-cent, and 86-cent Canadian stamps with a total value of $16.38. If the number of 66-cent stamps is 5 more than the number of 46-cent stamps, and the number of 86-cent stamps is 8 more than one half the number of 46-cent stamps. How many of each did Evan receive?

Stamps	Value of the Stamps	Number of Stamps	Total Value (in cents)
46-cent	46 ¢	x	$46x$
66-cent	66 ¢	$5 + x$	$66(5 + x)$
86-cent	86 ¢	$8 + \frac{1}{2}x$	$86(8 + \frac{1}{2}x)$
Total			1638 ¢

Let x = number of 46-cent stamps.

- Equation: $\mathbf{46x + 66(5 + x) + 86(8 + \frac{1}{2}x) = 1638}$ value of 46-cent + value of 66-cent + value of 86-cent = 1638 ¢
- Solution: $46x + 330 + 66x + 688 + 43x = 1638$ Remove parentheses & combine like terms.

  $155x = 620$

  $\mathbf{x = 4}$ 46-cent: 4

  $\mathbf{5 + x} = 5 + 4 = \mathbf{9}$ 66-cent: 9

  $\mathbf{8 + \frac{1}{2}x} = 8 + \frac{1}{2} \cdot 4 = \mathbf{10}$ 86-cent: 10

Concentration/Mixture Problems

Item	Concentration	Volume	Amount
A	concentration of A	volume of A	(concentration of A)(volume of A)
B	concentration of B	volume of B	(concentration of B)(volume of B)
Mixture	concentration of mixture	volume of mixture	(concentration of mixture)(volume of the mixture)

Let x = unknown

Amount of item A + Amount of item B = Amount of the mixture

Example: A **chicken meal** is **30%** protein and a **beef meal** is **40%** protein. Steve wants an **800 grams mixture** that is **35%** protein. How many grams of each meal should he have?

Meal	Concentration	Protein Volume	Amount
chicken meal	30% = 0.3	x	$0.3\,x$
beef meal	40% = 0.4	$800 - x$	$0.4\,(800 - x)$
Mixture	35% = 0.35	800	0.35 (800)

Let x = Protein volume of the chicken meal

Equation: $\mathbf{0.3\,x + 0.4\,(800 - x) = (0.35)(800)}$

Amount of chicken meal + Amount of beef meal = amount of the mixture

$0.3\,x + 320 - 0.4\,x = 280$

$-\,0.1\,x = -40$

$\mathbf{x = 400\text{ g}}$ chicken meal

$\mathbf{800 - x} = 800 - 400 = \mathbf{400\text{ g}}$ beef meal

Example: How much 5% salt solution must be added to 20 liters of 25% solution to make a 10% solution?

Solution	Concentration	Volume	Amount
5%	0.05	x	$0.05x$
25%	0.25	20	(0.25)(20)
10%	0.1	$20 + x$	$0.1(20 + x)$

Let x = Volume of 5% solution.

Equation: $\mathbf{0.05x + (0.25)(20) = 0.1\,(20 + x)}$ Amount of 5% + Amount of 25% = Amount of 10%

$0.05x + 5 = 2 + 0.1\,x$

$0.05\,x = 3$

$\mathbf{x = 60\text{ liters}}$ Volume of 5% solution.

2-3 SETS AND INEQUALITIES

Inequalities

- **An inequality** is a mathematical statement that contains $<$, $>$, $\geq$, or $\leq$ symbol.
- **Inequality symbols**

Symbols	Meaning	Example
>	is greater than	$15x + 7 > 0$
<	is less than	$4x - 3y < \frac{13}{25}$
≥	is greater than or equal to	$x + 5y \geq -12$
≤	Is less than or equal to	$3x - 14y \leq 67$

- **Compound inequality** is a statement that contains more than one inequality. $a < x < b$
- **The solution of an inequality** is the particular value of the variable in the inequality that makes the inequality true.

Example: Indicate if $x = 3$, -5 and $\frac{1}{2}$ are solutions of the inequality $\mathbf{6 - 2x < 5x}$.

1. For $x = 3$

$6 - 2 \cdot 3 \overset{?}{<} 5 \cdot 3$ — Substitute x for 3.

$0 \overset{\surd}{<} 15$ **True** — $x = 3$ is a solution.

2. For $x = -5$

$6 - 2(-5) \overset{?}{<} 5(-5)$ — Substitute x for -5.

$6 + 10 \overset{?}{<} -25$

$16 \overset{\times}{<} -25$ **False** — $x = -5$ is not a solution.

3. For $x = \frac{1}{2}$

$6 - 2 \cdot \frac{1}{2} \overset{?}{<} 5 \cdot \frac{1}{2}$ — Substitute x for $\frac{1}{2}$.

$6 - 1 \overset{?}{<} \frac{5}{2}$

$5 \overset{\times}{<} \frac{5}{2}$ **False** — $x = \frac{1}{2}$ is not a solution.

Intervals

- **Interval:** a set of numbers between or possibly including two given numbers.

- **Interval notation:**
  - **Open interval ( ):** the end points are not included.
  - **Closed interval [ ]:** the end points are included.
  - **Half-open interval (a, b]:** a is not included, but b is included.

    [a, b): a is included, but b is not included.
  - **Non-ending open interval (a, ∞):** a is not included and infinity is always excluded.

    (-∞, a): a is not included and infinity is always excluded.
  - **Non-ending half-open interval (-∞, b]:** b is included and infinity is always excluded.

    [b, ∞): b is included and infinity is always excluded.

- **Double inequality ($a < x < b$)** indicates "betweenness", meaning both $a < x$, $x < b$, and a must be less than b.

- **Strict inequalities:** an inequality that uses the symbols $<$ or $>$.

- **Weak inequalities:** an inequality that uses the symbol $\leq$ or $\geq$.

- **Graphing real-number inequalities**
  - **The empty circle ○ or open interval ( ):** the endpoints are excluded.
  - **The filled in circle ● or closed interval [ ]:** the endpoints are included.
  - Use a **heavy line** and an open or closed interval or an empty circle or filled-in circle to graph intervals.

- **Interval summary**

Inequality	Interval Notation	Set-Builder Notation	Example Empty/filled in circle	Graph Open/closed interval
$a < x < b$	(a, b)	$\{ x \mid a < x < b \}$	$2 < x < 5$	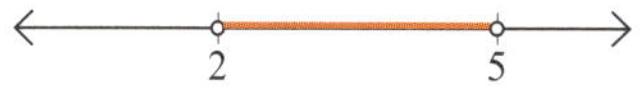
$a \leq x \leq b$	$[a, b]$	$\{ x \mid a \leq x \leq b \}$	$2 \leq x \leq 5$	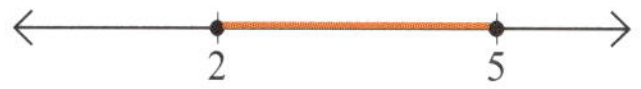
$a \leq x < b$	$[a, b)$	$\{ x \mid a \leq x < b \}$	$2 \leq x < 5$	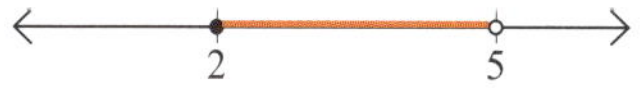
$a < x \leq b$	$(a, b]$	$\{ x \mid a < x \leq b \}$	$2 < x \leq 5$	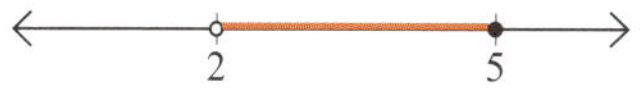
$a < x < \infty$	(a, ∞)	$\{ x \mid x > a \}$	$x > 2$	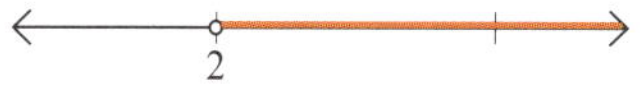
$a \leq x < \infty$	$[a, \infty)$	$\{ x \mid x \geq a \}$	$x \geq 2$	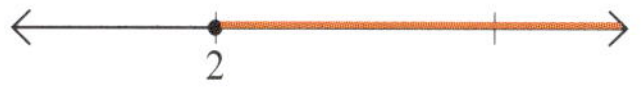
$-\infty < x < b$	$(-\infty, b)$	$\{ x \mid x < b \}$	$x < 5$	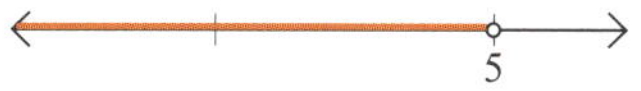
$-\infty < x \leq b$	$(-\infty, b]$	$\{ x \mid x \leq b \}$	$x \leq 5$	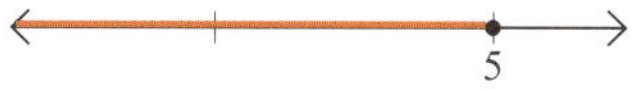
$-\infty < x < \infty$	$(-\infty, \infty)$	$\{ x \mid -\infty < x < \infty \}$	$-\infty < x < \infty$	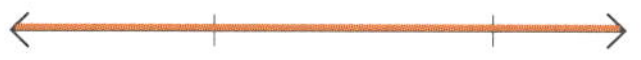

Example: Express the following in interval notation. **Solution**

1. $\{ x \mid x < -3 \}$ — **$(-\infty, -3)$**

2. $\{ x \mid -5 \leq x < 5 \}$ — **$[-5, 5)$**

3. 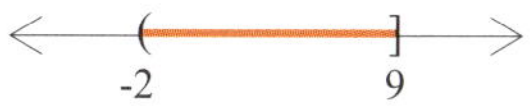

— **$(-2, 9]$**

4. 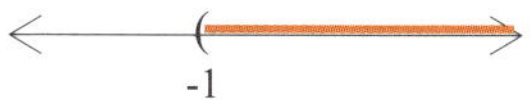

— **$(-1, \infty)$**

Example: Graph the following inequalities on a number line.

1. $\{ x \mid x < 2 \}$

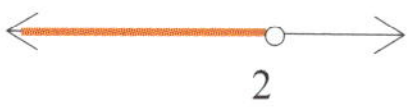

or
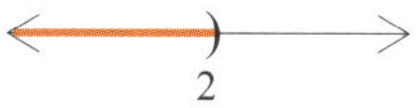

2. $\{ t \mid -4 \leq t < 3 \}$

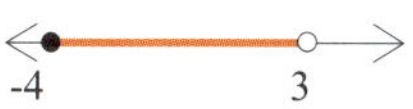

or
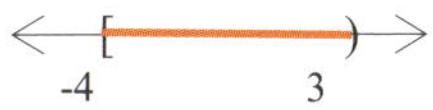

3. $\{ z \mid -2 < z \leq 7 \}$

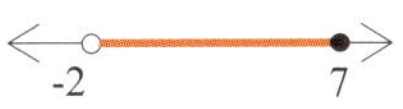

or
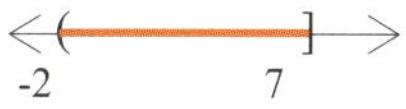

Properties of Inequalities

- **Addition property of inequality:** add or subtract the same value on each side of an inequality and the inequality remains true.

  If $a > b$, then $a + c > b + c$

  Example: $x - 4 > 3$
  $x - 4 + 4 > 3 + 4$
  $x > 7$

- **Subtraction property of inequality:** subtract the same value from each side of an inequality and the inequality remains true.

  If $a < b$, then $a - c < b - c$

  Example: $y + 2 < 3$
  $y + 2 - 2 < 3 - 2$
  $y < 1$

- **Multiplication property of inequality:** multiply the same positive value on each side of an inequality and the inequality remains true.

  If $a \geq b$, then $ac \geq bc$

  Example: $\frac{2}{3}x \geq 5$
  $\frac{2}{3}x \cdot \frac{3}{2} \geq 5 \cdot \frac{3}{2}$
  $x \geq \frac{15}{2}$

  Note: When multiplying each side of the inequality by a negative number, reverse the inequality sign.

  If $a > b$, then $a(-c) < b(-c)$

  Example: $-\frac{2}{3}x > 2$
  $-\frac{2}{3}x\left(-\frac{3}{2}\right) < 2\left(-\frac{3}{2}\right)$
  $x < -3$

- **Division property of equality:** divide the same positive value on each side of an inequality and the inequality remains true.

  If $a \leq b$, then $\frac{a}{c} \leq \frac{b}{c}$ $(c \neq 0)$

  Example: $4y \leq \frac{1}{3}$
  $\frac{4y}{4} \leq \frac{1}{3 \cdot 4}$, $y \leq \frac{1}{12}$

  Note: When dividing each side of the inequality by a negative number, reverse the inequality sign.

  If $a < b$, then $\frac{a}{-c} > \frac{b}{-c}$

  Example: $-4y \leq \frac{1}{3}$
  $-\frac{4y}{-4} \geq \frac{1}{3(-4)}$, $y \geq -\frac{1}{12}$

Solving Inequalities

- **Solving an inequality** is the process of finding a particular value for the variable in the inequality that makes the inequality true.
- **The procedure for solving linear inequalities** is similar to solving basic equations.

Example: Solve the inequality $\mathbf{6x + 1 \geq -17}$ and graph the solution set.

$6x + 1 - 1 \geq -17 - 1$ — Subtract 1 from both sides.

$6x \geq -18$ — Divide both sides by 6.

$x \geq -3$ $\quad$ $[-3, \infty)$ or $\{x \mid x \geq -3\}$

-3

Check:

Method I

Treat the inequality as an equation & check.

$6x + 1 = -17, \quad x = -3$

$6(-3) + 1 \overset{?}{=} -17$ — Replace x with -3.

$-18 + 1 \overset{?}{=} -17$

$-17 \overset{\surd}{=} -17$ — Correct!

Method II

Choose any number greater than -3 (say 0).

$6x + 1 \geq -17, \quad x = 0$

$6(0) + 1 \overset{?}{\geq} -17$ — Replace x with 0.

$1 \overset{\surd}{\geq} -17$ — Correct!

Example: Solve the following inequality and graph the solution set.

$\mathbf{4 - 2(x - 5) - 3x \geq 2x + 11}$ — Remove parenthesis.

$4 - 2x + 10 - 3x \geq 2x + 11$ — Combine like terms.

$14 - 5x \geq 2x + 11$ — Isolate x.

$-7x \geq -3$ — Divide both sides by -7.

$\frac{-7x}{-7} \leq \frac{-3}{-7}, \quad x \leq \frac{3}{7}$ — Reverse the symbol.

$\{x \mid x \leq \frac{3}{7}\}$ $\quad$ $(-\infty, \frac{3}{7}]$

$\frac{3}{7}$

Example: Solve the inequality $\frac{1}{2}(3 - x) - \frac{1}{3} > \frac{1}{4}$ and graph the solution set.

$\frac{12}{2}(3 - x) - \frac{1}{3} \cdot 12 > \frac{1}{4} \cdot 12$ — Multiply each term by the LCD.

$6(3 - x) - 4 > 3, \quad 18 - 6x - 4 > 3$

$14 - 6x > 3, \quad -6x > -11$

$x < \frac{11}{6}$ or $\{x \mid x < \frac{11}{6}\}$

$\frac{11}{6}$

Writing and Solving Inequalities

Example: If seven more than twice a number is greater than five times the number plus three, how large is the number?

- Let x = the number.
- Organize the facts:

  7 more than twice a number is greater than 5 times the number plus 3

  $+ \quad 2x \quad > \quad 5x \quad + 3$
- Inequality: $\mathbf{7 + 2x > 5x + 3}$ — Subtract $5x$ from both sides.

  $7 - 3x > 3$ — Subtract 7 from both sides.

  $-3x > -4$ — Divide both sides by -3.

  $x < \frac{4}{3}$, $\{x \mid x < \frac{4}{3}\}$ — Reverse the symbol.
- Check: Choose any number less than $\frac{4}{3}$ (say 0)

  $7 + 2 \cdot 0 \overset{?}{>} 5 \cdot 0 + 3$

  $7 \overset{\surd}{>} 3$ — Correct!

Example: Neal got an 81% on the midterm exam in Math. To get an A, the average of his midterm and final exam must be between 85% and 90%. For what range of scores on the final exam will Neal need to get an A?

- Facts and unknown:

Facts	85 % < the average of midterm and final exam < 90%
Unknown	Let x = the final exam score.

- Inequality: $\mathbf{85 < \frac{x+81}{2} < 90}$ — The average of midterm and final exam: $\frac{x+81}{2}$.

  $2(85) < 2\left(\frac{x+81}{2}\right) < 2(90)$ — Multiply 2 by each part.

  $170 < x + 81 < 180$ — Subtract 81 from each part.

  $170 - 81 < x + 81 - 81 < 180 - 81$
- Solution: $89 < x < 99$ — Neal's final exam score must be between 89% and 99%.

  $\mathbf{\{x \mid 89 < x < 99\}}$

2-4 INTERSECTIONS AND UNIONS

Intersections, Unions, and Subsets

- **Intersection of A and B ($A \cap B$):** the set of all elements contained in both A and B.

  Example: 1. If A = {red, ***green***, yellow, ***black***} and B = {white, ***black***, ***green***},
  then **A ∩ *B* = {black, green}**.

  2. If $A = \{1, 2, 3, \mathbf{4}, \mathbf{5}\}$ and $B = \{\mathbf{4}, \mathbf{5}, 6, 7, 8\}$,
  then **A ∩ B = {4, 5}**.

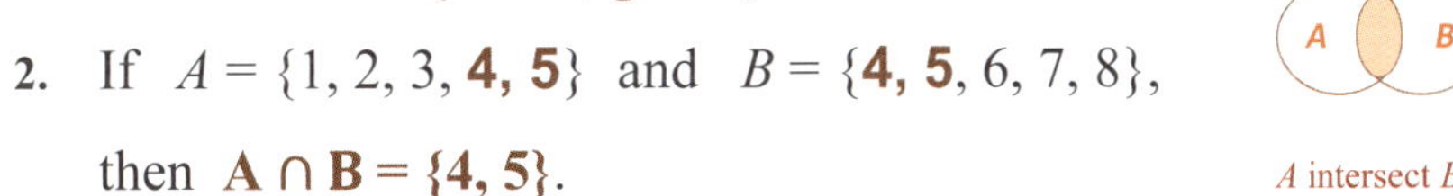

A intersect *B*

- **Union of A and B ($A \cup B$):** the set of all elements contained in A or B, or both.

  Example: 1. If A = {red, green, yellow} and B = {white, black},
  then **A ∪ B = { red, green, yellow, white, black}**.

  2. If $A = \{1, 3, 5\}$ and $B = \{2, 4, 6\}$,
  then **A ∪ B = {1, 2, 3, 4, 5, 6}**.

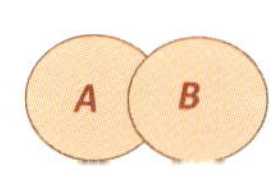

A union *B*

- **Empty set (or null set) ∅:** a set that contains no elements (disjoint).

  Example: If $A = \{ x \mid x = \text{Feb. } 30\}$, then **A = ∅**
  $B = \{ x \mid x = \text{Christmas day on Nov. } 25\} = \emptyset$

- Subset ($B \subset A$): a set B is a subset of a set A if each element of B is an element of A.

  A subset *B* is a portion of another set *A*.

  Example: If $A = \{4, \mathbf{5}, 8, \mathbf{10}, \mathbf{17}, 23\}$, $B = \{\mathbf{5}, \mathbf{10}, \mathbf{17}\}$,
  then $(B \subset A)$.

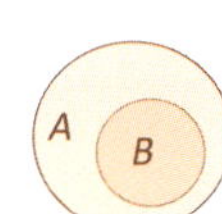

- $x \in A$: x is an element of the set A (or x belongs to A).
- $x \notin A$: x is not an element of the set A (or x does not belong to A).

  Example: $A = \{1, 2, 3, 4, 5\}$
  $3 \in A$: 3 is an element of A. $6 \notin A$: 6 is not an element of A.

- **Sets Summary**

Unions, Intersections, and Subsets		Example
union of A and B ($A \cup B$) OR	The set of all elements contained in A or B, or both.	If $A = \{2, 5\}$ and $B = \{1, 3, 4\}$ then $A \cup B = \{1, 2, 3, 4, 5\}$.
intersection of A and B ($A \cap B$) AND	The set of all elements contained in both A and B.	If $A = \{3, 6, 9\}$ and $B = \{5, 6, 7, 8, 9\}$ then $A \cap B = \{6, 9\}$.
empty set (or null set) ∅	A set that contains no elements.	If $A = \{ x \mid x = \text{Feb. } 30\}$, then $A = \emptyset$.
subset ($B \subset A$)	The subset B is a portion of another set A.	If $A = \{2, 5, 7, 11\}$, $B = \{5, 11\}$, then $(B \subset A)$.
$x \in A$	x is an element of the set A.	$\frac{2}{3}$ ∈ Rational numbers
$x \notin A$	x is not an element of the set A.	$\sqrt{5}$ ∉ Rational numbers

Example: Given $A = \{ a \mid a$ is a number between 6 and 10$\}$. 7, 8, 9

$B = \{ b \mid b$ is a prime number between 3 and 10$\}$. 5, 7

Review: A prime number is a whole number that only has two factors, 1 and itself.

List the elements in $A \cup B$ and $A \cap B$.

$A \cup B = \{5, 7, 8, 9\}$, $A \cap B = \{7\}$

Example: Let $A = \{2, 4, 6, 8\}$, $B = \{0, 1, 2, 3, 4\}$, and $C = \{-2, 3\}$. List the elements in the following.

Solution

1. $A \cup B$ $\{0, 1, 2, 3, 4, 6, 8\}$
2. $A \cap B$ $\{2, 4\}$
3. $A \cap C$ $\emptyset$

Example: Find the following sets.

1. $\{x, y, z\} \cap \{u, v, w, z, x, y\}$ $\{x, y, z\}$
2. $\{a, b, c\} \cup \emptyset$ $\{a, b, c\}$

- **Compound inequality review:** a statement that contains more than one inequality.
  $a < x < b$

  It means $a < x$ and $x < b$.

Example: Graph and write using interval notation. **Solution**

1. $-2 \le t$ and $t < 3$ **[-2, 3)**
2. $1 < b \le 5$ **(1, 5]**

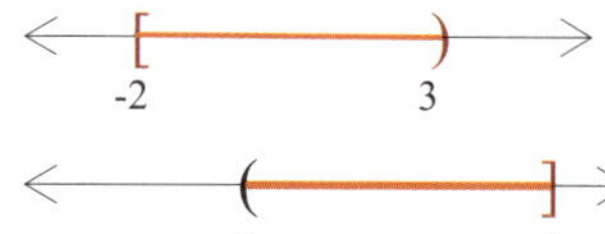

Example: Solve and sketch the graphs of the following inequalities.

1. $\mathbf{-3 \le 4 + 3x < 5}$

$-3 - 4 \le 4 + 3x - 4 < 5 - 4$ Subtract 4 from each term.

$-7 \le 3x < 1$ Divide each part by 3.

$\frac{-7}{3} \le x < \frac{1}{3}$

$\left\{x \mid \frac{-7}{3} \le x < \frac{1}{3}\right\}$ or $\left[\frac{-7}{3}, \frac{1}{3}\right)$

-2.33 0.33

$\left[\frac{-7}{3}, \frac{1}{3}\right)$ or [-2.33, 0.33)

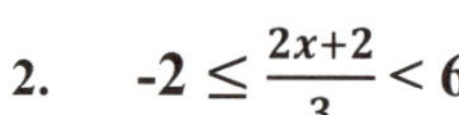

2. $\mathbf{-2 \le \frac{2x+2}{3} < 6}$

$-6 \le 2x + 2 < 18$ Multiply 3 by each term.

$-8 \le 2x < 16$ Subtract 2 from each term.

$-4 \le x < 8$ Divide each term by 2.

$\{x \mid -4 \le x < 8\}$ or $[-4, 8)$

Inequality and Unions/ Intersections

Intersections and inequalities

Example: Solve and sketch the graphs of $\mathbf{2x - 1 \le 3}$ and $\mathbf{4 + x < 5}$.

Tip: "and" means all x values that satisfy **both** inequalities (use intersection ∩).

- Solve each inequality and graph.

$2x - 1 \le 3$	$4 + x < 5$
$2x \le 4$	$x < 1$
$x \le 2$, $(-\infty, 2]$	$(-\infty, 1)$

- Solution: $\{x \mid x \le 2\} \cap \{x \mid x < 1\}$ or $\{x \mid x < 1\}$

The numbers common to both sets are those that are less than 1.

- Graph the intersect of the two solution sets.

$(-\infty, 2] \cap (-\infty, 1)$

Unions and inequalities

Example: Solve and sketch the graphs of $\mathbf{2 - 3x > 5}$ or $\mathbf{4 + x \ge 7}$.

Tip: "or" means x does not have to be in both solution sets to satisfy both inequalities (use union ∪).

- Solve each inequality and graph.

$2 - 3x > 5$	$4 + x \ge 7$
$-3x > 3$	$x \ge 3$
$x < -1$, $(-\infty, -1)$	$[3, \infty)$

- Graph the union of the two solution sets.

- The solution set: $\{x \mid x < -1 \text{ or } x \ge 3\}$ or $(-\infty, -1) \cup [3, \infty)$

Example: Solve and sketch the graphs of $2x - 3 \ge 1$ or $4 + 3x < 16$.

$2x \ge 4$	$3x < 12$
$x \ge 2$, $[2, \infty)$	$x < 4$, $(-\infty, 4)$

$[2, \infty) \cup (-\infty, 4)$

The solution set: $(-\infty, \infty)$, **or all real numbers**.

2-5 ABSOLUTE-VALUE EQUATIONS & INEQUALITIES

Absolute Value

- **Absolute value review:** geometrically, it is the distance of a number x from zero on the number line. It is symbolized by vertical bars, as in "$|x|$", "$|y|$" …

  Example: $|5|$ is 5 units away from 0.

- **No negatives for absolute value, $|-b| = |b|$:** Distance is always positive, and the absolute value is a distance, so the absolute value is never negative.

  Example: $|2|$ is 2 units away from 0.

  $|-2|$ is also 2 units away from 0.

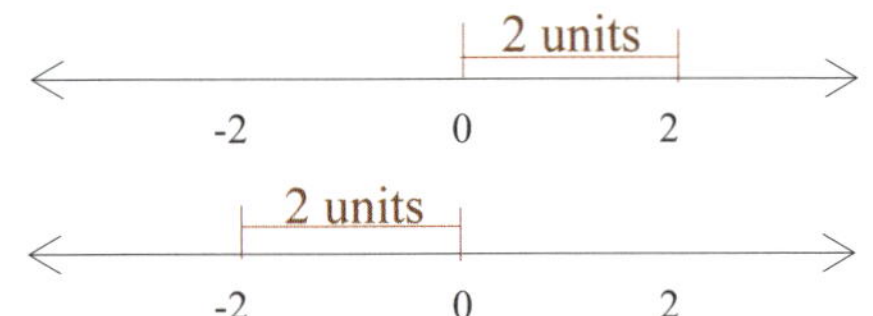

- **Properties of absolute value**

Absolute Value		Example
absolute value	$|x| = \begin{cases} x, & \text{if } x \geq 0 \\ -x, & \text{if } x < 0 \end{cases}$	If $|2x - 3| = 5$, then $2x - 3 = 5$ or $2x - 3 = -5$
properties	$|xy| = |x||y|$	$|-4a| = |-4||a| = 4|a|$
	$\left|\frac{x}{y}\right| = \frac{|x|}{|y|}$ $(y \neq 0)$	$\left|\frac{3x^3}{5y}\right| = \frac{|3x^3|}{|5y|} = \frac{3|x^3|}{5|y|}$

Example: Simplify the following.

1. $|-7x| = |-7||x| = 7|x|$ $\qquad |xy| = |x||y|$, $|-b| = |b|$

2. $\left|\frac{5x^2}{15x}\right| = \left|\frac{x^2}{3x}\right| = \left|\frac{x}{3}\right| = \frac{|x|}{|3|} = \frac{|x|}{3}$ $\qquad \left|\frac{x}{y}\right| = \frac{|x|}{|y|}$

3. $\left|\frac{-12a^5}{2}\right| = |-6a^5| = |-6|\,|a^5| = 6|a^5|$ $\qquad |xy| = |x||y|$, $|-b| = |b|$

Equations With Absolute Value

- **Absolute value equation:** an equation that includes absolute value(s).
- **$|x| = A$ is equivalent to $x = \pm A$:** **Example:** $|5t - 3| = 2$ is equivalent to $5t - 3 = \pm 2$
  $5t - 3 = 2,\ 5t - 3 = -2$
- **Procedure to solve an absolute value equation**

Steps	Example: $|2x - 3| - 5 = 0$
- Isolate the absolute value.	$|2x - 3| = 5$ +5 to both sides.
- Remove the absolute value symbol and set up two equations (one positive and one negative).	$2x - 3 = 5$ $2x - 3 = -5$ $|2x - 3| = 5$ is equivalent to $2x - 3 = \pm 5$.
- Solve two equations.	$2x = 8$ $2x = -2$ $x = 4$ $x = -1$
- Check.	$|2 \cdot 4 - 3| \stackrel{?}{=} 5$ $|2(-1) - 3| \stackrel{?}{=} 5$ $|5| \stackrel{\surd}{=} 5$ $|-5| \stackrel{\surd}{=} 5$ Correct!

The solution set: **{-1, 4}**

Example: Solve for x. $\mathbf{2|x + 1| - 3 = 5}$

- Isolate $|x|$.	$2|x + 1| = 8$ Add 3 to both sides. $|x + 1| = 4$ Divide both sides by 2.
- Remove the absolute value symbol and set up two equations.	$x + 1 = 4$ $x + 1 = -4$ $|x + 1| = 4$ is equivalent to $x + 1 = \pm 4$.
- Solve two equations.	$x = 3$ $x = -5$
- Check.	$2|3 + 1| - 3 \stackrel{?}{=} 5$ $2|-5 + 1| - 3 \stackrel{?}{=} 5$ $5 \stackrel{\surd}{=} 5$ $5 \stackrel{\surd}{=} 5$ Correct!

The solution set: **{-5, 3}**

Example: Solve for t. $\mathbf{|5t + 2| = -7}$

No solution   The absolute value of an expression is never negative.

- **Equations containing two absolute-value expressions**

Example: Solve for x. $|4x - 5| = |3x - 2|$

- Remove the absolute value symbol and set up two equations.
- Solve two equations.

+	−
$4x - 5 = 3x - 2$	$4x - 5 = -(3x - 2)$
$4x - 3x = -2 + 5$	$4x - 5 = -3x + 2$
$x = 3$	$x = 1$

- Check.

$\|4 \cdot 3 - 5\| \stackrel{?}{=} \|3 \cdot 3 - 2\|$	$\|4 \cdot 1 - 5\| \stackrel{?}{=} \|3 \cdot 1 - 2\|$
$\|12 - 5\| \stackrel{?}{=} \|9 - 2\|$	$\|-1\| \stackrel{?}{=} \|1\|$
$7 \stackrel{\surd}{=} 7$	$1 \stackrel{\surd}{=} 1$

Correct!

The solution set is **{1, 3}**

Example: Solve for x. $\left|\frac{6-8x}{5}\right| = \left|\frac{7+3x}{2}\right|$

$\left|\frac{6-8x}{5}\right| \cdot |10| = \left|\frac{7+3x}{2}\right| \cdot |10|$ — Multiply the LCD.

$\left|\frac{6-8x}{5} \cdot 10\right| = \left|\frac{7+3x}{2} \cdot 10\right|$ — $|xy| = |x||y|$

$|12 - 16x| = |35 + 15x|$ — $|12 - 16x| = |35 + 15x|$ is equivalent to $12 - 16x = \pm(35 + 15x)$.

$12 - 16x = 35 + 15x$	$12 - 16x = -(35 + 15x)$
$-31x = 23$	$12 - 16x = -35 - 15x$
	$-x = -47$
$x = \frac{-23}{31}$	$x = 47$

The solution set: $\left\{\frac{-23}{31}, 47\right\}$

Absolute Value Inequalities

- **$|x| < A$:** x is any value whose distance from zero is less than A units.

  It can be written as $\{x \mid -A < x < A\}$ or $(-A,\ A)$. $\because \pm x < A \begin{cases} x < A \\ -x < A,\ x > -A \end{cases}$

  Example: $|x| < 3$, x is less than 3 units away from zero, i.e.

  $\{x \mid -3 < x < 3\}$ or $(-3,\ 3)$

- **$|x| \le A$:** x is any value whose distance from zero is less than or equal to A units.

  It can be written as $\{x \mid -A \le x \le A\}$ or $[-A,\ A]$. $\because \pm x \le A \begin{cases} x \le A \\ -x \le A,\ x \ge -A \end{cases}$

  Example: $|x| \le 3$, x is less than or equal to 3 units away from zero, i.e.

  $\{x \mid -3 \le x \le 3\}$ or $[-3,\ 3]$

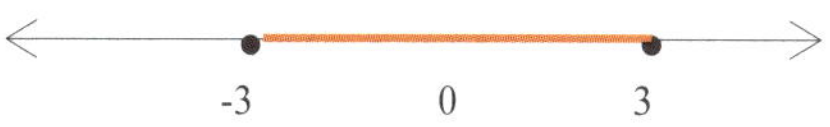

- **$|x| > A$:** x is any value whose distance from zero is greater than A units.

  It can be written as $\{x \mid x < -A \text{ or } x > A\}$ or $(-\infty,\ -A) \cup (A,\ \infty)$.

  $\because \pm x > A \begin{cases} x > A \\ -x > A,\ x < -A \end{cases}$

  Example: $|x| > 4$, x is any value whose distance from zero is greater than 4 units, i.e.

  $\{x \mid x < -4 \text{ or } x > 4\}$ or $(-\infty,\ -4) \cup (4,\ \infty)$

- **$|x| \ge A$:** x is any value whose distance from zero is at least A units. $\because \pm x \ge A \begin{cases} x \ge A \\ -x \ge A,\ x \le -A \end{cases}$

  It can be written as $\{x \mid x \le -A \text{ or } x \ge A\}$ or $(-\infty, -A] \cup [A,\ \infty)$.

  Example: $|x| \ge 4$, x is at least 4 units away from zero, i.e.

  $\{x \mid x \le -4 \text{ or } x \ge 4\}$ or $(-\infty, -4] \cup [4,\ \infty)$

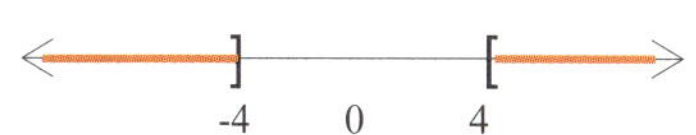

Absolute value inequalities summary

Absolute Value Inequality		Example	
$\lvert x\rvert < A$	$-A < x < A$ or $(-A,\ A)$	$\lvert x\rvert < 2$:	$\{x \mid -2 < x < 2\}$ or $(-2, 2)$
$\lvert x\rvert \le A$	$-A \le x \le A$ or $[-A,\ A]$	$\lvert x\rvert \le 2$:	$\{x \mid -2 \le x \le 2\}$ or $[-2, 2]$
$\lvert x\rvert > A$	$x < -A$ or $x > A$ or $(-\infty,\ -A) \cup (A,\ \infty)$	$\lvert x\rvert > 2$:	$\{x \mid x < -2 \text{ or } x > 2\}$ or $(-\infty, -2) \cup (2, \infty)$
$\lvert x\rvert \ge A$	$x \le -A$ or $x \ge A$ or $(-\infty, -A] \cup [A,\ \infty)$	$\lvert x\rvert \ge 2$:	$\{x \mid x \le -2 \text{ or } x \ge 2\}$ or $(-\infty, -2] \cup [2,\ \infty)$

Example

1. Solve for x: $|\mathbf{2x-3}| \leq \mathbf{5}$ — $|x| \leq a$: $-A \leq x \leq A$

$-5 \leq 2x - 3 \leq 5$ — Remove the absolute value symbol.

$-2 \leq 2x \leq 8$ — Isolate x term (add 3 to each term).

$\{x \mid -1 \leq x \leq 4\}$ **or** $[-1, 4]$ — Divide each term by 2.

2. Solve for x: $|\mathbf{3x-7}| > \mathbf{2}$ — $|x| > A$: $x < -A$ or $x > A$

$3x - 7 < -2$ | $3x - 7 > 2$ — Add 7 to both sides.

$3x < 5$ | $3x > 9$ — Divide 3 by both sides.

$\{x \mid x < \frac{5}{3}$ **or** $x > 3\}$ **or** $(-\infty, \frac{5}{3}) \cup (3, \infty)$

Unit 2 Summary

- **Equation:** a mathematical statement that contains two expressions separated by an equal sign.
- **Solution, root or zero of an equation:** a solution is the particular value of the variable in the equation that makes the equation true.
- **Solution Set { }:** the set of all values that makes the equation true.
- **Linear equation (or first-degree equation) in one variable:** an equation in which the highest **power** of the **variable** is **one**. (An equation whose graph is a straight line.)
- **Equations of different degrees**

Equation	Standard Form	Example	Comments
first-degree equation (linear equation)	$Ax + B = 0$ $(x = x^1)$	$5x + 4 = 0$	The highest power of x is 1.
second-degree equation (quadratic equation)	$Ax^2 + Bx + C = 0$	$2x^2 + 7x - 3 = 0$	The highest power of x is 2.
third-degree equation (cubic equation)	$Ax^3 + Bx^2 + Cx + D = 0$	$3x^3 + 4x^2 - 8x + 1 = 0$	The highest power of x is 3.
fourth-degree equation	$Ax^4 + Bx^3 + Cx^2 + Dx + E = 0$	$x^4 - 9x^3 + 3x^2 + 2x - 5 = 0$	The highest power of x is 4.

- **Higher-degree equations are nonlinear equations.**
- **A linear equation in two variables:** an equation that contains two variables in which the highest power (exponent) of two **variables** is one.
- **Formula:** an equation that contains more than one variable and is used to solve practical problems in everyday life.
- **An inequality:** a mathematical statement that contains $<$, $>$, $\geq$, or $\leq$ symbol.
- **Solution of an inequality:** the particular value(s) of the variable in the inequality that makes the inequality true.
- **Compound inequality:** a statement that contains more than one inequality. $a < x < b$
- **Absolute value equation:** an equation that includes absolute value(s).
- **$|x| = A$ is equivalent to $x = \pm A$.** **Example**: $|5t - 3| = 2$ is equivalent to $5t - 3 = \pm 2$.

- **Equations involving decimals**
  - Multiply each term by a power of 10 (10, 100, 1,000, etc.) to clear the decimals.
  - Collect the variable terms on one side of the equation and the constants on the other side.
  - Isolate the variable.

- **Equations involving fractions**
  - Multiply each term by the LCD.
  - Collect the variable terms on one side of the equation and the constants on the other side.
  - Isolate the variable.

- **Properties for solving equations**

Properties	Equality	Example
property of addition	$A = B,\ A + C = B + C$	Solve $y - 7 = 2$ $y - 7 + 7 = 2 + 7,\ \ y = \mathbf{9}$
property of subtraction	$A = B,\ A - C = B - C$	Solve $x + 3 = -8$ $x + 3 - 3 = -8 - 3,\ \ x = \mathbf{-11}$
property of multiplication	$A = B,\ \ A \cdot C = B \cdot C$ $(C \neq 0)$	Solve $\frac{-t}{6} = 7$ $\frac{-t}{6}(-6) = 7(-6),\ \ t = \mathbf{-42}$
property of division	$A = B,\ \ \frac{A}{C} = \frac{B}{C}$ $(C \neq 0)$	Solve $4a = -16$ $\frac{4a}{4} = \frac{-16}{4},\ \ a = \mathbf{-4}$

- **Equation-solving strategy**

Equation-Solving Strategy

- Clear the fractions or decimals if necessary.
- Remove parentheses.
- Combine like terms on each side of the equation if necessary.
- Collect the variable terms on one side of the equation and the numerical terms on the other side.
- Isolate the variable.
- Check the solution with the original equation.

- **Steps for solving word problems**

Steps for Solving Word Problems

- Organize the ***facts*** given from the problem.
- Identify and label the unknown quantity (***let x = unknown***).
- Draw a ***diagram*** if it will make the problem clearer.
- Convert words into a mathematical ***equation***.
- ***Solve*** the equation and find the solution(s).
- ***Check*** and state the ***answer***.

- **Sets Summary**

Unions, Intersections, and Subsets		Example
union of A and B ($A \cup B$) OR	The set of all elements contained in A or B, or both.	If $A = \{2, 5\}$ and $B = \{1, 3, 4\}$ then $A \cup B = \{1, 2, 3, 4, 5\}$.
intersection of A and B ($A \cap B$) AND	The set of all elements contained in both A and B.	If $A = \{3, 6, 9\}$ and $B = \{5, 6, 7, 8, 9\}$ then $A \cap B = \{6, 9\}$.
empty set (or null set) $\emptyset$	A set that contains no elements.	If $A = \{x \mid x = \text{Feb. } 30\}$, then $A = \emptyset$.
subset ($B \subset A$)	The subset B is a portion of another set A.	If $A = \{2, 5, 7, 11\}$, $B = \{5, 11\}$, then ($B \subset A$).
$x \in A$	x is an element of the set A.	$\frac{2}{3} \in$ Rational numbers
$x \notin A$	x is not an element of the set A.	$\sqrt{5} \notin$ Rational numbers

- **Properties of absolute value**

Absolute Value		Example
absolute value	$\lvert x\rvert = \begin{cases} x, & \text{if } x \geq 0 \\ -x, & \text{if } x < 0 \end{cases}$	If $\lvert 2x - 3\rvert = 5$ Then $2x - 3 = 5$ or $2x - 3 = -5$
properties	$\lvert xy\rvert = \lvert x\rvert\lvert y\rvert$	$\lvert -4a\rvert = \lvert -4\rvert\lvert a\rvert = 4\lvert a\rvert$
	$\left\lvert\frac{x}{y}\right\rvert = \frac{\lvert x\rvert}{\lvert y\rvert}$ $(y \neq 0)$	$\left\lvert\frac{3x^3}{5y}\right\rvert = \frac{\lvert 3x^3\rvert}{\lvert 5y\rvert} = \frac{3\lvert x^3\rvert}{5\lvert y\rvert}$

- **Procedure to solve an absolute value equation:**
  - Isolate the absolute value.
  - Remove the absolute value symbol and set up two equations (one positive and one negative.)
  - Solve two equations.
  - Check.

- **Absolute value inequalities summary**

Absolute Value Inequality		Example
$\lvert x\rvert < A$	$-A < x < A$ or $(-A, A)$	$\lvert x\rvert < 2$: $\{x \mid -2 < x < 2\}$ or $(-2, 2)$
$\lvert x\rvert \leq A$	$-A \leq x \leq A$ or $[-A, A]$	$\lvert x\rvert \leq 2$: $\{x \mid -2 \leq x \leq 2\}$ or $[-2, 2]$
$\lvert x\rvert > A$	$x < -A$ or $x > A$ or $(-\infty, -A) \cup (A, \infty)$	$\lvert x\rvert > 2$: $\{x \mid x < -2$ or $x > 2\}$ or $(-\infty, -2) \cup (2, \infty)$
$\lvert x\rvert \geq A$	$x \leq -A$ or $x \geq A$ or $(-\infty, -A] \cup [A, \infty)$	$\lvert x\rvert \geq 2$: $\{x \mid x \leq -2$ or $x \geq 2\}$ or $(-\infty, -2] \cup [2, \infty)$

- **Business formulas**

Application	Formula
Percent Increase	Percent increase = $\frac{\text{New value} - \text{Original value}}{\text{Original value}}$, $x = \frac{\text{N} - \text{O}}{\text{O}}$
Percent Decrease	Percent decrease = $\frac{\text{Original value} - \text{New value}}{\text{Original value}}$, $x = \frac{\text{O} - \text{N}}{\text{O}}$
Sales Tax	sales tax = sales × tax rate
Commission	commission = sales × commission rate
Discount	discount = original price × discount rate sale price = original price – discount
Markup	markup = original price × markup rate original price = selling price – markup
Simple Interest	interest = principle × interest rate × time, $I = Prt$ balance = principle + interest
Compound Interest	balance = principle (100% + interest rate)^t balance = $P(100\% + r)^t$

- **Recall some geometry formulas**

Name of the Figure	Formula	Figure
rectangle	$P = 2l + 2w$ $A = lw$	w, l
parallelogram	$P = 2a + 2b$ $A = bh$	h, a, b
circle	$C = \pi d = 2\pi r$ $A = \pi r^2$	r, d
triangle	$\angle X + \angle Y + \angle Z = 180^0$ $A = \frac{1}{2}bh$	X, h, Y, b, Z
trapezoid	$A = \frac{1}{2}h(b + B)$	b, h, B
cube	$V = s^3$	s
rectangular solid	$V = lwh$	h, l, w
cylinder	$V = \pi r^2 h$	r, h
sphere	$V = \frac{4}{3}\pi r^3$	r
cone	$V = \frac{1}{3}\pi r^2 h$	h, r
pyramid	$V = \frac{1}{3}lwh$	h, l, w

- **More formulas**

Application	Formula	Component
distance	$d = rt,\ r = \frac{d}{t},\ t = \frac{d}{r}$	d – distance r – speed t – time
simple interest	$I = Prt,\ P = \frac{I}{rt},\ t = \frac{I}{Pr}$	I – interest P – principle r – interest rate (%) t – time (years)
compound interest	$B = P(100\% + r)^t$	B – balance P – principle r – interest rate (%) t – time (years)
percent increase	$\frac{N - O}{O}$	N – new value O – original value
percent decrease	$\frac{O - N}{O}$	N – new value O – original value
sale price	$S = L - rL,\ L = \frac{S}{1-r}$	S – sale price L – list price r – discount rate
intelligence quotient (I.Q.)	$I = \frac{100m}{c}$	I – I.Q. m – mental age c – chronological age
temperature	$C = \frac{5}{9}(F - 32),\ F = \frac{9}{5}C + 32$	C – Celsius F – Fahrenheit

PRACTICE QUIZ

Unit 2 Equations and Inequalities

1. Solve the following equations.

a. $3(x - 2) + 4x - 7 = 3(5 - x)$

b. $0.3y - 0.27 = -4.36y$

c. $\frac{3x}{4} - \frac{2}{3} = \frac{x}{2} + \frac{1}{4}$

2. Five less than four times a number is nine more than the number divided by two. Find the number.

3. Find three consecutive even integers such that four times the first integer is two less than the sum of the second and third integers.

4. Two vehicles are 340 km apart and are traveling towards each other. Their speeds differ by 10 km per hour. What is the speed of each vehicle if they meet after 2 hours?

5. Alice boats at a speed of 26 km per hour in still water. The river flows at a speed of 12 km per hour. How long will it take Alice to boat 4 km downstream? 3 km upstream?

6. Tom purchased 46-cent, 66-cent, and 86-cent Canadian stamps with a total value of $6.80. If the number of 66-cent stamps is 3 more than the number of 46-cent stamps, and the number of 86-cent stamps is 2 more than one half the number of 46-cent stamps. How many stamps of each did Tom receive?

7. Solve the following inequalities and graph the solution sets.

a. $-7x - 3 \geq 11$

b. $3 - 2(4x - 5) + 7x > 2x + 10$

c. $\frac{3}{4}(5 - y) - \frac{5}{2} \leq \frac{1}{3}$

8. Amanda got a 78% on the midterm exam in English. To get a B+, the average of her midterm and final exam must be between 76% and 80%. For what range of scores on the final exam will Amanda need to get a B+?

9. Indicate whether each of the following is true or false.

a. $\frac{-5}{16} \in$ rational numbers

b. $\sqrt{13} \in$ rational numbers

10. **a.** Given $A = \{ a \mid a$ is a prime number between 10 and 18$\}$

$B = \{ b \mid b$ is a number between 12 and 16$\}$

List the numbers in $A \cup B$ and $A \cap B$

b. Given $A = \{3, 5, 7\}$, $B = \{1, 2, 3, 4, 5\}$ and $C = \{-3, -2\}$. List the elements in the following:

$A \cup B$

$A \cap B$

$A \cap C$

11. Solve the following and graph the solution set.

$-3 < \frac{1+2x}{3} \leq 1$

12. Solve the following equations.

a. $2|x + 3| - 4 = 6$

b. $|3x - 4| = |5x - 2|$

13. Solve the following inequalities.

a. $|3x - 4| \leq 7$

b. $|5x - 3| > 4$

UNIT 3 FUNCTIONS AND GRAPHS

3-1 GRAPHING EQUATIONS

The Coordinate Plane

- **The coordinate plane** (or Cartesian / rectangular coordinate system): a powerful tool to mark a point and the solution of a linear equation on a graph.
  - **Coordinate axes:**

    ***x* axis** – the horizontal line.

    ***y* axis** – the vertical line.
  - **The origin:** the intersection of the x and y axes where both lines are 0.

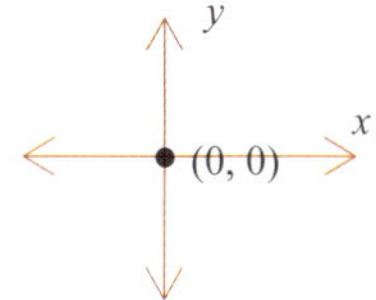

- **Ordered pair: (x, y):** Each point on the plane corresponds to an ordered pair.

Example: (2, 1)

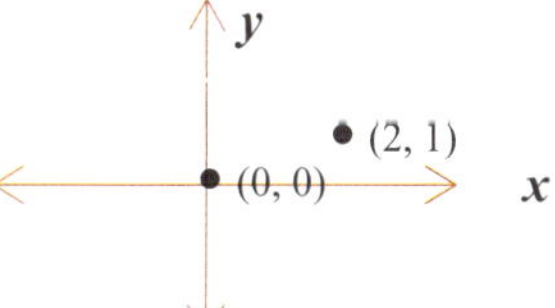

Example: (soda, \$0.90) , (juice, \$1.25)

- **Coordinate:** the numbers in an ordered pair.
- **Four quadrants**

Quadrant	(x, y)	Example
The 1st quadrant I	$(+x, +y)$	(+2, +3)
The 2nd quadrant II	$(-x, +y)$	(-2, +3)
The 3rd quadrant III	$(-x, -y)$	(-2, -3)
The 4th quadrant IV	$(+x, -y)$	(+2, -3)

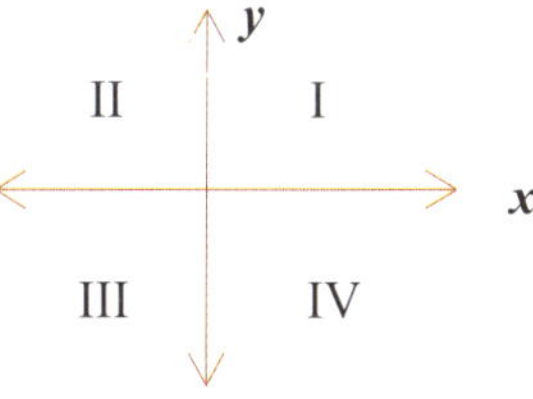

Example: Plot the points and name the quadrant.

(1, 3) (-3, 2) (-2, -2) (2, -1)

(1, 3): I , (-3, 2): II , (-2, -2): III , (2, -1): IV

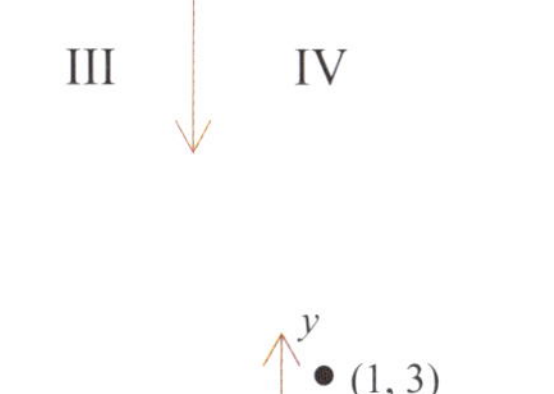

- ***x*-intercept:** the point at which the graph crosses the x-axis.

Example: $(x, y) =$ **(3, 0)**

- ***y*-intercept:** the point at which the graph crosses the y-axis.

Example: $(x, y) =$ **(0, 2)**

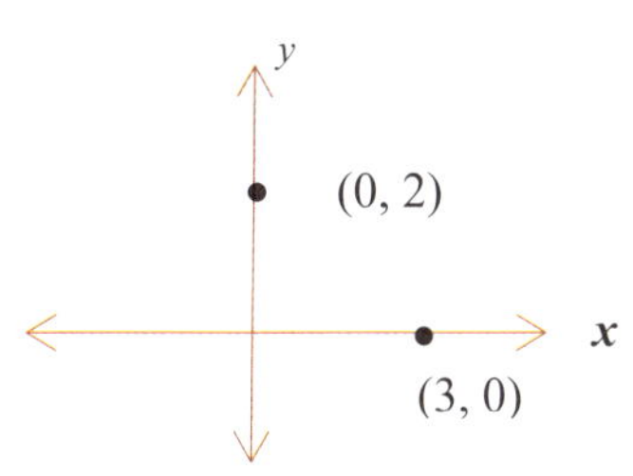

Points are on axes

Graphs of Linear Equations

- **A linear (first-degree) equation:** an equation whose graph is a straight line.
- **A linear (first-degree) equation in two variables:** a linear equation that contains two variables, such as $2x + y = 3$.
- **The standard form of linear equation in two variables:** $Ax + By = C$

Standard Form	Example
$Ax + By = C$	$5x - 7y = 4$

- **Solutions of equations:** Solutions for a linear equation in two variables are an ordered pair. They are the particular values of the variables in the equation that makes the equation true.

Example: Determine whether the given point is a solution.

1. **(2, -1): $2x - 3y = 7$** $\quad 2 \cdot 2 - 3(-1) \stackrel{?}{=} 7 \quad 7 \stackrel{\surd}{=} 7 \quad$ **Yes**
2. **(0, 3): $10p + 3q = -4$** $\quad 10 \cdot 0 + 3 \cdot 3 \stackrel{?}{=} -4 \quad 9 \neq -4 \quad$ **No**

- **The graph of an equation** is the diagram obtained by plotting the set of points where the equation is true (or satisfies the equation).
- **Procedure to graph a linear equation**

Steps

- Choose two values of x, calculate the corresponding y, and make a table.
- Plot these two points on the coordinate plane.
- Connect the points with a straight line.
  (Any two points determine a straight line.)
- Check with the third point.

Is third point (2, 1) on the line? Yes. Correct!

Example: Graph $2x - y = 3$

x	$y = 2x - 3$	(x, y)	
0	$2 \cdot 0 - 3 = -3$	(0, -3)	y-intercept
1	$2 \cdot 1 - 3 = -1$	(1, -1)	

Select x / Calculate y / Ordered pair

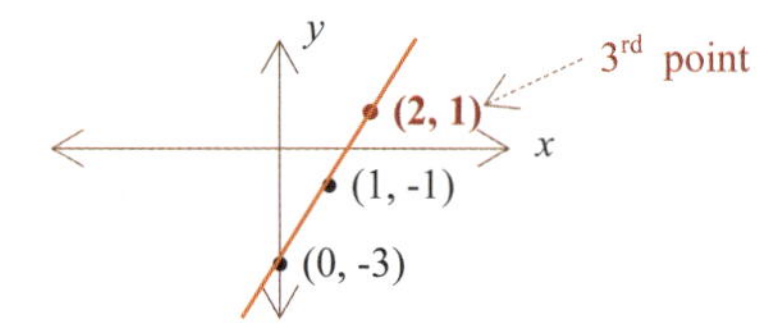

x	$y = 2x - 3$	(x, y)
2	$2 \cdot 2 - 3 = 1$	(2, 1)

Example: Graph $y = \frac{1}{2}x - 3$ and determine another point.

x	y	(x, y)
0	- 3	(0, -3)
2	- 2	(2, -2)

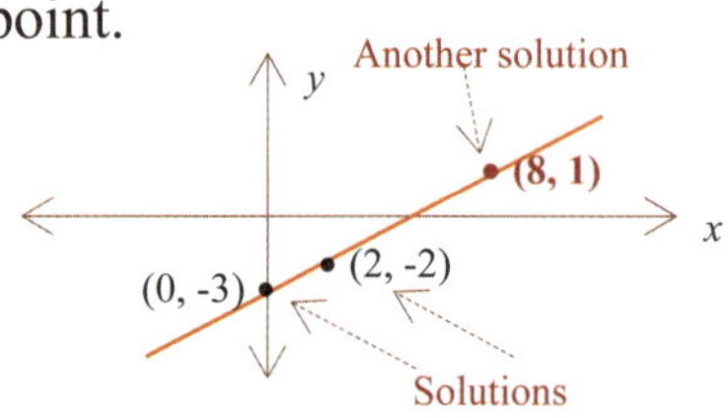

Graphing Nonlinear Equation With Two Variables

- **Nonlinear equation:** an equation whose graph is not a straight line.

  Example: $2x^2 - 5y = 3$, $3y^3 + 7x^2 - 3xy + 8 = 0$

  Recall: Higher-degree equations are nonlinear equations.

- **Procedure to graph a nonlinear equation with two variables**
  - Choose a few values of x, calculate the corresponding y, and make a table.
  - Plot these points on the coordinate plane (plot more points to get a cleaner shape of the graph).
  - Connect the points with a smooth curve.

Example: Graph the equation $\boldsymbol{y = 5 + x^2}$.

x	$y = 5 + x^2$	Ordered Pair
0	$5 + 0^2 = 5$	(0, 5)
1	$5 + 1^2 = 6$	(1, 6)
-1	$5 + (-1)^2 = 6$	(-1, 6)
2	$5 + 2^2 = 9$	(2, 9)
-2	$5 + (-2)^2 = 9$	(-2, 9)

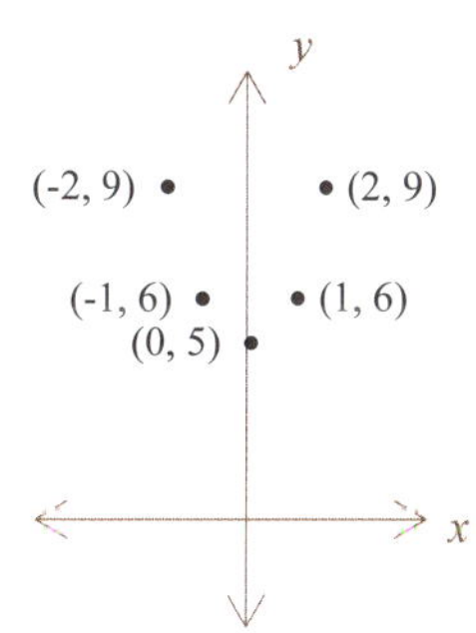

Example: Graph the equation $\boldsymbol{y = \frac{4}{x}}$.

x	$y = \frac{4}{x}$	Ordered Pair
1	$\frac{4}{1} = 4$	(1, 4)
-1	$\frac{4}{-1} = -4$	(-1, -4)
2	$\frac{4}{2} = 2$	(2, 2)
-2	$\frac{4}{-2} = -2$	(-2, -2)
4	$\frac{4}{4} = 1$	(4, 1)
-4	$\frac{4}{-4} = -1$	(-4, -1)

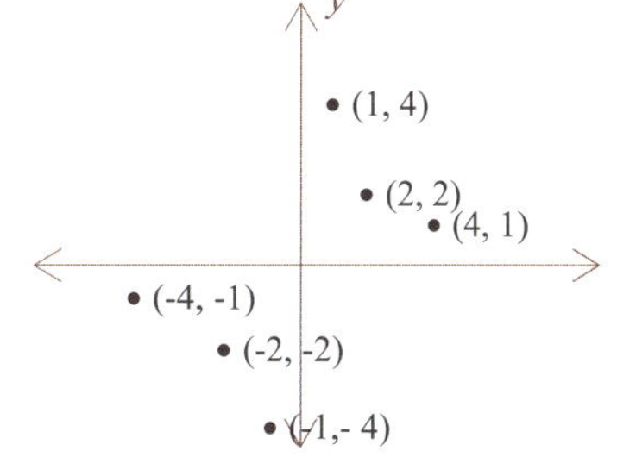

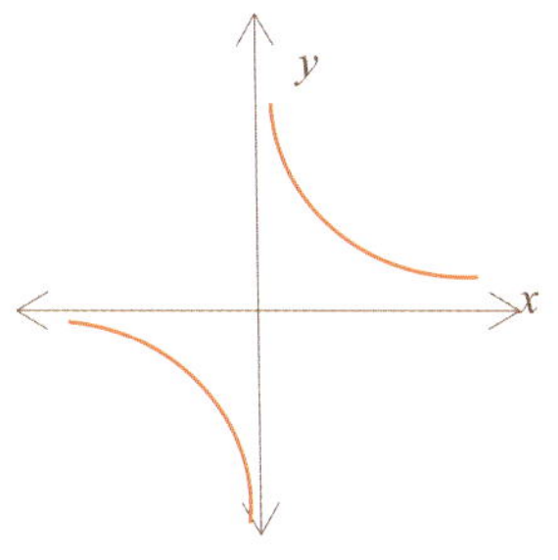

Example: Graph the equation $\boldsymbol{y = |x - 1|}$.

x	$y = \|x - 1\|$	Ordered Pair
0	$\|0 - 1\| = 1$	(0, 1)
1	$\|1 - 1\| = 0$	(1, 0)
-1	$\|-1 - 1\| = 2$	(-1, 2)
2	$\|2 - 1\| = 1$	(2, 1)
3	$\|3 - 1\| = 2$	(3, 2)

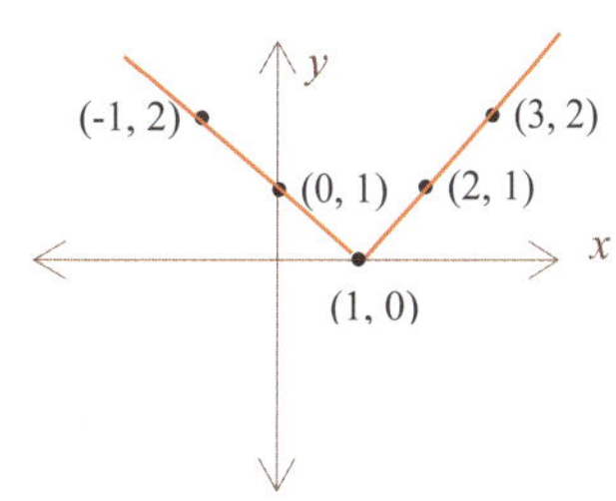

3-2 FUNCTIONS

Function

- **Function:** a special type of relation (or correspondence) which matches **each** element of the **domain** (x-value or first set) **with** exactly **one** element of the **range** (y-value or second set).

- **All functions are relations (correspondence), but not all relations are functions.**

Example: **1.** **Name (x)** **Social Security Number (y)**

Tom → 618-31-4123
Steve → 312-15-7432

This is a **function** (Since each person is assigned only one SSN number.)

2. **Name (x)** **Address (y)**

Adam → 123 First Ave.
Shawn → 234 Second Ave. (Home)
Shawn → 456 Univ. Way (Student residency)

This is **a relation but not a function.** (Shawn has two addresses.)

Example: Determine if the following relation (correspondence) is a function.

Domain (x)	Range (y)	Function	Comments
a → 1 b → 2 c → 3	1 2 3	Yes	Each value of x is assigned only one value of y.
3 → 4 -2 → 4 -2 → -3	4 -3	No	-2 is assigned more than one value of the range (4 and -3).
-5 → 2 4 → 2 0 → 3	2 3	Yes	-5 and 4 are assigned only one value of the range (2).

Example: Determine if the following relation (correspondence) is a function.

Domain (x)	Range (y)	Correspondence	Function	Comments
famous writers	a set of book titles	a book that the writer has published	No	Some writers have publised more than one book.
a set of numbers	a set of positive numbers	square each number and then divide by 3	Yes	$y = \frac{x^2}{3}$ The result will be a unique positive number.

Finding Function Values

- **Function notation:** The notation for a function is $f(x)$, $P(x)$, $g(x)$, $h(x)$, …

  Read $f(x)$ as "f of x". $f(x)$ does not mean f times x.

- **Function values:** The value of a function at "$x = a$" is denoted as "$f(a)$". $f(a)$ is the value of $f(x)$ when a is replaced by x in $f(x)$.

$$f(x)\,|_{\,x=a} = f(a), \quad \begin{cases} a \text{ is a constant} \\ \text{replace } x \text{ by } a \end{cases}$$

Example: $f(x) = 3x + 1$

If $x = 2$

$f(\ \ ) = 3(\ \ ) + 1$

$f(2) = 3(2) + 1 = 7$

(Substitute x for 2.)

If $x = -4$

$f(\ \ ) = 3(\ \ ) + 1$

$f(-4) = 3(-4) + 1 = -11$

(Substitute x for -4.)

Example: Evaluate the functions and simplify at the indicated values.

	Solution
1. $f(-2)$ for $f(x) = 3 - 5x$	$f(-2) = 3 - 5(-2) = 3 + 10 = \mathbf{13}$
2. $p(3)$ for $p(t) = 2t^2 - 7$	$p(3) = 2(3)^2 - 7 = 2 \cdot 9 - 7 = \mathbf{11}$
3. $f(a-2)$ for $f(x) = 8 + 3x^3$	$f(a-2) = \mathbf{8 + 3(a-2)^3}$ Replace $(a-2)$ by x in $f(x)$.
4. $g(0)$ for $g(r) = r^2 - 3r + 2$	$g(0) = 0^2 - 3 \cdot 0 + 2 = \mathbf{2}$

Example: Evaluate the functions and simplify at the indicated values.

$f(x) = 3x + 1$

	Solution
1. $f(-2)$	$f(-2) = 3(-2) + 1 = -6 + 1 = \mathbf{-5}$
2. $f(b+2)$	$f(b+2) = 3(b+2) + 1 = 3b + 6 + 1 = \mathbf{3b + 7}$
3. $f(a) + f(3)$	$f(a) + f(3) = (3a + 1) + (3 \cdot 3 + 1) = 3a + 1 + 10 = \mathbf{3a + 11}$
4. $f\left(\frac{1}{6}\right)$	$f\left(\frac{1}{6}\right) = 3\left(\frac{1}{6}\right) + 1 = \frac{1}{2} + 1 = \frac{3}{2} = \mathbf{1\frac{1}{2}}$

$h(r) = 3r^2 - 2$

1. $h(0)$	$h(0) = 3 \cdot 0^2 - 2 = \mathbf{-2}$
2. $h\left(\frac{-2}{3}\right)$	$h\left(\frac{-2}{3}\right) = 3\left(\frac{-2}{3}\right)^2 - 2 = 3\left(\frac{4}{9}\right) - 2 = \frac{4}{3} - 2 = \frac{4}{3} - \frac{6}{3} = \mathbf{-\frac{2}{3}}$

$g(x) = |x + 3| + 2x$

1. $g(-4)$	$g(-4) = |-4 + 3| + 2(-4) = |-1| - 8 = 1 - 8 = \mathbf{-7}$
2. $g(a - b)$	$g(a - b) = |a - b + 3| + 2(a - b)$

Graphing a Function

- **The graph of a function:** the diagram obtained by plotting the set of all points where the function $y = f(x)$ is true.
- **Procedure to graph a function:** (similar to graph an equation)
  - Choose a few values of x, calculate the corresponding values of functions $y = f(x)$ and make a table.
  - Plot these points on the coordinate plane.
  - Connect the points with a smooth curve.

Example: Graph the function $f(x) = 2x^2 + x - 1$.

x	$y = f(x) = 2x^2 + x - 1$	(x, y)
0	$2 \cdot 0^2 + 0 - 1 = -1$	(0, -1)
1	$2 \cdot 1^2 + 1 - 1 = 2$	(1, 2)
-1	$2 \cdot (-1)^2 + (-1) - 1 = 0$	(-1, 0)
2	$2 \cdot 2^2 + 2 - 1 = 9$	(2, 9)
-2	$2 \cdot (-2)^2 + (-2) - 1 = 5$	(-2, 5)

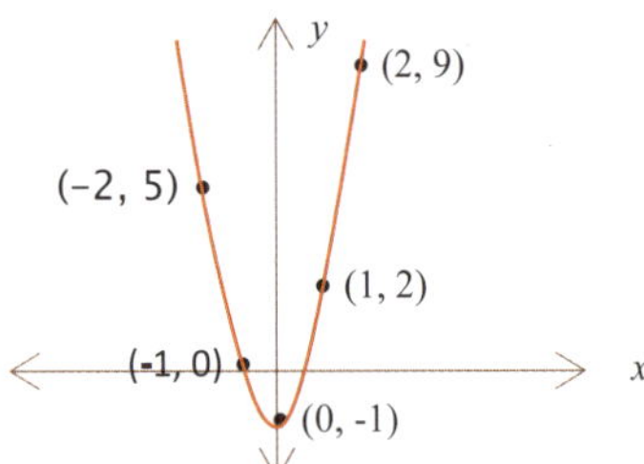

- **Identify the $f(x)$ in a graph**
  - Locate the x-value(s) on the x-axis, and plot vertical line(s) to the curve and draw a solid point.

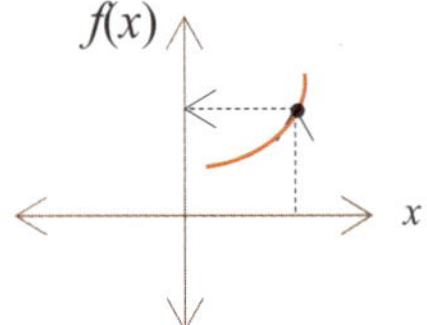

  - Plot horizontal line(s) from the point to the y-axis to determine $y = f(x)$ value(s).
    $f(x)$ is the y-value that is corresponded with x.

Example: The following graph shows the number of car rentals as a function of time in a vehicle rental store. How many cars were rented in 2011?

$f(2011) = 100$

(There were 100 cars rented in 2011.)

# of car rentals
f(x)
100
50
x (year)
2000
2005
2011

The Vertical Line Test

- **The vertical line test can determine whether a relation is a function.**
- **The vertical line test:** If a vertical line cuts the relation's graph more than once, then the relation is not a function.
- **Recall:** A **function** is a special type of relation which matches **each** element of the **domain** (x-value) **with** exactly **one** element of the **range** (y-value).

Example: Determine if the following graphs are functions.

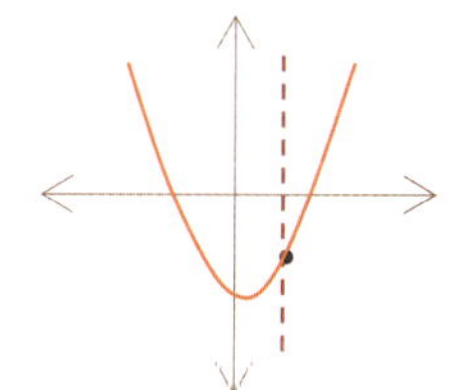

Yes, cuts once.

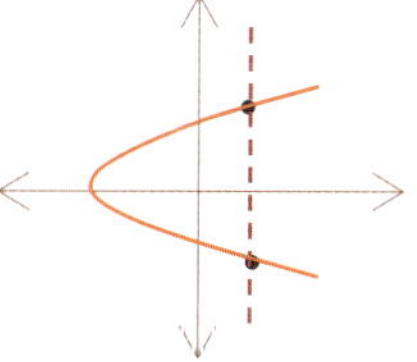

No, cuts twice.

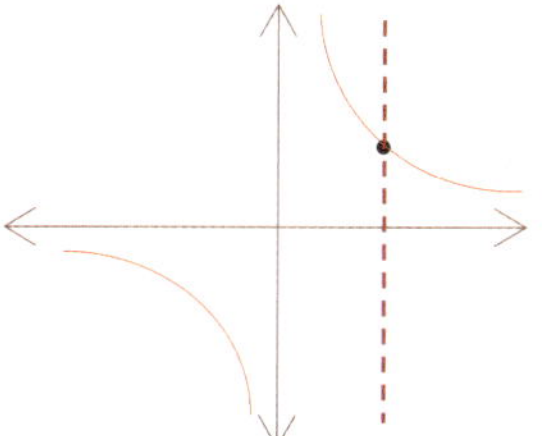

Yes, cuts once.

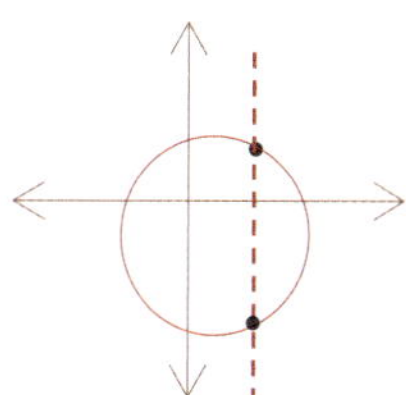

No, cuts twice.

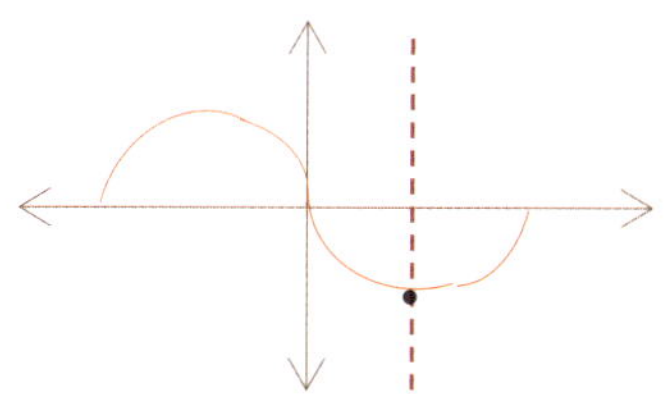

Yes, cuts once.

3-3 DOMAIN, RANGE, AND RELATION

Relation

- **Relation:** a set of ordered pairs (x, y).
- **Domain:** the set of the values of the independent variable (x-value) for which a function is defined.
- **Range:** the set of the values of the dependent variable (y-value) for which a function is defined.

Example

(3, 2)

domain range

Example

Domain	Range	Ordered Pair
2 - can of Coke	$1.50	(2-Coke, $1.50)
1 - can of juice	$1.25	(1-juice, $1.25)
3 - can of soup	$3.00	(3-soup, $3.00)

domain range (The range depends on the domain.)

- **Correspondence diagram:** an arrow points from each domain to the range.

Example: **Name (x)** **Age (y)**

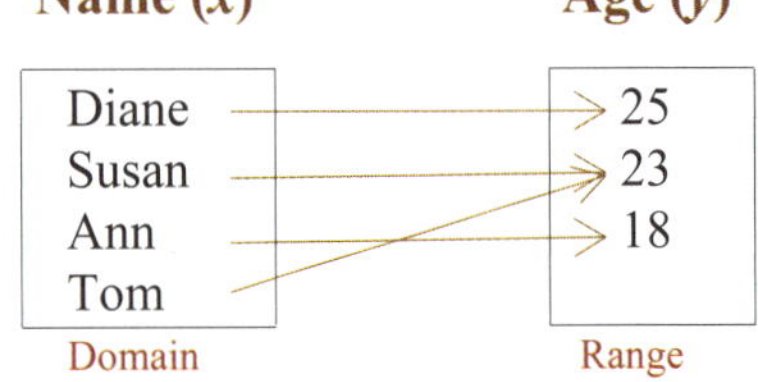

Example: Express the relation $R = \{(2, 4)\ (-1, 3)\ (5, -2)\ (-4, -3)\}$ as a table, correspondence diagram, and domain/range set.

- Table:

x	y
2	4
-1	3
5	-2
-4	-3

- Correspondence diagram:

- Domain: {2, -1, 5, -4}
  Range: {4, 3, -2, -3}

Finding Domain and Range

Example: Answer the following questions regarding each graph (a function) below.

a. $f(-2)$, **b.** the domain, **c.** all x-values such that $f(x) = 1$, and **d.** the range.

1.

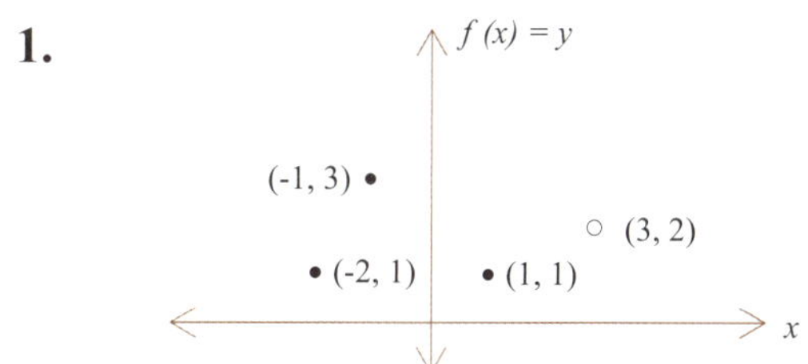

Open dot ○ : the point is not included.

$f(-2)$	**Domain** (x-values)	**All x-values such that $f(x) = 1$**	**Range** (y-values)
1	{-2, -1, 1}	When $y = 1$, $x = -2$ and 1	{1, 3}

2.

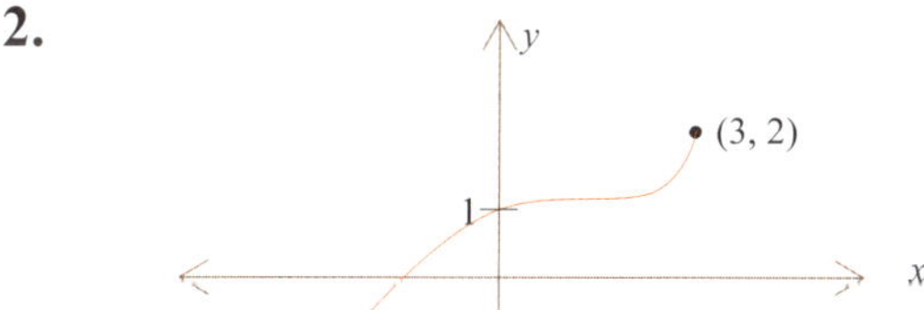

$f(-2)$	**Domain** (x-values)	**All x-values such that $f(x) = 1$**	**Range** (y-values)
-1	{-2, 3}	When $y = 1$, $x = 0$	{-1, 2}

Example: Identify the domain of the following functions.

$f(x)$	**Domain** (x-values)	**Comments**
$5 - 3x$	all real numbers	Since any real number can be used to calculate y. x: 0, 1 ; y: 5, 2 ……
$\frac{5}{3-x}$	$\{x \mid x$ is a real number and $x \neq 3\}$ or $(-\infty, 3) \cup (3, \infty)$	Find out what values of x "do not work" If $x = 3$, $\frac{5}{3-3} = \frac{5}{0}$ is undefined.
$\frac{3}{\lvert 3x-2 \rvert}$	$\{x \mid x$ is a real number and $x \neq \frac{2}{3}\}$ or $(-\infty, \frac{2}{3}) \cup (\frac{2}{3}, \infty)$	If $x = \frac{2}{3}$, $\frac{3}{\lvert 3(\frac{2}{3})-2 \rvert} = \frac{3}{0}$ is undefined.

Note: The **domain** x is the set of real numbers that will yield a real number for the range y.

(The set of the x-values for which a function is defined.)

3-4 LINEAR FUNCTIONS

Slope-Intercept Function of a Line

- **Slope-intercept form of a linear function**

Slope-Intercept Function of a Line	
$f(x) = mx + b$	m: the slope of the line b: y-intercept

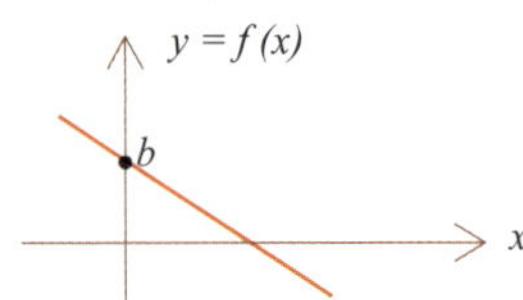

- **The y intercept**: the point at which the line crosses the y axis. $b = (0, y)$

Example: Identify the slope and y-intercept of the following equations.

1. $f(x) = -0.3x - 5$ — $f(x) = mx + b$

   The slope: $m = -0.3$

   y-intercept: $b = -5$ or $(0, -5)$

2. $2x + 3y = 4 - x - 4y$ — Combine like terms.

   $7y = -3x + 4$ — Divide both sides by 7.

   $y = \frac{-3}{7}x + \frac{4}{7}$ — $f(x) = mx + b$

   The slope: $m = \frac{-3}{7}$

   y-intercept: $b = \frac{4}{7}$ or $(0, \frac{4}{7})$

3. $3x + \frac{1}{2}y = 8$

   $3x \cdot 2 + \frac{1}{2}y \cdot 2 = 8 \cdot 2$ — Multiply 2 for each term.

   $6x + y = 16$

   $y = -6x + 16$ — $f(x) = mx + b$

   The slope: $m = -6$

   y-intercept: $b = 16$ or $(0, 16)$

Slope

- **Recall: The graph of a linear equation is a straight line.**
- **Slope (m):** The slope of a straight line is the rate of change. It is a measure of the "steepness" or incline of the line and indicates whether the line rises or falls.
- **A line with a positive slope rises from left to right and a line with a negative slope falls.**
- **The slope formula**

The Slope Formula	
slope $= \dfrac{\text{the change in } y}{\text{the change in } x} = \dfrac{\text{rise}}{\text{run}}$	The slope of the straight line that passes through two points (x_1, y_1) and (x_2, y_2): $m = \dfrac{y_2 - y_1}{x_2 - x_1}$ or $m = \dfrac{y_1 - y_2}{x_1 - x_2}$ $x_1 \neq x_2$

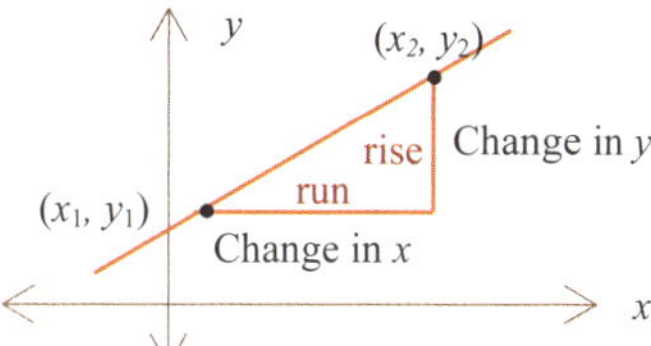

Example: Determine the slope containing points (2, -1) and (1, 3).

$$m = \frac{y_2 - y_1}{x_2 - x_1} = \frac{3 - (-1)}{1 - 2} = \frac{4}{-1} = -4$$

or $$m = \frac{y_1 - y_2}{x_1 - x_2} = \frac{-1 - 3}{2 - 1} = \frac{-4}{1} = -4$$

Example: Determine the slope of $5x - y - 7 = 0$.

x	$y = 5x - 7$	(x, y)
0	-7	$(x_1, y_1) = (0, -7)$
1	-2	$(x_2, y_2) = (1, -2)$
Choose	Calculate	

$$m = \frac{y_2 - y_1}{x_2 - x_1} = \frac{-2 - (-7)}{1 - 0} = \frac{5}{1} = 5 \qquad \text{or} \qquad m = \frac{y_1 - y_2}{x_1 - x_2} = \frac{-7 - (-2)}{0 - 1} = \frac{-5}{-1} = 5$$

Other points on the line will obtain the same slope m.

x	$y = 5x - 7$	(x, y)
2	3	(2, 3)
3	8	(3, 8)
Choose	Calculate	

$$m = \frac{8 - 3}{3 - 2} = \frac{5}{1} = 5$$

Example: Identify the slope (or rate of change).

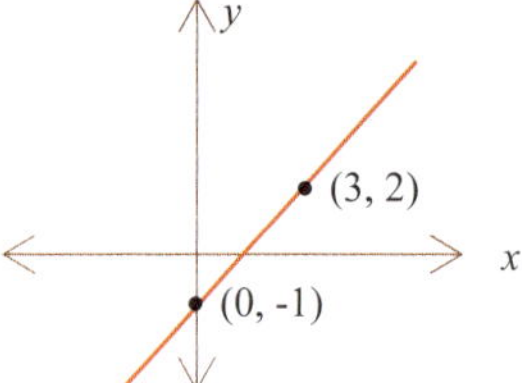

$$m = \frac{y_2 - y_1}{x_2 - x_1} = \frac{2-(-1)}{3-0} = \frac{3}{3} = \mathbf{1}$$

Example: Identify the slope.

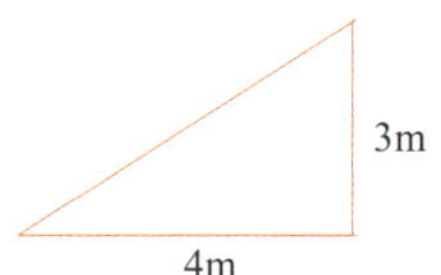

$$m = \frac{y_2 - y_1}{x_2 - x_1} = \frac{3}{4} = \mathbf{0.75}$$

Example: Tom purchased a car for \$23,000 in 2007. The car was worth \$19,000 in 2011. Find the average annual rate of change.

Year	*x*	*y*	(*x*, *y*)	Assuming
2007	7	\$23,000	(7, 23,000)	2000 = 0 , 2001 = 1, … 2007 = 7
2011	11	\$19,000	(11, 19,000)	2011 = 11

$$m = \frac{y_2 - y_1}{x_2 - x_1} = \frac{19{,}000-23{,}000}{11-7} = \frac{-4{,}000}{4} = \mathbf{-1{,}000}$$

The result means that the value of Tom's car decreased by \$1,000 per year.

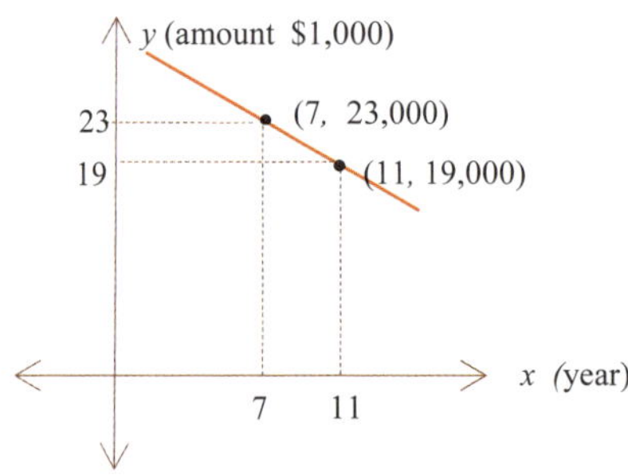

3-5 GRAPHING LINEAR EQUATIONS

Graphing Linear Equations Using the Intercept Method

- **Recall:** **The x-intercept** is the point at which the line crosses the x-axis. $(x, 0)$
  The y-intercept is the point at which the line crosses the y-axis. $(0, y)$

- **Procedures to graph a linear equation using the intercept method**

Steps

- Choose $x = 0$ and calculate the corresponding y.
- Choose $y = 0$ and calculate the corresponding x.
- Plot these two points on the coordinate plane.
- Connect the points with a straight line.
- Check with the third point.

Is third point (-1, -5) on the line? Yes. Correct!

Example: $2x - y = 3$

x	$y = 2x - 3$	(x, y)	Intercept
0	-3	(0, -3)	y-intercept
1.5	0	(1.5, 0)	x-intercept

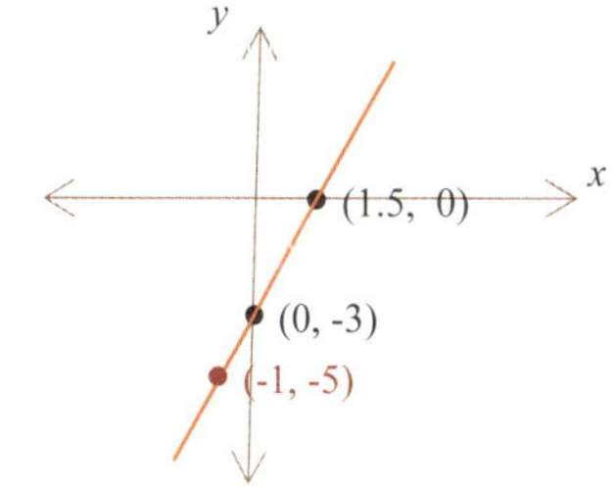

x	$y = 2x - 3$	(x, y)
-1	-5	(-1, -5)

Example: Graph the equation $x = 3y$.

- Choose $x = 0$ and calculate the corresponding y.
- Choose $x = 3$ and calculate the corresponding y.
- Plot (0, 0) and (3, 1).
- Connect two points with a straight line.
- Check (use the third point).
  Is third point (6, 2) on the line? Yes. Correct!

x	$y = \frac{x}{3}$	(x, y)
0	$\frac{0}{3} = 0$	(0, 0)
3	$\frac{3}{3} = 1$	(3, 1)

x	$y = \frac{x}{3}$	(x, y)
6	2	(6, 2)

Graphing Using the Slope and the *y* - Intercept

- **Recall: Slope-intercept function:** $f(x) = mx + b$
  $\begin{cases} m = \text{slope} \\ b = y\text{-intercept} \end{cases}$

- **The slope and a point can determine a straight line.**

Example: Graph the function using the slope and the *y*-intercept. $f(x) = \frac{-3}{5}x + 4$

- Plot the *y*-intercept (0, 4).
- Determine the rise and run: $m = \frac{-3}{5}$
  - The change in *y*: the rise (move 3 units down, ∵ *y* is negative).
  - The change in *x*: the run (move 5 units to the right, ∵ *x* is positive).
- Plot another point by moving 3 units down and 5 units to the right.
- Connect the two points with a line.

Starting point: y-intercept

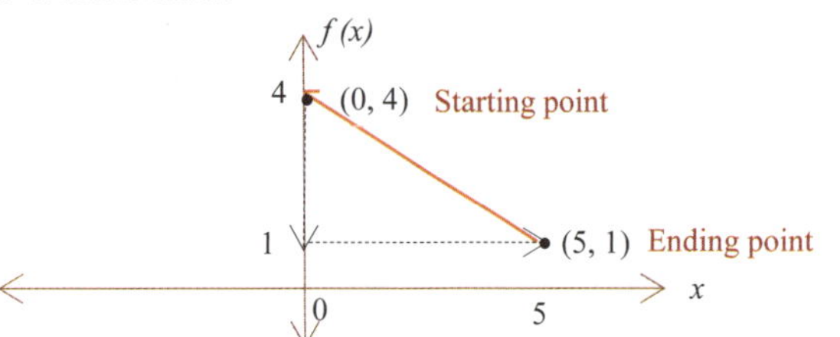

Example: Graph the function using the slope and the *y*-intercept. $-6x + 2 \cdot f(x) = -10$

- Convert to the slope-intercept form. $2 \cdot f(x) = 6x - 10$ Add 6*x* to both sides.
  $f(x) = 3x - 5$ Divide both sides by 2.
- *y*-intercept: (0, -5) $f(x) = mx + b$
- Slope: $m = 3 = \frac{3}{1}$

Move 3 units up and 1 unit to the right (both *x* & *y* are positive).

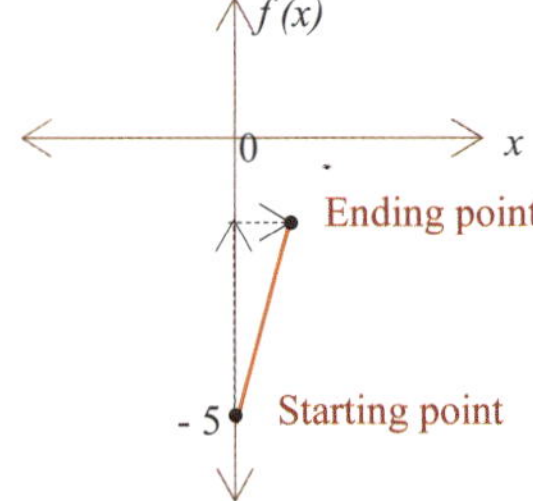

- **Tip:** $m = \frac{\text{rise}}{\text{run}} = \frac{\text{change in } y}{\text{change in } x}$ $\begin{cases} +y\text{: move up} \\ -y\text{: move down} \\ +x\text{: move to the right} \\ -x\text{: move to the left} \end{cases}$

+y
-x +x
-y

Vertical and Horizontal Lines

- **Horizontal line:** a line that is parallel to the x-axis. It has a slope of 0 and a y-intercept $(0, b)$, or $y = b$.

Example: $y = -3$

x	y	(x, y)
1	-3	(1, -3)
4	-3	(4, -3)

$$m = \frac{y_2 - y_1}{x_2 - x_1} = \frac{-3 - (-3)}{4 - 1} = \frac{0}{3} = \mathbf{0}$$

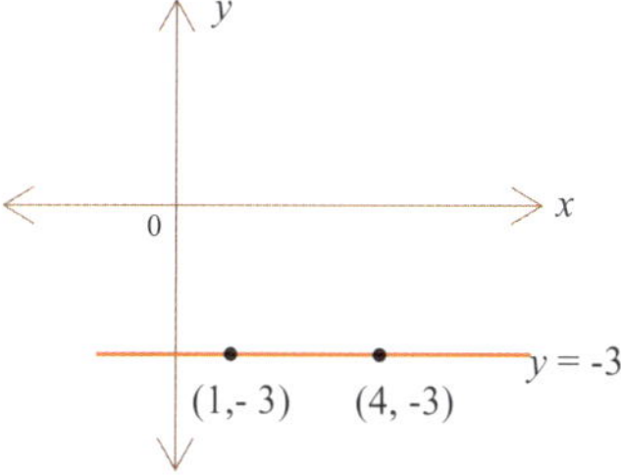

- **Vertical line:** a line that is parallel to the y-axis. It has an infinite slope with an x-intercept $(a, 0)$, or $x = a$.

Example: $x = -1$

x	y	(x, y)
-1	3	(-1, 3)
-1	-1	(-1, -1)

$$m = \frac{y_2 - y_1}{x_2 - x_1} = \frac{-1 - 3}{-1 - (-1)} = \frac{-4}{0} = \infty$$

Undefined

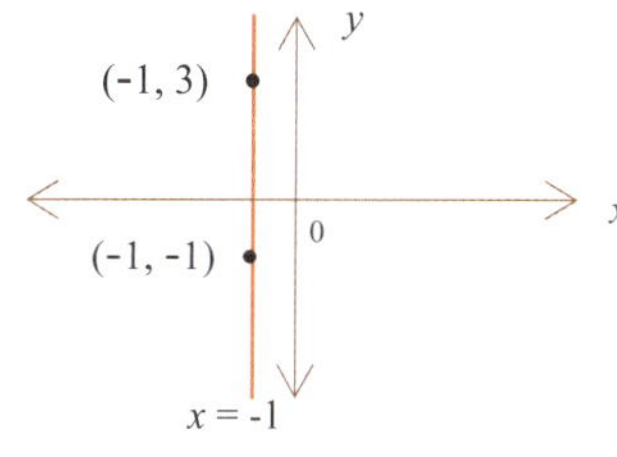

- **Horizontal and vertical line**

Line	Equation	m	Example	Graph
horizontal line	$y = b$	0	$y = 3$	
vertical line	$x = a$	∞	$x = -2$	

Example: Graph the function $\mathbf{2 + 5\,f(x) = 12}$ and determine the slope.

$5\,f(x) = 10$ Isolate $f(x)$.

$f(x) = 2$ or $y = 2$

Slope: $\boldsymbol{m = 0}$ Horizontal line

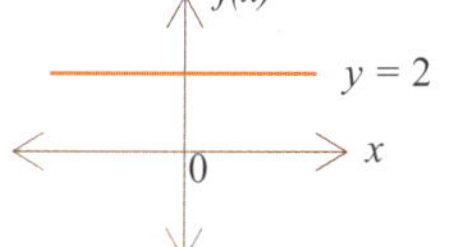

Perpendicular and Parallel Lines

- **Parallel lines** are always the same distance from each other and they will never intersect. Two parallel lines have the same slope $m_1 = m_2$.

  $L_1 \parallel L_2$ (Parallel symbol)

- **Perpendicular lines** intersect to form a 90-degree angle, and they have negative reciprocal slopes.

  $m_1 = -\frac{1}{m_2}$ $L_1 \perp L_2$ (Perpendicular symbol)

- **Parallel and perpendicular lines**

Line	Slope
Two parallel lines (∥)	$m_1 = m_2$
Two perpendicular lines (⊥)	$m_1 = -\frac{1}{m_2}$

Example: Determine if the graphs of two straight line equations are parallel or perpendicular.

1. $\mathbf{5y + 2x = 1}$ and $\mathbf{3 - 4x = 10y}$

$5y = -2x + 1$ | $10y = -4x + 3$ Convert to $f(x) = mx + b$.

$y = -\frac{2}{5}x + \frac{1}{5}$ | $y = -\frac{2}{5}x + \frac{3}{5}$

$m_1 = -\frac{2}{5}$ | $m_2 = -\frac{2}{5}$

$m_1 = m_2 = \frac{-2}{5}$, $\mathbf{L_1 \parallel L_2}$

2. $\mathbf{3x = 8 + y}$ and $\mathbf{3y + x + 4 = 0}$

$y = 3x - 8$ | $3y = -x - 4$ Convert to $f(x) = mx + b$.

$y = 3 \cdot x - 8$ | $y = -\frac{1}{3}x - \frac{4}{3}$

$m_1 = 3$ | $m_2 = -\frac{1}{3}$

$m_1 = \frac{-1}{m_2}$, $\mathbf{L_1 \perp L_2}$

3-6 STRAIGHT LINE EQUATIONS

Point-Slope Equation of a Line

- **Point-slope equation of a straight line**

Point-Slope Equation	
$y - y_1 = m\,(x - x_1)$	m – the slope of the line $(x_1,\ y_1)$ – the given point on the line (x, y) – any other point on the line

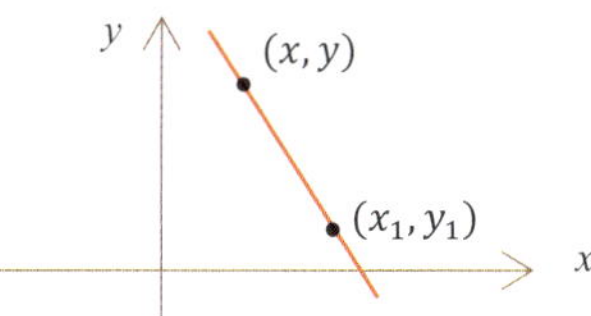

- **Derive:** from the slope formula $m = \frac{y_2 - y_1}{x_2 - x_1}$, let $x_2 = x$ and $y_2 = y$.

then $m = \frac{y - y_1}{x - x_1}$ Replace (x_2, y_2) by (x, y).

$m\,(x - x_1) = \frac{y - y_1}{x - x_1}(x - x_1)$ Multiply both sides by $x - x_1$.

point-slope equation: $y - y_1 = m\,(x - x_1)$

Example: Graph the line with slope $\frac{1}{3}$ that passes through the point (2, 3). Write an equation in point-slope form.

- Slope and point: $m = \frac{1}{3}$, $(x_1, y_1) = (2, 3)$
- Equation: $y - 3 = \frac{1}{3}(x - 2)$ Point-slope equation: $y - y_1 = m\,(x - x_1)$. Substitute $y_1 = 3$, $x_1 = 2$ and $m = \frac{1}{3}$.
- Graph: $m = \frac{1}{3}$ → The change in y (move 1 unit up). → The change in x (move 3 units to the right).

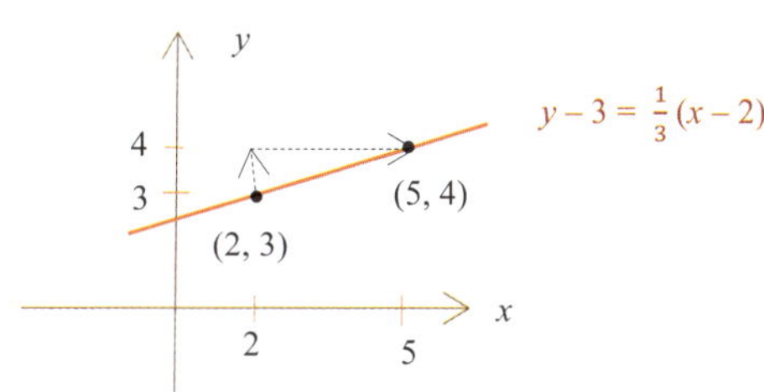

Finding an Equation of a Line

Straight-Line Equation	Equation	Example	
general form	$Ax + By = C$	$2x + y = 3$	$A = 2,\ B = 1,\ C = 3$
point-slope form	$y - y_1 = m(x - x_1)$	$y - 1 = -2\ (x + 5)$	$m = -2\quad y_1 = 1,\ x_1 = -5$
slope-intercept form	$y = mx + b$	$y = 8x - \frac{2}{7}$	$m = 8\ ,\ b = -\frac{2}{7}$

- **Finding an equation of a line when the slope and the y-intercept are given**

Example: Graph the line with slope -3 and y-intercept 5 and write the slope intercept equation.

$y = mx + b$ $m = -3,\quad b = 5$

$\mathbf{y = -3x + 5}$ $m = -3 = \frac{-3}{1}$ Move 3 units down and 1 unit to the right.

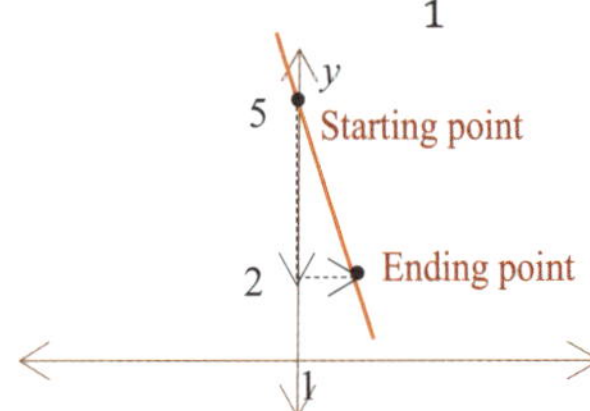

- **Finding an equation of a line when the slope and a point are given**

Example: Write an equation of the line passing the point (3, 2) with slope $m = -2$.

Start with: $y = mx + b$ Slope-intercept equation

Solve for b: $2 = -2 \cdot 3 + b$ Replace (x, y) by (3, 2) & m by -2.

$b = 8$

Equation of the line: $\mathbf{y = -2x + 8}$ $m = -2\ ,\quad b = 8$

- **Finding an equation of a line when two points are given**

Example: Write an equation of the line that passes through the points (1, 1) and (5, -7).

The slope: $m = \frac{y_2 - y_1}{x_2 - x_1} = \frac{-7-1}{5-1} = \frac{-8}{4} = -2$ Substitute $(x_1, y_1) = (1, 1)$, $(x_2, y_2) = (5, -7)$.

Start with: $y = mx + b$ Slope-intercept equation

Solve for b: $1 = -2 \cdot 1 + b$ Replace (x, y) by (1, 1) & m by – 2.

$b = 3$ Use $(x, y) = (5, -7)$ will get the same result.

Equation of the line: $\mathbf{y = -2x + 3}$ $m = -2\ ,\quad b = 3$

Example: Write an equation of the line passing through the points.

1. **(-5, 3) (4, 3)** and **2.** **(2, -1) (2, 3)**.

Solution:

1. $m = \frac{y_2 - y_1}{x_2 - x_1} = \frac{3-3}{4-(-5)} = \frac{0}{9} = 0$ Let $(x_1, y_1) = (-5, 3)$, $(x_2, y_2) = (4, 3)$.

$y = mx + b$ $y = 0 \cdot x + b$ $y = b$ $\mathbf{y = 3}$ (horizontal line)

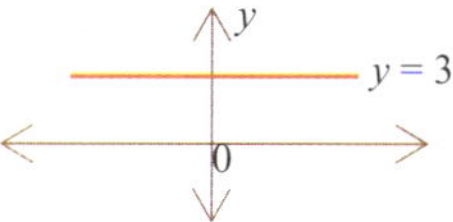

2. $m = \frac{y_2 - y_1}{x_2 - x_1} = \frac{3-(-1)}{2-2} = \frac{4}{0} = \infty$ undefined Let $(x_1, y_1) = (2, -1)$, $(x_2, y_2) = (2, 3)$.

$\mathbf{x = 2}$ (Vertical line)

(2, -1) (2, 3)

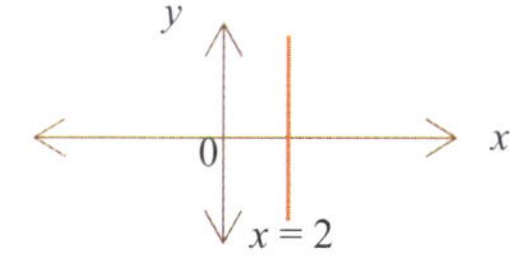

- **Find an equation of the line passing through a point and is parallel or perpendicular to a given line**

Example: Write an equation of the line passing through the point (1, -4) and is:

1. parallel to and **2.** perpendicular to the line $\mathbf{2x + 4y \quad 8 - 0}$.

Solution: $2x + 4y = 8$ Add 8 on both sides.

- Convert to slope-intercept form. $4y = -2x + 8$ Subtract $2x$ from both sides.

$y = -\frac{1}{2}x + 2$ Divide 4 on both sides.

- Determine the slope for the line 1. $m_1 = -\frac{1}{2}$ $y = mx + b$

1. A line L_2 is parallel to the line L_1 $(2x + 4y - 8 = 0)$ and has a slope of $m_2 = -\frac{1}{2}$.

Parallel: $m_1 = m_2$

- Start with: $y = mx + b$
- Solve for b: $-4 = -\frac{1}{2} \cdot 1 + b$ Replace (x, y) by $(1, -4)$ & m by $-\frac{1}{2}$.

$-8 = -1 + 2b$ Multiply 2 for each term.

$b = -\frac{7}{2}$

- Equation of the line: $\mathbf{y = -\frac{1}{2}x - \frac{7}{2}}$ $L_2 \parallel L_1$

2. A line L_2 is perpendicular to the line L_1 $(2x + 4y - 8 = 0)$ and has a slope of $m_2 = \frac{-1}{m_1}$,

or $m_2 = \frac{-1}{m_1} = \frac{(-1)}{\frac{-1}{2}} = 2$ $m_1 = \frac{-1}{2}$

- Start with: $y = mx + b$ Replace (x_1, y_1) by $(1, -4)$ & m by 2.
- Solve for b: $-4 = 2 \cdot 1 + b$, $b = -6$
- Equation of the line: $\mathbf{y = 2x - 6}$ $m = 2$, $b = -6$, $L_2 \perp L_1$

- **Applications**

Example: Tom bought a laptop for \$1,000. The value of the laptop decreases at a rate of \$100 per year. Write an equation for the value $f(t)$ of the laptop after t years. Graph the equation and determine the value of the laptop after 4 years.

- Equation: $f(t) = 1{,}000 - 100t$ $y = mx + b$, $f(t) = -100t + 1{,}000$
- Solve algebraically: $f(4) = 1{,}000 - 100t$ $t = 4$ years

$= 1{,}000 - 100\,(4)$

$= \$\,\mathbf{600}$

- Solve graphically:

t	$f(t) = 1{,}000 - 100t$
0	\$ 1,000
2	\$ 800

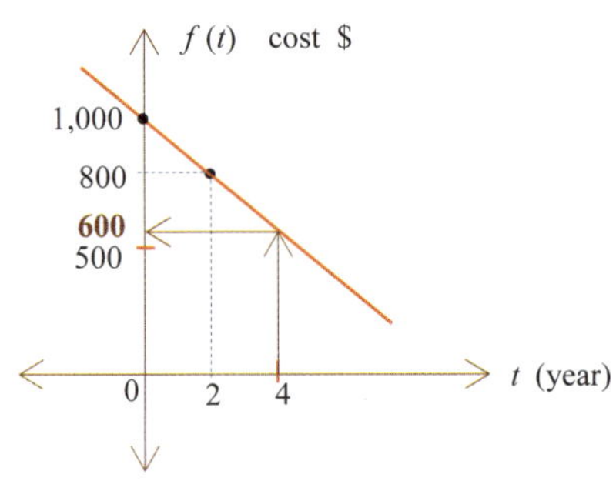

The laptop will be worth **\$600** after 4 years.

Unit 3 Summary

- **Ordered pair (x, y):** each point on the plane corresponds to an ordered pair.

  (x, y) — 1st coordinate (abscissa), 2nd coordinate (ordinate)

- **Four quadrants**

Quadrant	(x, y)	Example
The 1st quadrant I	$(+x, +y)$	(+2, +3)
The 2nd quadrant II	$(-x, +y)$	(-2, +3)
The 3rd quadrant III	$(-x, -y)$	(-2, -3)
The 4th quadrant IV	$(+x, -y)$	(+2, -3)

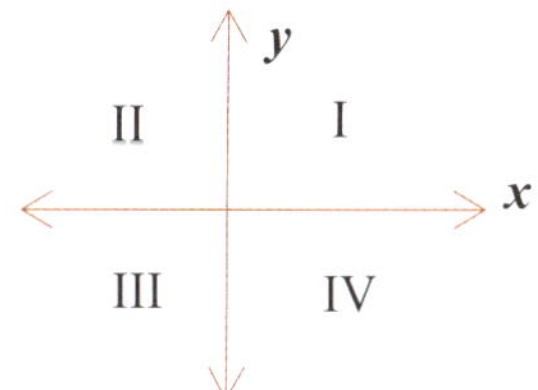

- **x-intercept $(x, 0)$:** the point at which the graph crosses the x-axis.
- **y-intercept $(0, y)$:** the point at which the graph crosses the y-axis.

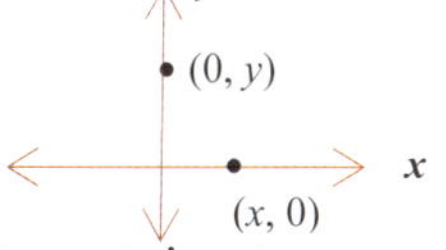

- **A linear (first-degree) equation in two variables:** a linear equation that contains two variables. (A linear equation whose graph is a straight line.)

Standard Form	Example
$Ax + By = C$	$5x - 7y = 4$

- **Nonlinear equation:** an equation whose graph is not a straight line.
- **Procedure to graph a nonlinear equation (or function) with two variables:**
  - Choose a few values of x, calculate the corresponding y, and make a table.
  - Plot these points on the coordinate plane (plot more points to get the cleaner shape of the graph).
  - Connect the points with a smooth curve.
- **Function:** a special type of relation (or correspondence) which matches **each** element of the **domain** with exactly **one** element of the **range**.
- **Relation:** a set of ordered pairs (x, y).
- **Domain:** the set of the values of the independent variable (x-value) for which a function is defined.
- **Range:** the set of the values of the dependent variable (y-value) for which a function is defined.
- **All functions are relations (correspondence), but not all relations are functions.**
- **Function notation:** the notation for a function is $f(x),\ P(x),\ g(x),\ h(x), \ldots$
- **Function values:**

$$f(x)\,|_{x=a} = f(a) \quad , \quad \begin{cases} a \text{ is a constant} \\ \text{replace } x \text{ by } a \end{cases}$$

- **The vertical line test:** If a vertical line cuts the relation's graph more than once, then the relation is not a function.

- **Slope-intercept form of a linear function**

Slope-Intercept Function of a Line	
$f(x) = mx + b$	m: the slope of the line b: y-intercept

- **Slope (m):** the slope of a straight line is the rate of change. It is a measure of the "steepness" or incline of the line and indicates whether the line rises or falls.

- **The slope formula**

The Slope Formula	
slope $= \frac{\text{the change in } y}{\text{the change in } x} = \frac{\text{rise}}{\text{run}}$	The slope of the straight line that passes through two points (x_1, y_1) and (x_2, y_2): $m = \frac{y_2 - y_1}{x_2 - x_1}$ or $m = \frac{y_1 - y_2}{x_1 - x_2}$ $x_1 \neq x_2$

- **Horizontal and vertical lines**

Line	Equation	m	Example	Graph
horizontal line	$y = b$	0	$y = 3$	3, 0
vertical line	$x = a$	∞	$x = -2$	-2, 0

- **Parallel and perpendicular lines**

Line	Slope
two lines are parallel (‖)	$m_1 = m_2$
two lines are perpendicular (⊥)	$m_1 = -\frac{1}{m_2}$

- **Equations of the straight lines**

Straight-Line Equation	Equation	Example	
general form	$Ax + By = C$	$2x + y = 3$	$A = 2,\ B = 1,\ C = 3$
point-slope form	$y - y_1 = m(x - x_1)$	$y - 1 = -2(x + 5)$	$m = -2\ \ y_1 = 1,\ x_1 = -5$
slope-intercept form	$y = mx + b$	$y = 8x - \frac{2}{7}$	$m = 8,\ b = -\frac{2}{7}$

PRACTICE QUIZ

Unit 3 Functions and Graphs

1. Graph the following equations.

   a. $3x - y = 2$

   b. $y = |x + 2|$

2. Evaluate the functions at the indicated values.

   a. $f(-3)$ for $f(x) = 7 + 5x^2$

   b. $q(0)$ for $q(r) = 5r^2 + 2r - 1$

3. Evaluate the functions and simplify at the indicated values.

   a. $f(x) = 5x - 3$, $f(a - 2) = ?$

   b. $h(x) = |x - 2| + 3x$, $h(5) = ?$

4. The following graph shows the number of bicycle rentals as a function of time in a rental store. How many bicycle rentals were there in 2012?

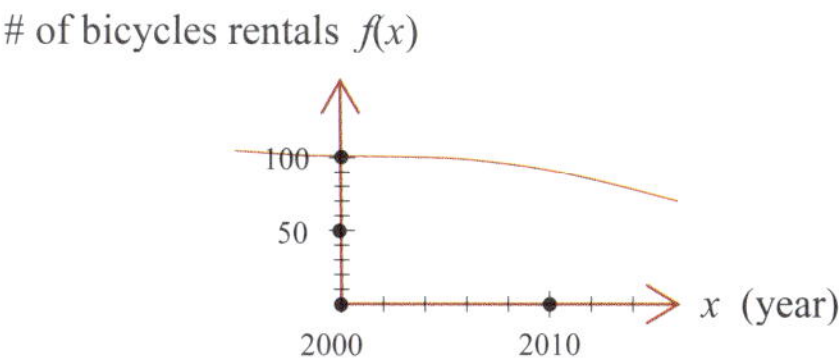

5. Given the relation: (3, 4), (-1, 6), (6, 3), (-4, 3)

   a. Identify the domain.

   b. Identify the range.

6. For the following functions, identify their domains.

   a. $f(x) = \frac{13}{5-x}$

   b. $f(x) = \frac{6}{|7x-5|}$

7. **a.** Identify the slope and y-intercept of $2x - \frac{1}{3}y = 5$.

b. Identify the slope of the line.

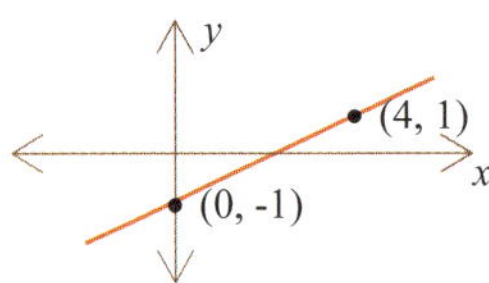

8. Mary purchased a laptop for $1,000 in 2008. The laptop was worth $500 in 2012. Find the average annual rate of change.

9. Graph using the slope and the y-intercept. $-4x + 2f(x) = -14$

10. Determine if the graphs of two straight line equations are parallel or perpendicular.

$2y + 7x = 1$ and $3 - 14x = 4y$

11. Write an equation of the line that passes through the points (2, 3) and (3, -4).

12. Write an equation of the line passing through the point (2, -3) and

a. parallel to and **b.** perpendicular to the line $9y = -3x + 1$.

13. Sam bought a car for $20,000. The value of the car decreases at a rate of $1,000 per year. Write an equation for the value $f(t)$ of the car after t years. Graph the equation and determine the value of the car after 5 years.

UNIT 4 SYSTEMS OF EQUATIONS & INEQUALITIES

4-1 SYSTEMS OF EQUATIONS

A System of Equations

- **A system of equations** is a group of two or more equations with the same variables (unknowns).

  Example: $\begin{cases} 2x^2 + 3y = 2 \\ 4x^2 - 5y = 7 \end{cases}$

- **A system of linear equations** is a group of two or more **first-degree** equations. (First-degree equation: The highest power of the variable is one.)

- **A system of two linear equations in two variables:** two linear equations in two unknowns.

  Example: $\begin{cases} x - y = 2 \\ 2x + y = 13 \end{cases}$

- **A system of linear equations**

	Standard Form	Example
2×2 system (2 equations, 2 unknowns)	$\begin{cases} A_1x + B_1y = C_1 \\ A_2x + B_2y = C_1 \end{cases}$	$\begin{cases} 3x - 4y = 5 \\ 5x + 7y = -2 \end{cases}$
3×3 system (3 equations, 3 unknowns)	$\begin{cases} A_1x + B_1y + C_1z = D_1 \\ A_2x + B_2y + C_2z = D_2 \\ A_3x + B_3y + C_3z = D_3 \end{cases}$	$\begin{cases} 2x - 3y + 4z = 7 \\ 4x - 2y - z = 3 \\ 5x - 6y + 2z = 2 \end{cases}$

- **The solutions for a system of equations:** the values for variables that make all equations in the system true.

  Example: Verify that the ordered pair (5, 3) is a solution of the system.

  $\begin{cases} x - y = 2 \\ 2x + y = 13 \end{cases}$

$x - y = 2$		$2x + y = 13$
$5 - 3 \stackrel{?}{=} 2$		$2(5) + 3 \stackrel{?}{=} 13$
√ $2 = 2$	**Yes!**	√ $13 = 13$

Replace (x, y) by (5, 3) in both equations.

(5, 3) makes both equations true, it is the solution of the system.

Solving Linear Systems by Graphing

- **Solving systems of equations – graphing method**: Graph both equations in the system on the coordinate plane. The point(s) at which the lines intersect will be the solution(s) to the system.

- **Procedure for graphing**

Example: Solve the following system graphically.

$$\begin{cases} x - y = 2 & (1) \\ x + y = 4 & (2) \end{cases}$$

- Graph $x - y = 2$ (1)

x	$y = x - 2$	(x, y)
0	-2	(0, -2)
2	0	(2, 0)

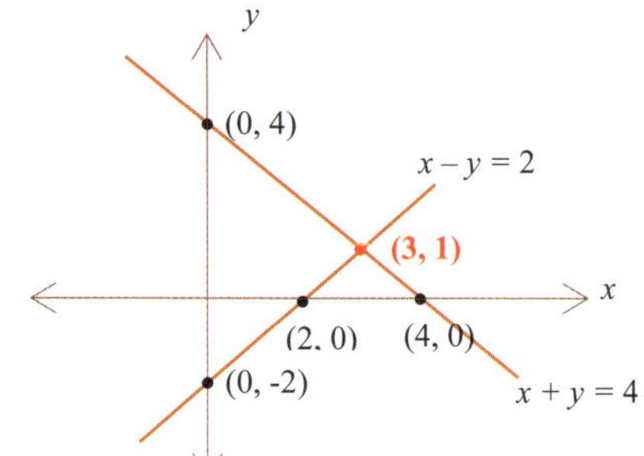

- Graph $x + y = 4$ (2)

x	$y = 4 - x$	(x, y)
0	4	(0, 4)
4	0	(4, 0)

- Find the intersection of two lines (x, y). $\mathbf{(x, y) = (3, 1)}$ Solution

- Check.

$x - y = 2$	$x + y = 4$
$3 - 1 \overset{?}{=} 2$	$3 + 1 \overset{?}{=} 4$
√	√
$2 = 2$	$4 = 4$

Correct!

Properties of a Linear System

- **Consistent and independent:** The system has one solution (the lines of equations intersect at one point). The equations in the system are independent.

  Example: (last example)

  $$\begin{cases} x - y = 2 \\ x + y = 4 \end{cases}$$

  Solution: $(x, y) = (3, 1)$

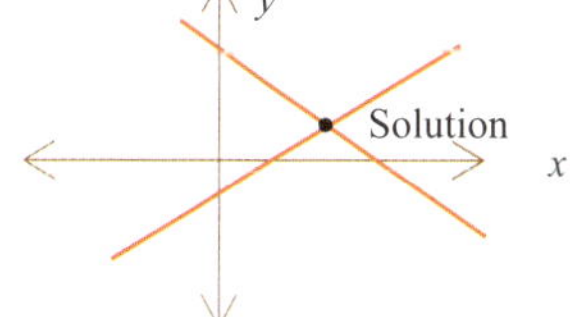

- **Consistent and dependent:** The system has infinite number of solutions (the lines of the equations coincide).

  Example: $\begin{cases} x - y = 2 & (1) \\ 2x - 2y = 4 & (2) \end{cases}$

$x - y = 2$ (1)		$2x - 2y = 4$ (2)	
x	$y = x - 2$	x	$y = x - 2$
0	-2	0	-2
2	0	2	0

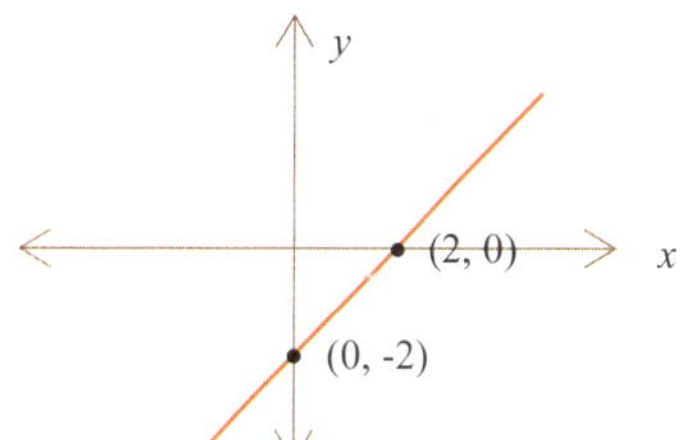

- **Inconsistent system:** the system has no solution, and the lines of the equations are parallel. (The solution set to the system is an empty set ∅.)

  Example: $\begin{cases} 2x + y = 6 & (1) \\ 2x + y = -8 & (2) \end{cases}$

$2x + y = 6$ (1)		$2x + y = -8$ (2)	
x	$y = 6 - 2x$	x	$y = -8 - 2x$
0	6	0	-8
3	0	-4	0

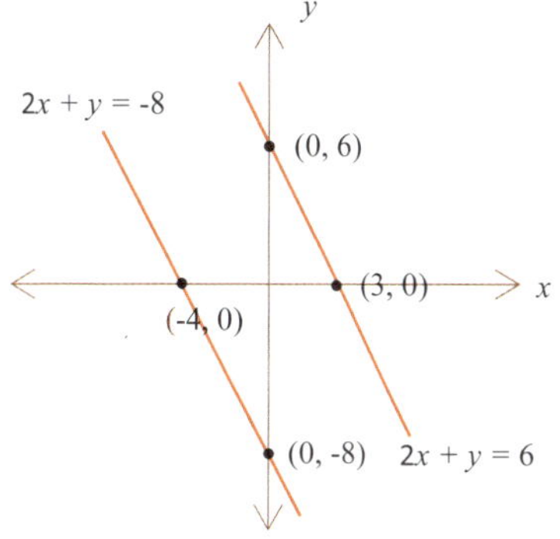

- **Properties of linear equations**

Property	Numbers of Solution	Lines	Graph
consistent & independent	one solution	lines intersect	
consistent & dependent	infinitely number of solutions	lines coincide (the same line)	
inconsistent	no solution ∅	lines are parallel	

4-2 SOLVING SYSTEMS BY SUBSTITUTION OR ELIMINATION

Solving Systems by Substitution

- **Substitution method**: Solve one variable in one equation and substitute the result into the other equation to solve another variable. (Objective is to eliminate one of the unknown variables).
- **Using the substitution method to solve systems**:

Steps	Example: $\begin{cases} x - 2y = 4 \\ 2x + y = 3 \end{cases}$
- Label the equation as (1) & (2).	$\begin{cases} x - 2y = 4 & (1) \\ 2x + y = 3 & (2) \end{cases}$
- Choose one equation and isolate one variable (x or y), and name the equation (3).	Choose (1) and isolate x. $x = 2y + 4$ (3)
- Substitute the isolated variable into the other equation.	Substitute x into (2) $2(2y + 4) + y = 3$ Replace x by $2y + 4$.
- Solve for the other variable.	$4y + 8 + y = 3$ Solve for y. $5y = -5$ $\mathbf{y = -1}$
- Substitute the solved value into equation (3) and solve for y or x.	$x = 2(-1) + 4$ $y = -1 \longrightarrow (3)$ $\mathbf{x = 2}$ The solution is **(2, -1)**

- Check.

$x - 2y = 4$	$2x + y = 3$
$2 - 2(-1) \stackrel{?}{=} 4$	$2(2) + (-1) \stackrel{?}{=} 3$
$2 + 2 \stackrel{\surd}{=} 4$	$4 - 1 \stackrel{\surd}{=} 3$

$x - 2y = 4$		$2x + y = 3$	
x	$y = \frac{x}{2} - 2$	x	$y = 3 - 2x$
0	-2	0	3
4	0	1	1

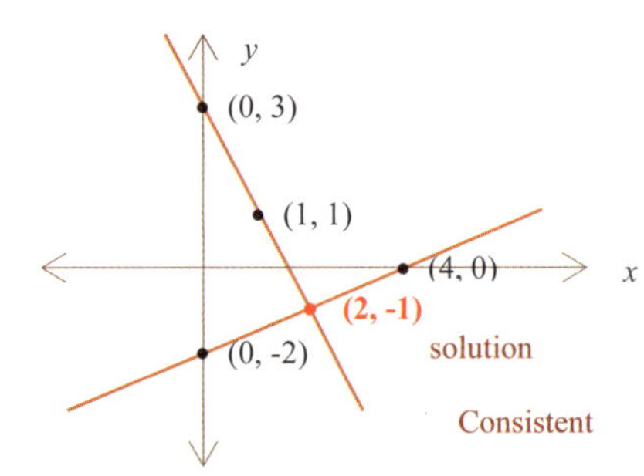

Solving Systems by Elimination

- **Elimination method**: Add or subtract the equations to eliminate one of the variables (unknowns), and then solve the resulting equation in one variable.
  Objective: eliminate one of the variables.
- **Using the elimination method to solve systems**:

Steps

Example: Solve $\begin{cases} 2x - 1 = -y \\ 3x = y + 4 \end{cases}$.

- Write the system of equations in standard form and label them as (1) and (2).

  Standard form: $\begin{cases} A_1x + B_1y = C_1 \\ A_2x + B_2y = C_2 \end{cases}$

  $\begin{cases} 2x + y = 1 & (1) \\ 3x - y = 4 & (2) \end{cases}$

- Add equations (1) and (2).

  $$\begin{array}{rl} & 2x + y = 1 \\ + & 3x - y = 4 \\ \hline & 5x \quad = 5 \end{array}$$

  Solve for x.

  $\mathbf{x = 1}$

- Substitute the isolated variable into (1) or (2).

  $2(1) + y = 1$ $\quad x = 1 \rightarrow (1)$

- Solve for the other variable.

  $\mathbf{y = -1}$ $\quad$ Solve for y.

  Solution: **(1, -1)**

- Check.

$2x - 1 = -y$	$3x = y + 4$
$2(1) - 1 \stackrel{?}{=} -(-1)$	$3(1) \stackrel{?}{=} -1 + 4$
√	√
$2 - 1 = 1$	$3 = 3$

Correct!

Example: Solve $\begin{cases} 2x - 5 = -y \\ -x + 3y = 1 \end{cases}$.

Steps	Solution
- Rewrite in standard form and label them as (1) and (2).	$\begin{cases} 2x + y = 5 & (1) \\ -x + 3y = 1 & (2) \end{cases}$
- Multiply one or both equations by the appropriate numbers to eliminate one variable (x or y).	$-2x + 6y = 2$ (3)

Multiply (2) by 2.

Note: if add equations (1) and (2), nothing cancels out:

$$\begin{array}{rl} & 2x + y = 5 \\ + & -x + 3y = 1 \\ \hline & x + 4y = 6 \end{array}$$

- Add equations (1) and (3) and solve for y.

  $$\begin{array}{rll} & 2x + y = 5 & (1) \\ + & -2x + 6y = 2 & (3) \\ \hline & 7y = 7 & \end{array}$$

  Solve for y.

  $\mathbf{y = 1}$

- Substitute $y = 1$ into equation (1) & solve for x.

  $2x + 1 = 5$ $\quad$ Replace y by 1.

  $\mathbf{x = 2}$ $\quad$ Solve for x.

  Solution: **(2, 1)**

Systems Involving Decimals or Fractions

- **System involving decimals:**

Example: Solve the system of equations by elimination. $\begin{cases} x - 2y = 3 \\ 0.4x + 0.2y = 0.2 \end{cases}$

Steps	Example	
- Label the equations as (1) & (2).	$\begin{cases} x - 2y = 3 & (1) \\ 0.4x + 0.2y = 0.2 & (2) \end{cases}$	
- Clear the decimals.	$4x + 2y = 2$ (3)	Multiply equation (2) by 10.
- Add equations (1) and (3) to eliminate y.	$\begin{array}{rl} & x - 2y = 3 \\ + & 4x + 2y = 2 \\ \hline & 5x \quad = 5 \end{array}$ $x = 1$	
- Substitute x into (1).	$1 - 2y = 3$	Replace x by 1.
- Solve for y.	$y = -1$	Solution: **(1, -1)**

- **System involving fractions**

Example: Solve the system of equations by elimination. $\begin{cases} \frac{2}{3}x + \frac{1}{2}y - 1 = 0 \\ \frac{2}{3}y - \frac{1}{3}x + 1 = 0 \end{cases}$

Steps	Solution	
- Write in standard form and label as (1) and (2).	$\begin{cases} \frac{2}{3}x + \frac{1}{2}y = 1 & (1) \\ \frac{-1}{2}x - \frac{2}{3}y = -1 & (2) \end{cases}$	
- Clear the fractions.	$6\left(\frac{2}{3}x\right) + 6\left(\frac{1}{2}y\right) = 1 \cdot 6$	Multiply (1) by the LCD.
	$4x + 3y = 6$ (3)	
	$6\left(-\frac{1}{2}x\right) - 6\left(\frac{2}{3}y\right) = -1 \cdot 6$	Multiply (2) by the LCD.
	$-3x - 4y = -6$ (4)	
- Multiply equation (3) by 3 and (4) by 4, and add them.	$\begin{array}{rl} & 12x + 9y = 18 \\ + & -12x - 16y = -24 \\ \hline & -7y = -6 \end{array}$ $y = \frac{6}{7}$	Multiply (3) by 3. Multiply (4) by 4.

- Substitute $\frac{6}{7}$ for y in equation (1), and solve for x.

$\frac{2}{3}x + \frac{1}{2}\left(\frac{6}{7}\right) = 1, \quad \frac{2}{3}x + \frac{3}{7} = 1$ — Multiply by the LCD: 21

$14x + 9 = 21, \quad x = \frac{6}{7}$

Solution: $\left(\frac{6}{7}, \frac{6}{7}\right)$

Applications

Example: Todd bought 5 apples and 4 oranges for \$3. Susan bought 7 apples and 4 oranges for \$4. How much does one apple and orange cost?

- List the facts.

	Apple	Orange	Price
Todd	5	4	\$ 3.00
Susan	7	4	\$ 4.00

- Label x and y. Let $x =$ the cost of one apple, $y =$ the cost of one orange.
- Write system of equations. $\begin{cases} 5x + 4y = 3 & (1) \\ 7x + 4y = 4 & (2) \end{cases}$
- Solve equations.

$$\begin{array}{r} 5x + 4y = 3 \\ -\ 7x + 4y = 4 \\ \hline -2x \quad = -1 \end{array} \qquad (1) - (2)$$

$$x = \frac{1}{2} = \$0.50$$

- Substitute $x = \frac{1}{2}$ into equation (1) and solve for y.

$$5\left(\frac{1}{2}\right) + 4y = 3 \qquad \text{Multiply 2 for each term.}$$

$$5 + 8y = 6$$

$$y = \frac{1}{8} \approx \$0.13$$

- Answer: One apple costs \$0.50 and one orange costs \$0.13. **$(x, y) = (\$0.50, \ \$0.13)$**

Example: The perimeter of a rectangular field is 400m. The length is 40m less than twice the width. Determine the dimension of the rectangular field.

- Facts:

width	w
length	$2w - 40 = l$
perimeter	$P = 400$m ($P = 2l + 2w$)

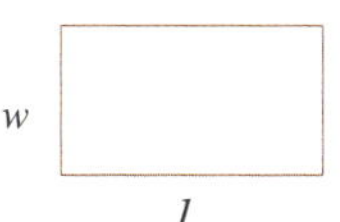

- Equations: $\begin{cases} 2l + 2w = 400 \\ l = 2w - 40 \end{cases}$
- Standard form: $\begin{cases} 2l + 2w = 400 & (1) \\ l - 2w = -40 & (2) \end{cases}$
- (1) + (2) :

$$\begin{array}{r} 2l + 2w = 400 \\ +\quad l - 2w = -40 \\ \hline 3l \quad = 360 \end{array}$$

$$l = \frac{360}{3} = 120 \qquad \boldsymbol{l = 120\text{m}}$$

- Substitute $l = 120$ into (1) and solve for w.

$$2(120) + 2w = 400$$

$$2w = 400 - 240$$

$$\boldsymbol{w = 80\ m}$$

- Answer: Length = 120 m, Width = 80 m

4-3 SYSTEMS OF LINEAR INEQUALITIES IN TWO VARIABLES

Linear Inequalities in Two Variables

- **A linear inequality:** a mathematical statement with an inequality symbol in which the highest power of the variable is one.
- **Inequality symbols review**

Symbol	Indication
$>$	greater than
$<$	less than
$\geq$	greater than or equal to
$\leq$	less than or equal to

- **A linear inequality in two variables:** a linear inequality contains two variables.
- **Standard linear inequality in two variables**

Standard Inequality	Example
$Ax + By > C$	$2x + 3y > 6$
$Ax + By < C$	$3x - 5y < 17$
$Ax + By \geq C$	$4x + 5y \geq 10$
$Ax + By \leq C$	$6x - 11y \leq 21$

- **Solutions of linear inequalities in two variables:** an ordered pair (x, y) that makes the inequality true.

Example: Determine if (1, 2) satisfies the inequality $3x + 5y < 17$.

$3(1) + 5(2) \overset{?}{<} 17$ Replace (x, y) by (1, 2).

$3 + 10 \overset{?}{<} 17$

$13 \overset{\surd}{<} 17$ Correct!

Yes, (1, 2) is a solution A true statement.

Graphing Linear Inequality in Two Variables

Procedure for graphing a linear inequality in two variables

Steps

- Change the inequality symbol to an equal sign.
- Graph the boundary line of the corresponding equation.

(Using x and y intercepts)

x	$y = x - 3$	(x, y)
0	-3	(0, -3)
3	0	(3, 0)

  - Draw a solid line if the inequality symbol is $\leq$ or $\geq$.
  - Draw a dashed line if the inequality symbol is $<$ or $>$.
- Choose a test point such as (0, 0).
  - If the test point satisfies the inequality, shade the side of the line that **contains** the test point.
  - If the test point does not satisfy the inequality, shade the side of the line that **does not contain** the test point.

Example: Graph $\boldsymbol{x - y \geq 3}$.

$x - y = 3$

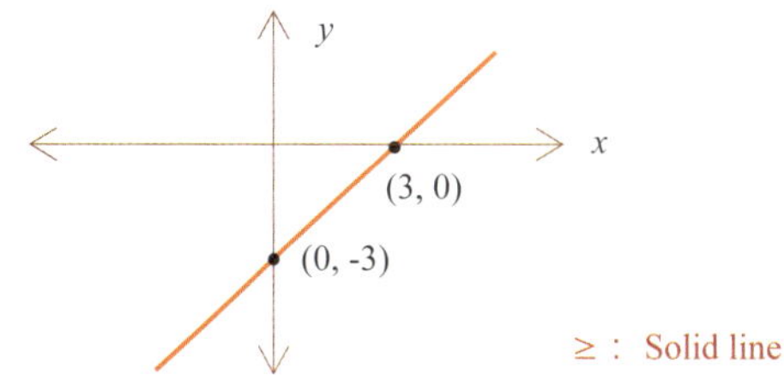

$\geq$: Solid line

Choose (0, 0)

$x - y \geq 3$

$0 - 0 \overset{?}{\geq} 3$ False

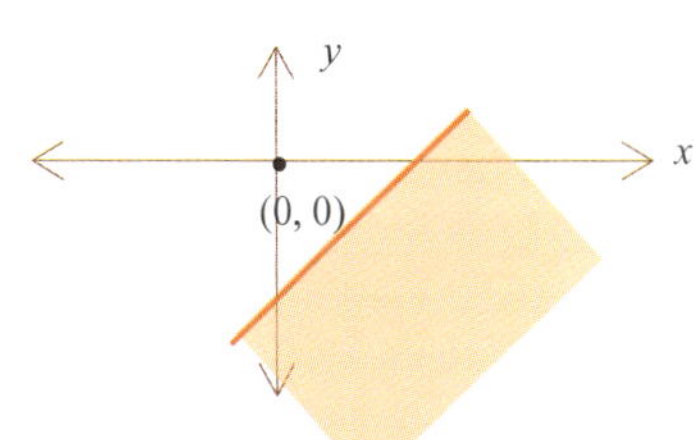

Shade the region that does not contain (0, 0).

Example: Graph the inequality $\boldsymbol{2x - y < 8}$.

- "<" changes to "="

$2x - y = 8$

- Draw a dashed boundary line (∵ the inequality symbol is <)

x	$y = 2x - 8$	(x, y)
0	-8	(0, -8)
4	0	(4, 0)

- Test point: choose (0, 0).

$2x - y < 8$

$2(0) - 0 \overset{?}{<} 8$

$0 \overset{\surd}{<} 8$ True.

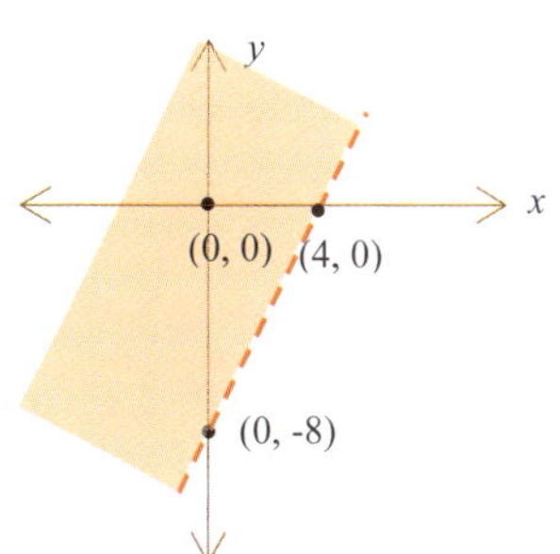

Shade the region that contains (0, 0).

Do not choose the point (0, 0) to test if it is on the solution line.

Example: Graph the inequality $y \geq 5x$.

- "$\geq$" changes to "="
- Draw a solid boundary line. (∵ the inequality symbol is $\geq$)

x	$y = 5x$	(x, y)
0	0	(0, 0)
1	5	(1, 5)

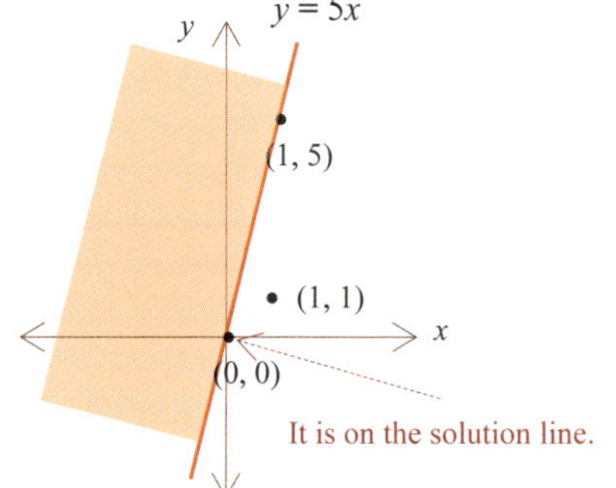

- Test point: choose (1, 1) $y \geq 5x$

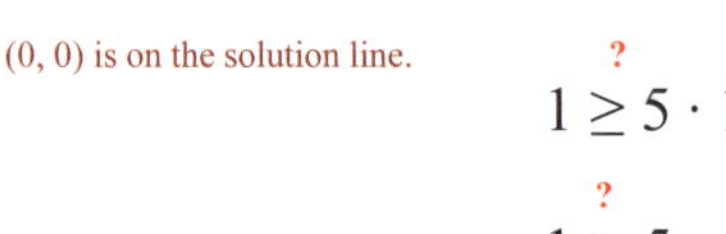

$1 \overset{?}{\geq} 5 \cdot 1$

$1 \overset{?}{>} 5$ False

Shade the region that not contains (1, 1).

Example: Write the linear inequalities whose graph is the shaded region.

1.

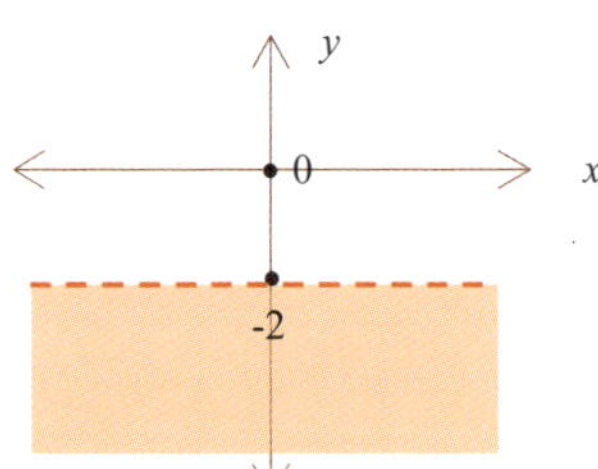

$\boldsymbol{y < -2}$

A dashed line: <

2.

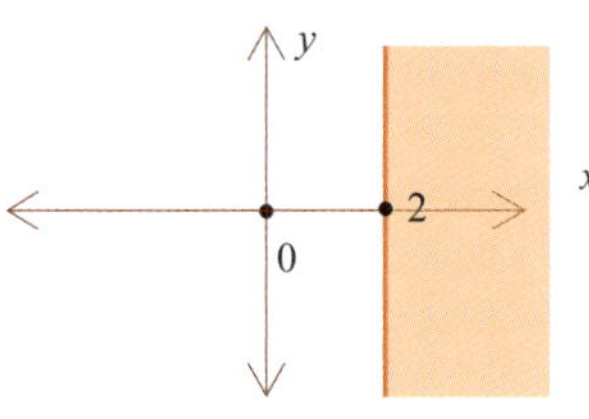

$\boldsymbol{x \geq 2}$

A solid line: $\geq$.

Systems of Linear Inequalities

- **A system of linear inequalities in two variables:** a group of two or more inequalities with the same two variables.

Standard Form	Example
$\begin{cases} A_1x + B_1y > C_1 \\ A_2x + B_2y \geq C_2 \end{cases}$	$2x + 3y < 4$ $3x - 5y \geq 8$

$<, >, \leq, \geq$

- **Solutions of a system of linear inequalities:** an ordered pair that satisfies both inequalities.
- **Graphing a system of linear inequalities in two variables**

Steps

Example: Graph $\begin{cases} x - y \geq 2 \\ 2x + y < 4 \end{cases}$

- Change the inequality symbols to equal signs and label with (1) and (2).

$\begin{cases} x - y = 2 & (1) \\ 2x + y = 4 & (2) \end{cases}$

- Graph the boundary lines of the corresponding equations.

(1)		(2)	
x	$y = x - 2$	x	$y = 4 - 2x$
0	-2	0	4
2	0	2	0

Draw a dashed line if the symbol is $<$ or $>$.
Draw a solid line if the symbol is $\leq$ or $\geq$.

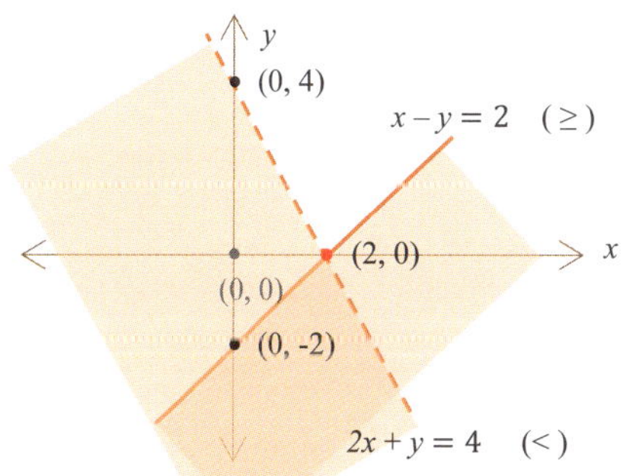

- Choose a test point (0, 0).

Test point (0, 0)

$x - y \geq 2$	$2x + y < 4$
$0 - 0 \overset{?}{\geq} 2$	$2 \cdot 0 + 0 \overset{?}{<} 4$
×	√
$0 \geq 2$ False	$0 < 4$ True
Shade the region that does not contain (0, 0), i.e. below $x - y = 2$.	Shade the region that contains (0, 0), i.e below $2x + y = 4$.

- The solution set is the region where the shading overlaps. The vertex is (2, 0).

The vertex is formed by an intersection of two boundary lines.

Example: Graph the system of inequalities $\begin{cases} x \leq 3 \\ 2 \leq y \leq 4 \\ x + 2y < 2 \end{cases}$. Find the coordinates of any vertices formed.

$x + 2y = 2$

x	$y = 1 - \frac{1}{2}x$
0	1
2	0

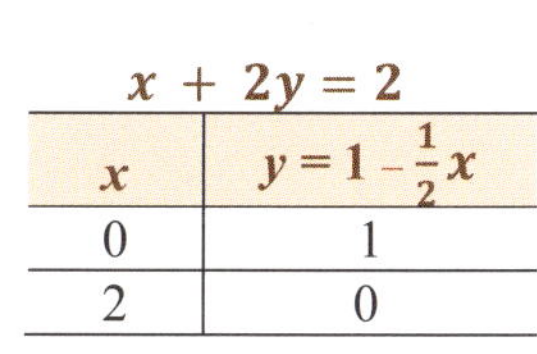

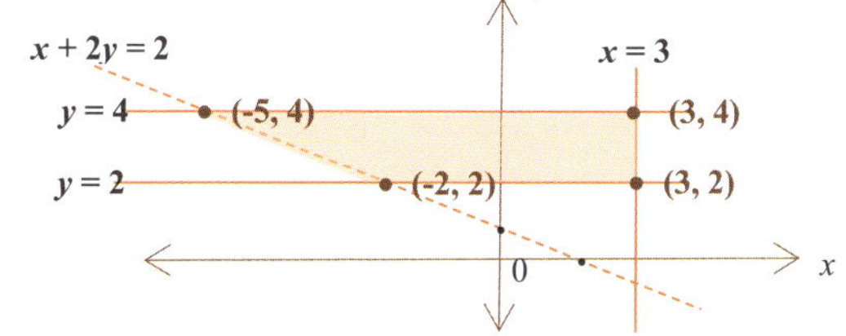

Vertices
(-5, 4)
(-2, 2)
(3, 4)
(3, 2)

Unit 4 Summary

- **A system of linear equations**

Property	Numbers of Solution	Graph
2×2 system (2 equations, 2 unknowns)	$\begin{cases} A_1x + B_1y = C_1 \\ A_2x + B_2y = C_2 \end{cases}$	$\begin{cases} 3x - 4y = 5 \\ 5x + 7y = -2 \end{cases}$
3×3 system (3 equations, 3 unknowns)	$\begin{cases} A_1x + B_1y + C_1z = D_1 \\ A_2x + B_2y + C_2z = D_2 \\ A_3x + B_3y + C_3z = D_3 \end{cases}$	$\begin{cases} 2x - 3y + 4z = 7 \\ 4x - 2y - z = 3 \\ 5x - 6y + 2z = 2 \end{cases}$

- **The solutions for a system of equations:** the values for variables that make all equations in the system true.
- **Solving systems of equations – graphing method:** Graph both equations in the system on the coordinate plane. The point(s) at which the lines intersect will be the solution(s) to the system.
- **Properties of linear equations**

Property	Numbers of Solution	Lines	Graph
consistent & independent	one solution	lines intersect	
consistent & dependent	infinite number of solutions	lines coincide (the same line)	
inconsistent	no solution $\emptyset$	lines are parallel	

- **Substitution method:** Solve for one variable in one equation and substitute the result into the other equation to solve another variable. (Objective is to eliminate one of the unknown variables).
- **Elimination method:** Add or subtract the equations to eliminate one of the variables (unknowns), then solve the resulting equation in one variable.
- **A linear inequality:** a mathematical statement with an inequality symbol in which the highest power of the variable is one.
- **Standard linear inequalities in two variables**

Standard Inequality	Example
$Ax + By > C$	$2x + 3y > 6$
$Ax + By < C$	$3x - 5y < 17$
$Ax + By \geq C$	$4x + 5y \geq 10$
$Ax + By \leq C$	$6x - 11y \leq 21$

- **Solutions of linear inequalities in two variables:** an ordered pair (x, y) that makes the inequality true.
- **Procedure for graphing a linear inequality in two variables**
  - Change the inequality symbol to an equal sign.
  - Graph the boundary line of the corresponding equation.
    - Draw a solid line if the inequality symbol is $<$ or $>$.
    - Draw a dashed line if the inequality symbol is $<$ or $>$.
  - Choose a test point such as (0, 0).
    - If the test point satisfies the inequality, shade the side of the line that **contains** the test point.
    - If the test point does not satisfy the inequality, shade the side of the line that **does not contain** the test point.
- **Do not choose the point (0, 0) to test if it is on the solution line.**
- **A system of linear inequalities in two variables**

Standard Form	Example
$\begin{cases} A_1x + B_1y > C_1 \\ A_2x + B_2y \geq C_2 \end{cases}$	$2x + 3y < 4$ $3x - 5y \geq 8$

$<, >, \leq, \geq$

- **Graphing a system of linear inequalities in two variables**
  - Change the inequality symbols to equal signs and label with (1) and (2).
  - Graph the boundary lines of the corresponding equations.
    - Draw a solid line if the inequality symbol is $\leq$ or $\geq$.
    - Draw a dashed line if the inequality symbol is $<$ or $>$.
  - Choose a test point (0, 0).
    - If the test point satisfies the inequality, shade the side of the line that contains the test point.
    - If the test point does not satisfy the inequality, shade the side of the line that does not contain the test point.
  - The solution set is the region where the shading overlaps.
  - A vertex is formed by an intersection of two boundary lines.

PRACTICE QUIZ

Unit 4 Systems of Equations & Inequalities

1. Solve the following system graphically.

$$\begin{cases} 2x - y = 1 \\ 3x + y = 4 \end{cases}$$

2. a. Solve the following system by substitution.

$$\begin{cases} 2x + y = 3 \\ 3x - 2y = 1 \end{cases}$$

b. Solve the following system by elimination.

$$\begin{cases} \frac{1}{3}x + \frac{1}{2}y - 3 = 0 \\ \frac{3}{4}x + \frac{1}{3}y - 2 = 0 \end{cases}$$

3. The perimeter of a rectangle field is 140m. The length is 10m more than 4 times the width. Determine the dimension of the rectangle field.

4. Graph the inequality.

a. $3x + y > 4$

b. $y \leq 3x$

5. Graph the system of inequalities $\begin{cases} 2x - y \leq -2 \\ 4x + y > 2 \end{cases}$

UNIT 5 POLYNOMIAL FUNCTIONS

5-1 ADDITION & SUBTRACTION OF POLYNOMIALS

Polynomials

Review basic algebraic terms

Algebraic Term	Description	Example
algebraic expression	A mathematical phrase that contains numbers, variables, and arithmetic operations.	$9x^2 - x + 3$ (arrows under 9 and -1)
coefficient	The number in front of a variable.	9, -1 $-x = (-1)(x)$
term	A term can be a constant, variable, or the product of a number and variable. (Terms are separated by a plus or minus sign.)	$9x^2$, $-x$, 3

Monomial: an algebraic expression consisting of just one term. (The prefix "mono" means one.)

Example: $3x$, $7y^2$

Binomial: an algebraic expression consisting of two terms. (The prefix "bi-" means two.)

Example: $ax + b$, $9t^2 - 2t$

Trinomial: an algebraic expression consisting of three terms. (The prefix "tri-" means three.)

Example: $ax^2 + bx + c$, $-4qp^2 + 3q + 5$

Polynomial: an algebraic expression consisting of two or more terms. (The prefix "poly-" means many.)

Example: $5x^2 - 2x + 6y + 1$, $-2a^2 - 2b + 6ab + a - 5$

Summary

Name	Example	Coefficient
monomial (one term)	$7a$	7
binomial (two terms)	$3x - 5$	3
trinomial (three terms)	$-4x^2 + xy + 7$	-4, 1
polynomial (two or more terms)	$2pq + 4p^3 + 11 + p$	2, 4, 1

Note: A polynomial uses only the operations of addition, subtraction, multiplication (no division), and non-negative integer exponents.

Example: $\frac{2x+7}{y-2}$, $\frac{3ab}{4a^2b+5+b^3}$, and $3x^2 - \frac{1}{x}y^{-2}$ are algebraic expressions but **not polynomials**.

division   negative exponent: $\frac{1}{x} = x^{-1}$

Degree of Polynomial

- **The degree of a term with one variable:** the exponent (power) of its variable.

  Example: $5x^2$ degree: **2**
  $-3t^7$ degree: **7**

- **The degree of a term with more variables:** the sum of the exponents of its variables.

  Example: $-3x^3y^5z^2$ degree: $3 + 5 + 2 =$ **10**

- **The degree of a polynomial with more variables:** the highest degree of any individual term.

  Example: $4ab^3 + 3a^2b^2c^3 - 5a + 1$ degree: **7**

  $2 + 2 + 3 = 7$

- **The leading term of a polynomial:** the term with the highest degree in the polynomial.

  Example: $4ab^3 + 3ab^2c^3 - 5a + 1$ leading term: $\mathbf{3ab^2c^3}$

  $1 + 2 + 3 = 6$
  $a = a^1$

- **The leading coefficient:** the coefficient of the leading term.

  Example: $4ab^3 + \mathbf{3}ab^2c^3 - 5a + 1$ leading coefficient: **3**

- **Examples of polynomial**

Polynomial	$3t^2 + t^3 - 5$	$2p^2q^3 + 5r - 7p^3q^2r$
term	$3t^2$, t^3, -5	$2p^2q^3$, $5r$, $-7p^3q^2r$
degree of the term	2, 3, 0	5, 1, 6
degree of the polynomial	3	6
leading term	t^3	$-7p^3q^2r$
leading coefficient	1	-7

- **Descending order:** the power of a variable decreases for each succeeding term.

  Example: $2x^3 + 5x^2 - x + 2$

  $-13ab^4 + 21b^3 - ab^2 + b - 34$ The descending order of power *b*.

- **Ascending order:** the power of a variable increases for each succeeding term.

  Example: $-9 + 7y + 4y^2 - 3y^3$

  $1 + \frac{2}{3}tu + 2t^2u^3 - 5t^3 + t^4$ The ascending order of power *t*.

Evaluating Polynomial Functions

- **Polynomial function:** The expression used to describe the function is a polynomial.

Example: $f(x) = 2x^3 - 3x^2 + 7x + 8$

$g(x) = -3x^4 + 5x^2 - 2$ ← Polynomials $f(x)$ & $g(x)$ are functions.

- **Evaluating polynomial functions**

Example: **1.** If $f(x) = 2x^3 + 1$, find $f(2)$ and $f(-1)$.

$\mathbf{f(2)} = 2(2)^3 + 1 = 16 + 1 = \mathbf{17}$ Replace x with 2.

$\mathbf{f(-1)} = 2(-1)^3 + 1 = -2 + 1 = \mathbf{-1}$ Replace x with -1.

2. If $R(x) = -8x^3 + x^2 + 2$, find $R(0)$ and $R\left(\frac{1}{2}\right)$.

$\mathbf{R(0)} = -8(0)^3 + (0)^2 + 2 = \mathbf{2}$ Replace x with 0.

$\mathbf{R\left(\frac{1}{2}\right)} = -8\left(\frac{1}{2}\right)^3 + \left(\frac{1}{2}\right)^2 + 2$ Replace x with $\frac{1}{2}$.

$= -1 + \frac{1}{4} + 2 = \mathbf{\frac{5}{4}}$

Example: The polynomial function $C(x) = 3{,}000 + 0.5x^2$ can be used to determine the total cost (in dollars) of producing x laptops in an electronics firm.

1. What is the total cost of producing 10 laptops?
2. Use the following graph to estimate $C(40)$.

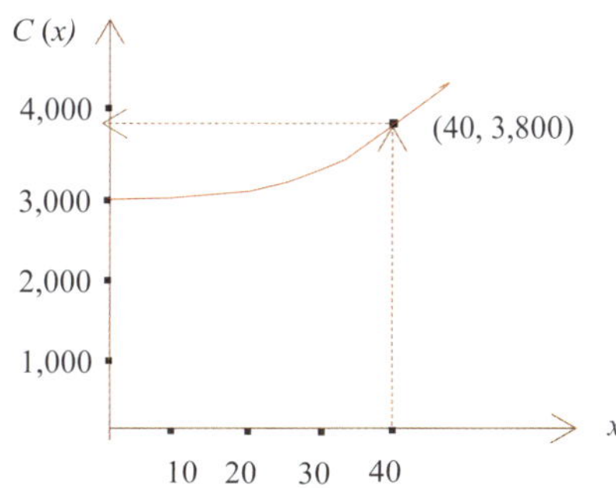

Solution: **1.** $\mathbf{C(10)} = 3{,}000 + 0.5(10)^2$ $C(x) = 3{,}000 + 0.5x^2$, replace x with 10.

$= \mathbf{\$3{,}050}$ ↑ x = number of laptops

2. $C(40)$: locate $x = 40$ on the x axis, move vertically to the graph, and then move horizontally to the $C(x)$ axis. Thus $\mathbf{C(40) \approx \$3{,}800}$.

Adding and Subtracting Polynomials

- **Adding or subtracting polynomials**

Example: Find the sum of $\mathbf{2x^3 - 3x^2 + x - 4}$ and $\mathbf{x^3 + 4x^2 + 2x + 1}$.

Steps	Solution
	$(2x^3 - 3x^2 + x - 4) + (x^3 + 4x^2 + 2x + 1)$
- Regroup like terms.	$= (2x^3 + x^3) + (-3x^2 + 4x^2) + (x + 2x) + (-4 + 1)$
- Combine like terms.	$= \mathbf{3x^3 + x^2 + 3x - 3}$

Example: Find the difference of $\mathbf{5x^2 + 4x - 2}$ and $\mathbf{2x^2 - 3x + 13}$.

Steps	Solution
	$(5x^2 + 4x - 2) - (2x^2 - 3x + 13)$
- Remove parentheses. (Reverse each sign in second parentheses.)	$= 5x^2 + 4x - 2 - 2x^2 + 3x - 13$
- Regroup like terms.	$= (5x^2 - 2x^2) + (4x + 3x) + (-2 - 13)$
- Combine like terms.	$= \mathbf{3x^2 + 7x - 15}$

- **Column method**

Example: Find the sum of $\mathbf{3x^3 - 5x^2 + 7x - 3}$ and $\mathbf{2x^3 + 3x + 5}$.

Steps

- Line up like terms in columns.
- Add.

Solution

$$\begin{array}{rrrrr} & 3x^3 & -\,5x^2 & +\,7x & -\,3 \\ + & 2x^3 & & +\,3x & +\,5 \\ \hline & \mathbf{5x^3} & \mathbf{-\,5x^2} & \mathbf{+10x} & \mathbf{+\,2} \end{array}$$

Leave space for the missing term.

Example: Find the difference of $(5x^2 - 2x + 3) - (2x^2 - 5)$.

Steps

- Line up like terms in columns:
- Change signs in minuend and add: (Leave space for the missing term.)

Solution

$$\begin{array}{rrrr} & 5x^2 & -\,2x & +\,3 \\ + & -\,2x^2 & & +\,5 \\ \hline & \mathbf{3x^2} & \mathbf{-\,2x} & \mathbf{+\,8} \end{array}$$

← Subtrahend
← Minuend
← Difference

- **The opposite of the polynomial:** $\mathbf{-p}$: the opposite of the polynomial
  $\mathbf{p}$: polynomial

$p + (-p) = 0$

Example: Write two expressions for the opposite of the polynomial.

$$\mathbf{7a^4b^2 - 3a^3b - 4a^2}$$

Solution: opposite expression: $\mathbf{-(7a^4b^2 - 3a^3b - 4a^2)}$
or $\mathbf{-7a^4b^2 + 3a^3b + 4a^2}$

Replace each term with its opposite.

5-2 MULTIPLYING POLYNOMIALS

Multiplication of Polynomials

- **Multiplying monomials**

Example: $(-2x^3y^2)(3x^2y^4) = (-2 \cdot 3)(x^3 \cdot x^2)(y^2 \cdot y^4)$ Multiply the coefficients and add exponents.

$= \mathbf{-6x^5y^6}$ $a^m \cdot a^n = a^{m+n}$

- **Multiplying monomial and binomial**

Example: $3x^3(5x^2 - 2x) = (3x^3)(5x^2) - (3x^3)(2x)$ Distributive property: $a(b + c) = ab + ac$

$= (3 \cdot 5)(x^{3+2}) - (3 \cdot 2)(x^{3+1})$ Multiply the coefficients and add exponents.

$= \mathbf{15x^5 - 6x^4}$ $a^m \cdot a^n = a^{m+n}$

Note: The distributive property can be used to multiply a polynomial by a monomial.

Example: $5ab^2(2a^2b + ab^2 - a)$ Distribute

$= (5ab^2)(2a^2b) + (5ab^2)(ab^2) + (5ab^2)(-a)$ Multiply the coefficients and add exponents.

$= \mathbf{10a^3b^3 + 5a^2b^4 - 5a^2b^2}$ $a^m \cdot a^n = a^{m+n}$

- **Multiplying binomial and polynomial**

Example: $(3a^2 + 5)(2a^2 + a - 3)$

$= (3a^2)(2a^2) + (3a^2)a + (3a^2)(-3) + 5(2a^2) + 5a + 5(-3)$ Distribute

$= 6a^4 + 3a^3 - 9a^2 + 10a^2 + 5a - 15$ Combine like terms.

$= \mathbf{6a^4 + 3a^3 + a^2 + 5a - 15}$

Tip: The distributive property is handy to get rid of parentheses.

- **Column method**

Example: Find the product: $2a^2 + a - 3$ and $3x^2 + 5$.

Steps	Solution
- Line up like terms in columns. (Leave space for the missing term.)	$2a^2 + a - 3$ $\times \quad 3a^2 \quad + 5$
	$10a^2 + 5a - 15$ ← 5 times $(2a^2 + a - 3)$
- Multiply.	$+ \; 6a^4 + 3a^3 - 9a^2$ ← $3a^2$ times $(2a^2 + a - 3)$
	$\mathbf{6a^4 + 3a^3 + a^2 + 5a - 15}$

Tip: the same as

$$\begin{array}{r} 213 \\ \times\ 102 \\ \hline 426 \\ +\ 213 \\ \hline 21726 \end{array}$$

FOIL Method to Multiply Binomials

- **The FOIL method:** an easy way to find the product of two binomials.

$(a + b)(c + d) = ac + ad + bc + bd$ F O I L			Example
F - First terms	first term × first term	$(a + b)(c + d)$	$(x + 2)(x + 3)$
O - Outer terms	outside term × outside term	$(a + b)(c + d)$	$(x + 2)(x + 3)$
I - Inner terms	inside term × inside term	$(a + b)(c + d)$	$(x + 2)(x + 3)$
L - Last terms	last term × last term	$(a + b)(c + d)$	$(x + 2)(x + 3)$

FOIL Method	Example
$(a + b)(c + d) = ac + ad + bc + bd$ F O I L	$(x + 2)(x + 3) = x{\cdot}x + x{\cdot}3 + 2{\cdot}x + 2{\cdot}3 = x^2 + 5x + 6$ F O I L

Tip: - Multiplication of binomials also uses distributive property.
- Each term of one binomial multiplied by each term of the other by repeatedly using the distributive property.
$(x + 2)(x + 3) = x(x + 3) + 2(x + 3) = x{\cdot}x + x{\cdot}3 + 2{\cdot}x + 2{\cdot}3$

- **Multiplying binomials (2 terms × 2 terms)**

Example: Find the following products.

1. $(2x - 3)(3x - 4) = \overset{F}{2x \cdot 3x} + \overset{O}{2x(-4)} - \overset{I}{3 \cdot 3x} - \overset{L}{3(-4)}$ FOIL
$= 6x^2 - 8x - 9x + 12$ $a^n a^m = a^{n+m}$
$= \mathbf{6x^2 - 17x + 12}$ Combine like terms.

2. $(3r - t)(5r + t^2) = 3r \cdot 5r + 3r \cdot t^2 - t \cdot 5r - t \cdot t^2$ FOIL
$= \mathbf{15r^2 + 3rt^2 - 5rt - t^3}$ $a^n a^m = a^{n+m}$

3. $(xy^2 + y)(2x^2y + x) = xy^2 \cdot 2x^2 y + xy^2 \cdot x + y \cdot 2x^2 y + y \cdot x$ FOIL
$= 2x^3 y^3 + x^2y^2 + 2x^2 y^2 + x y$ $a^n a^m = a^{n+m}$
$= \mathbf{2x^3 y^3 + 3x^2y^2 + x y}$ Combine like terms.

4. $(a + 2)(a + 1)(a - 1) = (a^2 + 3a + 2)(a - 1)$ FOIL: $(a + 2)(a + 1)$
$= a^3 - a^2 + 3a^2 - 3a + 2a - 2$ Distribute
$= \mathbf{a^3 + 2a^2 - a - 2}$ Combine like terms.

Special Binomial Products

- **Special binomial products – squaring binominals**

Special Products	Formula	Initial Expansion	Example
difference of squares	$(a+b)(a-b)=a^2-b^2$ It does not matter if $(a-b)$ comes first	$(a+b)(a-b)=a^2-ab+ba-b^2$ $=a^2-b^2$	$(x+2)(x-2)=x^2-2^2=x^2-4$ or $(x-2)(x+2)=x^2-2^2=x^2-4$ $(a=x,\ b=2)$
square of sum	$(a+b)^2 = a^2+2ab+b^2$ A perfect square trinomial	$(a+b)^2=(a+b)(a+b)$ $=a^2+ab+ba+b^2$ $=a^2+2ab+b^2$	$(x+3)^2=x^2+2\cdot x\cdot 3+3^2$ $=x^2+6x+9$
square of difference	$(a-b)^2 = a^2-2ab+b^2$ A perfect square trinomial	$(a-b)^2=(a-b)(a-b)$ $=a^2-ab-ba+b^2$ $=a^2-2ab+b^2$	$(x-4)^2=x^2-2\cdot x\cdot 4+4^2$ $=x^2-8x+16$

- **Special binomial products:** special forms of binomial products that are worth memorizing.
- **Memory aid:** $(a\pm b)^2=(a^2\pm ab+b^2)$ Notice the reversed plus or minus sign in the second term.

Example: Find the following products.

1. $(3y+4)(3y-4)=(3y)^2-4^2$ (a, b) — $(a+b)(a-b)=a^2-b^2$
   $=\mathbf{9y^2-16}$ — $a=3y$, $b=4$

2. $\left(5t+\frac{1}{2}\right)^2=(5t)^2+2(5t)\left(\frac{1}{2}\right)+\left(\frac{1}{2}\right)^2$ — $(a+b)^2=a^2+2ab+b^2$
   $=\mathbf{25t^2+5t+\frac{1}{4}}$ — $a=5t$, $b=\frac{1}{2}$

3. $(3q-\frac{1}{6}p)^2=(3q)^2-2(3q)\left(\frac{1}{6}p\right)+\left(\frac{1}{6}p\right)^2$ — $(a-b)^2=a^2-2ab+b^2$
   $=\mathbf{9q^2-qp+\frac{1}{36}p^2}$ — $a=3q$, $b=\frac{1}{6}p$

4. $(t+1)^3=(t+1)^2(t+1)$ — $a^na^m=a^{n+m}$
   $=(t^2+2t+1)(t+1)$ — $(a+b)^2=a^2+2ab+b^2$
   $=t^3+t^2+2t^2+2t+t+1$ — Distribute
   $=\mathbf{t^3+3t^2+3t+1}$ — Combine like terms.

5. $(2A-3+4B)(2A-3-4B)=(2A-3)^2-(4B)^2$ (a, b, a, b) — $(a+b)(a-b)=a^2-b^2$: $a=2A-3$, $b=4B$
   $=(2A)^2-2(2A)\cdot 3+3^2-16B^2$ — $(a-b)^2=a^2-2ab+b^2$: $a=2A$, $b=3$
   $=\mathbf{4A^2-12A+9-16B^2}$ — Simplify

- **Using function notation:**

Example: Given $f(x)=-3x+x^2$, find and simplify **1.** $f(u-1)$, and **2.** $f(a+h)-f(a)$.

1. $f(u-1)=-3(u-1)+(u-1)^2$ — Replace x with $(u-1)$
   $=-3u+1+u^2-2u+1$ — $(a-b)^2=a^2-2ab+b^2$
   $=\mathbf{u^2-5u+2}$ — Combine like terms.

2. $f(a+h)-f(a)=[-3(a+h)+(a+h)^2]-(-3a+a^2)$ — Replace x with $(a+h)$ and a.
   $=-3a-3h+a^2+2ah+h^2+3a-a^2$ — Remove parentheses.
   $=\mathbf{h^2+2ah-3h}$ — Combine like terms.

5-3 FACTORING

Highest / Greatest Common Factor

- **Greatest / highest common factor (GCF or HCF):** the largest factor of two or more terms.

Example	Factors	GCF or HCF
3	3	
6	$3 \cdot 2$	3
9	$3 \cdot 3$	
$2x^2y$	$2 \cdot x^2 \cdot y$	$2x^2y$
$8x^2y^3$	$2 \cdot 4 \cdot x^2 \cdot y \cdot y^2$	

- **Factoring a polynomial:** express a polynomial as a product of other polynomials. It is the reverse of multiplying.

Multiplying (or expanding) →

$$a(b + c + d) = ab + ac + ad$$

← Factoring

Example

Multiplying

$2ab(4a - 3ab + 1)$

$= 8a^2b - 6a^2b^2 + 2ab$

Factoring

$8a^2b - 6a^2b^2 + 2ab$

$= 2ab(4a) - 2ab(3ab) + 2ab \cdot 1$

$= 2ab(4a - 3ab + 1)$

GCF

$2ab$

Examples

Expression	Factoring	GCF
$-8x^2 - 4x$	$-4x \cdot 2x - 4x \cdot 1 = -4x(2x + 1)$	$-4x$
$3y^5 - 9y^3 + 6y$	$3y \cdot y^4 - 3 \cdot 3y \cdot y^2 + 3y \cdot 2 = 3y(y^4 - 3y^2 + 2)$	$3y$
$5a^3b + 10a^2b - 15ab$	$5ab \cdot a^2 + 5ab \cdot 2a - 5ab \cdot 3 = 5ab(a^2 + 2a - 3)$	$5ab$
$7x^2(x + 5) - (3x + 15)$	$7x^2(x + 5) - 3(x + 5) = (x + 5)(7x^2 - 3)$	$(x + 5)$
$2x^2 + 3y + 4$	Not factorable	No

Tip: Factor each term and pull out the GCF.

- **Negative of the greatest common factor**

Factoring	GCF	Factor Out a Negative GCF	Negative GCF
$2x - 4x^2 = 2x(1 - 2x)$	$2x$	$2x - 4x^2 = -2x(-1 + 2x)$	$-2x$
$3ab - 9ab^2 + 6a^2b = 3ab(1 - 3b + 2a)$	$3ab$	$3ab - 9ab^2 + 6a^2b = -3ab(-1 + 3b - 2a)$	$-3ab$

Factoring Polynomials by Grouping

Steps for factoring by grouping:

Steps	Example: $8y^2 - 2y + 12y - 3$
- Group terms with the GCF.	$8y^2 - 2y + 12y - 3 = (8y^2 - 2y) + (12y - 3)$
- Factor out the GCF from each group.	$= 2y(4y - 1) + 3(4y - 1)$
- Factor out the GCF again from the last step.	$= \mathbf{(4y - 1)(2y + 3)}$

Factoring completely: Continue factoring until no further factors can be found.

Example: Factor the following completely.

1. $6ab^2 - 3a^2b + 2b - a = (6ab^2 - 3a^2b) + (2b - a)$ Group terms with the GCF.
   $= 3ab(2b - a) + (2b - a) \cdot 1$ Factor out the GCF ; $(2b - a) = (2b - a) \cdot 1$
   $= \mathbf{(2b - a)(3ab + 1)}$ Factor out the GCF again.

2. $2ab + bc - 2bc + 4ab = (2ab + 4ab) + (bc - 2bc)$ Rearrange and group terms with the same pattern.
   $= 6ab - bc$ Combine like terms.
   $= \mathbf{b(6a - c)}$ Factor out the GCF.

3. $x^3 - xy^2 - x^2y + y^3 = (x^3 - x^2y) - (xy^2 - y^3)$ Group
   $= x^2(x - y) - y^2(x - y)$ Factor out the GCF.
   $= (x - y)(x^2 - y^2)$ $a^2 - b^2 = (a + b)(a - b)$
   $= (x - y)(x + y)(x - y)$ Keep factoring until cannot factor any further.
   $= \mathbf{(x - y)^2(x + y)}$

Tip: Recognize factoring patterns, such as $2b - a$, $x - y$, …

4. $32x^3y - 2xy^3 = 2xy(16x^2 - y^2)$ Factor out the GCF.
   $= 2xy[(4x)^2 - y^2)]$ $a^2 - b^2 = (a + b)(a - b)$
   $= \mathbf{2xy(4x + y)(4x - y)}$ $(4x + y)$ and $(4x - y)$ cannot be factored further.

Factoring $x^2 + bx + c$

Factoring $x^2 + bx + c$: Cross-multiplication method

Steps	Standard form	Example
	$x^2 + bx + c$	$x^2 + 3x + 2$
- Setting up two sets of parentheses.	$= (\quad)(\quad)$	$= (\quad)(\quad)$
	$x^2 + bx + c$	$x^2 + 3x + 2$
- Factor the first term x^2: $x^2 = x \cdot x$	x ╳ c_1	x ╳ 1
- Factor the last term c (by trial and error): $c = c_1 \cdot c_2$	x ╳ c_2	x ╳ 2
	$x \cdot x = x^2$ $\quad c_1 \cdot c_2 = c$	$x \cdot x = x^2$ $\quad 1 \cdot 2 = 2$
- Cross multiply and then add up to the middle term.	$(c_1)(x) + (c_2)(x) = bx$	$1 \cdot x + 2 \cdot x = 3x$
- Complete the parenthesis with $x + c_1$ and $x + c_2$.	$x^2 + bx + c$	$x^2 + 3x + 2$
	$= (x + c_1)(x + c_2)$	$= (x + 1)(x + 2)$

- Check using FOIL.

F O I L

$(x + 1)(x + 2) = x^2 + 2x + x + 2$

$(x + 1)(x + 2) = x^2 + 3x + 2$ √

Factoring $x^2 + bx + c$ Using the Cross-Multiplication Method	
In general	**Example**
$x^2 + bx + c = (\quad)(\quad)$	$x^2 - 5x + 6 = (\quad)(\quad)$
x ╳ c_1	x ╳ -2
x ╳ c_2	x ╳ -3
$x \cdot x = x^2$ $\quad c_1 \cdot c_2 = c$	$x \cdot x = x^2$ $\quad (-2)(-3) = 6$
$(c_1)(x) + (c_2)(x) \stackrel{?}{=} bx$	$-2 \cdot x + (-3)x \stackrel{?}{=} -5x$ yes!
$x^2 + bx + c = (x + c_1)(x + c_2)$	$x^2 - 5x + 6 = (x - 2)(x - 3)$

Summary: Factoring $x^2 + bx + c$	Example: $x^2 - 5x + 6$
$x^2 + (c_1 + c_2)x + c_1c_2 = (x + c_1)(x + c_2)$	$x^2 + [-2 + (-3)]x + 6 = (x - 2)(x - 3)$
x ╳ c_1	x ╳ -2
x ╳ c_2	x ╳ -3
Check: $c_1x + c_2x \stackrel{?}{=} bx$	Check: $-2x + (-3x) \stackrel{?}{=} -5x$ yes!

Tip: Cross multiply and then add up to the middle term.

Example: Factor the following:

Trial and Error Process

1. $x^2 - 6x + 8 = (\quad)(\quad)$

x ╳ -2

x ╳ -4

$x \cdot x = x^2$ $\quad (-2)(-4) = 8$

$-2 \cdot x + (-4)x \stackrel{?}{=} -6x$ yes!

Trial and error: $x^2 - 6x + 8$: x ╳ 2, x ╳ 4: $2x + 4x \stackrel{?}{=} -6x$ no

$x^2 - 6x + 8$: x ╳ 1, x ╳ 8: $1 \cdot x + 8x \stackrel{?}{=} -6x$ no

Answer: $x^2 - 6x + 8 = (x - 2)(x - 4)$ Check: $-2 + (-4) = -6$ √

2. $a^2 + 5a - 6 = (\quad)(\quad)$

a ╳ -1

a ╳ 6

$a \cdot a = a^2$ $\quad (-1)(6) = -6$

$(-1)a + 6a \stackrel{?}{=} 5a$ yes!

Trial and error: $a^2 + 5a - 6$: a ╳ 2, a ╳ -3: $2a + (-3)a \stackrel{?}{=} 5a$ no

$a^2 + 5a - 6$: a ╳ 1, a ╳ -6: $1 \cdot a + (-6)a \stackrel{?}{=} 5a$ no

Answer: $a^2 + 5a - 6 = (a - 1)(a + 6)$ Check: $-1 + 6 = 5$ √

5-4 FACTORING $ax^2 + bx + c$

Factoring Trinomials: $ax^2 + bx + c$

Procedure for factoring $ax^2 + bx + c$ using the cross-multiplication method

Steps	In general	Example
	$ax^2 + bx + c$	$2x^2 + x - 3$
- Setting up two sets of parenthesis.	$= (\quad)(\quad)$	$= (\quad)(\quad)$
	$ax^2 + bx + c$	$2x^2 + x - 3$
- Factor the first term ax^2: $ax^2 = a_1x \cdot a_2x$	$a_1x \quad c_1$	$x \quad -1$
- Factor the last term c (by trial and error):	$a_2x \quad c_2$	$2x \quad 3$
$c = c_1 \cdot c_2$	$a_1x \cdot a_2x = ax^2 \quad c_1 \cdot c_2 = c$	$x \cdot 2x = 2x^2 \quad -1 \cdot 3 = -3$
- Cross-multiply, then add up to the middle term.	$(a_1x)(c_2) + (a_2x)(c_1) = bx$	$3 \cdot x + (-1)(2x) = x$
- Complete the parenthesis with $(a_1x + c_1)$ and $(a_2x + c_2)$.	$ax^2 + bx + c$	$2x^2 + x - 3$
	$= \mathbf{(a_1x + c_1)(a_2x + c_2)}$	$= \mathbf{(x - 1)(2x + 3)}$

- Check using FOIL.

$$(x - 1)(2x + 3) = \overset{F}{2x^2} + \overset{O}{3x} \overset{I}{-2x} \overset{L}{-3}$$

$$(x - 1)(2x + 2) \overset{\surd}{=} 2x^2 + x - 3 \text{ (Original expression)}$$

Factoring $ax^2 + bx + c$ Using the Cross-Multiplication Method	
In general	**Example**
$ax^2 + bx + c = (\quad)(\quad)$	$3x^2 + 10x + 8 = (\quad)(\quad)$
$a_1x \quad c_1$	$3x \quad 4$
$a_2x \quad c_2$	$x \quad 2$
$a_1x \cdot a_2x = ax^2 \quad c = c_1 \cdot c_2$	$3x \cdot x = 3x^2 \quad 4 \cdot 2 = 8$
$(a_1x)(c_2) + (a_2x)(c_1) \overset{?}{=} bx$	$3x \cdot 2 + 4 \cdot x \overset{?}{=} 10x$ yes!
$ax^2 + bx + c = \mathbf{(a_1x + c_1)(a_2x + c_2)}$	$3x^2 + 10x + 8 = \mathbf{(3x + 4)(x + 2)}$

Summary: Factoring $ax^2 + bx + c$

$$a_1 a_2x^2 + (a_1c_2 + c_1a_2)x + c_1 c_2 = (a_1x + c_1)(a_2x + c_2)$$

$a_1x \quad c_1$

$a_2x \quad c_2$

Tip: Cross-multiply and then add up to the middle term.

More Examples for Factoring $ax^2 + bx + c$

Example: Factor the following.

$\mathbf{8x^2 + 10x - 25} = (\quad)(\quad)$

$2x \quad 5$
$4x \quad -5$

$2x \cdot 4x = 8x^2 \qquad 5(-5) = -25$

$(2x)(-5) + 5(4x) \overset{?}{=} 10x$ yes!

$8x^2 + 10x - 25 = \mathbf{(2x + 5)(4x - 5)}$

Trial and Error Process

1. $8x^2 + 10x - 25$
   $x \quad -5$
   $8x \quad 5$
   $x \cdot 5 + (-5)(8x) \overset{?}{=} 10x$ no
2. $8x^2 + 10x - 25$
   $4x \quad 5$
   $2x \quad -5$
   $(4x)(-5) + 5(2x) \overset{?}{=} 10x$ no
3. $8x^2 + 10x - 25$
   $8x \quad -25$
   $x \quad 1$
   $8x \cdot 1 + (-25)x \overset{?}{=} 10x$ no

Tip: Write the factors with their appropriate signs (+ or –) to get the right middle term.

Check: $(2x + 5)(4x - 5) = 8x^2 - 10x + 20x - 25$
F O I L

$(2x + 5)(4x - 5) \overset{\surd}{=} \mathbf{8x^2 + 10x - 25}$ Correct!

Example: Factor the following completely.

1. $\mathbf{3y^2(y + 4) + (y + 4)(y - 2)} = (y + 4)[3y^2 + (y - 2)]$ Factor out the GCF $(y + 4)$.

$= (y + 4)(3y^2 + y - 2)$

$y \quad 1$
$3y \quad -2$

$-2y + 3y = y$ √

$= \mathbf{(y + 4)(y + 1)(3y - 2)}$

2. $\mathbf{m^2 - m = -\frac{1}{4}}$

$m^2 - m + \frac{1}{4} = (\quad)(\quad)$ Write in standard form $(ax^2 + bx + c)$.

$m \quad -\frac{1}{2}$
$m \quad -\frac{1}{2}$

$-\frac{1}{2}m - \frac{1}{2}m = -m$

$m^2 - m + \frac{1}{4} = \left(m - \frac{1}{2}\right)\left(m - \frac{1}{2}\right)$

$= \mathbf{\left(m - \frac{1}{2}\right)^2}$

3. $\mathbf{3s^2 - 2st - 5t^2} = (\quad)(\quad)$

$s \quad t$
$3s \quad -5t$

$-5st + 3st = -2st$ √

$\mathbf{3s^2 - 2st - 5t^2 = (s + t)(3s - 5t)}$

4. $\mathbf{2q^4 + 14q^2 + 20} = 2(q^4 + 7q^2 + 10) = 2(\quad)(\quad)$ Factor out the GCF (2).

$q^2 \quad 2$
$q^2 \quad 5$

$2q^4 + 14q^2 + 20 = \mathbf{2(q^2 + 2)(q^2 + 5)}$

$5q^2 + 2q^2 = 7q^2$ √

Factoring Trinomials: AC Method

AC method for factoring trinomials: $ax^2 + bx + c$

Factoring $ax^2 + bx + c = 0$ by Grouping	Example
Steps	**Solve $14x - 6 = -12x^2$**
• Convert to standard form if necessary.	$12x^2 + 14x - 6 = 0$
• Factor out the greatest common factor (GCF).	$2(6x^2 + 7x - 3) = 0$
• Multiply a and c in $ax^2 + bx + c$.	$ac = 6\,(-3) = -18$
• Factor the product ac that sum to the middle coefficient b.	$9\,(-2) = -18,\ 9 + (-2) = 7$
• Rewrite the middle term as the sum using the factors found in last step.	$2(6x^2 + 7x - 3) = 0$
	$2\,(6x^2 + 9x - 2x - 3) = 0$
• Factor by grouping.	$2[3x(2x + 3) - (2x + 3)] = 0$
	$2\,(2x + 3)(3x - 1) = 0$ Factor out $(2x + 3)$.

Example: Factor $6x^2 - 8 = 2x$ using ac method.

Steps	**Solution**
	$6x^2 - 8 = 2x$
- Write in standard form:	$6x^2 - 2x - 8 = 0$
- Factor out the greatest common factor:	$2(3x^2 - 1x - 4) = 0$
- Multiply a and c in $ax^2 + bx + c$:	$ac = 3 \cdot (-4) = -12$
- Factor the product ac that sum to the middle coefficient b. (There are different pairs to get the product of ac of -12. Try to find two numbers that multiply to ac and added to obtain $b = -1$.)	

Some Factors of ac (-12)	Sum of Factors ($b = -1$)
-2 & 6	$-2 + 6 = 4$
-1 & 12	$-1 + 12 = 11$
-3 & 4	$-3 + 4 = 1$
3 & -4	$3 + (-4) = -1$ Correct!

The right choices are 3 and -4, since they both add up to $b = -1$. $3\,(-4) = -12$, $3 + (-4) = -1$

- Rewrite the middle term as $3x - 4x$.	$2(3x^2 - 1x - 4) = 0$
	$2(3x^2 + 3x - 4x - 4) = 0$
- Factor by grouping. Factor out $(x + 1)$	$2\,[3x\,(x + 1) - 4(x + 1) = 0$
	$\mathbf{2(x + 1)(3x - 4) = 0}$

5-5 FACTORING SPECIAL PRODUCTS

Special Factoring

- **Special factoring formulas**

Name	Formula	Example
difference of squares	$a^2 - b^2 = (a + b)(a - b)$	$n^2 - 25 = n^2 - 5^2 = (n + 5)(n - 5)$
square of sum (perfect square trinomial)	$a^2 + 2ab + b^2 = (a + b)^2$	$x^2 + 6x + 9 = (x + 3)^2$ $a = x,\ b = 3$ x ╳ 3 x ╳ 3 Check: $(x + 3)^2 = x^2 + 2 \cdot x \cdot 3 + 3^2 = x^2 + 6x + 9$ √
square of difference (perfect square trinomial)	$a^2 - 2ab + b^2 = (a - b)^2$	$25t^2 - 20t + 4 = (5t - 2)^2$ $a = 5t,\ b = 2$ $5t$ ╳ -2 $5t$ ╳ -2 Check: $(5t - 2)^2 = (5t)^2 - 2(5t)(2) + 2^2 = 25t^2 - 20t + 4$ √

Factoring (L → R)
$a^2 - b^2 = (a + b)(a - b)$
Multiplying (L ← R)

Note: The quickest way to factor an expression is to recognize it as a special product.

- **Memory aid:** $(a^2 \pm ab + b^2) = (a \pm b)^2$ Notice the plus or minus sign in the second term.
- **To use perfect square trinomial formulas:** Use cross-multiplication method to factor a perfect square. Then use the square formula to check.

Example: Factor the following completely.

1. $\mathbf{9x^2 - 16y^2} = 3^2x^2 - 4^2y^2 = (\overset{a}{3x})^2 - (\overset{b}{4y})^2$ $\qquad a^nb^n = (a\,b)^n$

   $= \mathbf{(3x + 4y)(3x - 4y)}$ $\qquad a^2 - b^2 = (a + b)(a - b):\ a = 3x,\ b = 4y$

2. $\mathbf{12x + 9 + 4x^2} = 4x^2 + 12x + 9$ $\qquad$ Rewrite in standard form: $ax^2 + bx + c$

   $2x$ ╳ 3
   $2x$ ╳ 3

   $= \mathbf{(2x + 3)^2}$ $\qquad 3(2x) + 3(2x) = 12x$

   Check: $(2x + 3)^2 = (2x)^2 + 2 \cdot 2x \cdot 3 + 3^2 = 4x^2 + 12x + 9$ √ $\qquad a^2 + 2ab + b^2 = (a + b)^2$

3. $\mathbf{25A^2 - 20AB + 4B^2 = (5A - 2B)^2}$

   $5A$ ╳ $-2B$
   $5A$ ╳ $-2B$ $\qquad (5A)(-2B) + (5A)(-2B) = -20AB$

   Check: $(5A - 2B)^2 = (5A)^2 - 2(5A)(2B) + (2B)^2 = 25A^2 - 20AB + 4B^2$ √ $\qquad a^2 - 2ab + b^2 = (a - b)^2:\ a = 5A,\ b = 2B$

4. $\mathbf{\frac{2}{16}x^2 - \frac{2}{9}y^2} = 2\left(\frac{1}{4^2}x^2 - \frac{1}{3^2}y^2\right)$ $\qquad$ Factor out the GCF (2). $\quad \frac{a^n}{b^n} = \left(\frac{a}{b}\right)^n$

   $= 2\left[\left(\frac{x}{4}\right)^2 - \left(\frac{y}{3}\right)^2\right]$ $\qquad a^2 - b^2 = (a + b)(a - b):\ a = \frac{x}{4},\ b = \frac{y}{3}$

   $= \mathbf{2\left[\left(\frac{x}{4} + \frac{y}{3}\right)\left(\frac{x}{4} - \frac{y}{3}\right)\right]}$

5. $\mathbf{-12x^2 + 36xy - 27y^2} = -3(4x^2 - 12xy + 9y^2)$ $\qquad$ Factor out the GCF (-3).

   $2x$ ╳ $-3y$
   $2x$ ╳ $-3y$ $\qquad (2x)(-3y) + (2x)(-3y) = -12xy$

   $= \mathbf{-3(2x - 3y)^2}$

   Check: $(2x - 3y)^2 = (2x)^2 - 2(2x)(3y) + (3y)^2 = 4x^2 - 12xy + 9y^2$ √ $\qquad a^2 - 2ab + b^2 = (a - b)^2:\ a = 2x,\ b = 3y$

More Examples for Special Factoring

- **Factoring by grouping**

Example:

1. $p^3 - p^2q - pq^2 + q^3 = (p^3 - p^2q) - (pq^2 - q^3)$ — Group.

$= p^2(p - q) - q^2(p - q)$ — Factor out the GCF (p^2 and q^2).

$= (p - q)(p^2 - q^2)$ — $a^2 - b^2 = (a + b)(a - b)$: $a = p$, $b = q$

$= (p - q)(p + q)(p - q)$ — Keep factoring until no further factors can be found.

$= (p - q)^2(p + q)$

2. $3s^2 - 18st + 27t^2 - 75u^2 = 3(s^2 - 6st + 9t^2 - 25u^2)$ — Factor out the GCF (3).

$= 3[(s^2 - 6st + 9t^2) - 5^2u^2]$

$s \quad -3t$
$s \quad -3t$ — $-3st + (-3st) = -6st$; $a^{mn} = (a^m)^n$

$= 3[(s - 3t)^2 - (5u)^2]$ — $a^2 - b^2 = (a + b)(a - b)$

($a = s - 3t$, $b = 5u$)

$= 3[(s - 3t) + 5u]\,[(s - 3t) - 5u]$ — $a = s - 3t$, $b = 5u$

- **Special factoring of higher degree**

Example: Factor the following completely.

1. $p^{10} + 22p^5 + 121 = p^{10} + 22p^5 + 121$

$p^5 \quad 11$
$p^5 \quad 11$ — $11p^5 + 11p^5 = 22p^5$

$= (p^5 + 11)^2$

Check: $(p^5 + 11)^2 = (p^5)^2 + 2(p^5)(11) + 11^2 = p^{10} + 22p^5 + 121$ √ — $a^2 + 2ab + b^2 = (a + b)^2$: $a = p^5$, $b = 11$

2. $u^4 - 81 = u^{2\cdot 2} - 9^2 = (u^2)^2 - 9^2$ — $a^{mn} = (a^m)^n$

$= (u^2 + 9)(u^2 - 9)$ — $a^2 - b^2 = (a + b)(a - b)$: $a = u^2$, $b = 9$

$= (u^2 + 9)(u^2 - 3^2)$ — $a^2 - b^2 = (a + b)(a - b)$: $a = u$, $b = 3$

$= (u^2 + 9)(u + 3)\,)(u - 3)$

3. $16y^8 - x^8 = 4^2y^{4\cdot 2} - x^{4\cdot 2} = (4y^4)^2 - (x^4)^2$ — $a^nb^n = (ab)^n$, $a^{mn} = (a^m)^n$

$= (4y^4 + x^4)(4y^4 - x^4)$ — $a^2 - b^2 = (a + b)(a - b)$: $a = 4y^4$, $b = x^4$

$= (4y^4 + x^4)[(2y^2)^2 - (x^2)^2]$ — $4y^4 = 2^2y^{2\cdot 2} = (2y^2)^2$

$= (4y^4 + x^4)(2y^2 + x^2)(2y^2 - x^2)$ — $a^2 - b^2 = (a + b)(a - b)$: $a = 2y^2$, $b = x^2$

Factoring the Sum & Difference of Cubes

- **Factoring a sum or difference of two cubes**

Name	Formula	Example
sum of cubes	$a^3 + b^3 = (a + b)(a^2 - ab + b^2)$	$27 + x^3 = 3^3 + x^3 = (3 + x)(3^2 - 3x + x^2)$ (with $a = 3$, $b = x$; a, b, a^2, ab, b^2 marked)
difference of cubes	$a^3 - b^3 = (a - b)(a^2 + ab + b^2)$	$27 - y^3 = 3^3 - y^3 = (3 - y)(3^2 + 3y + y^2)$

Note: $a^3 - b^3 \neq (a - b)^3$

- **Memory aid:** $a^3 \pm b^3 = (a \pm b)(a^2 \mp ab + b^2)$ — Notice the reversed plus or minus sign in the second term.

Example: Factor the following completely.

1. $x^3 + 125 = x^3 + 5^3 = (x + 5)(x^2 - 5x + 5^2)$ — $a^3 + b^3 = (a + b)(a^2 - ab + b^2)$: $a = x$, $b = 5$

$= \mathbf{(x + 5)(x^2 - 5x + 25)}$ (Not factorable)

2. $-2t^3 + 54 = -2(t^3 - 27) = -2(t^3 - 3^3)$ — Factor out -2. $(-2)(-27) = 54$

$= \mathbf{-2(t - 3)(t^2 + 3t + 9)}$ — $a^3 - b^3 = (a - b)(a^2 + ab + b^2)$: $a = t$, $b = 3$

3. $-wu^4 - 0.001wu = -wu(u^3 + 0.001)$ — Factor out $-wu$.

$= -wu(u^3 + 0.1^3)$ (with $a = u$, $b = 0.1$) — $0.1^3 = 0.001$

$= \mathbf{-wu(u + 0.1)(u^2 - 0.1u + 0.01)}$ ($0.1^2 = 0.01$) — $a^3 + b^3 = (a + b)(a^2 - ab + b^2)$: $a = u$, $b = 0.1$

4. $p^6 - 27q^6 = p^{2\cdot 3} - 3^3(q^2)^3 = (p^2)^3 - (3q^2)^3$ (with $a = p^2$, $b = 3q^2$) — $a^{mn} = (a^m)^n$

$= (p^2 - 3q^2)[(p^2)^2 + 3p^2q^2 + (3q^2)^2]$ — $a^3 - b^3 = (a - b)(a^2 + ab + b^2)$: $a = p^2$, $b = 3q^2$

$= \mathbf{(p^2 - 3q^2)(p^4 + 3p^2q^2 + 9q^4)}$ — $(a^m)^n = a^{mn}$

5. $7y^5 - 7y^2 = 7y^2(y^3 - 1) = 7y^2(y^3 - 1^3)$ — Factor out $7y^2$.

$= \mathbf{7y^2(y - 1)(y^2 + y + 1)}$ — $a^3 - b^3 = (a - b)(a^2 + ab + b^2)$: $a = y$, $b = 1$

6. $\frac{1}{64} + z^3 = \frac{1^3}{4^3} + z^3$

$= \left(\frac{1}{4}\right)^3 + z^3$ (with $a = \frac{1}{4}$, $b = z$) — $\frac{a^n}{b^n} = \left(\frac{a}{b}\right)^n$

$= \mathbf{\left(\frac{1}{4} + z\right)\left(\frac{1}{4^2} - \frac{1}{4}z + z^2\right)}$ — $a^3 + b^3 = (a + b)(a^2 - ab + b^2)$: $a = \frac{1}{4}$, $b = z$

Unit 5 Summary

- **Review basic algebraic terms**

Algebraic Term	Description	Example
algebraic expression	A mathematical phrase that contains numbers, variables, and arithmetic operations.	$9x^2 - x + 3$ ↑ ↑
coefficient	The number in front of a variable.	9, -1 $-x = (-1)(x)$
term	A term can be a constant, variable, or the product of a number and variable. (Terms are separated by a plus or minus sign.)	$9x^2$, $-x$, 3

- **Polynomial**

Name	Example	Coefficient
monomial (one term)	$7a$	7
binomial (two terms)	$3x - 5$	3
trinomial (three terms)	$-4x^2 + xy + 7$	-4, 1
polynomial (two or more terms)	$2pq + 4p^3 + 11 + p$	2, 4, 1

- **The degree of a term with one variable:** the exponent (power) of its variable.

  Example: $5x^2$ degree: **2**
  $-3t^7$ degree: **7**

- **The degree of a term with more variables:** the sum of the exponents of its variables.

  Example: $-3x^3y^5z^2$ degree: $3 + 5 + 2 = \mathbf{10}$

- **The degree of a polynomial with more variables:** the highest degree of any individual term.

  Example: $4ab^3 + 3a^2b^2c^3 - 5a + 1$ degree: **7**

- **The leading term of a polynomial:** the term with the highest degree in the polynomial.

  Example: $4ab^3 + 3ab^2c^3 - 5a + 1$ leading term: $\mathbf{3ab^2c^3}$

- **The leading coefficient:** the coefficient of the leading term.

  Example: $4ab^3 + 3ab^2c^3 - 5a + 1$ leading coefficient: **3**

- **Descending order:** the power of a variable decreases for each succeeding term.

- **Ascending order:** the power of a variable increases for each succeeding term.

- **The opposite of the polynomial:** $-p$: the opposite of the polynomial

  p: polynomial $p + (-p) = 0$

- **The FOIL method:** an easy way to find the product of two binomials.

$(a+b)(c+d) = ac + ad + bc + bd$
F O I L

Example

$(x+2)(x+3) = x \cdot x + x \cdot 3 + 2x + 2 \cdot 3$
F O I L
$= x^2 + 5x + 6$

- **Greatest / highest common factor (GCF or HCF):** the largest factor of two or more terms.

- **Negative of the greatest common factor**

Factoring	GCF	Factor Out a Negative GCF	Negative GCF
$2x - 4x^2 = 2x(1 - 2x)$	$2x$	$2x - 4x^2 = -2x(-1 + 2x)$	$-2x$
$3ab - 9ab^2 + 6a^2b = 3ab(1 - 3b + 2a)$	$3ab$	$3ab - 9ab^2 + 6a^2b = -3ab(-1 + 3b - 2a)$	$-3ab$

- **Factoring $x^2 + bx + c$**

Factoring $x^2 + bx + c$	Example: $x^2 - 5x + 6$
$x^2 + (c_1 + c_2)x + c_1c_2 = (x + c_1)(x + c_2)$	$x^2 + [-2 + (-3)]x + 6 = (x - 2)(x - 3)$
x — c_1; x — c_2	x — -2; x — -3
Check: $c_1x + c_2x \stackrel{?}{=} bx$	Check: $-2x + (-3x) \stackrel{?}{=} -5x$ yes!

- **Factoring $ax^2 + bx + c$**

Summary: Factoring $ax^2 + bx + c$
$a_1a_2x^2 + (a_1c_2 + c_1a_2)x + c_1c_2 = (a_1x + c_1)(a_2x + c_2)$
a_1x — c_1; a_2x — c_2

- **AC method for factoring trinomials: $ax^2 + bx + c$**

Factoring $ax^2 + bx + c = 0$ by Grouping	Example
Steps	**Solve $14x - 6 = -12x^2$**
• Convert to standard form if necessary.	$12x^2 + 14x - 6 = 0$
• Factor out the greatest common factor (GCF).	$2(6x^2 + 7x - 3) = 0$
• Multiply a and c in $ax^2 + bx + c$.	$ac = 6(-3) = -18$
• Factor the product ac that sum to the middle coefficient b.	$9(-2) = -18,\ 9 + (-2) = 7$
• Rewrite the middle term as the sum using the factors found in last step.	$2(6x^2 + 7x - 3) = 0$ $2(6x^2 + 9x - 2x - 3) = 0$
• Factor by grouping.	$2[3x(2x+3) - (2x+3)] = 0$ $2(2x+3)(3x-1) = 0$ Factor out $(2x+3)$.

- **Special factoring formulas**

Name	Formula	Example
difference of squares	$a^2 - b^2 = (a + b)(a - b)$	$n^2 - 25 = n^2 - 5^2 = (n + 5)(n - 5)$
square of sum (perfect square trinomial)	$a^2 + 2ab + b^2 = (a + b)^2$	$x^2 + 6x + 9 = (x + 3)^2$ $a = x,\ b = 3$ x ╳ 3 x 3 Check: $(x + 3)^2 = x^2 + 2 \cdot x \cdot 3 + 3^2 = x^2 + 6x + 9$ √
square of difference (perfect square trinomial)	$a^2 - 2ab + b^2 = (a - b)^2$	$25t^2 - 20t + 4 = (5t - 2)^2$ $a = 5t,\ b = 2$ $5t$ ╳ -2 $5t$ -2 Check: $(5t - 2)^2 = (5t)^2 - 2(5t)(2) + 2^2 = 25t^2 - 20t + 4$ √

Factoring (L → R)
$a^2 - b^2 = (a + b)(a - b)$
Multiplying (L ← R)

- **Factoring a sum or difference of two cubes**

Name	Formula	Example
sum of cubes	$a^3 + b^3 = (a + b)(a^2 - ab + b^2)$	$27 + x^3 = 3^3 + x^3 = (3 + x)(3^2 - 3x + x^2)$ ($a = 3$, $b = x$; a, b, a^2, ab, b^2)
difference of cubes	$a^3 - b^3 = (a - b)(a^2 + ab + b^2)$	$27 - y^3 = 3^3 - y^3 = (3 - y)(3^2 + 3y + y^2)$

PRACTICE QUIZ

Unit 5 Polynomial Functions

1. The function $f(x) = 2{,}000 + 0.6x^2$ can be used to determine the cost of producing x machines in a factory.
   - **a.** What is the total cost of producing 40 machines?
   - **b.** Use the following graph to estimate $f(30)$.

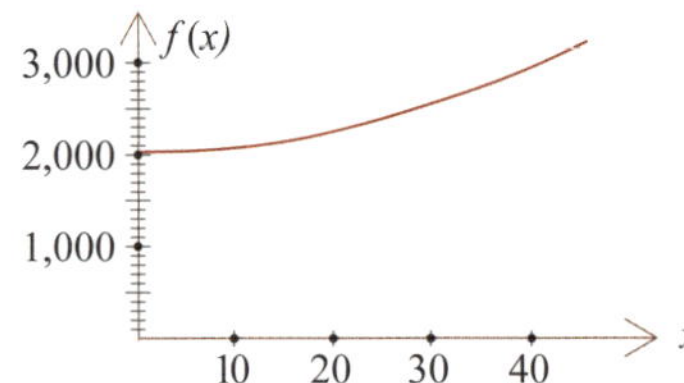

2. **a.** Find the sum of $5x^3 + 2x^2 - 4x + 1 = 0$ and $2x^3 - 4x^2 - x + 5 = 0$

   b. Find the difference of $7x^3 + 5x^2 + x - 5 = 0$ and $3x^3 - 2x^2 + 2x - 3 = 0$

3. Find the following products.
   - **a.** $\left(2t + \frac{1}{3}\right)(6t - 9)$
   - **b.** $(u + 2)^3$

4. Given $f(x) = 2x - x^2$, find $f(b + 2)$.

5. Factor the following completely.
   - **a.** $4c^2d - 2cd^2 + 2c - d$
   - **b.** $27x^3y - 3xy^3$
   - **c.** $x^2 - 2x - 3$
   - **d.** $3x^2 - 17x + 24 = 0$
   - **e.** $t^2 + \frac{2}{3}t = -\frac{1}{9}$

6. Factor the following completely.
   - **a.** $4x^2 - 9y^2$
   - **b.** $\frac{2}{9}u^2 - \frac{2}{25}v^2$
   - **c.** $t^4 - 16$
   - **d.** $x^6 - 8y^6$

UNIT 6 RATIONAL EXPRESSIONS

6-1 RATIONAL EXPRESSIONS & MULTIPLICATION

Rational Functions

Example

- **Rational number** $\left(\frac{a}{b}\right)$: the ratio or quotient of two numbers (a fraction). $\frac{2}{3}$, $\frac{-1}{5}$
- **Rational expression**: an expression that is a ratio or quotient of two polynomials. $\frac{2x-3}{7x+5}$
- **Rational function**: a function that is a ratio or quotient of two polynomials.

Rational Function	Example
$f(x) = \frac{a(x)}{b(x)}$ ← polynomials, $b(x) \neq 0$	$f(x) = \frac{4x+3}{5x-7}$, $f(x) = \frac{3y^2-2y+4}{5y-6}$

Example: For the following functions, identify their domains.

Rational Function	Restriction		Doman Set-Builder Notation	Doman Interval Notation
$f(x) = \frac{3x+1}{x-5}$	$x \neq 5$	$\left(\frac{3x+1}{5-5} = \frac{3x+1}{0}\text{ is undefined}\right)$	$\{x \mid x \neq 5\}$	$(-\infty, 5) \cup (5, \infty)$
$f(x) = \frac{5yt^2+2t-1}{11t}$	$t \neq 0$	$\left(\frac{5yt^2+2t-1}{0}\text{ is undefined}\right)$	$\{t \mid t \neq 0\}$	$(-\infty, 0) \cup (0, \infty)$
$f(x) = \frac{7y+4}{5y-3}$	$y \neq \frac{3}{5}$	$(5 \cdot \frac{3}{5} - 3 = 0)$	$\left\{y \mid y \neq \frac{3}{5}\right\}$	$\left(-\infty, \frac{3}{5}\right) \cup \left(\frac{3}{5}, \infty\right)$

- **Reducing rational expressions to lowest forms**

A rational expression reduced to lowest terms means that no common factors other than 1 occur in its top and bottom polynomials.

Example

$$\frac{2q^2}{6q^4} = \frac{\overset{1}{\cancel{2}}\cancel{q^2}}{\underset{3}{\cancel{6}}\cancel{q^2}q^2} = \frac{1}{3q^2}$$

Lowest terms

Example: Reduce to lowest terms (simplify).

1. $\frac{3b+9}{3} = \frac{3b}{3} + \frac{9}{3} = b + 3$

2. $\frac{3x^2+2x}{5x^3-7x^2} = \frac{\cancel{x}(3x+2)}{x^{\cancel{2}}(5x-7)} = \frac{3x+2}{x(5x-7)}$ — Factor, and then reduce.

3. $\frac{9y^2-3y}{18y} = \frac{\overset{1}{\cancel{3}}\cancel{y}(3y-1)}{\underset{6}{\cancel{18}}\cancel{y}} = \frac{3y-1}{6} = \frac{\overset{1}{\cancel{3}}y}{\underset{2}{\cancel{6}}} - \frac{1}{6} = \frac{y}{2} - \frac{1}{6}$

4. $\frac{3t^2-12}{(t-2)^2} = \frac{3(t^2-4)}{(t-2)^2} = \frac{3(t^2-2^2)}{(t-2)^2} = \frac{3(t+2)\cancel{(t-2)}}{(t-2)^{\cancel{2}}} = \frac{3(t+2)}{t-2}$ — $a^2 - b^2 = (a+b)(a-b)$

5. $\frac{a(2a-1)(2a+5)}{4a^2+8a-5} = \frac{a\cancel{(2a-1)}\cancel{(2a+5)}}{\cancel{(2a-1)}\cancel{(2a+5)}} = a$ — $4a^2 + 8a - 5 = (2a-1)(2a+5)$

6. $\frac{4(x^3-y^3)}{12(x-y)} = \frac{\overset{1}{\cancel{4}}\cancel{(x-y)}(x^2+xy+y^2)}{\underset{3}{\cancel{12}}\cancel{(x-y)}} = \frac{1}{3}(x^2+xy+y^2)$ — $a^3 - b^3 = (a-b)(a^2+ab+b^2)$

Multiplying Rational Expressions

- **Multiplying fractions:** $\left(\frac{2}{3}\right)\left(\frac{4}{5}\right) = \frac{2 \cdot 4}{3 \cdot 5} = \frac{8}{15}$

- **Multiplying rational expressions:** $\frac{N_1}{D_1} \cdot \frac{N_2}{D_2} = \frac{N_1 N_2}{D_1 D_2}$ (Numerator, Denominator) $\frac{N_1}{D_1}$ *and* $\frac{N_2}{D_2}$ are rational expressions. $(D_1 D_2 \neq 0)$

Steps

- Multiply the numerators.
- Multiply the denominators.
- Simplify (cancel or reduce common factors) if possible.

Example: $\frac{2x^2}{3y^3} \cdot \frac{3x}{4y} = \frac{(2x^2)(3x)}{(3y^3)(4y)} = \frac{6x^3}{12y^4} = \frac{\mathbf{x^3}}{\mathbf{2y^4}}$ $a^n a^m = a^{n+m}$

- **Note:** It is more efficient to reduce or cancel common factors before multiplying.

Example: $\frac{3}{8} \cdot \frac{4}{9} = \frac{1 \cdot 1}{2 \cdot 3} = \frac{\mathbf{1}}{\mathbf{6}}$

$\frac{x^2}{y} \cdot \frac{y^4}{4x} = \frac{\mathbf{xy^3}}{\mathbf{4}}$

Example: Perform the indicated operations and simplify.

1. $\frac{2a^2b}{b^2} \cdot \frac{b^3}{4a^2b} = \frac{1 \cdot b}{2} = \frac{\mathbf{b}}{\mathbf{2}}$

2. $\frac{x^2-xy+y^2}{(x-y)^2} \cdot \frac{x^2-y^2}{x^3+y^3} = \frac{(x^2-xy+y^2)}{(x-y)^2} \cdot \frac{(x+y)(x-y)}{x^3+y^3}$ $a^2 - b^2 = (a+b)(a-b)$

$= \frac{(x^2-xy+y^2)}{(x-y)} \cdot \frac{(x+y)}{x^3+y^3}$ $(a+b)(a^2 - ab + b^2) = a^3 + b^3$

$= \frac{\mathbf{1}}{\mathbf{x-y}}$

3. $\frac{b^2-2b-8}{b-2} \cdot \frac{b^2-4}{b+2} = \frac{(b+2)(b-4)}{b-2} \cdot \frac{(b+2)(b-2)}{b+2}$ $a^2 - b^2 = (a+b)(a-b)$

$= \mathbf{(b - 4)(b + 2)}$

4. $\frac{3x^3+3y^3}{4(x^2-y^2)} \cdot \frac{(x+y)}{3(x^2-xy+y^2)} = \frac{3(x^3+y^3)}{4(x+y)(x-y)} \cdot \frac{(x+y)}{3(x^2-xy+y^2)}$ $a^2 - b^2 = (a+b)(a-b)$

$= \frac{(x^3+y^3)}{4(x-y)} \cdot \frac{1}{(x^2-xy+y^2)}$

$= \frac{(x+y)(x^2-xy+y^2)}{4(x-y)} \cdot \frac{1}{x^2-xy+y^2}$ $a^3 + b^3 = (a+b)(a^2 - ab + b^2)$

$= \frac{\mathbf{x+y}}{\mathbf{4(x-y)}}$

Dividing Rational Expressions

Example

- **Dividing fractions:** to divide by a fraction, multiply by its reciprocal. $\frac{3}{4} \div \frac{5}{2} = \frac{3}{4} \cdot \frac{2}{5} = \frac{3}{10}$

- **Dividing rational expressions:** $\frac{N_1}{D_1} \div \frac{N_2}{D_2} = \frac{N_1}{D_1} \cdot \frac{D_2}{N_2}$ $\frac{N_1}{D_1}$ and $\frac{N_2}{D_2}$ are rational , $D_1, D_2, N_2 \neq 0$

Steps

- Write as multiplication of the reciprocal. $\div \longrightarrow \times$, $\frac{N_2}{D_2} \longrightarrow \frac{D_2}{N_2}$
- Simplify (cancel or reduce common factors) if possible.
- Multiply.

Example: Perform the indicated operations and simplify.

1. $\frac{y^2}{x^3} \div \frac{10y}{2} = \frac{y^2}{x^3} \cdot \frac{2}{10y} = \frac{y \cdot 1}{x^3 \cdot 5} = \frac{y}{5x^3}$ $\div \longrightarrow \times$, $\frac{10y}{2} \longrightarrow \frac{2}{10y}$

2. $\frac{5a^2-ab}{a^2-b^2} \div \frac{5a^2-ab}{a-b} = \frac{5a^2-ab}{a^2-b^2} \cdot \frac{a-b}{5a^2-ab}$ $\div \longrightarrow \times$, $\frac{5a^2-ab}{a-b} \longrightarrow \frac{a-b}{5a^2-ab}$

$= \frac{a-b}{(a+b)(a-b)}$ $a^2-b^2 = (a+b)(a-b)$

$= \frac{1}{(a+b)}$

3. $\frac{x^2-16}{x^2+4x+4} \div \frac{x-4}{3x+6} = \frac{x^2-4^2}{x^2+4x+4} \cdot \frac{3x+6}{x-4}$ $\div \longrightarrow \times$, $\frac{x-4}{3x+6} \longrightarrow \frac{3x+6}{x-4}$

$= \frac{(x+4)(x-4)}{(x+2)^2} \cdot \frac{3(x+2)}{x-4}$ $a^2-b^2 = (a+b)(a-b)$

$= \frac{3(x+4)}{x+2}$

4. $\frac{x^2-1}{3} \div \frac{x+1}{5} = \frac{x^2-1}{3} \cdot \frac{5}{x+1}$ $\div \longrightarrow \times$, $\frac{x+1}{5} \longrightarrow \frac{5}{x+1}$

$= \frac{(x+1)(x-1)}{3} \cdot \frac{5}{x+1}$ $a^2-b^2 = (a+b)(a-b)$

$= \frac{5(x-1)}{3}$

6-2 ADDING & SUBTRACTING RATIONAL EXPRESSIONS

Adding / Subtracting Like Rational Expressions

Example

- **Like rational expressions:** rational expressions that have the same denominator. $\frac{3x^2}{x+2}$, $\frac{5x}{x+2}$
- **Unlike rational expressions:** rational expressions that have different denominators. $\frac{7x+3}{x-2}$, $\frac{3x-5}{x^2+5}$
- **Adding or subtracting like rational expressions**

$\frac{N_1}{D}+\frac{N_2}{D}=\frac{N_1+N_2}{D}$, $\frac{N_1}{D}-\frac{N_2}{D}=\frac{N_1-N_2}{D}$ $\frac{N_1}{D}$ *and* $\frac{N_2}{D}$ are rational expressions. $D \neq 0$

Steps

- Combine the numerators.
- Denominators do not change.
- Simplify (cancel or reduce common factors) if possible.

Example

$$\frac{3x}{2(x+4)}+\frac{5x}{2(x+4)}=\frac{3x+5x}{2(x+4)}=\frac{8x}{2(x+4)}=\frac{4x}{x+4}$$

Example: Add or subtract as indicated and simplify.

1. $\frac{x^2+2xy+y^2}{x^2-y^2}-\frac{x+y}{x^2-y^2}=\frac{(x^2+2xy+y^2)-(x+y)}{x^2-y^2}$ Combine numerators.

$=\frac{(x+y)^2-(x+y)\cdot 1}{(x+y)(x-y)}$ $a^2+2ab+b^2=(a+b)^2$; $a^2-b^2=(a+b)(a-b)$

$=\frac{(x+y)[(x+y)-1]}{(x+y)(x-y)}$ Factor out $(x+y)$.

$=\frac{x+y-1}{x-y}$

2. $\frac{3a+9b}{2a-5b}+\frac{4(a+3b)}{2a-5b}-\frac{5a^3}{2a-5b}=\frac{3a+9b+4(a+3b)-5a^3}{2a-5b}$ Combine numerators.

$=\frac{3(a+3b)+4(a+3b)-5a^3}{2a-5b}$ Factor out 3.

$=\frac{7(a+3b)-5a^3}{2a-5b}$ Combine like terms.

3. $\frac{3}{m}-\frac{2}{-m}=\frac{3}{m}+\frac{2}{m}=\frac{3+2}{m}=\frac{5}{m}$ Combine numerators.

4. $\frac{2}{x-y}-\frac{1}{y-x}=\frac{2}{x-y}-\frac{1}{-(x-y)}$ Factor out (-1).

$=\frac{2}{x-y}+\frac{1}{x-y}=\frac{3}{x-y}$ Combine numerators.

Least Common Denominator (LCD)

- **Least common multiple (LCM):** the lowest number that is divisible by each given number without a remainder.

  Example: The LCM of 2 and 3 is 6.

  - Multiples of 2: 2, 4, **6**, 8, 10, **12**, …
  - Multiples of 3: 3, **6**, 9, **12**, 15, …
  - Common multiples of 2 and 3 are 6 and 12, …
  - The least common multiple (LCM) of 2 and 3 is **6**.

    The common multiple 12 is not the smallest (least).

- **Find the LCM:** Use repeated division (or upside-down division). The product of all the prime numbers around the outside is the LCM.

  Example: Find the LCM of 30 and 45.

```
5 | 30  45
3 |  6   9   ←  30 ÷ 5 = 6    45 ÷ 5 = 9
     2   3   ←  6 ÷ 3 = 2     9 ÷ 3 = 3
```

(Stop dividing since 2 and 3 are prime numbers)

$\text{LCM} = 5 \times 3^2 \times 2 = \mathbf{90}$

- **The least common denominator (LCD):** the least common multiple (LCM) of the **denominators** of two or more given fractions.

- **Find the LCD:** Use repeated division to find the LCM for all **denominators** of given fractions.

  Example: Find the LCD for $\frac{4}{8}$, $\frac{5}{16}$ and $\frac{2}{42}$.

```
2 | 8  16  42
2 | 4   8  21   ←  8 ÷ 2 = 4, 16 ÷ 2 = 8, 42 ÷ 2 = 21
2 | 2   4  21   ←  4 ÷ 2 = 2, 8 ÷ 2 = 4, move down 21
    1   2  21   ←  2 ÷ 2 = 1, 4 ÷ 2 = 2, move down 21
```

$\text{LCD} = 2^4 \times 21 = \mathbf{336}$

Finding the LCM & LCD for Expressions

- **The LCM for algebraic expressions:** the smallest expression that is divisible by each of the given expressions. LCM – the least common multiple

- **Finding the LCM for expressions**
  - Factor each term.
  - The LCM is the product of all **unique factors** with the highest exponent.

Example: Find the LCM for $2x^4y^2$, $6x^2y^3$ and $8xy$.

Expression	Factor	Factor With the Highest Exponent
$8xy$	$2^3 \cdot x \cdot y$	2^3
$6x^2y^3$	$2 \cdot 3 \cdot x^2 \cdot y^3$	$3y^3$
$2x^4y^2$	$2 \cdot x^4 \cdot y^2$	x^4

LCM = $2^3 \cdot 3y^3 \cdot x^4 = \mathbf{24x^4y^3}$

Example: Find the LCM for $3x(x^2-4)$ and $x^2(x+2)$.

Expression	Factor	Factor With the Highest Exponent
$3x(x^2-4)$	$3 \cdot x \cdot (x+2) \cdot (x-2)$	$3(x+2)(x-2)$
$x^2(x+2)$	$x^2 \cdot (x+2)$	x^2

LCM = $\mathbf{3x^2(x+2)(x-2)}$

- **Finding the LCD for rational expressions** LCD – the least common denominator
  - Factor each given denominator.
  - Find the product of all **unique factors** with the highest exponent.

Example: Find the LCD for the following fractions.

1. $\frac{7a}{9b^2}$, $\frac{5}{27a^2b}$ and $\frac{4ab}{6a^4b^2}$

Denominator	Factor	Factor With the Highest Exponent
$9b^2$	$3^2 \cdot b^2$	b^2
$27a^2b$	$3^3 \cdot a^2 \cdot b$	3^3
$6a^4b^2$	$3 \cdot 2 \cdot a^4 \cdot b^2$	$2a^4$

LCD = $2 \cdot 3^3 \cdot a^4 \cdot b^2 = \mathbf{54a^4b^2}$

2. $\frac{5ab}{3a^3(a^2-8a+16)}$ and $\frac{7a^2+b}{a(a-4)^4}$

Denominator	Factor	Factor With the Highest Exponent
$3a^3(a^2-8a+16)$ a -4 a -4	$3 \cdot a^3 \cdot (a-4)^2$	$3a^3$
$a(a-4)^4$	$a \cdot (a-4)^4$	$(a-4)^4$

LCD = $\mathbf{3a^3(a-4)^4}$

Adding/Subtracting Unlike Rational Expressions

- **Adding or subtracting unlike fractions** (with different denominators)

$$\frac{2}{3}+\frac{1}{4}=\frac{2\cdot 4}{3\cdot 4}+\frac{1\cdot 3}{4\cdot 3}=\frac{8}{12}+\frac{3}{12}=\frac{8+3}{12}=\frac{11}{12}$$

LCD = 12

$$\frac{5}{12}-\frac{3}{8}=\frac{5\cdot 2}{12\cdot 2}-\frac{3\cdot 3}{8\cdot 3}=\frac{10}{24}-\frac{9}{24}=\frac{10-9}{24}=\frac{1}{24}$$

2 | 12 8
2 | 6 4
3 2 LCD = $2^3\cdot 3=24$

- **Adding or subtracting unlike rational expressions**

Steps

- Determine the LCD.
- Rewrite expressions with the LCD.
- Combine the numerators.
- Simplify if possible.

Example: $\frac{5x^2+1}{3x}+\frac{7x^2-1}{4x}$

LCD = $3\cdot 4\cdot x=12x$

$$\frac{5x^2+1}{3x}+\frac{7x^2-1}{4x}=\frac{4(5x^2+1)}{4\cdot 3x}+\frac{3(7x^2-1)}{3\cdot 4x}$$

$$=\frac{4(5x^2+1)+3(7x^2-1)}{12x}=\frac{20x^2+4+21x^2-3}{12x}$$

$$=\frac{41x^2+1}{12x}=\frac{41x^2}{12x}+\frac{1}{12x}=\frac{41x}{12}+\frac{1}{12x}$$

Example: Add or subtract and simplify.

1. $\frac{3a}{a-3}+\frac{5}{a+3}-\frac{2}{a^2-9}=\frac{3a(a+3)}{(a-3)(a+3)}+\frac{5(a-3)}{(a+3)(a-3)}-\frac{2}{(a+3)(a-3)}$ $a^2-9=a^2-3^2$, LCD = $(a+3)(a-3)$

$=\frac{3a(a+3)+5(a-3)-2}{(a+3)(a-3)}$ Combine the numerators.

$=\frac{3a^2+9a+5a-15-2}{(a+3)(a-3)}$

$=\frac{3a^2+14a-17}{(a+3)(a-3)}$ Combine like terms.

2. $\frac{2x}{3x^2+2x-1}-\frac{3}{x+1}=\frac{2x}{(x+1)(3x-1)}-\frac{3}{x+1}$ LCD = $(x+1)(3x-1)$

x 1
$3x$ -1

$=\frac{2x}{(x+1)(3x-1)}-\frac{3(3x-1)}{(x+1)(3x-1)}$ Rewrite with the LCD.

$=\frac{2x-[3(3x-1)]}{(x+1)(3x-1)}$ Combine the numerators.

$=\frac{2x-9x+3}{(x+1)(3x-1)}$ Distribute

$=\frac{-7x+3}{(x+1)(3x-1)}$ Combine like terms.

6-3 POLYNOMIAL DIVISION

Dividing Polynomials

- **Dividing a monomial by a monomial**

Monomial: one term

Example: $\dfrac{-12x^2y^5}{4x^3y^2}$

Steps	Solution
- Divide coefficients.	$\dfrac{-12x^2y^5}{4x^3y^2} = \left(\dfrac{-12}{4}\right)\left(\dfrac{x^2y^5}{x^3y^2}\right)$
- Divide like variables. (apply $\frac{a^m}{a^n} = a^{m-n}$)	$= -3\left(\dfrac{x^2}{x^3}\right)\left(\dfrac{y^5}{y^2}\right)$
	$= -3\left(\dfrac{y^3}{x}\right)$

- **Dividing a polynomial by a monomial**

Example: $\dfrac{12x^2+4x-2}{4x}$

Steps	Solution
- Split the polynomial into three parts.	$\dfrac{12x^2+4x-2}{4x} = \dfrac{12x^2}{4x} + \dfrac{4x}{4x} - \dfrac{2}{4x}$
- Divide a monomial by a monomial.	$= 3x + 1 - \dfrac{1}{2x}$
	Cancel or reduce common factors.

Example: $\dfrac{3y^2+3y+2y+2}{y+1}$

Steps	Solution
- Group.	$\dfrac{3y^2+3y+2y+2}{y+1} = \dfrac{(3y^2+3y)+(2y+2)}{y+1}$
- Factor out the GCF.	$= \dfrac{3y(y+1)+2(y+1)}{y+1}$
- Split the polynomial into two parts.	$= \dfrac{3y(y+1)}{y+1} + \dfrac{2(y+1)}{y+1}$
- Divide a monomial by a monomial.	$= 3y + 2$

Long Division of Polynomials

- **Division of whole numbers (long division):**

$$\begin{array}{r} \text{Quotient} \\ \text{Divisor}\overline{)\text{Dividend}} \\ -\underline{\qquad\qquad} \\ \text{Remainder} \end{array}$$

Example:

$$\begin{array}{r} 3 \\ 4\overline{)15} \\ -\underline{12} \\ 3 \end{array}$$

- **Polynomial long division** works more conveniently for more general polynomials.

Example: $\frac{6x^2+9x+2}{3x}$

Steps	Solution	Dividing whole numbers
- Write in divisor$\overline{)\text{dividend}}$ form.	$3x\overline{)6x^2+9x+2}$	$3\overline{)692}$
- Divide the first term.	$\begin{array}{r} 2x \\ 3x\overline{)6x^2+9x+2} \\ -\ \underline{6x^2} \end{array}$ $(3x)(2x)=6x^2$	$\begin{array}{r} 2 \\ 3\overline{)692} \\ -\ \underline{6} \end{array}$ $2\cdot 3=6$
- Divide the second term.	$\begin{array}{r} \mathbf{2x+3} \\ 3x\overline{)6x^2+9x+2} \\ \underline{6x^2} \\ 9x \\ -\ \underline{9x} \\ \mathbf{2} \end{array}$ Bring 9x down; $(3x)(3)=9x$	$\begin{array}{r} 230 \\ 3\overline{)692} \\ \underline{6} \\ 9 \\ \underline{-9} \\ 2 \end{array}$ Bring 9 down; $3\cdot 3=9$

remainder

Quotient + $\frac{\text{remainder}}{\text{divisor}}$

$$\frac{6x^2+9x+2}{3x} = \mathbf{(2x+3)} + \frac{\mathbf{2}}{\mathbf{3x}}$$

(quotient: $2x+3$; remainder: 2; divisor: $3x$)

$$692 \div 3 = \mathbf{230} + \frac{\mathbf{2}}{\mathbf{3}}$$

Tip: Continue until the degree of the remainder is less than the degree of the divisor.

(i.e. $2 = 2\cdot x^0$ and $3x = 3x^1$)

$0 < 1$

- Check: Dividend = Quotient · Divisor + Remainder

$$6x^2+9x+2 \stackrel{?}{=} (2x+3)(3x)+2$$

$$6x^2+9x+2 \stackrel{\surd}{=} 6x^2+9x+2 \quad \text{Correct!}$$

$$692 \stackrel{?}{=} 230\cdot 3+2$$

$$692 \stackrel{\surd}{=} 692$$

Missing Terms in Long Division

Missing terms in long division: If there is a missing consecutive power term in a polynomial (i.e. if there are x^3 and x, but not x^2), insert the missing power term with a coefficient of 0.

Example: $\dfrac{5-3a^2+a^3}{1+a}$

Steps	Solution
- Rewrite both polynomials in descending order. Descending order: Ax^3+Bx^2+Cx+D , $Ax+B$	$\dfrac{a^3-3a^2+5}{a+1}$
- Write in divisor$\overline{)\text{Dividend}}$ form and insert a 0 coefficient for the missing power term.	$a+1\overline{)\,a^3-3a^2+\mathbf{0a}+5}$ ↑ Missing power
- Divide as usual.	see below

$$
\begin{array}{r}
a^2-4a+4 \\
a+1\overline{)\,a^3-3a^2+0a+5} \\
-\underline{\;a^3+a^2\qquad\qquad} \\
-4a^2+0a \\
-\underline{-4a^2-4a} \\
4a+5 \\
-\underline{4a+4} \\
1
\end{array}
$$

- Solution. $\dfrac{5-3a^2+a^3}{1+a}=\left(a^2-4a+4\right)+\dfrac{1}{a+1}$ Quotient + $\dfrac{\text{remainder}}{\text{divisor}}$

- Check: Dividend = Quotient · Divisor + Remainder

$$5-3a^2+a^3\overset{?}{=}(a^2-4a+4)(a+1)+1$$

$$5-3a^2+a^3\overset{?}{=}(a^3+a^2-4a^2-\cancel{4a}+\cancel{4a}+4)+1$$

$$5-3a^2+a^3\overset{\surd}{=}a^3-3a^2+5$$ Correct!

Synthetic Division

Synthetic Division: a shortcut method of dividing a polynomial by a binomial of the form **$(x - a)$**, by using only the coefficients of the terms.

Steps / **Example**

$(x-a)$

$$(3x^4 - 40 + 4x - 2x^2) \div (x - 2)$$

- Rewrite the polynomial in descending order. Insert a zero coefficient for the missing power.

$$x - 2\,\overline{)\,3x^4 + 0x^3 - 2x^2 + 4x - 40}$$

Missing power ($0x^3$)

- Set up the synthetic coefficients. $(a = 2)$

a in the divisor: 2 | The coefficient of the dividend: 3 0 -2 4 -40

- Bring down the leading coefficient and multiply it by *a* in $(x - a)$. Place the product beneath the second coefficient.

2 | 3 0 -2 4 -40 (2nd coefficient: 0)

2×3: 3 6

- Add the numbers in column 2.

2 | 3 0 -2 4 -40
   6 +
3 6 (0 + 6)

- Repeat until the last column done.

$2 \times 6 = 12$, $-2 + 12 = 10$
$2 \times 10 = 20$, $4 + 20 = 24$
$2 \times 24 = 48$, $-40 + 48 = 8$

2	3	0	-2	4	-40
		6	12 +	20 +	48 +
	3	6	**10**	**24**	**8**
	x^3	x^2	x	constant	remainder

- Write out the answer.

Quotient + $\frac{\text{remainder}}{\text{divisor}}$

Answer: $(3x^3 + 6x^2 + 10x + 24) + \frac{8}{x-2}$

One less than the degree of the dividend

Example: Divide. $(6 + 4x^3 - 2x - 2x^2) \div (x + 1)$

$$x + 1\,\overline{)\,4x^3 - 2x^2 - 2x + 6}$$

-1	4	-2	-2	6
-1×4		-4	6	-4
	4	**-6**	**4**	**2**
	x^2	x	constant	remainder

Write in descending order.

$(x - a)$: $x + 1 = x - (-1)$, $\therefore a = -1$

The synthetic coefficients

$-1 \times 4 = -4$, $-2 + (-4) = -6$
$-1 \times (-6) = 6$, $-2 + 6 = 4$
$-1 \times 4 = -4$, $6 + (-4) = 2$

Answer: $(4x^2 - 6x + 4) + \frac{2}{x+1}$

Quotient + $\frac{\text{remainder}}{\text{divisor}}$

6-4 COMPLEX RATIONAL EXPRESSIONS

Simplify Complex Rational Expressions — Method I

- **Complex fraction:** a fraction that contains another fraction in its numerator or denominator (or both).

  Example: $\dfrac{\frac{3}{4}}{\frac{3}{2}} = \frac{3}{4} \div \frac{3}{2}$ (fractions) — $\rightarrow \div$

- **Complex rational expression:** a rational expression whose numerator or denominator (or both) contains rational expressions.

  $\dfrac{\frac{N_1}{D_1}}{\frac{N_2}{D_2}}$ $\frac{N_1}{D_1}$ and $\frac{N_2}{D_2}$ are rational expressions. D_1, D_2 & $N_2 \neq 0$

  Example

  $\dfrac{\frac{5}{x} - \frac{3xy^2}{y}}{\frac{3}{y} + \frac{4}{yx}}$

- **Simplifying a complex rational expression — method I:** multiplying the LCD.

Examples: Simplify the following.

1. $\dfrac{\frac{1}{w} - 3}{\frac{1}{w} + w} = \left(\dfrac{\frac{1}{w} - 3}{\frac{1}{w} + w}\right) \cdot \dfrac{w}{w} = \dfrac{\frac{w}{w} - 3w}{\frac{w}{w} + w^2}$ Multiply num. & den. by the LCD. (w)

$= \dfrac{1-3w}{1+w^2}$ Simplify.

2. $\dfrac{\frac{1}{a^2} + \frac{2}{b}}{\frac{3a}{b^2} - \frac{1}{a^2}} = \dfrac{\left(\frac{1}{a^2} + \frac{2}{b}\right)(a^2b^2)}{\left(\frac{3a}{b^2} - \frac{1}{a^2}\right)(a^2b^2)}$ Multiply num. & den. by the LCD. (a^2b^2)

$= \dfrac{\frac{a^2b^2}{a^2} + \frac{2(a^2b^2)}{b}}{\frac{3a(a^2b^2)}{b^2} - \frac{(a^2b^2)}{a^2}}$

$= \dfrac{b^2 + 2a^2b}{3a^3 - b^2}$ Simplify.

$= \dfrac{b(b+2a^2)}{3a^3-b^2}$ Factor out b.

Simplify Complex Rational Expressions
Method II

Simplifying a complex rational expression — method II: multiply the reciprocal of the denominator $(\div \to \times)$.

$$\frac{\frac{N_1}{D_1}}{\frac{N_2}{D_2}} = \frac{N_1}{D_1} \div \frac{N_2}{D_2} = \frac{N_1}{D_1} \cdot \frac{D_2}{N_2}$$

$\frac{N_1}{D_1}$ and $\frac{N_2}{D_2}$ are rational expressions.

$$\frac{\frac{3}{4}}{\frac{3}{2}} = \frac{3}{4} \div \frac{3}{2} = \frac{3}{4} \cdot \frac{2}{3} = \frac{1}{2}$$

Examples: Simplify the following.

1. $\dfrac{\frac{1}{w} - 3}{\frac{1}{w} + w} = \dfrac{\frac{1}{w} - \frac{3}{1}}{\frac{1}{w} + \frac{w}{1}} = \dfrac{\frac{1}{w} - \frac{3w}{w}}{\frac{1}{w} + \frac{w^2}{w}}$ — Multiply num. & den. by the LCD. LCD = w

$= \dfrac{\frac{1-3w}{w}}{\frac{1+w^2}{w}}$ — Rewrite to get a single rational expression in the den. & num.

$= \dfrac{1-3w}{w} \div \dfrac{1+w^2}{w}$ — $\text{——} \to \div$

$= \dfrac{1-3w}{w} \cdot \dfrac{w}{1+w^2}$ — $\div \to \times$, $\frac{1+w^2}{w} \to \frac{w}{1+w^2}$

$= \dfrac{1-3w}{1+w^2}$

2. $\dfrac{\frac{y^2-2y-8}{2y+6y^2}}{\frac{3y^2+4y-4}{3y+1}} = \dfrac{y^2-2y-8}{2y+6y^2} \div \dfrac{3y^2+4y-4}{3y+1}$ — $\text{——} \to \div$

$= \dfrac{y^2-2y-8}{2y+6y^2} \cdot \dfrac{3y+1}{3y^2+4y-4}$ — $\div \to \times$, $\frac{3y^2+4y-4}{3y+1} \to \frac{3y+1}{3y^2+4y-4}$

$= \dfrac{(y+2)(y-4)}{2y(1+3y)} \cdot \dfrac{3y+1}{(y+2)(3y-2)}$ — Factor: $y^2 - 2y - 8$ (y, y; 2, -4), $3y^2 + 4y - 4$ (y, $3y$; 2, -2)

$= \dfrac{y-4}{2y(3y-2)}$ — Simplify.

3. $\dfrac{\frac{3}{t+2} - \frac{1}{t-1}}{4t} = \dfrac{\frac{3(t-1)}{(t+2)(t-1)} - \frac{1(t+2)}{(t-1)(t+2)}}{\frac{4t}{1}}$ — The LCD = $(t+2)(t-1)$.

$= \dfrac{\frac{3(t-1)-(t+2)}{(t+2)(t-1)}}{\frac{4t}{1}}$ — Rewrite to get a single rational expression in the den. & num.

$= \dfrac{3(t-1)-(t+2)}{(t+2)(t-1)} \div \dfrac{4t}{1}$ — $\text{——} \to \div$

$= \dfrac{3(t-1)-(t+2)}{(t+2)(t-1)} \cdot \dfrac{1}{4t}$ — $\div \to \times$, $\frac{4t}{1} \to \frac{1}{4t}$

$= \dfrac{3t-3-t-2}{(t+2)(t-1)} \cdot \dfrac{1}{4t}$ — Distribute

$= \dfrac{2t-5}{4t(t+2)(t-1)}$ — Combine like terms.

6-5 RATIONAL EQUATIONS

Rational Equations

- **Review** — **Example**
  - **Expression:** a mathematical statement that contains numbers, variables, and arithmetic operations (without an equal sign). — $2ab^2 + 3a$
  - **Equation:** a mathematical statement that contains two expressions and separated by an equal sign. — $3x^2 + 4x = 2$
  - **Rational (fractional) expression:** an expression that is a ratio or quotient of two polynomials. — $\frac{2x-3}{7x+5}$
- **Rational (fractional) equation:** an equation that contains rational expressions.

Example

Rational Expression	Rational Equation
$\frac{5x^2+3x}{4-x}$	$\frac{3}{x}+\frac{2}{5x}=7$
$\frac{a^2+b^2}{2ab-b}-\frac{3a^2}{4a}$	$\frac{2ab+3}{4a}-\frac{5a+7}{4}=\frac{3ab}{5a}$

- **Solving a rational equation**

Steps	**Example:** Solve $\frac{1}{x}+\frac{3}{2x}=5$.
- Find the least common denominator (LCD).	LCD $= 2x$
- Multiply each term by the LCD.	$\frac{1}{x}\cdot 2x+\frac{3}{2x}\cdot 2x = 5\cdot 2x$ $2+3=10x$
- Solve the variable.	$5 = 10x$ $x=\frac{1}{2}$
- Check.	$\frac{1}{\frac{1}{2}}+\frac{3}{2\cdot\frac{1}{2}} \stackrel{?}{=} 5$ $\frac{1}{\frac{1}{2}}=1\div\frac{1}{2}=1\cdot\frac{2}{1}=2$ $2+3 \stackrel{\surd}{=} 5$ Correct!

Note: Checking is necessary, not optional (check for a valid solution rather than errors).

Solving Rational Equations

Example: Solve the following.

1. $\frac{3}{a-2} = \frac{5}{a+4}$ LCD = $(a-2)(a+4)$

$\frac{3}{a-2}(a-2)(a+4) = \frac{5}{a+4}(a-2)(a+4)$ Multiply each term by the LCD.

$3(a+4) = 5(a-2)$ Distribute

$3a + 12 = 5a - 10$ Solve for a: add 10, subtract $3a$.

$22 = 2a$, $\boldsymbol{a = 11}$ Divide by 2.

Check: $\frac{3}{11-2} \overset{?}{=} \frac{5}{11+4}$, $\frac{3}{9} \overset{?}{=} \frac{5}{15}$

$\frac{1}{3} \overset{\surd}{=} \frac{1}{3}$ Correct!

2. $\frac{2-t}{t+5} = 2 + \frac{7}{t+5}$ LCD = $t + 5$

$\frac{2-t}{t+5}\cdot(t+5) = 2(t+5) + \frac{7}{t+5}\cdot(t+5)$ Multiply each term by the LCD.

$2 - t = 2t + 10 + 7$ Solve for t: add t, subtract 17.

$-15 = 3t$, $\boldsymbol{t = -5}$ Divide by 3.

Check: $\frac{2-(-5)}{-5+5} \overset{?}{=} 2 + \frac{7}{-5+5}$, $\frac{7}{0} = 2 + \frac{7}{0}$ **No solution** (undefined)

3. $\frac{5}{x+2} + \frac{2x}{x^2-4} = \frac{3}{x-2}$ $x^2 - 4 = x^2 - 2^2 = (x+2)(x-2)$

LCD $= (x+2)(x-2)$

$\frac{5}{x+2}\cdot(x-2)(x+2) + \frac{2x}{x^2-4}(x-2)(x+2) = \frac{3}{x-2}(x-2)(x+2)$

Multiply each term by the LCD.

$5(x-2) + 2x = 3(x+2)$ Distribute

$5x - 10 + 2x = 3x + 6$ Solve for x: subtract $3x$, add 10.

$4x = 16$, $\boldsymbol{x = 4}$ Divide by 4.

Check: $\frac{5}{4+2} + \frac{2\cdot 4}{4^2-4} \overset{?}{=} \frac{3}{4-2}$, $\frac{5}{6} + \frac{8}{12} \overset{?}{=} \frac{3}{2}$

$\frac{5\cdot 2}{6\cdot 2} + \frac{8}{12} \overset{?}{=} \frac{18}{12}$, $\frac{18}{12} \overset{\surd}{=} \frac{18}{12}$ Correct!

6-6 APPLICATIONS OF RATIONAL EQUATIONS

Applications

- **Mathematical model:** uses mathematical language to describe the behavior of a real-life phenomenon.
- **World-problem solving strategy review**

Procedure for Solving Word Problems

- **Organize** the **facts** given from the problem.
- Identify and label the unknown quantity (**let x = unknown**).
- Draw a **diagram** if it will make the problem clearer.
- Convert the wording into a mathematical **equation**.
- **Solve** the equation and find the solution(s).
- **Check** and state the **answer.**

Example: Tom plans to plant a flower garden in his backyard. If the size of the garden is as indicated in the following figure, what is the total **total area** of the garden?

- Diagram.

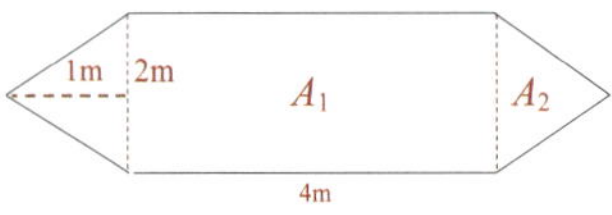

- Organize the facts.

rectangle	width (w) = 2m , length (l) = 4m
triangle	base (b) = 2m , height (h) = 1m
total area	$A = A_1 + 2A_2$

1 rectangle 2 triangles

1m
2m

Recall: Area of a rectangle $A = wl$, area of a triangle $A = \frac{1}{2}bh$

- Equation: $\boldsymbol{A = wl + 2\left(\frac{1}{2}bh\right)}$

- Solution: $A = (2)(4) + 2 \cdot \frac{1}{2}(2)(1)$ $w = 2\text{m},\ l = 4\text{m},\ b = 2\text{m},\ h = 1\text{m}$

  $\boldsymbol{A = 10\ \text{m}^2}$

- Check. $10 \overset{?}{=} (2)(4) + 2 \cdot \frac{1}{2}(2)(1)$

  $10 \overset{\checkmark}{=} 8 + 2$ Correct!

- Answer: The total area of the garden is 10 m^2.

Number Problems

Example: Three divided by one more than a number is equal to the quotient of two and the same number less than 3. What is the number?

- Facts: $\frac{3}{x+1}$ $\frac{2}{3-x}$ Let x = number
- Equation: $\frac{3}{x+1} = \frac{2}{3-x}$ LCD = $(x+1)(3-x)$
- Solve for x. $\frac{3}{x+1}(x+1)(3-x) = \frac{2}{3-x}(x+1)(3-x)$ × LCD

$3(3-x) = 2(x+1)$ Solve for x.

$9 - 3x = 2x + 2$, $\boldsymbol{x = \frac{7}{5}}$

Example: The quotient of 5 and the product of a number and 4 is equal to the quotient of 7 and 5 times that number less than 2. What is the number?

- Facts: $\frac{5}{4x}$ $\frac{7}{2-5x}$ Let x = number
- Equation: $\frac{5}{4x} = \frac{7}{2-5x}$ LCD = $4x(2-5x)$
- Solve for x. $\frac{5}{4x} \cdot 4x(2-5x) = \frac{7}{2-5x} \cdot 4x(2-5x)$ × LCD

$5(2-5x) = 28x$

$10 - 25x = 28x$, $\boldsymbol{x = \frac{10}{53}}$

Example: The difference between the reciprocals of two consecutive **positive even** integers is four over thirty. What are the two integers?

English Phrase	Algebraic Expression	Example
two consecutive integers	x, $x+1$	If $x = \mathbf{1}$, $x+1 = \mathbf{2}$
two consecutive **odd** integers	x, $x+2$	If $x = \mathbf{1}$, $x+2 = \mathbf{3}$
two consecutive **even** integers	x, $x+2$ or $2x$, $2x+2$	If $x = \mathbf{2}$, $x+2 = \mathbf{4}$ If $x = \mathbf{2}$, $2x = \mathbf{4}$, $2x+2 = \mathbf{6}$

- Equation: $\frac{1}{x} - \frac{1}{x+2} = \frac{4}{30}$ Let x = 1st even integer , $x+2$ = 2nd even integer
- Solve for x. $\frac{1}{x} \cdot 30x(x+2) - \frac{1}{x+2} \cdot 30x(x+2) = \frac{4}{30} \cdot 30x(x+2)$ LCD = $30x(x+2)$

$30(x+2) - 30x = 4x(x+2)$

$30x + 60 - 30x = 4x^2 + 8x$

$4x^2 + 8x - 60 = 0$, $4(x^2 + 2x - 15) = 0$ Factor.

$\frac{4}{4}(x^2 + 2x - 15) = \frac{0}{4}$ Divide by 4.

$(x-3)(x+5) = 0$ Factor.

$x - 3 = 0$ or $x + 5 = 0$ Zero product property.

So $\boldsymbol{x = 3}$ or $x = -5$ Ignore the negative answer.

The two integers are $\boldsymbol{x = 3}$ and $\boldsymbol{x + 2 = 5}$

Work Problems

The formula for "work" problems that involve two people is:

$$\frac{1}{t_A} + \frac{1}{t_B} = \frac{1}{t}$$

Time:
- t_A – time required when person A works alone
- t_B – time required when person B works alone
- t – time required when two people work together

Rate:
- $1/t_A$ – person A can finish 1 job every t_A hours
- $1/t_B$ – person B can finish 1 job every t_B hours

Example: **Tom** can paint a room in **2 hours**. **Susan** can paint a room in **3 hours**. **How long** will it take both of them to paint a room **together**?

- Organize the facts

Time to Paint a Room	Part of Job Finished in 1 hour	Comments
Tom: 2 hours	$\frac{1}{2}$ job	If Tom can finish the job in 2 hours, he can finish ½ of the job in 1 hour.
Susan: 3 hours	$\frac{1}{3}$ job	If Susan can finish the job in 3 hours, she can finish 1/3 of the job in 1 hour.
Together: t hours	$\frac{1}{2}+\frac{1}{3}=\frac{1}{t}$	If Tom and Susan work together, they can finish the job in t hours, and they can finish $1/t$ of the job in 1 hour.

Let t = time needed to paint a room together.

- Equation: $\frac{1}{2}+\frac{1}{3}=\frac{1}{t}$ $\qquad \frac{1}{t_A}+\frac{1}{t_B}=\frac{1}{t}$, $t_A=2$, $t_B=3$
- Solve for x. $\frac{1}{2}\cdot 6t+\frac{1}{3}\cdot 6t=\frac{1}{t}\cdot 6t$ $\qquad$ Multiply each term by the LCD. $(6t)$

  $3t+2t=6$, $\boldsymbol{t=1.2}$ **hours**
- Answer: It will take Tom and Susan 1.2 hours to paint a room together.

Example: **Jason** can plow the snow from the school's parking lot **3 fewer hours than Shawn**. If they work **together**, they can finish the job in **2 hours**. **How long** will it take **each** of them to finish the job alone?

- Organize the facts

Time to Finish the Job	Part of Job Finished in 1 hour	Comments
Shawn: t hours	$\frac{1}{t}$ job	If Shawn can finish the job in t hours, he can finish $1/t$ of the job in 1 hour.
Jason: $t-3$ hours	$\frac{1}{t-3}$ job	If Jason can finish the job in $(t-3)$ hours, he can finish $1/(t-3)$ of the job in 1 hour.
Together: 2 hours	$\frac{1}{t}+\frac{1}{t-3}=\frac{1}{2}$	If Shawn and Jason work together, they can finish the job in 2 hours, and they can finish 1/2 of the job in 1 hour.

Let t = time required for Shawn to finish the job alone.

- Equation: $\frac{1}{t}+\frac{1}{t-3}=\frac{1}{2}$ $\qquad \frac{1}{t_A}+\frac{1}{t_B}=\frac{1}{t}$, $t_A=t$, $t_B=t-3$. $t=2$
- Solve for t. $\frac{1}{t}\cdot 2t(t-3)+\frac{1}{t-3}\cdot 2t(t-3)=\frac{1}{2}\cdot 2t(t-3)$ $\qquad$ LCD $=2t(t-3)$

  $2(t-3)+2t=t(t-3)$ $\qquad$ Distribute.

  $2t-6+2t=t^2-3t$ $\qquad$ Subtract $4t$, add 6.

  $t^2-7t+6=0$ $\qquad$ Factor.

  $(t-1)(t-6)=0$, $t-1=0$ or $t-6=0$ $\qquad$ Zero product property
  - Shawn: $t=1$, $\boldsymbol{t=6}$ $\qquad$ $t=1$ hour is not possible (2 people can finish the job in 2 hours.)
  - Jason: $\boldsymbol{t-3}=6-3=\boldsymbol{3}$
- Answer: It will take Shawn 6 hours and Jason 3 hours to clean the school's parking lot.

Proportions

- **Ratio, rate, and proportion**

	Representation		Example
Ratio	a to b or $a{:}b$ or $\frac{a}{b}$	with the same unit.	5 to 9 or 5:9 or $\frac{5\text{ m}}{9\text{ m}}$
Rate	a to b or $a{:}b$ or $\frac{a}{b}$	with different units.	3 to 7 or 3:7 or $\frac{3\text{ cm}}{7\text{ m}}$
Proportion	$\frac{a}{b} = \frac{c}{d}$	an equation with a ratio on each side.	$\frac{3\text{ cm}}{7\,m} = \frac{1\text{ cm}}{5\text{ m}}$

Note: The units for both numerators must match and the units for both denominators must match.

Example: $\frac{\text{in}}{\text{ft}} = \frac{\text{in}}{\text{ft}}$, $\frac{\text{minutes}}{\text{hours}} = \frac{\text{minutes}}{\text{hours}}$

- **Solving a proportion:**
  - Cross multiply: multiply along two diagonals. $\frac{a}{b} = \frac{c}{d}$
  - Solve for the unknown.

Example

$$\frac{x}{9} = \frac{2}{6}$$

$$6 \cdot x = 2 \cdot 9$$

$$x = \frac{2 \cdot 9}{6} = \frac{18}{6} = 3$$

- **Application**

Example: To determine the number of moose in an area, a conservationist catches **50 moose, tags** them, and lets them loose. Later, **20 moose** are caught; **5** of them are **tagged. How many moose** are in the area?

- Equation: $\frac{x \text{ moose}}{50 \text{ tagged moose}} = \frac{20 \text{ moose}}{5 \text{ tagged moose}}$ Let $x =$ the numbers of moose
- Cross multiply. $\frac{x}{50} = \frac{20}{5}$
- Solve for x. $5 \cdot x = 20 \cdot 50$

$$x = \frac{20 \cdot 50}{5} = \mathbf{200}$$

- Answer: There are 200 moose in the area.

Motion Problems

- **Motion formulas**

distance = speed · time $d = r\,t$ $t = \frac{d}{r}$ $r = \frac{d}{t}$

- **Table for motion problem**

Condition	Distance (d)	Speed or Rate (r)	Time (t) $t = \frac{d}{r}$
A	d	r	$\frac{d}{r}$
B	d	r	$\frac{d}{r}$
Total			

Example: **Bob** biked **twice** as fast the **150 km** to town **B** than he did the **60 km** to town **A**. If the **total trip** took **4.5 hours**, then **how fast** was he biking **to** town **A**?

- Table:

Condition	Distance (d) km	Speed (r) km/h	Time (t) h $t = \frac{d}{r}$
To town A	60 km	r	$\frac{60 \text{ km}}{r}$
To town B	150 km	$2r$	$\frac{150 \text{ km}}{2r}$
Total			4.5 h

- Equation: $\frac{\mathbf{60}}{\boldsymbol{r}} + \frac{\mathbf{150}}{\mathbf{2}\boldsymbol{r}} = \mathbf{4.5}$ time to A + time to B = 4.5 h

- Solve for r: $\frac{60}{r} \cdot 2r + \frac{150}{2r} \cdot 2r = (4.5)(2r)$ Multiply by the LCD. $(2r)$

$120 + 150 = 9\,r$ Combine like terms.

$270 = 9\,r$ $r = 30$ km/h Divide by 9.

- Answer: To town A: $\boldsymbol{r} = \mathbf{30}$ **km/h** To town B: $2r = (2)(30) = 60$ km/h

Example: John **boats** at a **speed** of **30** km per hour in still water. The **river** flows at a **speed** of **10** km per hour. **How long** will it take John to boat **2 km downstream? 2 km upstream?**

Condition	Speed (r)	Distance (d)	Time $\left(t = \frac{d}{r}\right)$
Downstream	$r = 30 + 10 = 40$ km/h	$d = 2$ km	$\frac{2 \text{ km}}{40 \text{ km/h}}$
Upstream	$r = 30 - 10 = 20$ km /h	$d = 2$ km	$\frac{2 \text{ km}}{20 \text{ km/h}}$

Downstream (fast): speed of boat + speed of river
Upstream (slower): speed of boat – speed of river

Downstream: $t = \frac{d}{r} = \frac{2 \text{ km}}{40 \text{ km/h}} = \mathbf{0.05\ h}$

Upstream: $t = \frac{d}{r} = \frac{2 \text{ km}}{20 \text{ km/h}} = \mathbf{0.1\ h}$

Unit 6 Summary

- **Rational expression:** an expression that is a ratio or quotient of two polynomials.
- **Rational function:** a function that is a ratio or quotient of two polynomials.

Rational Function	Example
$f(x) = \frac{a(x)}{b(x)}$ ← polynomials, $b(x) \neq 0$	$f(x) = \frac{4x+3}{5x-7}$, $f(x) = \frac{3y^2-2y+4}{5y-6}$

- **Multiplying rational expressions:** $\frac{N_1}{D_1} \cdot \frac{N_2}{D_2} = \frac{N_1 N_2}{D_1 D_2}$ — $\frac{N_1}{D_1}$ *and* $\frac{N_2}{D_2}$ are rational expressions. $(D_1 D_2 \neq 0)$
- **Dividing rational expressions:** $\frac{N_1}{D_1} \div \frac{N_2}{D_2} = \frac{N_1}{D_1} \cdot \frac{D_2}{N_2}$ — $\frac{N_1}{D_1}$ *and* $\frac{N_2}{D_2}$ are rational expressions. $(D_1,\ D_2,\ N_2 \neq 0)$
- **Like rational expressions:** rational expressions that have the same denominator.
- **Unlike rational expressions:** rational expressions that have different denominators.
- **Adding or subtracting like rational expressions**

$$\frac{N_1}{D} + \frac{N_2}{D} = \frac{N_1 + N_2}{D} \ , \quad \frac{N_1}{D} - \frac{N_2}{D} = \frac{N_1 - N_2}{D}$$

$\frac{N_1}{D}$ *and* $\frac{N_2}{D}$ are rational expressions. $(D \neq 0)$

- **Find the LCD** — **Example**: Find LCD for $\frac{4}{8}$, $\frac{5}{16}$ and $\frac{2}{42}$

```
2 | 8  16  42
2 | 4   8  21   ←  8 ÷ 2 = 4, 16 ÷ 2 = 8, 42 ÷ 2 = 21
2 | 2   4  21   ←  4 ÷ 2 = 2, 8 ÷ 2 = 4, move down 21
    1   2  21   ←  2 ÷ 2 = 1, 4 ÷ 2 = 2, move down 21
```

LCD = $2^4 \times 21 =$ **336**

- **Adding or subtracting unlike rational expressions**
  - Determine the LCD.
  - Rewrite expressions with the LCD.
  - Combine the numerators.
  - Simplify if possible.
- **Complex rational expression:** a rational expression whose numerator or denominator (or both) contains rational expressions.

$$\frac{\frac{N_1}{D_1}}{\frac{N_2}{D_2}}$$

$\frac{N_1}{D_1}$ and $\frac{N_2}{D_2}$ are rational expressions, D_1, D_2 & $N_2 \neq 0$

- **Simplifying a complex rational expression — method I:** multiply by the LCD.
- **Simplifying a complex rational expression — method II:** multiply by the reciprocal of the denominator $(\div \rightarrow \times)$.

$$\frac{\frac{N_1}{D_1}}{\frac{N_2}{D_2}} = \frac{N_1}{D_1} \div \frac{N_2}{D_2} = \frac{N_1}{D_1} \cdot \frac{D_2}{N_2}$$

$\frac{N_1}{D_1}$ and $\frac{N_2}{D_2}$ are rational expressions.

- **Rational (fractional) equation:** an equation that contains rational expressions.
- **Polynomial long division** **Example:** $\frac{6x^2+9x+2}{3x}$

Steps	Solution	Dividing whole numbers
- Write in divisor$\overline{)\text{dividend}}$ form.	$3x\overline{)6x^2+9x+2}$	$3\overline{)692}$
- Divide the first term.	$\begin{array}{r} 2x \\ 3x\overline{)6x^2+9x+2} \\ -\ 6x^2 \end{array}$ $(3x)(2x)=6x^2$	$\begin{array}{r} 2 \\ 3\overline{)692} \\ -\ 6 \end{array}$ $3 = 6$
- Divide the second term.	$\begin{array}{r} \mathbf{2x+3} \\ 3x\overline{)6x^2+9x+2} \\ 6x^2 \\ \hline 9x \\ -\ 9x \\ \hline \mathbf{2} \end{array}$ Bring $9x$ down; $(3x)(3)=9x$; Remainder	$\begin{array}{r} 230 \\ 3\overline{)692} \\ 6 \\ \hline 9 \\ -\ 9 \\ \hline 2 \end{array}$ Bring 9 down; $3 \cdot 3 = 9$; Remainder

$$\text{Quotient} + \frac{\text{remainder}}{\text{divisor}}$$

$$\frac{6x^2+9x+2}{3x} = (2x+3) + \frac{2}{3x}$$

(quotient: $(2x+3)$; remainder: 2; divisor: $3x$)

$$692 \div 3 = 230 + \frac{2}{3}$$

- Check: Dividend = Quotient · Divisor + Remainder

$$\begin{array}{r} \text{Quotient} \\ \text{Divisor}\overline{)\text{Dividend}} \\ - \\ \hline \text{Remainder} \end{array}$$

- **Missing terms in long division:** If there is a missing consecutive power term in a polynomial, insert the missing power term with a coefficient of 0.
- **Solving a rational equation**
  - Find the least common denominator (LCD).
  - Multiply each term by the LCD.
  - Solve the variable.
  - Check.

- **Synthetic division:** a shortcut method of dividing a polynomial by a binomial of the form $(x - a)$, by using only the coefficients of the terms.

Steps

- Rewrite the polynomial in descending order. Insert a zero coefficient for the missing power.
- Set up the synthetic coefficients. $(a = 2)$
- Bring down the leading coefficient and multiply it by a in $(x - a)$. Place the product beneath the second coefficient.
- Add column 2.
- Repeat until the last column done.
  $2 \times 6 = 12$, $-2 + 12 = 10$
  $2 \times 10 = 20$, $4 + 20 = 24$
  $2 \times 24 = 48$, $-40 + 48 = 8$
- Write out the answer.

Quotient + $\frac{\text{remainder}}{\text{divisor}}$

Example

$(x - a)$

$(3x^4 - 40 + 4x - 2x^2) \div (x - 2)$

$x - 2 \overline{)\, 3x^4 + 0x^3 - 2x^2 + 4x - 40}$

Missing power

a in the divisor — The coefficient of the dividend

2	3	0	-2	4	-40

2	3	0	-2	4	-40
	3	6			

2×3

2	3	0	-2	4	-40
		6 +			
	3	**6** (0 + 6)			

2	3	0	-2	4	-40
		6	12 +	20 +	48 +
	3	6	**10**	**24**	**8**
	x^3	x^2	x	constant	remainder

Answer: $(3x^3 + 6x^2 + 10x + 24) + \frac{8}{x-2}$

One less than the degree of the dividend.

- **The formula for "work" problems that involve two people**

$$\frac{1}{t_A} + \frac{1}{t_B} = \frac{1}{t}$$

Time:
- t_A – time required when person A works alone
- t_B – time required when person B works alone
- t – time required when two people work together

Rate:
- $1/t_A$ – person A can finish 1 job every t_A hours
- $1/t_B$ – person B can finish 1 job every t_B hours

- **Ratio, rate and proportion**

	Representation		Example
Ratio	a to b or $a{:}b$ or $\frac{a}{b}$	with the same unit.	5 to 9 or 5:9 or $\frac{5\text{ m}}{9\text{ m}}$
Rate	a to b or $a{:}b$ or $\frac{a}{b}$	with different units.	3 to 7 or 3:7 or $\frac{3\text{ cm}}{7\text{ m}}$
Proportion	$\frac{a}{b} = \frac{c}{d}$	an equation with a ratio on each side.	$\frac{3\text{ cm}}{7\ m} = \frac{1\text{ cm}}{5\text{ m}}$

- **Motion formulas**

distance = speed · time $\quad d = r\,t \quad t = \frac{d}{r} \quad r = \frac{d}{t}$

PRACTICE QUIZ

Unit 6 Rational Expressions

1. Reduce to lowest terms.

a. $\frac{2x^2-8x}{24x}$

b. $\frac{b(b+1)(3b-7)}{3b^2-4b-7}$

2. Perform the indicated operations and simplify.

a. $\frac{x^2-4x-5}{x-3} \cdot \frac{x^2-9}{x-5}$

b. $\frac{y^2-1}{2} \div \frac{y+1}{3}$

c. $\frac{5}{x} - \frac{3}{-x}$

3. Find the LCD for the following.

$\frac{3x}{4x^2}$, $\frac{7}{12x^2y}$ and $\frac{3xy}{2x^4y^2}$

4. Perform the indicated operations and simplify.

$\frac{2b}{b-2} - \frac{1}{b+2} + \frac{3}{b^2-4}$

5. Simplify: $\frac{27y^2-9y-36}{3y}$

6. Divide using long division.

a. $6y^2 - 3y + 4$ by $3y$

b. $x^3 + 2x^2 + 3$ by $x - 1$

7. Use synthetic division to divide.

$2x^3 - 3x^2 + 5x - 7$ by $x - 2$

8. Simplify the following.

a. $\dfrac{\frac{1}{x}+5}{\frac{1}{x}+x}$

b. $\dfrac{\frac{2}{y+3}-\frac{1}{y-2}}{3y}$

9. Solve the following.

a. $\frac{2}{y}-\frac{3}{4y}=7$

b. $\frac{3-x}{x+4}=3-\frac{1}{x+4}$

10. It takes Tim 4 hours to clean a house and it takes 3 hours for Amanda to do the same job. How long will it take for both of them to clean the house together?

11. Watermelon is on sale at 2 for $7; how much will it cost for 12 watermelons?

12. Evan walked the 20km to location B twice as fast as he did the 15 km to location A. If the total trip took 5 hours, then how fast was he walking to location A?

UNIT 7 RADICALS

7-1 ROOTS AND RADICALS

Square Roots

- **Square root ($\sqrt{\ }$):** a number with the symbol $\sqrt{\ }$ that is the opposite of the square of a number, such as $\sqrt{4} = 2$ and $2^2 = 4$, respectively.

Square (2^2) →
2 4
← Square root ($\sqrt{4}$)

- **Perfect square:** a number that is the exact square of a whole number.

Examples

Square Root	Perfect Square
$\sqrt{64} = 8$	$8^2 = 64$
$-\sqrt{121} = -11$	$-(11)^2 = -121$
$\sqrt{\frac{4}{9}} = \frac{\sqrt{4}}{\sqrt{9}} = \frac{2}{3}$	$2^2 = 4$ $3^2 = 9$
$\sqrt{0.16} = 0.4$	$0.4^2 = 0.16$
$\sqrt{0} = 0$	$0^2 = 0$

- **Using a calculator**: $\sqrt{25} = ?$ [2nd F] [$\sqrt{\ }$] 25 [=] (The display reads 5.)

  Or [2nd F] 25 [$\sqrt{\ }$] [=] for some calculators.

- **Each positive number has two square roots**, one positive and one negative.

Example: $\sqrt{4} = 2$ and $\sqrt{4} = -2$ or $\sqrt{4} = \pm 2$

$\because$ $2^2 = 4$ and $(-2)^2 = 4$, so 2 and -2 are both square roots of 4.

Square Roots	Example
If $x^2 = A$, Then $\begin{cases} x = \sqrt{A} & \text{The principal square root (positive root)} \\ x = -\sqrt{A} & \text{Negative root} \end{cases}$ This can be written as $x = \pm\sqrt{A}$. ($A \geq 0$)	If $x^2 = 9$, Then $\begin{cases} x = \sqrt{9} = 3 \\ x = -\sqrt{9} = -3 \end{cases}$ This can be written as $x = \pm\sqrt{9} = \pm 3$.

Note: All **even** indexed radicals have 2 possible answers – positive and negative roots.

Square Root Functions

- **Square root function:** $f(x) = \sqrt{x}$

Example: Given the function $f(x) = \sqrt{2x+5}$,

1. Determine the function values $f(2)$, $f(0)$, and $f(-3)$.

$f(2) = \sqrt{2 \cdot 2 + 5} = \sqrt{9} = \mathbf{3}$ — Replace x with 2.

$f(0) = \sqrt{2 \cdot 0 + 5} = \sqrt{\mathbf{5}}$ — Replace x with 0.

$f(-3) = \sqrt{2(-3) + 5} = \sqrt{\mathbf{-1}}$ It is not a real number. — Replace x with -3.

2. Identify the **domain** of the function $f(x) = \sqrt{2x+5}$.

$2x + 5 \geq 0$

$2x \geq -5$ — Subtract 5.

$x \geq -\frac{5}{2}$ — Divide by 2.

Domain $= \{x \mid x \geq -\frac{5}{2}\} = \left[-\frac{5}{2}, \infty\right)$

Review: The domain is the set of x-values for which a function is defined.

- **Graphing square root function**

Example: Graph $f(x) = -\sqrt{2x}$.

x	$y = -\sqrt{2x}$	(x, y)
0	$-\sqrt{2 \cdot 0} = 0$	(0, 0)
2	$-\sqrt{2 \cdot 2} = -2$	(2, -2)
8	$-\sqrt{2 \cdot 8} = -\sqrt{16} = -4$	(8, -4)

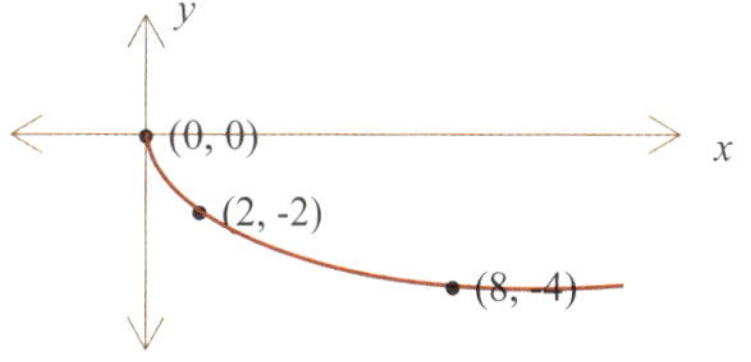

- **Finding $\sqrt{x^2}$:** $\sqrt{x^2} = |x|$ — x is any real number

Use the absolute value sign to ensure that the positive root is non-negative (x^2 never represents a negative number).

Example:

1. $2\sqrt{9} = 2\sqrt{3^2} = 2 \cdot 3 = \mathbf{6}$
2. $2\sqrt{(-3)^2} = 2 \cdot 3 = \mathbf{6}$
3. $\sqrt{0^2} = \mathbf{0}$
4. $\sqrt{(-17x)^2} = \sqrt{(-17)^2 x^2} = \sqrt{(-17)^2}\,\sqrt{x^2} = \mathbf{17|x|}$ — Split -17 and x.
5. $\sqrt{a^2 - 4a + 4} = \sqrt{(a-2)^2} = |a - 2|$ — Factor, $\sqrt{x^2} = |x|$

$a \quad -2$

$a \quad -2$

Radical

- **A radical (root)** is an expression that uses a root, such as square root, cube root, etc.

  The "radical" comes from the Latin word "radic", meaning "root."

Examples

$\sqrt{2x+3}$, $\sqrt[3]{5a}$, $\sqrt[7]{\frac{2w-3}{4t}}$

- **Radical notation for the *n*th root** $\sqrt[n]{\ }$

$\sqrt[n]{a}$ $\begin{cases} \sqrt{\ } & \text{– the radical sign} \\ a & \text{– the radicand (a real number)} \\ n & \text{– the index (a positive integer > 1)} \end{cases}$

$\sqrt[n]{a}$ – radical or radical expression

Example

1. $\sqrt[3]{5a}$ $\begin{cases} 5a \text{ – radicand} \\ 3 \text{ – index} \end{cases}$

2. $\sqrt[7]{\frac{2w-3}{4t}}$ $\begin{cases} \frac{2w-3}{4t} \text{ – radicand} \\ 7 \text{ – index} \end{cases}$

- **Rational (fractional) exponent notation** $a^{\frac{1}{n}}$

A fractional power or a number is raised to a fraction.

Example

$7^{\frac{1}{3}}$

- Rational exponent and radical are both used to indicate the *n*th root.

*n*th Root	Example
Radical notation → $\sqrt[n]{a} = a^{\frac{1}{n}}$ ← Rational exponent notation	$\sqrt[3]{7} = 7^{\frac{1}{3}}$
Note: if $n = 2$, write $\sqrt{a}$ rather than $\sqrt[2]{a}$	Omit 2 in $\sqrt[2]{5}$, write $\sqrt{5}$

- ***n*th root to the *n*th power**

$\sqrt[n]{a}^{\,n} = a$ $\quad \because \sqrt[n]{a}^{\,n} = (a^n)^{\frac{1}{n}} = a^{\frac{n}{n}} = a^1 = a$ $\quad$ **Note:** $\sqrt[n]{a}^{\,n} = \sqrt[n]{a^n}$

Example

$\sqrt{7}^{\,2} = (7^2)^{\frac{1}{2}} = 7^{\frac{2}{2}} = 7^1 = 7$

- **The cube root**

$\sqrt[3]{a} = b$ means $a = b^3$

$\because$ *if* $\sqrt[3]{a}^{\,3} = b^3$, then $a = b^3$

Example

$\sqrt[3]{8} = 2$ means $8 = 2^3$

$\because$ if $\sqrt[3]{8}^{\,3} = 2^3$, then $8 = 2^3$

Example: Find each root.

1. $\sqrt[3]{64} = \sqrt[3]{4^3} = \mathbf{4}$ $\qquad \sqrt[n]{a^n} = a$; [2nd F] [$\sqrt[3]{\ }$] 64 [=] → 4

2. $\sqrt[3]{0.027(a+3)^3} = \sqrt[3]{(0.3)^3(a+3)^3}$ $\qquad 0.3^3 = 0.027$; [2nd F] [$\sqrt[3]{\ }$] .027 [=] → 0.3

   $= \sqrt[3]{(0.3)^3}\ \sqrt[3]{(a+3)^3}$ $\qquad \sqrt[n]{a^n} = a$

   $= \mathbf{0.3\,(a+3)}$

- ***n*th root**

$\sqrt[n]{a} = b$ means $a = b^n$

$\because$ *if* $\sqrt[n]{a}^{\,n} = b^n$, then $a = b^n$

Example

$\sqrt[4]{16} = 2$ means $16 = 2^4$

$\because$ if $\sqrt[4]{16}^{\,4} = 2^4$, then $16 = 2^4$

Odd and Even Roots

- **If the index n is an *even* natural number:** $\sqrt[n]{a^n} = |a|$
- **If the index n is an *odd* natural number:** $\sqrt[n]{a^n} = a$

Natural numbers: 1, 2, 3, …

Example

$\sqrt[4]{-3^4} = |-3| = 3$

$\sqrt[5]{6^5} = 6$ $a = 6$

$\sqrt[5]{-6^5} = -6$ $a = -6$

$\sqrt[5]{0^5} = 0$ $a = 0$

Example: Find each root.

1. $\sqrt{(-2)^2} = \sqrt[2]{(-2)^2} = |-2| = \mathbf{2}$ — $n = 2$ is even ; $\sqrt[n]{a^n} = |a|$
2. $\sqrt[8]{(3y)^8} = \mathbf{3|y|}$ — Use an | | when a variable is involved.
3. $\sqrt[5]{-32} = \sqrt[5]{-2^5} = \mathbf{-2}$ — Rewrite 32 as a perfect 5th power. 2^5; $n = 5$ is odd; $a = -2$; $\sqrt[n]{a^n} = a$
4. $\sqrt[177]{(9a-4)^{177}} = \mathbf{9a - 4}$ — $n = 177$ is odd ; $\sqrt[n]{a^n} = a$
5. $\sqrt[11]{-1} = \sqrt[11]{(-1)^{11}} = \mathbf{-1}$ — $n = 11$ is odd; $\sqrt[n]{a^n} = a$; $1^n = 1$
6. $\sqrt[4]{\frac{1}{16}} = \sqrt[4]{\frac{1}{2^4}} = \frac{\sqrt[4]{1}}{\sqrt[4]{2^4}} = \mathbf{\frac{1}{2}}$ — $2^4 = 16$; $\sqrt[n]{\frac{a}{b}} = \frac{\sqrt[n]{a}}{\sqrt[n]{b}}$
7. $\sqrt[5]{243t^5} = \sqrt[5]{3^5 t^5} = \sqrt[5]{3^5}\sqrt[5]{t^5} = \mathbf{3t}$ — $3^5 = 243$; $\sqrt[n]{ab} = \sqrt[n]{a}\sqrt[n]{b}$; $\sqrt[n]{a^n} = a$

5 [2nd F] [$\sqrt[x]{\ }$] 243 [=] → 3

or 5 [MATH] [5] 243 [Enter] → 3 (T1-83 Plus)

- **Find the function values**

Example: Given the function $f(x) = -\sqrt[3]{4y+1}$, determine the function values $f(0)$ and $f(31)$.

$f(0) = -\sqrt[3]{4 \cdot 0 + 1} = -\sqrt[3]{1} = \mathbf{-1}$ — Replace y with 0.

$f(31) = -\sqrt[3]{4 \cdot 31 + 1}$ — Replace y with 31.

$= -\sqrt[3]{125} = -\sqrt[3]{5^3} = \mathbf{-5}$ — $\sqrt[n]{a^n} = a$; 3 [2nd F] [$\sqrt[x]{\ }$] 125 [=] → 5

or [MATH] [4] 125 [Enter] → 5 (T1-83 Plus)

7-2 RATIONAL EXPONENTS

Powers of Roots

- **Review:** $\sqrt[n]{a}$ — $\sqrt{\ }$ – the radical sign; a – the radicand; n – the index
  - Rational exponent notation: $a^{\frac{1}{n}}$
  - Radical notation: $\sqrt[n]{\ }$

- **The index of a radical**

Index n	Read	Example	Read
$a^{\frac{1}{2}} = \sqrt{a}$	the square root of a	$3^{\frac{1}{2}} = \sqrt{3}$	the square root of 3
$a^{\frac{1}{3}} = \sqrt[3]{a}$	the cube root of a	$5^{\frac{1}{3}} = \sqrt[3]{5}$	the cube root of 5
$a^{\frac{1}{4}} = \sqrt[4]{a}$	the fourth root of a	$7^{\frac{1}{4}} = \sqrt[4]{7}$	the fourth root of 7
$a^{\frac{1}{n}} = \sqrt[n]{a}$	the nth root of a	$2^{\frac{1}{11}} = \sqrt[11]{2}$	the 11th root of 2
$a^{\frac{m}{n}} = \sqrt[n]{a}^{\,m}$	the nth root of a to the mth power	$7^{\frac{5}{6}} = \sqrt[6]{7}^{\,5}$	the 6th root of 7 to the 5th power

rational exponent notation ($a^{\frac{m}{n}}$) — radical notation ($\sqrt[n]{a}^{\,m}$)

- **Powers of roots**

The nth Root to the mth Power	Example
$a^{\frac{m}{n}} = (\sqrt[n]{a})^m = \sqrt[n]{a}^{\,m} = \sqrt[n]{a^m}$ m – power	$7^{\frac{2}{3}} = (\sqrt[3]{7})^2 = \sqrt[3]{7}^{\,2} = \sqrt[3]{7^2}$

Example: Rewrite **without** rational exponents.

1. $(81)^{\frac{1}{4}} = \sqrt[4]{81} = \sqrt[4]{3^4} = \mathbf{3}$ Rewrite 81 as 3^4; $\sqrt[n]{a}^{\,n} = a$

2. $(x^2y^3)^{\frac{1}{7}} = \sqrt[7]{\mathbf{x^2y^3}}$ $a^{\frac{1}{n}} = \sqrt[n]{a}$

3. $(8)^{\frac{2}{3}} = \sqrt[3]{8^2} = (\sqrt[3]{8})^2 = (\sqrt[3]{2^3})^2 = 2^2 = \mathbf{4}$ $a^{\frac{m}{n}} = \sqrt[n]{a}^{\,m} = (\sqrt[n]{a})^m$; $\sqrt[n]{a}^{\,n} = a$; Rewrite 8 as 2^3

Example: Rewrite the radicals using rational exponents.

1. $(\sqrt[9]{3a^4b^5})^7 = \mathbf{(3a^4b^5)^{\frac{7}{9}}}$ $(\sqrt[n]{a})^m = a^{\frac{m}{n}}$

2. $(\sqrt{5p^5q})^3 = \mathbf{(5p^5q)^{\frac{3}{2}}}$ $n = 2$: $(\sqrt{5p^5q})^3$; $(\sqrt[n]{a})^m = a^{\frac{m}{n}}$

3. $\sqrt[3]{2t} = \mathbf{(2t)^{\frac{1}{3}}}$ $\sqrt[n]{a} = a^{\frac{1}{n}}$

4. $\dfrac{2w}{\sqrt[5]{7t}} = \mathbf{\dfrac{2w}{(7t)^{1/5}}}$ $\sqrt[n]{a} = a^{\frac{1}{n}}$

Exponents & Rules

- **Exponents: review of basic rules**

Name	Rule	Example
zero exponent a^0	$a^0 = 1$ ($a \neq 0$, 0^0 is undefined)	$(15)^0 = 1$
one exponent a^1	$a^1 = a$ (But $1^n = 1$)	$7^1 = 7$, $1^{13} = 1$
negative exponent a^{-n}	$a^{-n} = \frac{1}{a^n}$	$5^{-2} = \frac{1}{5^2} = \frac{1}{25}$
	$\frac{1}{a^{-n}} = a^n$	$\frac{1}{6^{-2}} = 6^2 = 36$
	$\left(\frac{a}{b}\right)^{-n} = \left(\frac{b}{a}\right)^n$	$\left(\frac{4}{5}\right)^{-3} = \left(\frac{5}{4}\right)^3$

Example: Express each of the following in positive exponential form.

1. $(-0.1356)^0 = \mathbf{1}$ — $a^0 = 1$
2. $64^{-1/3} = \frac{1}{64^{1/3}} = \frac{1}{\sqrt[3]{64}} = \frac{1}{\sqrt[3]{4^3}} = \mathbf{\frac{1}{4}}$ — $a^{-n} = \frac{1}{a^n}$, $a^{\frac{1}{n}} = \sqrt[n]{a}$, $\sqrt[n]{a}^n = a$
3. $-5p^{-3/4}\, q^{2/5}\, r^{-1/2} = \mathbf{\frac{-5\, q^{2/5}}{p^{3/4}\, r^{1/2}}}$ — $a^{-n} = \frac{1}{a^n}$
4. $\left(\frac{4cd}{3ab}\right)^{-4/7} = \mathbf{\left(\frac{3ab}{4cd}\right)^{4/7}}$ — $\left(\frac{a}{b}\right)^{-n} = \left(\frac{b}{a}\right)^n$

- **Exponent rules review**

Name	Rule	
product of like bases	$a^m a^n = a^{m+n}$	
quotient of like bases	$\frac{a^m}{a^n} = a^{m-n}$	
power of a power	$(a^m)^n = a^{m\,n}$	
power of a product	$(a \cdot b)^n = a^n b^n$	$(a^m \cdot b^n)^p = a^{mp} b^{np}$
power of a quotient	$\left(\frac{a}{b}\right)^n = \frac{a^n}{b^n}$	$\left(\frac{a^m}{b^n}\right)^p = \frac{a^{mp}}{b^{np}}$

Example: Express each of the following in positive exponential form.

1. $\mathbf{10^{1/2}\, 10^{-2/3}} = 10^{1/2-2/3} = 10^{3/6-4/6} = 10^{-1/6} = \mathbf{\frac{1}{10^{1/6}}}$ — $a^m a^n = a^{m+n}$, $a^{-n} = \frac{1}{a^n}$
2. $\mathbf{\frac{w^{5/7}}{w^{2/7}}} = w^{5/7-2/7} = \mathbf{w^{3/7}}$ — $\frac{a^m}{a^n} = a^{m-n}$
3. $\mathbf{(y^{-2/3})^{4/5}} = y^{(-2/3)(4/5)} = y^{-8/15} = \mathbf{\frac{1}{y^{8/15}}}$ — $(a^n)^m = a^{n\,m}$, $a^{-n} = \frac{1}{a^n}$
4. $\mathbf{(u \cdot v)^{3/5}} = \mathbf{u^{3/5}\, v^{3/5}}$ — $(a \cdot b)^n = a^n b^n$
5. $\mathbf{(a^2 \cdot b^{-3})^{2/5}} = a^{2\cdot(2/5)} \cdot b^{-3\cdot(2/5)} = a^{4/5} \cdot b^{-6/5} = \mathbf{\frac{a^{4/5}}{b^{6/5}}}$ — $(a^m \cdot b^n)^p = a^{mp} b^{np}$, $a^{-n} = \frac{1}{a^n}$
6. $\left(\frac{x}{y}\right)^{-3} = \left(\frac{y}{x}\right)^3 = \mathbf{\frac{y^3}{x^3}}$ — $\left(\frac{a}{b}\right)^{-n} = \left(\frac{b}{a}\right)^n$, $\left(\frac{a}{b}\right)^n = \frac{a^n}{b^n}$
7. $\left(\frac{t^5}{u^{-2}}\right)^2 = \frac{t^{5\cdot 2}}{u^{(-2)(2)}} = \frac{t^{10}}{u^{-4}} = \mathbf{t^{10}u^4}$ — $\left(\frac{a^m}{b^n}\right)^p = \frac{a^{mp}}{b^{np}}$, $\frac{1}{a^{-n}} = a^n$

Simplifying Radical Expressions

Example

- **A radical expression** is an algebraic expression containing a radical sign $\sqrt[n]{}$. — $\sqrt[3]{7xy^2}$
- **Simplifying radical expressions**

Example: Express in simplest radical form.

1. $\sqrt[10]{x^2} = (x)^{\frac{2}{10}} = x^{\frac{1}{5}} = \sqrt[5]{x}$ — $\sqrt[n]{a^m} = a^{\frac{m}{n}}$

2. $\sqrt[5]{32x^{10}y^2} = (2^5 x^{10} y^2)^{\frac{1}{5}}$ — $\sqrt[n]{a} = a^{\frac{1}{n}}$

   $= 2^{5\cdot\frac{1}{5}} x^{10\cdot\frac{1}{5}} y^{2\cdot\frac{1}{5}} = 2x^2\sqrt[5]{y^2}$ — $(a^m \cdot b^n)^p = a^{mp} b^{np}$, $a^{\frac{1}{n}} = \sqrt[n]{a}$

3. $\sqrt[4]{3a}\sqrt{2a} = (3a)^{\frac{1}{4}}(2a)^{\frac{1}{2}} = (3a)^{\frac{1}{4}}(2a)^{\frac{2}{4}}$ — $\sqrt[n]{a} = a^{\frac{1}{n}}$, $LCD = 4$

   $= [(3a)^1(2a)^2]^{\frac{1}{4}} = \sqrt[4]{(3a)(2a)^2}$ — $a^{mp} b^{np} = (a^m \cdot b^n)^p$, $\sqrt[n]{a^m} = a^{\frac{m}{n}}$

   $= \sqrt[4]{12a^3}$ — $a^m a^n = a^{m+n}$

4. $\sqrt[6]{\sqrt[3]{a}} = \sqrt[6]{a^{\frac{1}{3}}} = (a^{\frac{1}{3}})^{\frac{1}{6}}$ — $\sqrt[n]{a} = a^{\frac{1}{n}}$

   $= a^{\frac{1}{3}\cdot\frac{1}{6}} = a^{\frac{1}{18}} = \sqrt[18]{a}$ — $(a^n)^m = a^{nm}$, $a^{\frac{1}{n}} = \sqrt[n]{a}$

5. $\dfrac{3y^{\frac{1}{2}}}{4y^{\frac{2}{3}}} = \dfrac{3}{4}y^{\frac{1}{2}-\frac{2}{3}} = \dfrac{3}{4}y^{\frac{3}{6}-\frac{4}{6}}$ — $\dfrac{a^m}{a^n} = a^{m-n}$, $LCD = 6$

   $= \dfrac{3}{4}y^{\frac{-1}{6}} = \dfrac{3}{4y^{\frac{1}{6}}} = \dfrac{3}{4\sqrt[6]{y}}$ — $a^{-n} = \dfrac{1}{a^n}$, $a^{\frac{1}{n}} = \sqrt[n]{a^n}$

6. $x^{\frac{3}{4}} y^{\frac{4}{3}} z^{\frac{1}{2}} = x^{\frac{9}{12}} y^{\frac{16}{12}} z^{\frac{6}{12}}$ — $LCD = 12$

   $= (x^9 y^{16} z^6)^{\frac{1}{12}} = \sqrt[12]{x^9y^{16}z^6}$ — $a^{nm} = (a^n)^m$, $a^{\frac{1}{n}} = \sqrt[n]{a}$

7. $2\left(\dfrac{a^{1/3}b^{1/3}}{c^{1/6}d^{1/6}}\right)^2 = \dfrac{(a^{1/3})^2(b^{1/3})^2}{(c^{1/6}d^{1/6})^2} = \dfrac{(a^{2/3})(b^{2/3})}{c^{2/6}d^{2/6}}$ — $\left(\dfrac{a^m}{b^n}\right)^p = \dfrac{a^{mp}}{b^{np}}$

   $= \dfrac{(a^{2/3})(b^{2/3})}{(c^{1/3})(d^{1/3})} = \left(\dfrac{(a^2)(b^2)}{(c^1)(d^1)}\right)^{\frac{1}{3}}$ — $a^{mp} b^{np} = (a^m \cdot b^n)^p$

   $= \sqrt[3]{\dfrac{a^2b^2}{cd}}$ — $a^{\frac{1}{n}} = \sqrt[n]{a}$

7-3 SIMPLIFY RADICALS USING PRODUCT & QUOTIENT RULES

Product and Quotient Rules

- **Product and quotient rule for radicals**

Name	Rule	Example
product rule	$\sqrt[n]{ab} = \sqrt[n]{a} \cdot \sqrt[n]{b}$ $a \geq 0$, $b \geq 0$	$\sqrt{12} = \sqrt{4 \cdot 3} = \sqrt{4}\sqrt{3} = \sqrt{2^2}\sqrt{3} = 2\sqrt{3}$
quotient rule	$\sqrt[n]{\frac{a}{b}} = \frac{\sqrt[n]{a}}{\sqrt[n]{b}}$ $a \geq 0$, $b > 0$, $b \neq 0$	$\sqrt[3]{\frac{8}{27}} = \frac{\sqrt[3]{8}}{\sqrt[3]{27}} = \frac{\sqrt[3]{2^3}}{\sqrt[3]{3^3}} = \frac{2}{3}$

Read $\sqrt[n]{ab} = \sqrt[n]{a}\sqrt[n]{b}$: The nth root of the product of a and b is the product of the nth root of a and the nth root of b.

$\sqrt[n]{\frac{a}{b}} = \frac{\sqrt[n]{a}}{\sqrt[n]{b}}$: The nth root of $\frac{a}{b}$ is the nth root of a over the nth root of b.

- **Simplifying radical expressions:** a radical expression is in simplest form if it satisfies the following conditions.

A radical expression is in simplest form when:	Simplest Form	Not Simplest Form
The exponent (m) of the radical is less than the index (n). $m < n$ $\sqrt[n]{a}^m$	$\sqrt[5]{x^3}$ or $\sqrt[5]{a}^3$ $3 < 5$	$\sqrt[7]{x^8}$ $8 > 7$
No fractions appear within a radical sign.	$\sqrt[3]{2y}$	$\sqrt[4]{\frac{2}{3xy}}$
No radicals appear in the denominator of a fraction.	$\frac{\sqrt{3}}{5}$	$\frac{\sqrt{3}}{\sqrt{8}}$

- **Tips:** To use the product and quotient rule for radicals, factor out any perfect square, perfect cube, and perfect 4th power, perfect 5th power, etc.
  - Perfect square: a number that is the exact square of a whole number.
  - Perfect cube: a number that is the exact cube of a whole number.
  - Perfect nth power: a number that is the exact nth power of a whole number.

Examples

Perfect Square	Perfect Cube	Perfect 4th Power	Perfect 5th Power	… …
$2^2 = 4$	$2^3 = 8$	$2^4 = 16$	$2^5 = 32$	
$3^2 = 9$	$3^3 = 27$	$3^4 = 81$	$3^5 = 243$	
$4^2 = 16$	$4^3 = 64$	$4^4 = 256$	$4^5 = 1024$	
$5^2 = 25$	$5^3 = 125$	$5^4 = 625$	$5^5 = 3125$	
$6^2 = 36$	$6^3 = 216$	$6^4 = 1296$	$6^5 = 7776$	
$7^2 = 49$	$7^3 = 343$	$7^4 = 2401$	$7^5 = 16807$	
$8^2 = 64$	$8^3 = 512$	$8^4 = 4096$	$8^5 = 32768$	
… …	… …	… …	… …	

2 [y^x] 5 [=] → 32

or 2 [^] 5 [Enter] → 32

Simplifying Radicals

Example: Simplify.

1. $\sqrt{18x^3} = \sqrt{2 \cdot 9\,x^2 \cdot x}$ — Factor out a perfect square: $9 = 3^2$

$= \sqrt{(3x)^2}\,\sqrt{2x} = 3|x|\sqrt{2x}$ — $\sqrt[n]{ab} = \sqrt[n]{a}\,\sqrt[n]{b}$; $\sqrt[n]{a^n} = a$

2. $\sqrt[3]{40} = \sqrt[3]{5 \cdot 8} = \sqrt[3]{5 \cdot 2^3}$ — Factor out a perfect cube: $8 = 2^3$

$= \sqrt[3]{5}\,\sqrt[3]{2^3} = 2\sqrt[3]{5}$ — $\sqrt[n]{ab} = \sqrt[n]{a}\,\sqrt[n]{b}$; $\sqrt[n]{a^n} = a$

3. $\sqrt[3]{24x^5y} = \sqrt[3]{3 \cdot 8x^3x^2y} = \sqrt[3]{3x^2y}\,\sqrt[3]{8x^3}$ — $\sqrt[n]{ab} = \sqrt[n]{a}\,\sqrt[n]{b}$; regroup

$= \sqrt[3]{3x^2y}\,\sqrt[3]{(2x)^3} = 2x\sqrt[3]{3x^2y}$ — $8 = 2^3$; $\sqrt[n]{a^n} = a$

4. $\sqrt[4]{x^2}\,\sqrt[4]{16x^6} = \sqrt[4]{x^2 \cdot 16x^6}$ — $\sqrt[n]{a}\,\sqrt[n]{b} = \sqrt[n]{ab}$; $a^m a^n = a^{m+n}$

$= \sqrt[4]{2^4 \cdot x^8}$ — Rewrite 16 as a perfect 4th power: $16 = 2^4$

$= \sqrt[4]{2^4}\,\sqrt[4]{x^8} = 2\,\sqrt[4]{x^8}$ — $\sqrt[n]{ab} = \sqrt[n]{a}\,\sqrt[n]{b}$; $\sqrt[n]{a^n} = a$

$= 2\,x^{\frac{8}{4}} = 2x^2$ — $\sqrt[n]{a^m} = a^{\frac{m}{n}}$

5. $\sqrt{\frac{9}{49}} = \frac{\sqrt{9}}{\sqrt{49}} = \frac{\sqrt{3^2}}{\sqrt{7^2}} = \frac{3}{7}$ — $\sqrt[n]{\frac{a}{b}} = \frac{\sqrt[n]{a}}{\sqrt[n]{b}}$; $\sqrt[n]{a^n} = a$

6. $\sqrt[5]{\frac{32}{243}} = \frac{\sqrt[5]{32}}{\sqrt[5]{243}} = \frac{\sqrt[5]{2^5}}{\sqrt[5]{3^5}} = \frac{2}{3}$ — $\sqrt[n]{\frac{a}{b}} = \frac{\sqrt[n]{a}}{\sqrt[n]{b}}$; $2^5 = 32$; $3^5 = 243$

5 [2nd F] [$\sqrt[x]{\ }$] 243 [=] → 3

7. $\sqrt{\frac{54a^8}{6a^4}} = \sqrt{\frac{9a^8}{a^4}} = \sqrt{3^2a^4}$ — $\frac{a^m}{a^n} = a^{m-n}$

$= \sqrt{3^2(a^2)^2} = \sqrt{3^2}\cdot\sqrt{(a^2)^2} = 3a^2$ — $\sqrt[n]{ab} = \sqrt[n]{a}\,\sqrt[n]{b}$; $\sqrt[n]{a^n} = a$

8. $\frac{\sqrt[3]{81a^5b^8}}{\sqrt[3]{3a^2b^2}} = \sqrt[3]{\frac{81a^5b^8}{3a^2b^2}} = \sqrt[3]{27a^3b^6} = \sqrt[3]{3^3a^3b^6}$ — $\frac{\sqrt[n]{a}}{\sqrt[n]{b}} = \sqrt[n]{\frac{a}{b}}$; $\frac{a^m}{a^n} = a^{m-n}$

$= \sqrt[3]{3^3}\,\sqrt[3]{a^3}\,\sqrt[3]{b^6} = 3\,a\,b^{\frac{6}{3}} = 3ab^2$ — $\sqrt[n]{ab} = \sqrt[n]{a}\,\sqrt[n]{b}$; $\sqrt[n]{a^n} = a$; $\sqrt[n]{a^m} = a^{\frac{m}{n}}$

9. $\frac{\sqrt[5]{a^2b^4}}{\sqrt[3]{ab}} = \frac{(a^2b^4)^{\frac{1}{5}}}{(ab)^{\frac{1}{3}}} = \frac{a^{\frac{2}{5}}\,b^{\frac{4}{5}}}{a^{\frac{1}{3}}\,b^{\frac{1}{3}}}$ — $\sqrt[n]{a} = a^{\frac{1}{n}}$; $(a^m \cdot b^n)^p = a^{mp}\,b^{np}$

$= \left(a^{\frac{2}{5}-\frac{1}{3}}\right)\left(b^{\frac{4}{5}-\frac{1}{3}}\right) = \left(a^{\frac{6}{15}-\frac{5}{15}}\right)\left(b^{\frac{12}{15}-\frac{5}{15}}\right)$ — $\frac{a^m}{a^n} = a^{m-n}$; LCD = 15

$= a^{\frac{1}{15}}\,b^{\frac{7}{15}} = (a^1\,b^7)^{\frac{1}{15}} = \sqrt[15]{ab^7}$ — $a^{\frac{1}{n}} = \sqrt[n]{a}$

7-4 OPERATIONS WITH RADICALS

Adding and Subtracting Radicals

- **Add and subtract radical expressions** by combining the like radicals (or like terms).
- **Like radicals** are radicals with exactly the same index (n) and radicand (a). $\sqrt[n]{a}$

Example

Like Radicals	$4\sqrt[3]{5a}$ and $-6\sqrt[3]{5a}$	The same index (3) and radicand ($5a$)
Unlike Radicals	$7x\sqrt[3]{6x}$ and $5x\sqrt[7]{6x}$	The same radicand but different index (3 and 7)

Tips:
- Combine expressions: $7ab - 2ab + 3ab = ab\,(7 - 2 + 3) = 8ab$
- Combine radicals: $7\sqrt{ab} - 2\sqrt{ab} + 3\sqrt{ab} = \sqrt{ab}\,(7 - 2 + 3) = 8\sqrt{ab}$

Example: Perform the indicated operations and simplify.

1. $5\sqrt{3} + 4\sqrt{3} - 2\sqrt{3} = \sqrt{3}\,(5 + 4 - 2) = 7\sqrt{3}$ Factor out $\sqrt{3}$.

2. $3\sqrt{256} + \sqrt{64} = 3\sqrt{64 \cdot 4} + \sqrt{64}$ Rewrite: $256 = 64 \cdot 4$

 $= 3\sqrt{64}\sqrt{4} + \sqrt{64}$ $\sqrt[n]{ab} - \sqrt[n]{a}\sqrt[n]{b}$

 $= \sqrt{64}\,(3\sqrt{4} + 1)$ Factor out $\sqrt{64}$.

 $= \sqrt{8^2}\,(3 \cdot 2 + 1) = 8 \cdot 7 = 56$ $\sqrt[n]{a^n} = a$

3. $9\sqrt{35x^3} - 2\sqrt{7x^3} = 9\sqrt{5 \cdot 7x^3} - 2\sqrt{7x^3}$ Rewrite: $35 = 5 \cdot 7$

 $= 9\sqrt{5}\sqrt{7x^3} - 2\sqrt{7x^3}$ $\sqrt[n]{ab} = \sqrt[n]{a}\sqrt[n]{b}$

 $= \sqrt{7x^3}\,(9\sqrt{5} - 2)$ Factor out $\sqrt{7x^3}$.

 $= \sqrt{7x \cdot x^2}\,(9\sqrt{5} - 2)$ $a^m a^n = a^{m+n}$

 $= x\sqrt{7x}\,(9\sqrt{5} - 2)$ $\sqrt[n]{a^n} = a$

4. $2\sqrt[3]{16y} - 3\sqrt[3]{54y^4} = 2\sqrt[3]{2 \cdot 8y} - 3\sqrt[3]{2 \cdot 27y \cdot y^3}$ Rewrite: $y^4 = y^1y^3$; $16 = 2 \cdot 8$; $54 = 2 \cdot 27$

 $= 2\sqrt[3]{2y}\sqrt[3]{2^3} - 3\sqrt[3]{2y}\sqrt[3]{3^3}\sqrt[3]{y^3}$ $\sqrt[n]{ab} = \sqrt[n]{a}\sqrt[n]{b}$; regroup

 $= 2\sqrt[3]{2y} \cdot 2 - 3 \cdot \sqrt[3]{2y} \cdot 3 \cdot y$ $\sqrt[n]{a^n} = a$

 $= 4\sqrt[3]{2y} - 9y\sqrt[3]{2y}$

 $= \sqrt[3]{2y}\,(4 - 9y)$ Factor out $\sqrt[3]{2y}$.

Multiplying Radicals

- **Multiplying radical expressions** is based on the product rule and distributive property.
- **Review:**
  - **Product rule:** $\sqrt[n]{a}\sqrt[n]{b} = \sqrt[n]{ab}$ **Note:** $\sqrt[n]{a}\sqrt[n]{b} = \sqrt[n]{ab}$ (Multiply →; ← Simplify)
  - **Distributive property:** $a(b+c) = ab + ac$

Example: Find the following products.

1. $2\sqrt{3}\,(3\sqrt{2}+\sqrt{3}) = 2\sqrt{3}\cdot 3\sqrt{2} + 2\sqrt{3}\sqrt{3} = 6\sqrt{3\cdot 2} + 2\sqrt{3^2}$ Distributive property
   $= 6\sqrt{6} + 2\cdot 3 = \mathbf{6(\sqrt{6}+1)}$ $\sqrt[n]{ab} = \sqrt[n]{a}\sqrt[n]{b};\ \sqrt[n]{a^n} = a$
2. $\sqrt[4]{2}\,(\sqrt[4]{8} - 3\sqrt[4]{3}) = \sqrt[4]{2}\sqrt[4]{8} - 3\sqrt[4]{2}\sqrt[4]{3} = \sqrt[4]{16} - 3\sqrt[4]{6}$ Distribute, $\sqrt[n]{a}\sqrt[n]{b} = \sqrt[n]{ab}$
   $= \sqrt[4]{2^4} - 3\sqrt[4]{6} = \mathbf{2 - 3\sqrt[4]{6}}$ $\sqrt[n]{a^n} = a$
3. $2\sqrt[3]{x}\left(\sqrt[3]{x^2} + \sqrt[3]{x^2y^3} - 3\sqrt[3]{x^2}\right) = 2\sqrt[3]{x}\sqrt[3]{x^2} + 2\sqrt[3]{x}\sqrt[3]{x^2y^3} + 2\sqrt[3]{x}(-3\sqrt[3]{x^2})$ Distribute
   $= 2\sqrt[3]{x\,x^2} + 2\sqrt[3]{x\,x^2y^3} - 6\sqrt[3]{x\,x^2}$ $\sqrt[n]{a}\sqrt[n]{b} = \sqrt[n]{ab}$
   $= 2\sqrt[3]{x^3} + 2\sqrt[3]{x^3y^3} - 6\sqrt[3]{x^3}$ $a^m a^n = a^{m+n}$
   $= 2x + 2\sqrt[3]{x^3}\sqrt[3]{y^3} - 6x$ $\sqrt[n]{a^n} = a$
   $= 2xy - 4x = \mathbf{2x(y-2)}$ Factor out $2x$.
4. $(\sqrt{3} - \sqrt{2})(3\sqrt{2} + \sqrt{3}) = 3\sqrt{3}\sqrt{2} + \sqrt{3}\sqrt{3} - 3\sqrt{2}\sqrt{2} - \sqrt{2}\sqrt{3}$ FOIL
   $= 3\sqrt{6} + \sqrt{3^2} - 3\sqrt{2^2} - \sqrt{6}$ $\sqrt[n]{a}\sqrt[n]{b} = \sqrt[n]{ab};\ \sqrt[n]{a^n} = a$
   $= 3\sqrt{6} + 3 - 3\cdot 2 - \sqrt{6} = \mathbf{2\sqrt{6} - 3}$ Combine like radicals.
5. $(\sqrt{2} - \sqrt{5})^2 = \sqrt{2}^2 - 2\sqrt{2}\sqrt{5} + \sqrt{5}^2 = 2 - 2\sqrt{10} + 5 = \mathbf{7 - 2\sqrt{10}}$ $(a-b)^2 = a^2 - 2ab + b^2$

- **Conjugates** are two binomials (2 terms) whose only difference is the sign of one term.
  (Switch the middle sign of a pair of binomials, then conjugate to $(a + b)$ is $(a - b)$.)

Example:

Conjugates	Switch the middle sign
$3-4$	$3+4$
$2x+\sqrt{5}$	$2x-\sqrt{5}$
$\sqrt{a}-\sqrt{b}$	$\sqrt{a}+\sqrt{b}$
$5+7i$	$5-7i$

Example: Find the following products.

1. $(\sqrt{5}+\sqrt{3})(\sqrt{5}-\sqrt{3}) = \sqrt{5}^2 - \sqrt{3}^2 = 5 - 3 = \mathbf{2}$ $(a+b)(a-b) = a^2 - b^2$
   or $= \sqrt{5}^2 - \sqrt{5}\sqrt{3} + \sqrt{3}\sqrt{5} - \sqrt{3}^2 = \sqrt{5}^2 - \sqrt{3}^2$ FOIL
2. $(\sqrt{a} - \sqrt{3})(\sqrt{a} + \sqrt{3}) = \sqrt{a}^2 - \sqrt{3}^2 = \mathbf{a - 3}$ $(a+b)(a-b) = a^2 - b^2$

Tip: The radicals will disappear if a pair of conjugates are mulitplied.

7-5 DIVIDING RADICALS

Rationalizing Denominators

Rationalize the denominator by getting rid of the radicals in the denominator to satisfy the simplest condition – no radical appears in the denominator.

Rationalize a monomial by multiplying both denominator (bottom) and numerator (top) by the root in the denominator.

In General

$$\frac{a}{\sqrt{b}} = \frac{a\sqrt{b}}{\sqrt{b}\sqrt{b}} = \frac{a\sqrt{b}}{\sqrt{b^2}} = \frac{a\sqrt{b}}{b}$$

Multiply by $\sqrt{b}$ to get a perfect square. $\sqrt{b}^{2} = \sqrt[2]{b^2} = b$

Example

$$\frac{2}{\sqrt{6}} = \frac{2\sqrt{6}}{\sqrt{6}\sqrt{6}} = \frac{2\sqrt{6}}{\sqrt{6^2}} = \frac{2\sqrt{6}}{6} = \frac{\sqrt{6}}{3}$$

Example:

$$\sqrt{\frac{3a^3}{7a^8}} = \sqrt{\frac{3a^3}{7a^3a^5}} = \sqrt{\frac{3}{7a^5}}$$

$a^m a^n = a^{m+n}$; $\frac{\sqrt[n]{a}}{\sqrt[n]{b}} = \sqrt[n]{\frac{a}{b}}$

$$= \frac{\sqrt{3}}{\sqrt{7a^5}} = \frac{\sqrt{3}}{\sqrt{7a^5}}\frac{\sqrt{7a^5}}{\sqrt{7a^5}} = \frac{\sqrt{3\cdot 7a^5}}{\sqrt{(7a^5)(7a^5)}}$$

Multiply by $\sqrt{7a^5}$; $\sqrt[n]{a}\,\sqrt[n]{b} = \sqrt[n]{ab}$

$$= \frac{\sqrt{21a\cdot a^4}}{\sqrt{(7a^5)^2}} = \frac{\sqrt{21a}\sqrt{(a^2)^2}}{\sqrt{(7a^5)^2}} = \frac{a^2\sqrt{21a}}{7a^5} = \frac{\sqrt{21a}}{7a^3}$$

$a^m a^n = a^{m+n}$; $a^{nm} = (a^n)^m$; $\sqrt[n]{a^n} = a$

Rationalize a binomial (two terms) in denominator by multiplying both denominator and numerator by the ***conjugate*** of the denominator.

In General

1. $$\frac{a}{\sqrt{b}+\sqrt{c}} = \frac{a(\sqrt{b}-\sqrt{c})}{(\sqrt{b}+\sqrt{c})(\sqrt{b}-\sqrt{c})}$$ Multiply by $(\sqrt{b}-\sqrt{c})$.

$$= \frac{a(\sqrt{b}-\sqrt{c})}{(\sqrt{b})^2-(\sqrt{c})^2}$$ $(a+b)(a-b) = a^2-b^2$: $a = \sqrt{b}$, $b = \sqrt{c}$; $\sqrt[n]{a^n} = a$

$$= \frac{a(\sqrt{b}-\sqrt{c})}{b-c}$$

2. $$\frac{a}{\sqrt{b}-\sqrt{c}} = \frac{a(\sqrt{b}+\sqrt{c})}{(\sqrt{b}-\sqrt{c})(\sqrt{b}+\sqrt{c})}$$ Multiply by $(\sqrt{b}+\sqrt{c})$.

$$= \frac{a(\sqrt{b}+\sqrt{c})}{(\sqrt{b})^2-(\sqrt{c})^2}$$ $a^2-b^2 = (a+b)(a-b)$: $a = \sqrt{b}$, $b = \sqrt{c}$; $\sqrt[n]{a^n} = a$

$$= \frac{a(\sqrt{b}+\sqrt{c})}{b-c}$$

Example

1. $$\frac{4}{\sqrt{6}+\sqrt{2}} = \frac{4(\sqrt{6}-\sqrt{2})}{(\sqrt{6}+\sqrt{2})(\sqrt{6}-\sqrt{2})}$$ Multiply by $(\sqrt{6}-\sqrt{2})$.

$$= \frac{4(\sqrt{6}-\sqrt{2})}{(\sqrt{6})^2-(\sqrt{2})^2}$$ $(a+b)(a-b) = a^2-b^2$: $a = \sqrt{6}$, $b = \sqrt{2}$; $\sqrt[n]{a^n} = a$

$$= \frac{4(\sqrt{6}-\sqrt{2})}{6-2} = \sqrt{6}-\sqrt{2}$$

2. $$\frac{5}{\sqrt{10}-\sqrt{5}} = \frac{5(\sqrt{10}+\sqrt{5})}{(\sqrt{10}-\sqrt{5})(\sqrt{10}+\sqrt{5})}$$ Multiply by $(\sqrt{10}+\sqrt{5})$.

$$= \frac{5(\sqrt{10}+\sqrt{5})}{(\sqrt{10})^2-(\sqrt{5})^2}$$ $(a+b)(a-b) = a^2-b^2$: $a = \sqrt{10}$, $b = \sqrt{5}$; $\sqrt[n]{a^n} = a$

$$= \frac{5(\sqrt{10}+\sqrt{5})}{10-5} = \sqrt{10}+\sqrt{5}$$

Dividing Radicals

- **Dividing radical expressions** is based on the quotient rule.
- **Recall quotient rule:** $\frac{\sqrt[n]{a}}{\sqrt[n]{b}} = \sqrt[n]{\frac{a}{b}}$

  Note: $\frac{\sqrt[n]{a}}{\sqrt[n]{b}} = \sqrt[n]{\frac{a}{b}}$ (Dividing →; ← Simplify)

- **Tip:** Multiply both denominator and numerator by a radical to get a perfect square, perfect cube, perfect 4th power, perfect 5th power, etc. in the denominator.

Example: Perform the indicated operations (rationalize each denominator).

1. $\sqrt{\frac{5}{3}} = \frac{\sqrt{5}}{\sqrt{3}} = \frac{\sqrt{5}\sqrt{3}}{\sqrt{3}\sqrt{3}}$ — $\sqrt[n]{\frac{a}{b}} = \frac{\sqrt[n]{a}}{\sqrt[n]{b}}$; multiply by $\sqrt{3}$ to get a perfect square.

   $= \frac{\sqrt{5 \cdot 3}}{\sqrt{3}^2} = \frac{\sqrt{15}}{3}$ — $\sqrt[n]{a^n} = a$

2. $\frac{\sqrt[3]{2x}}{\sqrt[3]{y}} = \frac{\sqrt[3]{2x}\,\sqrt[3]{y^2}}{\sqrt[3]{y^1}\,\sqrt[3]{y^2}} = \frac{\sqrt[3]{2xy^2}}{\sqrt[3]{y^1\,y^2}}$ — Multiply by $\sqrt[3]{y^2}$ to get a perfect cube; $\sqrt[n]{a}\,\sqrt[n]{b} = \sqrt[n]{ab}$

   $= \frac{\sqrt[3]{2xy^2}}{\sqrt[3]{y^{1+2}}} = \frac{\sqrt[3]{2xy^2}}{\sqrt[3]{y^3}} = \frac{\sqrt[3]{2xy^2}}{y}$ — $a^m a^n = a^{m+n}$; $\sqrt[n]{a^n} = a$

3. $\frac{3x}{\sqrt{2} - \sqrt{x}} = \frac{3x(\sqrt{2} + \sqrt{x})}{(\sqrt{2} - \sqrt{x})(\sqrt{2} + \sqrt{x})}$ — Multiply by $\sqrt{2} + \sqrt{x}$.

   $= \frac{3x(\sqrt{2} + \sqrt{x})}{(\sqrt{2})^2 - (\sqrt{x})^2}$ — Distribute; $(a + b)(a - b) = a^2 - b^2$

   $= \frac{3x\sqrt{2} + 3x\sqrt{x}}{2 - x}$ — $\sqrt[n]{a^n} = a$

4. $\frac{2\sqrt{3} + \sqrt{2}}{\sqrt{2} - \sqrt{3}} = \frac{(2\sqrt{3} + \sqrt{2})(\sqrt{2} + \sqrt{3})}{(\sqrt{2} - \sqrt{3})(\sqrt{2} + \sqrt{3})}$ — Multiply by $\sqrt{2} + \sqrt{3}$.

   $= \frac{2\sqrt{3}\sqrt{2} + 2\sqrt{3}\sqrt{3} + \sqrt{2}\sqrt{2} + \sqrt{2}\sqrt{3}}{(\sqrt{2})^2 - (\sqrt{3})^2}$ — FOIL; $(a + b)(a - b) = a^2 - b^2$

   $= \frac{2\sqrt{3 \cdot 2} + 2\sqrt{3 \cdot 3} + \sqrt{2 \cdot 2} + \sqrt{2 \cdot 3}}{2 - 3} = \frac{2\sqrt{6} + 6 + 2 + \sqrt{6}}{2 - 3}$ — $\sqrt[n]{a}\,\sqrt[n]{b} = \sqrt[n]{ab}$

   $= \frac{3\sqrt{6} + 8}{-1} = -(3\sqrt{6} + 8)$ — Combine like radicals.

5. $\frac{3a}{\sqrt[4]{2a^3b^2}} = \frac{3a\sqrt[4]{2^3a^1b^2}}{\sqrt[4]{2a^3b^2}\,\sqrt[4]{2^3a^1b^2}}$ — Multiply by $\sqrt[4]{2^3a^1b^2}$ to get a perfect 4th power.

   $= \frac{3a\sqrt[4]{2^3a^1b^2}}{\sqrt[4]{(2 \cdot 2^3)(a^3a^1)(b^2b^2)}} = \frac{3a\sqrt[4]{2^3ab^2}}{\sqrt[4]{2^4a^4b^4}}$ — $a^m a^n = a^{m+n}$

   $= \frac{3a\sqrt[4]{8ab^2}}{\sqrt[4]{2^4}\,\sqrt[4]{a^4}\,\sqrt[4]{b^4}} = \frac{3a\sqrt[4]{8ab^2}}{2ab} = \frac{3\sqrt[4]{8ab^2}}{2b}$ — $\sqrt[n]{ab} = \sqrt[n]{a}\,\sqrt[n]{b}$; $\sqrt[n]{a^n} = a$

7-6 SOLVING EQUATIONS WITH RADICALS

Square Root Equations

- **A square root equation** is an equation containing a square root.

Example

$\sqrt{x} - 5 = 3$

- **To solve a square root equation**

Steps

- Isolate the square root term (on one side of the equation).
- Get rid of the square root by squaring both sides.
- Solve for x :
- Check.

Example: Solve $\sqrt{x} - 2 = 3$.

$\sqrt{x} = 3 + 2$ Add 2.

$\sqrt{x} = 5$

$\sqrt{x}^2 = 5^2$ Square both sides.

$x = 25$ $\sqrt[n]{a^n} = a,\ \sqrt{x}^2 = \sqrt[2]{x^2}$

$\sqrt{25} - 2 \overset{?}{=} 3$ Replace x by 25 in the equation.

$\sqrt{5^2} - 2 \overset{?}{=} 3$

$5 - 2 \overset{\surd}{=} 3$ Correct!

Example: Solve for x.

$$\frac{5}{\sqrt{4-3x}} = 1$$

$$\frac{5}{\sqrt{4-3x}} \cdot \sqrt{4-3x} = 1 \cdot \sqrt{4-3x}$$ Multiply by $\sqrt{4-3x}$.

$$\sqrt{4-3x} = 5$$

$$\sqrt{4-3x}^2 = 5^2$$ Square both sides ; $\sqrt[n]{a^n} = a$

$$4 - 3x = 25$$ Solve for x ; subtract 4.

$$-3x = 21$$ Divide by -3.

$$x = -7$$

Check: $\frac{5}{\sqrt{4-3(-7)}} \overset{?}{=} 1$ Replace x by -7 in the equation.

$$\frac{5}{\sqrt{25}} \overset{?}{=} 1$$

$$\frac{5}{5} \overset{\surd}{=} 1$$ Correct!

Square Root Equations & Extraneous Solutions

Example: Solve the following equation. $\sqrt{3x+7} - x = 3$

$\sqrt{3x+7} = 3 + x$	Isolate the $\sqrt{\ }$ term: add x
$\sqrt{3x+7}^2 = (3+x)^2$	Square both sides ; $\sqrt[n]{a^n} = a$
$3x + 7 = 9 + 6x + x^2$	$(a+b)^2 = a^2 + 2ab + a^2$
$x^2 + 3x + 2 = 0$	Combine like terms: subtract $3x$; subtract 7.
$(x+1)(x+2) = 0$	Factor.
$(x+1) = 0$, $(x+2) = 0$	Zero product property
$\mathbf{x = -1}$ or $\mathbf{x = -2}$	Solve for x.

Check:

$x = -1$	$x = -2$	$\sqrt{3x+7} - x = 3$
$\sqrt{3(-1)+7} - (-1) \stackrel{?}{=} 3$	$\sqrt{3(-2)+7} - (-2) \stackrel{?}{=} 3$	Replace x by -1 and -2 in the equation.
$\sqrt{4} + 1 \stackrel{?}{=} 3$	$\sqrt{1} + 2 \stackrel{?}{=} 3$	
$2 + 1 = 3$ √	$1 + 2 = 3$ √	Correct!

- **The squaring, cubing, etc. process can sometimes create extraneous solutions** that do not satisfy the original equation. So always check solutions. Checking is necessary, not optional.
- **An extraneous solution** (false solution) is a solution that does not satisfy the original equation.

Example:

$\mathbf{x = -3}$	Original equation
$x^2 = (-3)^2$	Square both sides.
$x^2 = 9$	Take the square root of both sides.
$\sqrt{x^2} = \pm\sqrt{9}$	If $x^2 = A$, then $\sqrt{x^2} = \pm\sqrt{A}$.
$x = \pm 3$	

Solutions $\begin{cases} x = 3, & \text{an extraneous solution (discard it, } 3 \neq -3) \\ \mathbf{x = -3}, & \text{the solution of the original equation} \end{cases}$

Example: $\mathbf{1 + x - \sqrt{5 - x} = 0}$

$1 + x = \sqrt{5-x}$	Isolate the $\sqrt{\ }$ term: add $\sqrt{5-x}$.
$(1+x)^2 = \sqrt{5-x}^2$	Square both sides.
$1 + 2x + x^2 = 5 - x$	$\sqrt[n]{a^n} = a$, $(a+b)^2 = a^2 + 2ab + b^2$
$x^2 + 3x - 4 = 0$, $(x-1)(x+4) = 0$	Factor.
$\mathbf{x = 1}$ or $x = -4$	Solve for x (zero product property).

Check:

$x = 1$	$x = -4$	$1 + x - \sqrt{5-x} = 0$
$1 + 1 - \sqrt{5-1} \stackrel{?}{=} 0$	$1 + (-4) - \sqrt{5-(-4)} \stackrel{?}{=} 0$	Replace x by 1 and -4 in the equation.
$2 - 2 = 0$ √ True	$-3 - 3 \neq 0$	False (an extraneous solution)

Radical Equations

- **A radical equation** is an equation containing **radical expressions.**

  (Expressions containing radical signs $\sqrt[n]{\ }$)

  Example

  $\sqrt[3]{x} - 2x = 7$

- **Solve a radical equation** by generalizing the squaring property to other powers.

  Tips:
  - Get rid of a square root by squaring.
  - Get rid of a cube root by cubing.
  - Get rid of the 4th root by raising to the 4th power.

    … …
  - Get rid of the *n*th root by raising to the nth power. $\sqrt[n]{a}^n = a$

Radical Equation	Do	Example	Solution
square root equation	squaring	$\sqrt{x} = 2,\quad \sqrt{x}^2 = 2^2$	$x = 4$
cube root equation	cubing	$\sqrt[3]{x} = 2,\quad \sqrt[3]{x}^3 = 2^3$	$x = 8$
4th root equation	raising to the 4th power	$\sqrt[4]{x} = 2,\quad \sqrt[4]{x}^4 = 2^4$	$x = 16$
5th root equation	raising to the 5th power	$\sqrt[5]{x} = 2,\quad \sqrt[5]{x}^5 = 2^5$	$x = 32$
***n*th root equation**	raising to the *n*th power	$\sqrt[n]{x} = 2,\quad \sqrt[n]{x}^n = 2^n$	$x = 2^n$

- **Procedure to solve a radical equation**

Steps

- Isolate the radical term (on one side of the equation).
- Get rid of the radical by raising the power of both sides to *n*.
- Solve for variable.
- Check.

Example Solve $\sqrt[3]{a} - 1 = 2$

$\sqrt[3]{a} = 2 + 1$ Isolate $\sqrt[3]{a}$.

$\sqrt[3]{a} = 3$

$\sqrt[3]{a}^3 = 3^3$ Cube both sides.

$a = 27$ $\sqrt[n]{a}^n = a$

$\sqrt[3]{27} - 1 \overset{?}{=} 2$ Replace *a* by 27.

$\sqrt[3]{3^3} - 1 \overset{?}{=} 2$, $3 - 1 \overset{\surd}{=} 2$ Correct!

Example: $3 + \sqrt[4]{a + 2} = 5$

$\sqrt[4]{a + 2} = 2$ Isolate $\sqrt[4]{a + 2}$.

$\sqrt[4]{a + 2}^4 = 2^4$ Raise to the 4th power.

$a + 2 = 16$, $a = 14$ $\sqrt[n]{a}^n = a$ Solve for *a*.

Check: $3 + \sqrt[4]{14 + 2} \overset{?}{=} 5$

$3 + \sqrt[4]{16} \overset{?}{=} 5$

$3 + \sqrt[4]{2^4} \overset{?}{=} 5$, $3 + 2 \overset{\surd}{=} 5$ Correct!

Equations With Two Radicals

Equations with two radicals perform the same steps as equations with one radical term.

Example: Solve the following equations.

$\mathbf{\sqrt{7+2a}-\sqrt{a+15}+1=0}$	Isolate one $\sqrt{\ }$ term.
$\sqrt{7+2a}=\sqrt{a+15}-1$	Add $\sqrt{a+15}$; subtract 1.
$\sqrt{7+2a}^{\,2}=(\sqrt{a+15}-1)^2$	Square both sides.
$7+2a=\sqrt{a+15}^{\,2}-2\sqrt{a+15}\cdot 1+1^2$	$(a-b)^2=a^2-2ab+b^2$: $a=\sqrt{a+15}$; $b=1$
$7+2a=a+15-2\sqrt{a+15}+1$	
$7+2a=a+16-2\sqrt{a+15}$	$15+1=16$
$2\sqrt{a+15}=9-a$	Isolate $\sqrt{\ }$ again: add $2\sqrt{a+15}$; subtract $2a$ & 7.
$2^2\sqrt{a+15}^{\,2}=(9-a)^2$	Square both sides.
$4(a+15)=9^2-18a+a^2$	$(a-b)^2=a^2-2ab+b^2$
$4a+60=81-18a+a^2$	Combine like terms: subtract 4a & 60. Write in descending order.
$a^2-22a+21=0$	Factor.
$(a-1)(a-21)=0$, $(a-1)=0$ ¦ $(a-21)=0$	Zero product rule
$a=1$ ¦ $a=21$	Solve for a.

Check: $\sqrt{7+2a}-\sqrt{a+15}+1=0$ — Original equation

$a=1$	$a=21$
$\sqrt{7+2\cdot 1}-\sqrt{1+15}+1\overset{?}{=}0$	$\sqrt{7+2\cdot 21}-\sqrt{21+15}+1\overset{?}{=}0$
$\sqrt{9}-\sqrt{16}+1\overset{?}{=}0$	$\sqrt{49}-\sqrt{36}+1\overset{?}{=}0$
$3-4+1\overset{\surd}{=}0$	$7-6+1\overset{?}{=}0$
$-1+1\overset{\surd}{=}0$	$2\neq 0$

Solution: $\mathbf{a=1}$ — $a=21$ is an extraneous solution.

7-7 COMPLEX NUMBERS

Complex Number System

- Recall **an even root of a negative number is not a real number**.

  Such as $x = \sqrt{-1}$ is not real, $\because$ $x^2 = -1$ has no real solution (no real number squared gives -1.)

- **The complex number system** is an expanded number system that is larger than the real number system and includes an even root of a negative number such as $\sqrt{-1}$.

- **A complex number** is an expression of the form $A + iB$, which is the sum of a real number A and an imaginary number Bi.

Complex Number		Example	
$A + iB$	A – real part iB – imaginary part A and B are real numbers	$3 + 7i$	3 – real part $7i$ – imaginary part

- **Imaginary unit (i)**: the square root of negative one.

Imaginary Unit	
$i = \sqrt{-1}$, $i^2 = -1$	$(i^2 = \sqrt{-1}^{\,2} = -1)$

- **Examples of complex numbers**

Complex Number	Real Part	Imaginary Part
$-4 + \sqrt{3}\,i$	-4	$\sqrt{3}\,i$
$6 - \pi\,i$	6	$-\pi\,i$
$\frac{\sqrt{2}}{3} - \frac{1}{2}i$	$\frac{\sqrt{2}}{3}$	$-\frac{1}{2}i$
$-7\,i$	0	$-7\,i$

Note: Either part can be 0.

- **Extended number system**

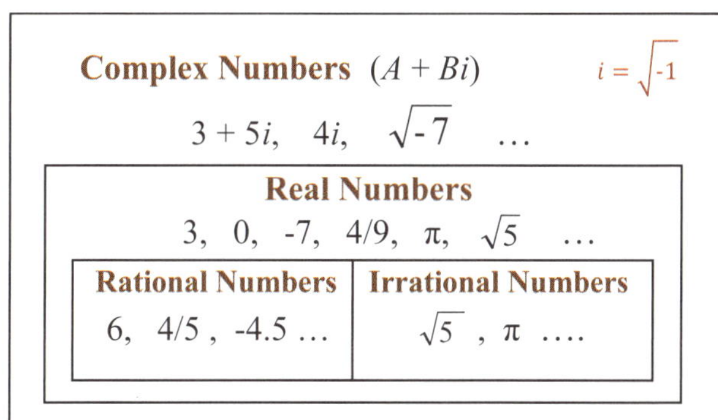

Imaginary Unit i

- **Powers of imaginary unit i**

Powers of i	
$i = \sqrt{-1}$	i
$i^2 = \left(\sqrt{-1}\right)^2 = -1$	$i^2 = -1$
$i^3 = i^2 \cdot i = (-1)\, i = -i$	$i^3 = -i$
$i^4 = i^2 \cdot i^2 = (-1)(-1) = 1$	$i^4 = 1$
$i^5 = i^4 \cdot i = (1)\, i$	$i^5 = i$
$i^6 = i^4 \cdot i^2 = (1)(-1) = -1$	$i^6 = -1$
$i^7 = i^6 \cdot i^1 = (-1)\, i$	$i^7 = -i$
$i^8 = i^4 \cdot i^4 = 1 \cdot 1$	$i^8 = 1$

One cycle (i through i^4)

Another cycle (i^5 through i^8)

… …

Note: i, -1, $-i$ and 1 keep repeating.

Example: Write in terms of i.

1. $\sqrt{-13} = \sqrt{(-1)(13)} = \mathbf{\sqrt{13}\, i}$ $\qquad i = \sqrt{-1}$

2. $-\sqrt{-20} = -\sqrt{(-1)(4 \cdot 5)}$

$= -\sqrt{-1}\sqrt{4}\sqrt{5} = \mathbf{-2\sqrt{5}\, i}$ $\qquad i = \sqrt{-1}$

Example: Simplify the following.

1. $-5\, i^4 = -5 \cdot 1 = \mathbf{-5}$ $\qquad i^4 = 1$

2. $3 + 4 \cdot i^3 = 3 + 4\,(-i) = \mathbf{3 - 4i}$ $\qquad i^3 = -i$

3. $7\, i^{13} = 7\, i^5 \cdot i^8 = 7 \cdot i^5 \cdot 1$ $\qquad a^m a^n = a^{m+n}$; $i^8 = 1$

$= 7 \cdot i \cdot 1 = \mathbf{7i}$ $\qquad i^5 = i$

- **A shortcut for powers of imaginary unit i**

Power of i	Example
$i^n = i^R$ R = the remainder of $n \div 4$	$i^{23} = i^3 = -i$ $\qquad 23 \div 4 = 5$ R 3 ($4 \overline{)23}$, 20, 3) Proof: $i^{23} = (i^4)^5 \cdot i^3 = 1^5 \cdot i^3 = i^3$ $\qquad (i^4 = 1)$

$a^{nm} = (a^n)^m$; $1^n = 1$

Example: Simplify the following.

1. $i^{85} = i^1 = \mathbf{i}$ $\qquad 85 \div 4 = 21\ R\ 1$

2. $i^{91} = i^3 = \mathbf{-i}$ $\qquad 91 \div 4 = 22\ R\ 3$ $\qquad i^3 = -i$

(Long division: $4 \overline{)85}$ = 21; 8; 5; 4; 1)

Operations With Complex Numbers

- **Add and subtract complex numbers** by combining real numbers together and imaginary numbers together (combine like terms).

Adding/Subtracting Complex Numbers	Example
$(A + Bi) + (C + Di) = (A + C) + (B + D)\,i$	$(2 + 5i) + (1 - 3i) = (2 + 1) + (5 - 3)\,i = 3 + 2i$
$(A + Bi) - (C + Di) = (A - C) + (B - D)\,i$ Or remove parentheses and combine like terms.	$(7 + 6i) - (2 + 3i) = (7 - 2) + (6 - 3)\,i = 5 + 3i$ or $(7 + 6i) - (2 + 3i) = 7 + 6i - 2 - 3i = 5 + 3i$

Example: Perform the indicated operations and simplify.

1. $\mathbf{(-2 - 3i) + (6 - 7i)} = (-2 + 6) + [-3 + (-7)]i = 4 - 10i = \mathbf{2(2 - 5i)}$
2. $\mathbf{(4 + 9i) - (5 - 6i)} = (4 - 5) + [9 - (-6)]i = \mathbf{-1 + 15i}$

   or $\mathbf{(4 + 9i) - (5 - 6i)} = 4 + 9i - 5 + 6i = \mathbf{-1 + 15i}$ Treat i as a variable.

- Multiply complex numbers using the FOIL method.

Multiplying Complex Numbers	Example
$(A + Bi)(C + Di) = AC + ADi + BCi + BDi^2$ F O I L $(i^2 = -1)$ $= AC + (AD + BC)i + BD(-1)$ $= (AC - BD) + (AD + BC)\,i$	$(4 + 3i)(3 + 7i) = 12 + 28i + 9i + 21i^2$ F O I L $= 12 + 37i - 21$ $(i^2 = -1)$ $= -9 + 37i$

Example: Perform the indicated operations and simplify.

1. $\mathbf{(3 - 4i)(4 + 5i)} = 12 + 15i - 16i - 20i^2$ FOIL

   $= 12 - i - 20(-1)$ $i^2 = -1$

   $= \mathbf{32 - i}$

2. $\mathbf{4i(3 - 2i)} = 12i - 8i^2 = 12i - 8(-1) = \mathbf{8 + 12i}$ Distribute, $i^2 = -1$

3. $\mathbf{2i - (3 - 2i)^2} = 2i - [3^2 - 2 \cdot 3(2i) + (2i)^2]$ $(a - b)^2 = a^2 - 2ab + b^2$, $a = 3,\ b = 2i$

   $= 2i - (9 - 12i + 4i^2)$

   $= 2i - 9 + 12i - 4i^2$

   $= 14i - 9 - 4(-1)$ $i^2 = -1$

   $= \mathbf{-5 + 14i}$

4. $\mathbf{\sqrt{-81} \cdot \sqrt{-4}} = \sqrt{(-1)(81)} \cdot \sqrt{(-1)(4)} = \sqrt{-1}\sqrt{9^2} \cdot \sqrt{-1}\sqrt{2^2}$

   $= (i\,9) \cdot (i\,2) = i^2\,18 = (-1)\,18 = \mathbf{-18}$ $i^2 = -1$

Note: $\sqrt[n]{a}\sqrt[n]{b} = \sqrt[n]{ab}$ This rule applies only when both a and b are non-negative.

$\sqrt{-81}\sqrt{-4} = \sqrt{(-81)(-4)} = \sqrt{9^2 \cdot 2^2} = 9 \cdot 2 = 18$ Incorrect!

Complex Conjugates and Division

Example

- **Review conjugates:** $A + B$ and $A - B$ — $3 + \sqrt{2}$ and $3 - \sqrt{2}$

- **Complex conjugates**: each complex number has a complex conjugate.

Complex Conjugates	Example
Conjugates $A + Bi$ and $A - Bi$	Conjugates $4 + 3i$ and $4 - 3i$

Tip: Change the sign of the imaginary part.

Example

Complex Number	Complex Conjugate
$11 + 7i$	$11 - 7i$
$-2 - 5i$	$-2 + 5i$
$-21i$ $(0 - 21i)$	$21i$ $(0 + 21i)$

- **To divide complex numbers,** rationalize the denominator to get rid of the imaginary number in the denominator.

Steps — **Example**: $\frac{-3}{2+i}$

- Multiply the nominator and denominator by the conjugate of the denominator. $\frac{-3}{2+i} = \frac{-3(2-i)}{(2+i)(2-i)}$ Multiply by $(2 - i)$.

- Apply $(a + b)(a - b) = a^2 - b^2$. $a = 2$, $b = i$ $= \frac{-6+3i}{2^2-i^2}$

- Simplify. $= \frac{-6+3i}{4-(-1)}$ $i^2 = -1$

- Write in the $A + Bi$ form. $= \frac{-6 + 3i}{5}$

$$= \frac{-6}{5} + \frac{3}{5}i$$

Complex Division and Solution

- **Complex division**

Example: Simplify and write the answer in the form $A + Bi$.

1. $\frac{2-3i}{3-4i} = \frac{(2-3i)(3+4i)}{(3-4i)(3+4i)}$ Multiply by $(3 + 4i)$ (the conjugate of $(3 - 4i)$).

$= \frac{6+8i-9i-12i^2}{3^2-(4i)^2}$ FOIL ; $(a+b)(a-b) = a^2 - b^2$

$= \frac{6-i-12(-1)}{9-4^2 i^2}$ $i^2 = -1$

$= \frac{6-i+12}{9-16(-1)} = \frac{18-i}{25}$

$= \frac{18}{25} - \frac{1}{25}i$ $A + Bi$

2. $\frac{2}{5i} = \frac{2i}{5i \cdot i} = \frac{2i}{5i^2}$ Multiply by i.

$= \frac{2i}{5(-1)}$ $i^2 = -1$

$= -\frac{2}{5}i$ $A + Bi$ $(0 - \frac{2}{5}i)$

3. $\frac{2-3i}{4i} = \frac{(2-3i)i}{4i \cdot i}$ Multiply by i.

$= \frac{2i-3i^2}{4(-1)}$ $i^2 = -1$

$= \frac{2i-3(-1)}{-4}$

$= \frac{2i+3}{-4}$

$= \frac{-3}{4} - \frac{1}{2}i$ $A + Bi$

- **Complex solution**

Example: Determine whether the complex number **(2 – *i*)** is a solution of the equation.

$\mathbf{y^2 - 4y + 5 = 0}$.

$(2-i)^2 - 4(2-i) + 5 \stackrel{?}{=} 0$ Replace y with $(2 - i)$.

$(2^2 - 2i + 2i + i^2) - 8 + 4i + 5 \stackrel{?}{=} 0$ $(a-b)^2 = a^2 - 2ab + b^2$; combine like terms.

$i^2 + 1 \stackrel{?}{=} 0$ $i^2 = -1$

$-1 + 1 \stackrel{\checkmark}{=} 0$ **Yes, (2 – *i*) is a solution.**

Unit 7 Summary

- **Square roots**

Square Roots		Example
If $x^2 = A$,		If $x^2 = 9$,
Then $\begin{cases} x = \sqrt{A} \\ x = -\sqrt{A} \end{cases}$	The principal square root (positive root) Negative root	Then $\begin{cases} x = \sqrt{9} = 3 \\ x = -\sqrt{9} = -3 \end{cases}$
This can be written as $x = \pm\sqrt{A}$.	$(A \geq 0)$	This can be written as $x = \pm\sqrt{9} = \pm 3$.

- **Radical (root)** is an expression that uses a root, such as square root, cube root, etc.

- **Radical notation for the *n*th root** $\sqrt[n]{}$

$\sqrt[n]{a}$ $\begin{cases} \sqrt{} \text{ – the radical sign} \\ a \text{ – the radicand} \quad \text{(a real number)} \\ n \text{ – the index} \quad \text{(a positive integer > 1)} \end{cases}$

$\sqrt[n]{a}$ – radical or radical expression

- **Rational (fractional) exponent notation $a^{\frac{1}{n}}$** is a fractional power or a number is raised to a fraction.

*n*th Root	Example
Radical notation → $\sqrt[n]{a} = a^{\frac{1}{n}}$ ← Rational exponent notation	$\sqrt[3]{7} = 7^{\frac{1}{3}}$
Note: if $n = 2$, write $\sqrt{a}$ rather than $\sqrt[2]{a}$.	Omit 2 in $\sqrt[2]{5}$, write $\sqrt{5}$.

- ***n*th root to the *n*th power**

$\sqrt[n]{a}^{\,n} = a$ Note: $\sqrt[n]{a}^{\,n} = \sqrt[n]{a^n}$

Example

$\sqrt{7}^{\,2} = (7^2)^{\frac{1}{2}} = 7^{\frac{2}{2}} = 7^1 = 7$

- ***n*th root**

$\sqrt[n]{a} = b$ means $a = b^n$

Example

$\sqrt[4]{16} = 2$ means $16 = 2^4$

- **If the index *n* is an *even* natural number:** $\sqrt[n]{a}^{\,n} = |a|$

- **If the index *n* is an *odd* natural number:** $\sqrt[n]{a}^{\,n} = a$

Natural numbers: 1, 2, 3, …

Example

$\sqrt[4]{3}^{\,4} = |\text{-}3| = 3$

$\sqrt[5]{6}^{\,5} = 6$ $a = 6$

$\sqrt[5]{-6}^{\,5} = -6$ $a = -6$

$\sqrt[5]{0}^{\,5} = 0$ $a = 0$

- **Index of a radical (*n*)**

Index n	Read	Example	Read
$a^{\frac{1}{2}} = \sqrt{a}$	the square root of *a*	$3^{\frac{1}{2}} = \sqrt{3}$	the square root of 3
$a^{\frac{1}{3}} = \sqrt[3]{a}$	the cube root of *a*	$5^{\frac{1}{3}} = \sqrt[3]{5}$	the cube root of 5
$a^{\frac{1}{4}} = \sqrt[4]{a}$	the fourth root of *a*	$7^{\frac{1}{4}} = \sqrt[4]{7}$	the fourth root of 7
$a^{\frac{1}{n}} = \sqrt[n]{a}$	the *n*th root of *a*	$2^{\frac{1}{11}} = \sqrt[11]{2}$	the 11th root of 2
$a^{\frac{m}{n}} = \sqrt[n]{a}^{\,m}$	the *n*th root of *a* to the *m*th power	$7^{\frac{5}{6}} = \sqrt[6]{7}^{\,5}$	the 6th root of 7 to the 5th power

rational exponent notation ↑ ↑ radical notation

- **Powers of roots**

The *n*th Root to the *m*th Power	Example
$a^{\frac{m}{n}} = (\sqrt[n]{a})^m = \sqrt[n]{a}^m = \sqrt[n]{a^m}$　　m – power	$7^{\frac{2}{3}} = (\sqrt[3]{7})^2 = \sqrt[3]{7}^2 = \sqrt[3]{7^2}$

- **A radical expression** is an algebraic expression containing a radical sign $\sqrt[n]{}$.
- **Product and quotient rule for radicals**

Name	Rule	Example
product rule	$\sqrt[n]{ab} = \sqrt[n]{a} \cdot \sqrt[n]{b}$　　$a \geq 0$,　$b \geq 0$	$\sqrt{12} = \sqrt{4 \cdot 3} = \sqrt{4}\sqrt{3} = \sqrt{2^2}\sqrt{3} = 2\sqrt{3}$
quotient rule	$\sqrt[n]{\frac{a}{b}} = \frac{\sqrt[n]{a}}{\sqrt[n]{b}}$　　$a \geq 0$,　$b > 0$,　$b \neq 0$	$\sqrt[3]{\frac{8}{27}} = \frac{\sqrt[3]{8}}{\sqrt[3]{27}} = \frac{\sqrt[3]{2^3}}{\sqrt[3]{3^3}} = \frac{2}{3}$

- **Simplifying radical expressions**

A radical expression is in simplest form when:	Simplest Form	Not Simplest Form
The exponent (m) of the radical is less than the index (n). $m < n$　$\sqrt[n]{a}^m$	$\sqrt[5]{x^3}$ or $\sqrt[5]{a}^3$　$3 < 5$	$\sqrt[7]{x^8}$　$8 > 7$
No fractions appear within a radical sign.	$\sqrt[3]{2y}$	$\sqrt[4]{\frac{2}{3xy}}$
No radicals appear in the denominator of a fraction.	$\frac{\sqrt{3}}{5}$	$\frac{\sqrt{3}}{\sqrt{8}}$

- **To add and subtract radical expressions** by combining the like radicals (or like terms).
- **Like radicals** are radicals with exactly the same index (n) and radicand (a).　　$\sqrt[n]{a}$
- **Conjugates** are two binomials (2 terms) whose only difference is the sign of one term.
  (Switch the middle sign of a pair of binomials, then conjugate to $(a + b)$ is $(a - b)$.)
- **Rationalize the denominator** by getting rid of the radicals in the denominator to satisfy the simplest condition — no radical appears in the denominator.
- **A square root equation** is an equation containing a square root.　　**Example** $\sqrt{x} - 5 = 3$
- **The squaring, cubing, etc. process can sometimes create extraneous solutions** that do not satisfy the original equation. So always check solutions.　　Checking is necessary, not optional.
- **A radical equation** contains **radical expressions.**　　**Example** $\sqrt[3]{x} - 2x = 7$
  (Expressions containing radical signs $\sqrt[n]{}$)
- **Solve a radical equation** by generalizing the squaring property to other powers.

Radical Equation	Do	Example	Solution
square root equation	squaring	$\sqrt{x} = 2$,　$\sqrt{x}^2 = 2^2$	$x = 4$
cube root equation	cubing	$\sqrt[3]{x} = 2$,　$\sqrt[3]{x}^3 = 2^3$	$x = 8$
4th root equation	raising to the 4th power	$\sqrt[4]{x} = 2$,　$\sqrt[4]{x}^4 = 2^4$	$x = 16$
5th root equation	raising to the 5th power	$\sqrt[5]{x} = 2$,　$\sqrt[5]{x}^5 = 2^5$	$x = 32$
*n*th root equation	raising to the *n*th power	$\sqrt[n]{x} = 2$,　$\sqrt[n]{x}^n = 2^n$	$x = 2^n$

- **The complex number system** is an expanded number system that is larger than the real number system and includes an even root of a negative number such as $\sqrt{-1}$.

Complex Number		Example	
$A + iB$	A – real part iB – imaginary part A and B are real numbers	$3 + 7i$	3 – real part $7i$ – imaginary part

- **Imaginary unit (i):** the square root of negative one.

Imaginary Unit		
$i = \sqrt{-1}$,	$i^2 = -1$	$(i^2 = \sqrt{-1}^{\,2} = -1)$

- **Extended number system**

Complex Numbers $(A + Bi)$ $\quad i = \sqrt{-1}$

$3 + 5i$, $4i$, $\sqrt{-7}$ ...

Real Numbers

3, 0, -7, 4/9, π, $\sqrt{5}$ ...

Rational Numbers	Irrational Numbers
6, 4/5 , -4.5 ...	$\sqrt{5}$, π ....

- **Shortcut for powers of imaginary unit i**

Power of i	Example	
$i^n = i^R$ R = the remainder of $n \div 4$	$i^{23} = i^3 = -i$	$23 \div 4 = 5$, 20, remainder 3

- **Adding and subtracting complex numbers**

Adding/Subtracting Complex Numbers	Example
$(A + Bi) + (C + Di) = (A + C) + (B + D)\,i$	$(2 + 5i) + (1 - 3i) = (2 + 1) + (5 - 3)\,i = 3 + 2i$
$(A + Bi) - (C + Di) = (A - C) + (B - D)\,i$ Or remove parentheses and combine like terms	$(7 + 6i) - (2 + 3i) = (7 - 2) + (6 - 3)\,i = 5 + 3i$ or $(7 + 6i) - (2 + 3i) = 7 + 6i - 2 - 3i = 5 + 3i$

- **Multiplying complex numbers**

Multiplying Complex Numbers	Example
$(A + Bi)(C + Di) = AC + ADi + BCi + BDi^2$ F O I L $(i^2 = -1)$ $= AC + (AD + BC)i + BD(-1)$ $= (AC - BD) + (AD + BC)\,i$	$(4 + 3i)(3 + 7i) = 12 + 28i + 9i + 21i^2$ F O I L $= 12 + 37i - 21$ $(i^2 = -1)$ $= -9 + 37i$

- **Complex conjugates:** each complex number has a complex conjugate.

Complex Conjugates	Example
Conjugates $A + Bi$ and $A - Bi$	Conjugates $4 + 3i$ and $4 - 3i$

- **To divide complex numbers:** Rationalize the denominator to get rid of the imaginary number in the denominator.

PRACTICE QUIZ

Unit 7 Radicals

1. Given the function $f(x) = \sqrt{5x+2}$,

a. determine the function values $f(3)$ and $f(0)$.

b. identify the domain.

2. Find each root.

a. $\sqrt[4]{\frac{1}{81}}$

b. $\sqrt[3]{8u^3}$

3. Given the function $f(x) = -\sqrt[3]{7x-1}$,

determine the function value $f(4)$.

4. Express each of the following in positive exponential form.

a. $-3x^{-2/3}\,y^{3/4}\,z^{-1/5}$

b. $(u^{-3} \cdot v^{2})^{3/4}$

c. $\left(\frac{x^3}{y^{-4}}\right)^3$

d. $\left(\frac{a}{b}\right)^{-4}$

e. $(-37.56891)^0$

5. Express in simplest radical form.

a. $\sqrt[4]{16x^8y^3}$

b. $\sqrt[5]{\sqrt[4]{b}}$

c. $u^{\frac{2}{3}}\,v^{\frac{1}{2}}\,w^{\frac{3}{4}}$

d. $\left(\frac{a^{1/4}b^{1/4}}{c^{1/12}d^{1/12}}\right)^3$

6. Simplify the following.

a. $\sqrt[3]{56x^4y}$

b. $\frac{\sqrt[4]{32a^7b^9}}{\sqrt[4]{2a^3b^4}}$

7. Perform the indicated operations and simplify.

a. $4\sqrt{15y^3} - 3\sqrt{5y^3}$

b. $3\sqrt[3]{a}(\sqrt[3]{a^2} + \sqrt[3]{a^2b^3} - 5\sqrt[3]{a^2})$

c. $\frac{\sqrt[3]{5y}}{\sqrt[3]{x}}$

8. Solve the following equations:

a. $2 + \sqrt[4]{7x + 13} = 4$

b. $\sqrt{x - 6} - \sqrt{x + 9} + 3 = 0$

9. Simplify and write the answer in the form $A + Bi$.

$\frac{3 - 4i}{5 - 2i}$

UNIT 8 QUADRATIC EQUATIONS AND INEQUALITIES

8-1 SOLVING QUADRATIC EQUATIONS

Incomplete Quadratic Equations

- **A quadratic equation:** an equation that has a squared term, such as $2x^2 + 7x - 3 = 0$.

Quadratic Equations in Standard Form	
$ax^2 + bx + c = 0$	$a \neq 0$

- **Incomplete quadratic equation**

Incomplete Quadratic Equation		Example	a	b	c
$ax^2 + bx = 0$	$(c = 0)$	$7x^2 - 4x = 0$	7	-4	0
$ax^2 + c = 0$	$(b = 0)$	$3x^2 + 16 = 0$	3	0	16

- **Zero-product property**

Zero-Product Property
If $A \cdot B = 0$, then either $A = 0$ or $B = 0$ (or both)
(A and B are algebraic expressions.)

Note: "or" means possibility of both.

- **Solving incomplete quadratic equations**

Incomplete Quadratic Equation	Steps	Example
Use the zero-product property to solve $ax^2 + bx = 0$.	- Express in $ax^2 + bx = 0$ - Factor: $x(ax + b) = 0$ - Apply the zero-product property: $x = 0$ | $ax + b = 0$ - Solve for x: $x = 0$ | $x = -\frac{b}{a}$	**Solve $9x^2 = -5x$** $9x^2 + 5x = 0$ Add $5x$ $x(9x + 5) = 0$ $x = 0$ | $9x + 5 = 0$ $x = 0$ | $x = -\frac{5}{9}$
Use the square root method to solve $ax^2 - c = 0$ (or $ax^2 = c$).	- Express in $ax^2 = c$ - Divide both sides by a: $x^2 = \frac{c}{a}$ - Take the square root of both sides: $x = \pm\sqrt{\frac{c}{a}}$	**Solve $7x^2 - 4 = 0$** $7x^2 = 4$ $x^2 = \frac{4}{7}$ $x = \pm\sqrt{\frac{4}{7}} \approx \pm 0.76$ Exact solutions; Approximate solutions

Quadratic Equations

- **Solve a quadratic equation:** a quadratic equation can be written as:

$(x + a)(x + b) = 0$ Factor.

Set each term equal to zero: $x + a = 0$ | $x + b = 0$ Zero-product property

Solutions: $x = -a$ | $x = -b$ Solve for a and b.

Example: Solve for x. $\mathbf{(x + 5)(x - 7) = 0}$

$x + 5 = 0$ | $x - 7 = 0$ Zero-product property

$x = -5$ | $x = 7$ Solve for x.

The solution set is **{-5, 7}**.

- **The x-intercepts of a quadratic equation:** the solutions of a quadratic equation.

Recall: The x-intercept is the point at which the graph crosses the x-axis.

- **To find the x-intercept $(x, 0)$:** solve for x in the quadratic equation $x^2 + bx + c = 0$

$\because$ All points on the x-axis (the x-intercepts) have a y-coordinate that is zero, $x^2 + bx + c = 0$ is $x^2 + bx + c = y$ with $y = 0$.

Example: **1.** Solve the quadratic equation $\mathbf{x^2 - 2x - 8 = 0}$.

2. Identify the x-intercepts of $f(x) = \mathbf{x^2 - 2x - 8}$.

Solution: **1.** $\mathbf{x^2 - 2x - 8 = 0}$

$(x + 2)(x - 4) = 0$ Factor.

$x + 2 = 0$ | $x - 4 = 0$ Zero-product property

$\mathbf{x = -2}$ | $\mathbf{x = 4}$

2. $f(x) = \mathbf{x^2 - 2x - 8}$

x	$y = x^2 - 2x - 8$	(x, y)
0	$0^2 - 2 \cdot 0 - 8 = -8$	(0, -8)
1	$1^2 - 2 \cdot 1 - 8 = -9$	(1, -9)
-1	$(-1)^2 - 2(-1) - 8 = -5$	(-1, -5)
2	$2^2 - 2 \cdot 2 - 8 = -8$	(2, -8)
-2	$(-2)^2 - 2(-2) - 8 = 0$	(-2, 0)
4	$4^2 - 2 \cdot 4 - 8 = 0$	(4, 0)

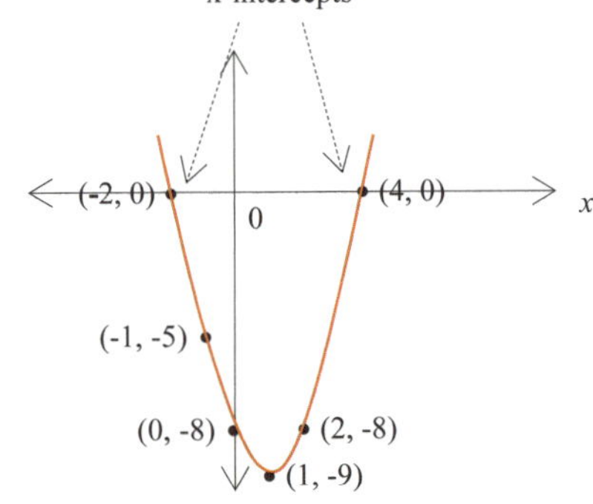

Tips: - Choose points on both sides of the axis.
- The solutions of $f(x) = x^2 - 2x - 8$ are the first coordinates of the x-intercepts.

x-intercepts: **(-2, 0) , (4, 0)**

Example: Solve $(y + 3)^2 = 2$

$\sqrt{(y+3)^2} = \pm\sqrt{2}$ Take the square root of both sides.

$y + 3 = \sqrt{2}$ | $y + 3 = -\sqrt{2}$

$y = \sqrt{2} - 3 \approx -1.586$ | $y = -\sqrt{2} - 3 \approx -4.414$ Subtract 3.

Solutions: $\mathbf{y = -3 \pm \sqrt{2}}$ or $\mathbf{y \approx \begin{cases} -1.586 \\ -4.414 \end{cases}}$

Exact solutions Approximate solutions

8-2 COMPLETING THE SQUARE

Completing the Square

- **Completing the square** can be used to solve quadratic equations that are not factorable.
- **Completing the square**: the process of finding a number to add to a quadratic equation and to form a perfect square, such as: $x^2 + 10x + \boxed{?} = (x+5)^2$
- **Procedure to complete the square – Case I: $x^2 + bx + c = 0$**

Steps

- Express in the form $x^2 + bx = -c$.
- Add $\square$ to both sides of the equation.
- Determine $\left(\frac{b}{2}\right)^2$ (Take half of the coefficient of x and square it.)
- Add $\left(\frac{b}{2}\right)^2$ to both sides of the equation.
  $x^2 + bx + \left(\frac{b}{2}\right)^2 = -c + \left(\frac{b}{2}\right)^2$
- Factor the left side.
- Take the square root of both sides.
- Solve for x.

Example: Solve $x^2 + 10x - 1 = 0$.

$x^2 + 10x = 1$ Add 1.

$x^2 + 10x + \square = 1 + \square$

$\left(\frac{b}{2}\right)^2 = \left(\frac{10}{2}\right)^2 = 25$

$x^2 + 10x + \boxed{25} = 1 + \boxed{25}$

$(x+5)^2 = 26$

$\sqrt{(x+5)^2} = \pm\sqrt{26}$

$x + 5 = \pm\sqrt{26}$

$x + 5 = \sqrt{26}$ | $x + 5 = -\sqrt{26}$

$x = -5 + \sqrt{26}$ | $x = -5 - \sqrt{26}$

Solutions: $x = -5 \pm \sqrt{26}$

- **Procedure to complete the square – Case II: $Ax^2 + Bx + C = 0$**

Steps

- Express in the form $Ax^2 + Bx = -C$.
- Make the coefficient of x^2 equal to 1.
- Add $\square$ to both sides of the equation.
- Determine $\left(\frac{b}{2}\right)^2$.
- Add $\left(\frac{b}{2}\right)^2$ to both sides of the equation.
- Factor the left side.
- Take the square root of both sides.
- Solve for x.

Example: Solve $2x^2 + 4x - 70 = 0$.

Method 1

$2x^2 + 4x = 70$

$\frac{2x^2}{2} + \frac{4x}{2} = \frac{70}{2}$ Divide by 2.

$x^2 + 2x + \square = 35 + \square$

$\left(\frac{b}{2}\right)^2 = \left(\frac{2}{2}\right)^2 = 1$

$x^2 + 2x + \boxed{1} = 35 + \boxed{1}$

$(x+1)^2 = 36$

$\sqrt{(x+1)^2} = \pm\sqrt{36}$

Method 2

$2x^2 + 4x = 70$ Add 70.

$2(x^2 + 2x) = 70$ Factor out 2.

$2(x^2 + 2x + \square) = 70 + 2 \cdot \square$ Add $2 \cdot \square$ to the right side.

$\left(\frac{b}{2}\right)^2 = \left(\frac{2}{2}\right)^2 = 1$

$2(x^2 + 2x + \boxed{1}) = 70 + 2 \cdot \boxed{1}$

$2(x+1)^2 = 72$ Divide by 2.

$\sqrt{(x+1)^2} = \pm\sqrt{36}$

$x + 1 = \pm 6$

$x + 1 = 6$ | $x + 1 = -6$

Solutions: $x = 5$ | $x = -7$

Example: **1.** Solve $\mathbf{x^2 - 4x + 9 = 0}$ by completing the square.

2. Identify the x-intercepts of $f(x) = \mathbf{x^2 - 4x + 9}$.

Steps	**Solution**	
1.	$\mathbf{x^2 - 4x + 9 = 0}$	
- Express in the form $x^2 + bx = -c$.	$x^2 - 4x = -9$	Subtract 9.
- Determine $\left(\frac{b}{2}\right)^2$.	$\left(\frac{-4}{2}\right)^2 = 4$	$b = -4$
- Add $\left(\frac{b}{2}\right)^2$ to both sides of the equation.	$(x^2 - 4x + 4) = -9 + 4$	
- Factor the left side.	$(x-2)^2 = -5$	
- Take the square root of both sides.	$\sqrt{(x-2)^2} = \pm\sqrt{-5}$	
- Solve for x.	$x - 2 = \pm\sqrt{-5}$	
	$x = 2 \pm \sqrt{-5}$	Add 2.
	$= 2 \pm \sqrt{(-1)\cdot 5}$	$\sqrt{-1} = i$
	$= 2 \pm i\sqrt{5}$	

Solutions: $x = 2 + i\sqrt{5}$ or $x = 2 - i\sqrt{5}$

$\mathbf{x = 2 \pm i\sqrt{5}}$

2. $f(x) = \mathbf{x^2 - 4x + 9}$.

$f(x) = x^2 - 4x + 9$

x	$y = x^2 - 4x + 9$	(x, y)
0	$0^2 - 4 \cdot 0 + 9 = 9$	(0, 9)
1	$1^2 - 4 \cdot 1 + 9 = 6$	(1, 6)
-1	$(-1)^2 - 4(-1) + 9 = 14$	(-1, 14)
2	$2^2 - 4 \cdot 2 + 9 = 5$	(2, 5)
3	$3^2 - 4 \cdot 3 + 9 = 6$	(3, 6)
4	$4^2 - 4 \cdot 4 + 9 = 9$	(4, 9)
5	$5^2 - 4 \cdot 5 + 9 = 14$	(5, 14)

Tip: Choose points on both sides of the y-axis.

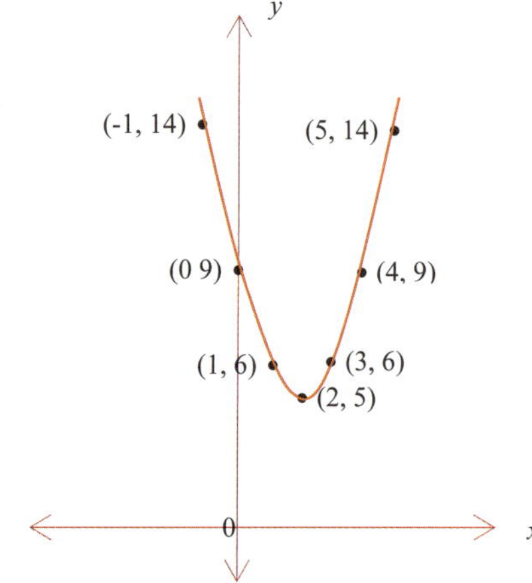

No x-intercepts (x are non-real complex numbers).

The graph does not cross the x-axis anywhere.

Applications

- **Simple interest:** interest computed on the original principal.
- **Compound interest:** interest computed on both the principal and the past interest earned.
- **Compound interest formula**

Formula	Component
$A = P(1+r)^t$	A – new value P – starting principal r – interest rate t – time (years)

Example: $100 grows to $121 in 2 years. Calculate interest rate r.

$$A = P(1+r)^t$$

A = $121, P = $100, t = 2 years

$$\mathbf{121 = 100(1+r)^2}$$

$$\frac{121}{100} = (1+r)^2$$

Divide by 100.

$$\pm\sqrt{\frac{121}{100}} = \sqrt{(1+r)^2}$$

Take the square root of both sides.

$$\pm\sqrt{\frac{121}{100}} = 1 + r$$

$$-1 \pm\sqrt{\frac{121}{100}} = r$$

Subtract 1

Solve for r.

$$r = -1 + \sqrt{\frac{121}{100}} \qquad\qquad r = -1 - \sqrt{\frac{121}{100}}$$

$$= -1 + \sqrt{\frac{11^2}{10^2}} \qquad\qquad = -1 - \sqrt{\frac{11^2}{10^2}}$$

$$= -1 + \frac{11}{10} \qquad\qquad = -1 - \frac{11}{10}$$

$$= -\frac{10}{10} + \frac{11}{10} \qquad\qquad = -\frac{10}{10} - \frac{11}{10}$$

$$= \frac{1}{10} = 0.1 \;\checkmark \qquad\qquad = \frac{-21}{10} \;\times$$

Interest rate cannot be negative, eliminate it.

$\mathbf{r = 0.1}$ **or 10 %**

Interest rate is 10%.

8-3 THE QUADRATIC FORMULA

Methods to Solve Quadratic Equations

- **Methods for solving quadratic equations**

Quadratic Equation	Method
$ax^2 + c = 0$ (no x term)	Square root method
$ax^2 + bx = 0$ ($c = 0$)	Zero-product property
$ax^2 + bx + c = 0$	Try factoring first.
$ax^2 + bx + c = 0$ Not factorable (or does not factor easily)	Completing the square or quadratic formula

- **Factoring:** fast and easy to use, but is limited in scope. (Some quadratic equations are not factorable.)
- **Completing the square**: can be used to solve all quadratic equations, but is tedious.
- **The quadratic formula**: a general formula that can be used to solve any quadratic equation.

The Quadratic Formula		
quadratic equation:	$ax^2 + bx + c = 0$	
solutions:	$x = \frac{-b \pm \sqrt{b^2 - 4ac}}{2a}$	($a \neq 0$)

Note: The plus or minus sign (±) shows that the quadratic formula gives two solutions.

$x = \frac{-b + \sqrt{b^2 - 4ac}}{2a}$ and $x = \frac{-b - \sqrt{b^2 - 4ac}}{2a}$

The Quadratic Formula

Solving quadratic equations using the quadratic formula

Example: Use the quadratic formula to solve $x^2 + 5x = -4$.

Steps	Solution	
	$x^2 + 5x = -4$	
- Write in standard form $(ax^2 + bx + c = 0)$.	$1x^2 + 5x + 4 = 0$	Add 4.
- Identify a, b, and c.	$a = 1,\ b = 5,\ c = 4$	
- Substitute the values of a, b, and c into the formula and calculate.	$x = \frac{-b \pm \sqrt{b^2 - 4ac}}{2a} = \frac{-5 \pm \sqrt{5^2 - 4 \cdot 1 \cdot 4}}{2 \cdot 1}$ $x = \frac{-5 \pm \sqrt{25 - 16}}{2} = \frac{-5 \pm \sqrt{9}}{2} = \frac{-5 \pm 3}{2}$ $x = \frac{-5 \pm 3}{2}$	
- Solve for x.	$x = \frac{-5 + 3}{2} = -1$ ¦ $x = \frac{-5 - 3}{2} = -4$	

Solutions: $\boldsymbol{x = -4}$ **or** $\boldsymbol{-1}$

Example: Use the quadratic formula to solve $\boldsymbol{-6x = 3 - 4x^2}$.

Steps	Solution	
	$-6x = 3 - 4x^2$	
- Write in standard form.	$4x^2 - 6x - 3 = 0$	Add $4x^2$; subtract 3.
- Identify a, b and c.	$a = 4,\ b = -6,\ c = -3$	
- Substitute a, b, and c into the formula.	$x = \frac{-b \pm \sqrt{b^2 - 4ac}}{2a}$ $= \frac{-(-6) \pm \sqrt{(-6)^2 - 4 \cdot 4 \cdot (-3)}}{2 \cdot 4}$	
- Solve for x.	$= \frac{6 \pm \sqrt{36 + 48}}{8} = \frac{6 \pm \sqrt{84}}{8}$ $= \frac{6 \pm \sqrt{21 \cdot 4}}{8} = \frac{6 \pm 2\sqrt{21}}{8}$	Divide by 2.

Solutions: $\boldsymbol{x = \frac{3 \pm \sqrt{21}}{4}}$

Example: **1.** Use the quadratic formula to solve $(x-3)(x-4)-8=0$.

2. Identify the x-intercepts of $f(x)=(x-3)(x-4)-8$.

Solution: **1.** $x^2-4x-3x+12-8=0$ FOIL

$x^2-7x+4=0$ Standard form

$x=\dfrac{-b\pm\sqrt{b^2-4ac}}{2a}$ $a=1,\ b=-7,\ c=4$

$=\dfrac{-(-7)\pm\sqrt{(-7)^2-4\cdot1\cdot4}}{2\cdot1}$

$=\dfrac{7\pm\sqrt{49-16}}{2}=\dfrac{7\pm\sqrt{33}}{2}$

2. The x-intercepts: $\left(\frac{7+\sqrt{33}}{2},\ 0\right)$ or $\left(\frac{7-\sqrt{33}}{2},\ 0\right)$

Example: Use the quadratic formula to solve the following.

1. $2x(x-1)+(x+3)=x^2+x$ Remove parentheses.

$2x^2-2x+x+3=x^2+x$ Write in standard form.

$x^2-2x+3=0$ Subtract x^2 and x.

$x=\dfrac{-b\pm\sqrt{b^2-4ac}}{2a}=\dfrac{-(-2)\pm\sqrt{(-2)^2-4\cdot1\cdot3}}{2\cdot1}$ $a=1,\ b=-2,\ c=3$

$=\dfrac{2\pm\sqrt{4-12}}{2}=\dfrac{2\pm\sqrt{-8}}{2}$

$=\dfrac{2\pm\sqrt{(-1)\cdot2\cdot4}}{2}=\dfrac{2\pm i2\sqrt{2}}{2}$ $\sqrt{-1}=i$; divide by 2.

$x=1\pm i\sqrt{2}$

2. $\dfrac{1}{t}+\dfrac{1}{t-1}=\dfrac{1}{5}$ LCD = $5t(t-1)$

$\dfrac{1}{t}5t(t-1)+\dfrac{1}{t-1}5t(t-1)=\dfrac{1}{5}5t(t-1)$ Multiply by the LCD.

$5(t-1)+5t=t(t-1)$ Distribute

$5t-5+5t=t^2-t$

$t^2-11t+5=0$ Write in standard form.

$t=\dfrac{-b\pm\sqrt{b^2-4ac}}{2a}=\dfrac{-(-11)\pm\sqrt{(-11)^2-4\cdot1\cdot5}}{2\cdot1}$ $a=1,\ b=-11,\ c=5$

$=\dfrac{11\pm\sqrt{121-20}}{2}$

$t=\dfrac{11\pm\sqrt{101}}{2}$ Exact solutions. $t\approx\begin{cases}10.525\\0.475\end{cases}$ Approximate solutions.

8-4 APPLICATIONS OF QUADRATIC EQUATIONS

Quadratic Applications

Recall steps for solving word problems

Procedure for Solving Word Problems

- **Organize** the **facts** given from the problem.
- Identify and **label** the **unknown** quantity (let x = unknown).
- Draw a **diagram** if it will make the problem clearer.
- Convert the wording into a mathematical **equation**.
- **Solve** the equation.
- **Check** and **answer** the question.

Example: Evan is going to replace old carpet in his bedroom, which is a rectangle and has a length 2 meters greater than its width. If the area of his bedroom is 48 square meters, what will be the dimensions (length and width) of the carpet?

Steps	Solution
- List the facts and label the unknown.	**Facts**: Area $A = 48\text{m}^2$; Length = Width + 2m **Unknowns**: Width = x, Length = $x + 2$m
- Draw a diagram.	Width = x; Length = $x + 2$
- Write an equation.	$x(x+2) = 48$ (Area: $A = lw$)
- Solve the equation.	$x^2 + 2x = 48$ Distribute
- Standard form:	$x^2 + 2x - 48 = 0$
- Factor:	$(x+8)(x-6) = 0$
- Zero-product property:	$x + 8 = 0$ | $x - 6 = 0$
- Solutions:	$x = -8$ | $x = 6$ (Since the width of a rectangle cannot be negative, eliminate $x = -8$.)
- Check.	$6(6+2) \stackrel{?}{=} 48$, $48 \stackrel{\surd}{=} 48$
- Answer (the size of the carpet):	**Width** = x = **6m** **Length** = $x + 2 = 6 + 2$ = **8m**

More Examples

Example: Alice plans to make a circular flower garden in her yard. If the area is 36 square meters and she is going to put a statue in the middle of the circle, what will be the distance from the edge of the circle to the statue (radius r)?

Steps | **Solution**

- List the facts and label the unknown.

Fact	Area $A = 36\text{m}^2$
Unknown	Radius $r = ?$

- Diagram.

- Equation: $A = \pi r^2$ — The area of a circle: $A = \pi r^2$
- Solve for r. $r^2 = \dfrac{A}{\pi}$ — Divide both sides by π.

$$r = \pm\sqrt{\frac{A}{\pi}}$$ Take the square root of both sides.

$$= \pm\sqrt{\frac{36}{\pi}} \approx \pm 3.385 \text{ m}$$ Area $A = 36 \text{ m}^2$

- Solution: $\mathbf{r \approx 3.385 \text{ m}}$ — The radius cannot be negative, eliminate -3.385m.
- Answer: the distance from the edge of the circle to the statue is 3.385 m.

Example: Tom is going to make a small square table for his kids. If the diagonal of the square is 3 inches, what is the side of this square table?

Steps | **Solution**

- List the facts and label the unknown.

Fact	The diagonal of a square = 3″.
Unknown	The side $x = ?$

- Diagram.

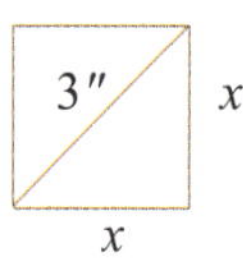

- Equation: $x^2 + x^2 = 3^2$ — Pythagorean theorem

- Solve for x: $x^2 + x^2 = 3^2$, $2x^2 = 9$

$$x^2 = \frac{9}{2}$$

$$x = \pm\sqrt{\frac{9}{2}} = \pm\sqrt{4.5} \approx \pm 2.12$$ Take the square root of both sides.

- Solution: **$x = 2.12''$** The side of the table cannot be negative, eliminate -2.12″.
- Answer: the side of the table is about 2.12 inches.

Example: The product of two consecutive integers is 156. Find the two integers.

Steps **Solution**

- List the facts and label the unknown.

Unknowns	Let 1st integer $= x$, 2nd integer $= x + 1$
Organize Facts	$x \cdot (x + 1) = 156$ (· = product, = = is)

- Equation: $x\,(x + 1) = 156$
- Solve for x. $x^2 + x - 156$ Does not factor easily.

$x^2 + x - 156 = 0$ Standard form: $ax^2 + bx + c = 0$

$$x = \frac{-b \pm \sqrt{b^2 - 4ac}}{2a}$$ Quadratic formula

$$= \frac{-1 \pm \sqrt{1^2 - 4 \cdot 1 \cdot (-156)}}{2 \cdot 1}$$ $a = 1$, $b = 1$, $c = -156$

$$= \frac{-1 \pm \sqrt{625}}{2}$$

$$= \frac{-1 \pm 25}{2}$$

$$x = \frac{-1 + 25}{2} = 12 \quad | \quad x = \frac{-1 - 25}{2} = -13$$

Solutions: **$x = 12$** or **-13**

Answer: **the first integer x is 12 or -13.**

Tips: - If the first integer is $x = 12$, the second consecutive integer is $x + 1 = 12 + 1 = 13$.
- If the first integer is $x = -13$, the second consecutive integer is $x + 1 = -13 + 1 = -12$.

8-5 DISCRIMINANT OF QUADRATIC EQUATIONS

The Discriminant & Solutions

- **Discriminant:** The expression that appears under the square root sign in the quadratic formula. It can predict the type of quadratic solution without solving it.

Quadratic Formula	Discriminant
$x = \frac{-b \pm \sqrt{b^2 - 4ac}}{2a}$	$b^2 - 4ac$

- **Three cases:** A quadratic equation may have one or two real solutions, or two complex solutions.

Recall the number system

Complex Numbers $(a + i\,b)$
$3 + 5i$, $4i$, $\sqrt{-7}$ …

Real Numbers

Rational Numbers	Irrational Numbers
6, 4/5 , -4.5	$\sqrt{5}$, π ….

$\sqrt{-1} = i$

- **If $(b^2 - 4ac) = 0$, there is one real solution**

In general

$$x = \frac{-b \pm \sqrt{b^2 - 4ac}}{2a} = \frac{-b \pm \sqrt{0}}{2a} = \frac{-b}{2a}$$

One real solution

Example: $x^2 - 4x + 4 = 0$

$$x = \frac{-(-4) \pm \sqrt{(-4)^2 - 4 \cdot 1 \cdot 4}}{2 \cdot 1}$$

$$= \frac{4 \pm \sqrt{0}}{2} = \frac{4}{2} = 2$$

One real solution

$ax^2 + bx + c = 0$

$b^2 - 4ac = 0$

- **If $(b^2 - 4ac) > 0$, there are two unequal real solutions**

In general

$$x = \frac{-b \pm \sqrt{b^2 - 4ac}}{2a}$$

$$x = \frac{-b + \sqrt{b^2 - 4ac}}{2a} \quad\Big|\quad x = \frac{-b - \sqrt{b^2 - 4ac}}{2a}$$

Two real solutions

Example: $x^2 + 5x + 4 = 0$

$$x = \frac{-5 \pm \sqrt{5^2 - 4 \cdot 1 \cdot 4}}{2 \cdot 1}$$

$$= \frac{-5 \pm \sqrt{9}}{2} = \frac{-5 \pm 3}{2}$$

$b^2 - 4ac = 9 > 0$

$$x = \frac{-5+3}{2} = -1 \quad\Big|\quad x = \frac{-5-3}{2} = -4$$

Two real solutions

- **If $(b^2 - 4ac) < 0$, there are two unequal complex solutions**

$$x = \frac{-b \pm \sqrt{-(b^2 - 4ac)}}{2a} \qquad b^2 - 4ac < 0$$

$$= \frac{-b \pm \sqrt{-1}\sqrt{b^2 - 4ac}}{2a}$$

$$= \frac{-b \pm i\sqrt{b^2 - 4ac}}{2a}$$

Two non-real

Example: $x^2 - 4x + 9 = 0$

$$x = \frac{-(-4) \pm \sqrt{(-4)^2 - 4 \cdot 1 \cdot 9}}{2 \cdot 1}$$

$$= \frac{4 \pm \sqrt{-20}}{2} = \frac{4 \pm \sqrt{-1}\sqrt{20}}{2} \qquad b^2 - 4ac = -20 < 0$$

$$= \frac{4 \pm i\sqrt{4 \cdot 5}}{2} = 2 \pm i\sqrt{5} \qquad \sqrt{-1} = i$$

Divide by 2.

Two non-real

- **Discriminant and solutions**

Discriminant: $b^2 - 4ac$	Solution	Example	$b^2 - 4ac$
$(b^2 - 4ac) = 0$	one real solution	$x^2 - 4x + 4 = 0$ $x = 2$	$(-4)^2 - 4(1)(4) = 0$
$(b^2 - 4ac) > 0$	two real solutions	$x^2 + 5x + 4 = 0$ $x = -4$ or -1	$5^2 - 4(1)(4) = 9 > 0$
$(b^2 - 4ac) < 0$	two non-real (complex solutions)	$x^2 - 4x + 9 = 0$ $x = 2 \pm i\sqrt{5}$	$(-4)^2 - 4(1)(9) = -20 < 0$

Example: Use the discriminant to determine the nature of the solutions to the equations.

1. $2y^2 = 5$

- Write in standard form. — $2y^2 + 0y - 5 = 0$ $ax^2 + by + c = 0$
- Identify a, b, and c. — $a = 2,\ b = 0,\ c = -5$
- Calculate the discriminant. ($b^2 - 4ac$) — $b^2 - 4ac = 0^2 - 4 \cdot 2 \cdot (-5) = 40$
- It has **two real solutions.** — $b^2 - 4ac = 40 > 0$

2. $n^2 - 3\sqrt{2}n + 7 = 0$

- Identify a, b, and c. — $a = 1,\ b = -3\sqrt{2},\ c = 7$
- Calculate the discriminant. — $b^2 - 4ac = (-3\sqrt{2})^2 - 4 \cdot 1 \cdot 7$

$$= (-3)^2\sqrt{2}^2 - 4 \cdot 1 \cdot 7$$

$$= 18 - 28$$

$$= -10$$

- It has **two non-real solutions.** (Complex solutions) — $b^2 - 4ac = -10 < 0$

Writing Equation From Solutions

- **Writing equation from solutions:** applying the zero-product property in reverse.
- **Recall zero-product property:** If $A \cdot B = 0$, then either $A = 0$ or $B = 0$ (A and B are algebraic expressions.)
- **Zero-product property in reverse:** If $A = 0$ or $B = 0$, then $A \cdot B = 0$
- **Steps for writing equation from solutions**

Steps	**Example**: **-5** or **7** are solutions
- Let x = two solutions.	$x = -5$ | $x = 7$
- Make one side zero.	$x + 5 = 0$ (Add 5.) | $x - 7 = 0$ Subtract 7.
- Apply the zero-product property in reverse.	$(x + 5)(x - 7) = 0$
- Use FOIL.	$x^2 - 7x + 5x - 35 = 0$ FOIL
	Equation: $\mathbf{x^2 - 2x - 35 = 0}$

Example: Write a quadratic equation having the given numbers as solutions.

1. $\mathbf{-\sqrt{2}}$ **and** $\mathbf{3\sqrt{2}}$

$x = -\sqrt{2}$ \| $x = 3\sqrt{2}$ — Let x = two solutions.

$x + \sqrt{2} = 0$ \| $x - 3\sqrt{2} = 0$ — Make one side zero.

$(x + \sqrt{2})(x - 3\sqrt{2}) = 0$ — Apply the zero-product property in reverse.

$x^2 - 3\sqrt{2}\,x + \sqrt{2}\,x - 3\sqrt{2}\sqrt{2} = 0$ — FOIL

Equation: $\mathbf{x^2 - 2\sqrt{2}\,x - 6 = 0}$

2. **5 - only solution** (A double solution)

$x = 5$ \| $x = 5$ — Let $x = 5$.

$x - 5 = 0$ \| $x - 5 = 0$ — Make one side zero.

$(x - 5)(x - 5) = 0$ — Apply the zero-product property in reverse.

$x^2 - 5x - 5x + 25 = 0$ — FOIL

Equation: $\mathbf{x^2 - 10x + 25 = 0}$

3. $\mathbf{\frac{-a}{2}}$ **and** $\mathbf{\frac{b}{3}}$

$x = \frac{-a}{2}$ \| $x = \frac{b}{3}$ — Let x = two solutions.

$x + \frac{a}{2} = 0$ \| $x - \frac{b}{3} = 0$ — Make one side zero.

$2x + a = 0$ \| $3x - b = 0$ — Multiply 2 or 3.

$(2x + a)(3x - b) = 0$ — Apply the zero-product property in reverse.

$6x^2 - 2bx + 3ax - ab = 0$ — FOIL

Equation: $\mathbf{6x^2 + (3a - 2b)x - ab = 0}$

8-6 SOLVING EQUATIONS IN QUADRATIC FORM

Equations in Quadratic Form

- **Recall quadratic equation:** $ax^2 + bx + c = 0$
- **Equations in quadratic form** are equations that are not really quadratic but can be reduced to the quadratic form by using proper substitution.

  Example: Although $x^4 + bx^2 + c = 0$ is a fourth-degree equation (in one variable), it has a form similar to a quadratic equation.
- **Substitution:**

  $x^4 + bx^2 + c = 0$

  $(x^2)^2 + bx^2 + c = 0$ — Replace x^4 with $(x^2)^2$.

  Equation in quadratic form: $u^2 + bu + c = 0$ — Let $u = x^2$ (let u = middle term's variable).
- **Solving equations in quadratic form**

Steps

- Rewrite: $x^4 = (x^2)^2$.
- **Let** $u = x^2$. (Let u = middle term's variable.)
- Factor.
- Apply the zero-product property:
- Substitute x^2 back for u (to find x).
- Solve for x.

Example: Solve $x^4 - 5x^2 + 6 = 0$.

$(x^2)^2 - 5x^2 + 6 = 0$

$u^2 - 5u + 6 = 0$ — Equation in quadratic form. (Solve it like normal.)

$(u - 2)(u - 3) = 0$

$u - 2 = 0$	$u - 3 = 0$
$u = 2$	$u = 3$
$x^2 = 2$	$x^2 = 3$
$x = \pm\sqrt{2}$	$x = \pm\sqrt{3}$

Take the square root of both sides.

Steps

- Let $u = \sqrt{y}$. (Let u = middle term's variable.)
- Factor.
- Apply the zero-product property.
- Substitute $\sqrt{y}$ back for u (to find y).
- Solve for y.
- Check.

Example: Solve $y + 2\sqrt{y} - 3 = 0$.

$u^2 + 2u - 3 = 0$ — $u = \sqrt{y}$, $u^2 = \sqrt{y}^2 = y$

$(u - 1)(u + 3) = 0$

$u - 1 = 0$	$u + 3 = 0$
$u = 1$	$u = -3$
$\sqrt{y} = 1$	$\sqrt{y} = -3$
$y = 1$	$y = 9$

$u = \sqrt{y}$; Square both sides.

$y + 2\sqrt{y} - 3 = 0$ — Original equation..

$1 + 2\sqrt{1} - 3 \stackrel{?}{=} 0$	$9 + 2\sqrt{9} - 3 \stackrel{?}{=} 0$
$1 + 2 - 3 \stackrel{?}{=} 0$	$9 + 2 \cdot 3 - 3 \stackrel{?}{=} 0$
$0 = 0$ ✓	$12 \neq 0$

An extraneous solution.

Solution: $y = 1$

Solving Equations in Quadratic Form

Example: Solve $t^{-2} - 7t^{-1} - 8 = 0$ by factoring.

	$t^{-2} - 7t^{-1} - 8 = 0$
- Let $u = t^{-1}$. (Let u = middle term's variable.)	$u^2 - 7u - 8 = 0$ $u = t^{-1}$, $u^2 = (t^{-1})^2 = t^{-2}$
- Factor.	$(u + 1)(u - 8) = 0$
- Apply the zero-product property.	$(u + 1) = 0$	$(u - 8) = 0$
	$u = -1$	$u = 8$
- Substitute $t^{-1} = \frac{1}{t}$ back for u.	$\frac{1}{t} = -1$	$\frac{1}{t} = 8$
- Solve for t.	$t = -1$	$t = \frac{1}{8}$

Example: Determine the x-intercepts of the function.

$$f(x) = (x^2 - 2)^2 - (x^2 - 2) - 6$$

- Let $f(x) = 0$.	$(x^2 - 2)^2 - (x^2 - 2) - 6 = 0$
- Let $u = x^2 - 2$. (Let u = middle term's variable.)	$u^2 - u - 6 = 0$
- Factor.	$(u + 2)(u - 3) = 0$
- Apply the zero-product property.	$(u + 2) = 0$	$(u - 3) = 0$
	$u = -2$	$u = 3$
- Substitute $x^2 - 2$ back for u.	$x^2 - 2 = -2$	$x^2 - 2 = 3$ $u = x^2 - 2$
- Solve for x.	$x^2 = 0$	$x^2 = 5$
	$x = 0$	$x = \pm\sqrt{5}$ Take the square root.
- The x-intercepts of the function:	$(0, 0)$, $(-\sqrt{5}, 0)$, $(\sqrt{5}, 0)$

Summary: Substitution for variable

Equation in Quadratic Form	Substitution	Quadratic Form
$5t^4 - 2t^2 + 7 = 0$	Let $u = t^2$	$5u^2 - 2u + 7 = 0$
$a^6 - 5a^3 + 4 = 0$	Let $u = a^3$	$u^2 - 5u + 4 = 0$
$2w^{-2} - 7w^{-1} + 5 = 0$	Let $u = w^{-1}$ $u^2 = w^{-2}$	$2u^2 - 7u + 5 = 0$
$7x + 4\sqrt{x} = 3$	Let $u = \sqrt{x}$ $u^2 = x$	$7u^2 + 4u - 3 = 0$
$(x^2 + 3x)^2 - 5(x^2 + 3x) + 4 = 0$	Let $u = x^2 + 3x$	$u^2 - 5u + 4 = 0$
$3b^{1/2} - b^{1/4} = 2$	Let $u = b^{1/4}$ $u^2 = (b^{1/4})^2 = b^{1/2}$	$3u^2 - u = 2$
$2t^{2/3} + 3t^{1/3} - 5 = 0$	Let $u = t^{1/3}$ $u^2 = (t^{1/3})^2 = t^{2/3}$	$2u^2 + 3u - 5 = 0$

(Let u = middle term's variable.)

8-7 QUADRATIC AND RATIONAL INEQUALITIES

Quadratic Inequalities

- **Review inequality symbols**

Symbol	Meaning
$>$	is greater than
$<$	is less than
$\geq$	is greater than or equal to
$\leq$	is less than or equal to

- **Quadratic inequality**: an inequality written in one of the following forms.

Standard Quadratic Inequality	Example
$Ax^2 + Bx + C > 0$	$3x^2 + 5x + 7 > 0$
$Ax^2 + Bx + C < 0$	$7x^2 - 4x + 3 < 0$
$Ax^2 + Bx + C \geq 0$	$4x^2 + 11x - 6 \geq 0$
$Ax^2 + Bx + C \leq 0$	$2x^2 - 3x - 2 \leq 0$

Procedure for Solving Quadratic Inequalities

- Convert the given inequality to standard form.
- Solve the related quadratic equation ($Ax^2 + Bx + C = 0$) and find the cut points (x-intercepts).
- Use cut points to divide the number line into intervals (create a sign chart).
- Test each interval and determine the solution set (pick test values within each interval).
- Graph and write the solution(s).

- **Graphing real-number inequalities (review)**
  - **The empty circle ○ or open interval ( ) :** the endpoints are excluded.
  - **The filled in circle ● or closed interval [ ]:** the endpoints are included.
  - Use a **heavy line** (shade) and open or closed interval, or use an empty circle versus filled-in circle to graph the intervals.

Solving Quadratic Inequalities

Example: Solve $x^2 - 3x < 4$ and graph the solution set.

Steps	Solution	
	$x^2 - 3x < 4$	
- Convert to standard form. $(Ax^2 + Bx + C < 0)$	$x^2 - 3x - 4 < 0$	Subtract 4.
- Solve the related equation and find the cut points (x-intercepts).	$x^2 - 3x - 4 = 0$	
	$(x - 4)(x + 1) = 0$	Factor.
	$x - 4 = 0$ ¦ $x + 1 = 0$	Zero-product property
Cut points:	$x = 4$ ¦ $x = -1$	

- Use cut points to divide the number line into three distinct intervals (create a sign chart).

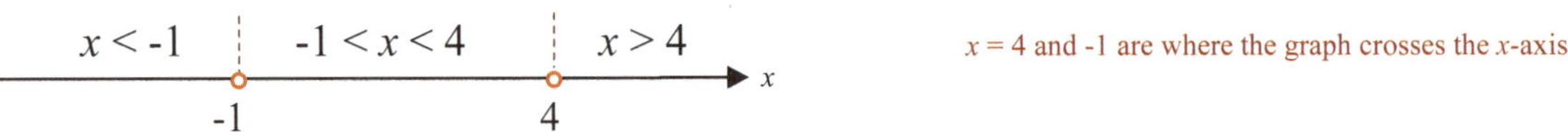

$x = 4$ and -1 are where the graph crosses the x-axis.

Note: The open circles ○ are used because the sign of the inequality is "less than" (<).

- Test each interval and determine the solution sets (pick a number within each interval).

Test $x < -1$: pick any value less than -1, say $x = -2$.	Test $x > 4$: pick any value great than 4, say $x = 5$.	Test $-1 < x < 4$: pick any value between -1 and 4, say $x = 1$.
$x^2 - 3x < 4$	$x^2 - 3x < 4$	$x^2 - 3x < 4$
$(-2)^2 - 3(-2) \overset{?}{<} 4$	$5^2 - 3 \cdot 5 \overset{?}{<} 4$	$1^2 - 3 \cdot 1 \overset{?}{<} 4$
$4 + 6 \overset{?}{<} 0$	$25 - 15 \overset{?}{<} 4$	$1 - 3 \overset{?}{<} 4$
× $10 < 4$, false	× $10 < 4$, false	√ $-2 < 4$, true

- **Graph** (shade) the solution set on the number line (on the sign chart).

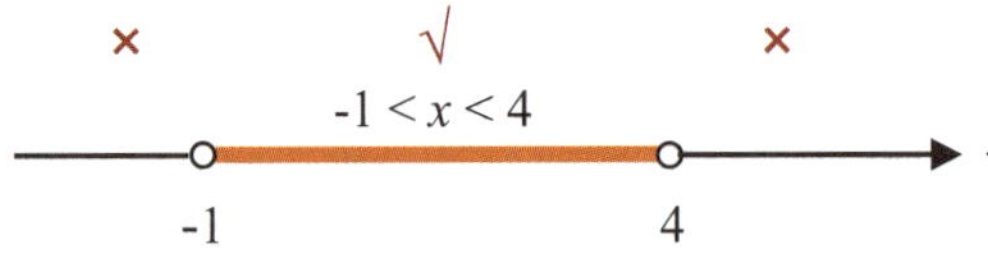

- Solution set: $\{ x \mid -1 < x < 4 \}$ **or** $(-1, 4)$

Example: Solve $2x^2 - 7x \geq -3$ and graph the solution set.

Steps	Solution	
	$2x^2 - 7x \geq -3$	
- Convert to standard form.	$2x^2 - 7x + 3 \geq 0$	Add 3 to both sides.
- Solve the related equation.	$2x^2 - 7x + 3 = 0$	
	$(2x - 1)(x - 3) = 0$	Factor.
	$2x - 1 = 0$ ¦ $x - 3 = 0$	Zero-product property
- Cut points:	$x = \frac{1}{2}$ ¦ $x = 3$	

- Intervals:

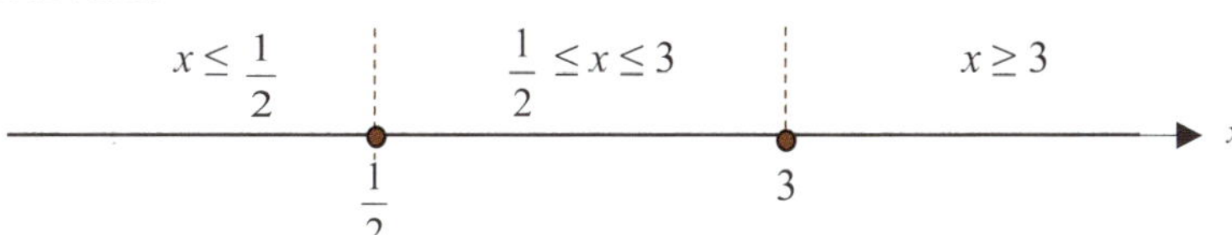

Note: The closed circles • are used because the sign of the inequality is "great than or equal to" (≥).

- Test.

Test $x \leq \frac{1}{2}$: pick any value less than $\frac{1}{2}$, say $x = 0$.	Test $x \geq 3$: pick any value great than 3, say $x = 4$.	Test $\frac{1}{2} \leq x \leq 3$: pick any value between $\frac{1}{2}$ and 3, say $x = 1$.
$2x^2 - 7x \geq -3$	$2x^2 - 7x \geq -3$	$2x^2 - 7x \geq -3$
$2 \cdot 0^2 - 7 \cdot 0 \overset{?}{\geq} -3$	$2 \cdot 4^2 - 7 \cdot 4 \overset{?}{\geq} -3$	$2 \cdot 1^2 - 7 \cdot 1 \overset{?}{\geq} -3$
$0 - 0 \overset{?}{\geq} -3$	$32 - 28 \overset{?}{\geq} -3$	$2 - 7 \overset{?}{\geq} -3$
√ $0 > -3$, true	√ $4 > -3$, true	× $-5 > -3$, false

- Graph.

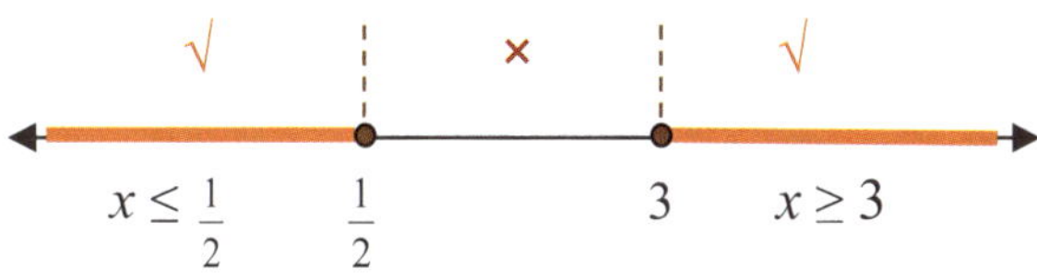

Solution set: $\{x \mid x \leq \frac{1}{2}$ **or** $x \geq 3\}$ **or** $(-\infty, \frac{1}{2}] \cup [3, \infty)$

Rational Inequalities

- **Rational inequality**: an inequality involving fractional expression(s).

  Examples: $\frac{x}{x-2} \geq 0$, $\frac{x+5}{x-4} \geq 0$

- **Analyzing and graphing a rational inequality/function**

  Example: $\frac{x}{x-2} \geq \mathbf{0}$ $f(x) = \frac{x}{x-2}$

x	$y = f(x) = \frac{x}{x-2}$
0	0
1	-1
-1	0.33
2	∞
3	3
4	2
5	1.67

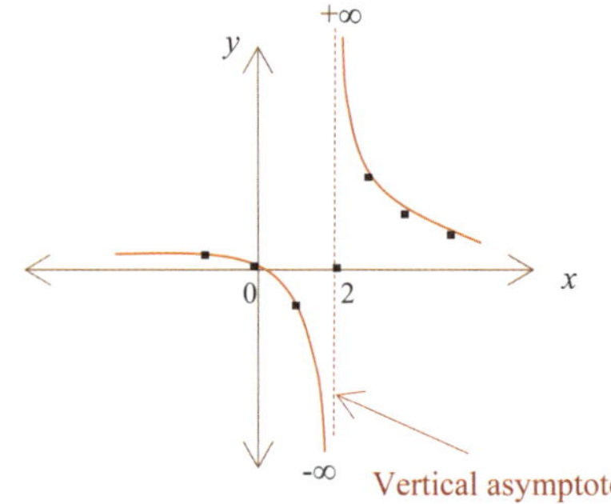

- Where is this $\left(\frac{x}{x-2} \geq \mathbf{0}\right)$ true?
- Or when is $\frac{x}{x-2}$ positive? ($\geq \mathbf{0}$)
- Or, graphically, for what x is $f(x) = \frac{x}{x-2}$ above the x–axis?
- Or where can $f(x) = \frac{x}{x-2}$ change its sign (from negative to positive, or vice versa)?
- $f(x) = \frac{x}{x-2}$ changes sign (crosses the x-axis) when $x = 0$ (the numerator = 0) and when $x = 2$ (the denominator = 0, or $f(x) = \infty$ or undefined).
- **The graph of** $f(x) = \frac{x}{x-2}$ has a vertical asymptote at points where the denominator is 0. The sign of $f(x)$ might change from $-\infty$ to $+\infty$ (it is undefined for $f(x) = \frac{x}{x-2}$).

- **Cut points (or critical points) of rational inequalities:** the points where the rational inequality changes sign or is 0 (the numerator) and undefined (the denominator).

  Example: The cut points for $\frac{x}{x-2} \geq \mathbf{0}$ are $x = 0$ and $x = 2$.

Solving Rational Inequalities

Example: Solve $\frac{x+5}{x-4} \geq 0$ and graph the solution set.

Steps	**Solution**	
- Find the cut points:	$\frac{x+5}{x-4} \geq 0$	
Set the numerator = 0	$x + 5 = 0, \quad x = -5$	Subtract 5.
Set the denominator = 0	$x - 4 = 0, \quad x = 4$	Add 4.

- Use cut points to divide the number line into intervals (create a sign chart).

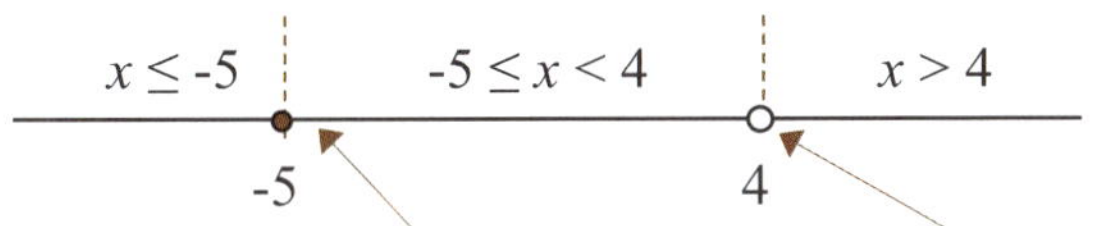

Note: -5 is included. 4 is not included (since $x = 4$ is undefined).

- Test each interval and determine the solution sets.

Test $x \leq -5$: pick $x = -6$	Test $x > 4$: pick $x = 5$	Test $-5 \leq x < 4$: pick $x = 1$
$\frac{x+5}{x-4} \geq 0$	$\frac{x+5}{x-4} \geq 0$	$\frac{x+5}{x-4} \geq 0$
$\frac{-6+5}{-6-4} \overset{?}{\geq} 0$	$\frac{5+5}{5-4} \overset{?}{\geq} 0$	$\frac{1+5}{1-4} \overset{?}{\geq} 0$
√	√	×
$\frac{-1}{-10} = \frac{1}{10} > 0$, true	$\frac{10}{1} = 10 > 0$, true	$\frac{6}{-3} = -2 > 0$, false

- Graph:

- Solution sets: $\{ x \mid x \leq -5$ **or** $x > 4 \}$ **or** $(-\infty, -5] \cup (4, \infty)$

Unit 8 Summary

- **A quadratic equation**: an equation that has a squared term.

Quadratic Equations in Standard Form	
$ax^2 + bx + c = 0$	$a \neq 0$

- **Zero-product property**

Zero-Product Property
If $A \cdot B = 0$, then either $A = 0$ or $B = 0$ (or both)
(A and B are algebraic expressions.)

- **Solving incomplete quadratic equations**

Incomplete Quadratic Equation	Steps	Example
Use the zero-product property to solve $ax^2 + bx = 0$.	- Express in $ax^2 + bx = 0$ - Factor: $x(ax + b) = 0$ - Apply the zero-product property: $x = 0$ ¦ $ax + b = 0$ - Solve for x: $x = 0$ ¦ $x = -\frac{b}{a}$	**Solve $9x^2 = -5x$** $9x^2 + 5x = 0$ Add 5x. $x(9x + 5) = 0$ $x = 0$ ¦ $9x + 5 = 0$ $x = 0$ ¦ $x = -\frac{5}{9}$
Use the square root method to solve $ax^2 - c = 0$ (or $ax^2 = c$).	- Express in $ax^2 = c$ - Divide both sides by a: $x^2 = \frac{c}{a}$ - Take the square root of both sides: $x = \pm\sqrt{\frac{c}{a}}$	**Solve $7x^2 - 4 = 0$** $7x^2 = 4$ $x^2 = \frac{4}{7}$ $x = \pm\sqrt{\frac{4}{7}} \approx \pm 0.76$ Exact solutions / Approximate solutions

- **The x-intercepts of a quadratic equation** are the solutions of a quadratic equation.

- **Completing the square** is the process of finding a number to add to a quadratic equation and to form a perfect square, such as: $x^2 + 10x + \boxed{?} = (x + 5)^2$

- **Procedure to complete the square – Case I: $x^2 + bx + c = 0$**
  - Express in the form $x^2 + bx = -c$.
  - Add $\square$ to both sides of the equation.
  - Determine $\left(\frac{b}{2}\right)^2$ (Take half of the coefficient of x and square it.)
  - Add $\left(\frac{b}{2}\right)^2$ to both sides of the equation. $x^2 + bx + \left(\frac{b}{2}\right)^2 = -c + \left(\frac{b}{2}\right)^2$
  - Factor the left side.
  - Take the square root of both sides.
  - Solve for x.

- **Procedure to complete the square - Case II: $Ax^2 + Bx + C = 0$**
  - Express in the form $Ax^2 + Bx = - C$.
  - Make the coefficient of x^2 equal to 1.
  - Add $\square$ to both sides of the equation.
  - Determine $\left(\frac{b}{2}\right)^2$.
  - Add $\left(\frac{b}{2}\right)^2$ to both sides of the equation.
  - Factor the left side.
  - Take the square root of both sides.
  - Solve for x.

- **Simple interest**: interest computed on the original principal.
- **Compound interest**: interest computed on both the principal and the past interest earned.
- **Compound interest formula**

Formula	Component
$A = P(1 + r)^t$	A – new value P – starting principal r – interest rate t – time (year)

- **Methods for solving quadratic equations**

Quadratic Equation	Method
$ax^2 + c = 0$ (no x term)	square root method
$ax^2 + bx = 0$ ($c = 0$)	zero-product property
$ax^2 + bx + c = 0$	try factoring first
$ax^2 + bx + c = 0$ Not factorable (or does not factor easily)	completing the square or quadratic formula

- **The quadratic formula**: a general formula that can be used to solve any quadratic equation.

The Quadratic Formula		
Quadratic equation:	$ax^2 + bx + c = 0$	
The solutions:	$x = \frac{-b \pm \sqrt{b^2 - 4ac}}{2a}$	$(a \neq 0)$

- **Discriminant**

Quadratic Formula	Discriminant
$x = \frac{-b \pm \sqrt{b^2 - 4ac}}{2a}$	$b^2 - 4ac$

- **Discriminant and solutions**

Discriminant: $b^2 - 4ac$	Nature of Solution	Example	$b^2 - 4ac$
$(b^2 - 4ac) = 0$	One real solution	$x^2 - 4x + 4 = 0$ $x = 2$	$(-4)^2 - 4(1)(4) = 0$
$(b^2 - 4ac) > 0$	Two real solutions	$x^2 + 5x + 4 = 0$ $x = -4$ or -1	$5^2 - 4(1)(4) = 9 > 0$
$(b^2 - 4ac) < 0$	Two non-real (complex solutions)	$x^2 - 4x + 9 = 0$ $x = 2 \pm i\sqrt{5}$	$(-4)^2 - 4(1)(9) = -20 < 0$

- **Writing equation from solutions:** applying the zero-product property in reverse.
- **Zero-product property in reverse:** If $A = 0$ or $B = 0$, then $A \cdot B = 0$ (A and B are algebraic expressions.)
- **Equations in quadratic form:** equations that are not really quadratic but can be reduced to the quadratic form by using proper substitution.
- **Substitution for variable** (Let u = middle term's variable)

Equation in Quadratic Form	Substitution	Quadratic Form
$5t^4 - 2t^2 + 7 = 0$	Let $u = t^2$	$5u^2 - 2u + 7 = 0$
$a^6 - 5a^3 + 4 = 0$	Let $u = a^3$	$u^2 - 5u + 4 = 0$
$2w^{-2} - 7w^{-1} + 5 = 0$	Let $u = w^{-1}$ $u^2 = w^{-2}$	$2u^2 - 7u + 5 = 0$
$7x + 4\sqrt{x} = 3$	Let $u = \sqrt{x}$ $u^2 = x$	$7u^2 + 4u - 3 = 0$
$(x^2 + 3x)^2 - 5(x^2 + 3x) + 4 = 0$	Let $u = x^2 + 3x$	$u^2 - 5u + 4 = 0$
$3b^{1/2} - b^{1/4} = 2$	Let $u = b^{1/4}$ $u^2 = (b^{1/4})^2 = b^{1/2}$	$3u^2 - u = 2$
$2t^{2/3} + 3t^{1/3} - 5 = 0$	Let $u = t^{1/3}$ $u^2 = (t^{1/3})^2 = t^{2/3}$	$2u^2 + 3u - 5 = 0$

- **Quadratic inequality**: an inequality written in one of the following forms.

Standard Quadratic Inequality	Example
$Ax^2 + Bx + C > 0$	$3x^2 + 5x + 7 > 0$
$Ax^2 + Bx + C < 0$	$7x^2 - 4x + 3 < 0$
$Ax^2 + Bx + C \geq 0$	$4x^2 + 11x - 6 \geq 0$
$Ax^2 + Bx + C \leq 0$	$2x^2 - 3x - 2 \leq 0$

Procedure for Solving Quadratic Inequalities

- Convert the given inequality to standard form.
- Solve the related quadratic equation ($Ax^2 + Bx + C = 0$) and find the cut points (x-intercepts).
- Use cut points to divide the number line into intervals (create a sign chart).
- Test each interval and determine the solution set (pick test values within each interval).
- Graph and write the solution(s).

- **Rational inequality:** an inequality involving fractional expression(s).
- **Cut points (or critical points) of rational inequalities:** the points where the rational inequality is 0 (the numerator) or undefined (the denominator).

PRACTICE QUIZ

Unit 8 Quadratic Equations and Inequalities

1. Solve the following equation: $(x + 5)^2 = 3$

2. Solve the following by completing the square. $x^2 + 4x - 3 = 0$

3. 5,000 grows to \$5,500 in 2 years. Calculate interest rate r.

4. Use the quadratic formula to solve the following.

   a. $x^2 - 4x + 1 = 0$

   b. $3x(x + 2) - (x - 5) = x^2 - x$

5. How much fencing would be required for a rectangular field of area 4,000 m^2 if the length is 30m more than the width?

6. Find the length of the side of a square with diagonal equal to 10m.

7. The product of two consecutive integers is 132. Find the two integers.

8. Use the discriminant to determine the nature of the solutions of $x^2 + 5\sqrt{3}x - 4 = 0$

9. Solve $m^{-2} - 6m^{-1} - 7 = 0$.

10. Solve $x^2 + 2x - 8 \geq 0$ and graph the solution set.

UNIT 9 CONICS

- **A conic section:** a curve obtained as the intersection of a plane with a cone.
- **Slicing a cone** (or a double cone) can generate a circle, a parabola, an ellipse or a hyperbola.

The intersection of a plane with a double cone.

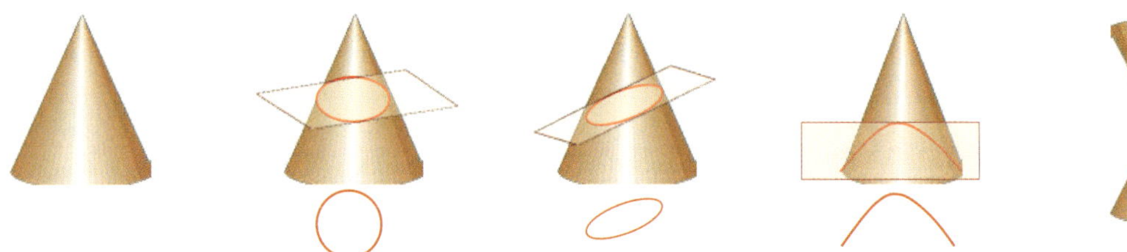

9-1 CIRCLES

The Distance Formula

- **Distance formula** can determine the distance between any two points on a coordinate plane.
- **The distance (d) between two points (x_1, y_1) and (x_2, y_2)**

Distance Formula	Example
$d = \sqrt{(x_2 - x_1)^2 + (y_2 - y_1)^2}$	$(x_1, y_1) = (1, 4)$, $(x_2, y_2) = (5, 1)$ $d = \sqrt{(5-1)^2 + (1-4)^2} = \sqrt{16+9} = 5$

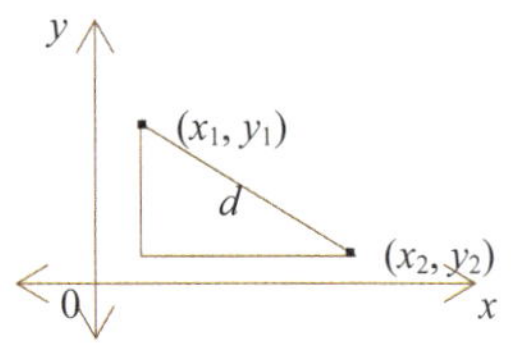

Note: It does not matter which point is (x_1, y_1) and which is (x_2, y_2).

Tip: The Pythagorean theorem is the basis for calculating distance between two points. The hypotenuse is the distance between the two points.

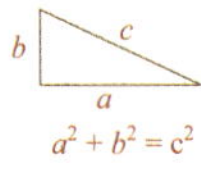

Example: Find the distance between the points (-3, 2) and (4, -3).

- Let: $(x_1, y_1) = (-3, 2)$, $(x_2, y_2) = (4, -3)$

  $d = \sqrt{(4-(-3))^2 + (-3-2)^2} = \sqrt{49+25} = \mathbf{\sqrt{74}}$

- Let: $(x_1, y_1) = (4, -3)$, $(x_2, y_2) = (-3, 2)$

  $d = \sqrt{(-3-4)^2 + (2-(-3))^2} = \sqrt{49+25} = \mathbf{\sqrt{74}}$

$d = \sqrt{(x_2 - x_1)^2 + (y_2 - y_1)^2}$

- **The midpoint formula for a segment** determines the midpoint of a line segment.

Midpoint Formula	Example
$\left(\frac{x_1 + x_2}{2}, \frac{y_1 + y_2}{2}\right)$	$(x_1, y_1) = (4, 3)$, $(x_2, y_2) = (-4, 1)$ midpoint $= \left(\frac{4+(-4)}{2}, \frac{3+1}{2}\right) = \mathbf{(0, 2)}$

A midpoint divides a line segment into two equal parts.

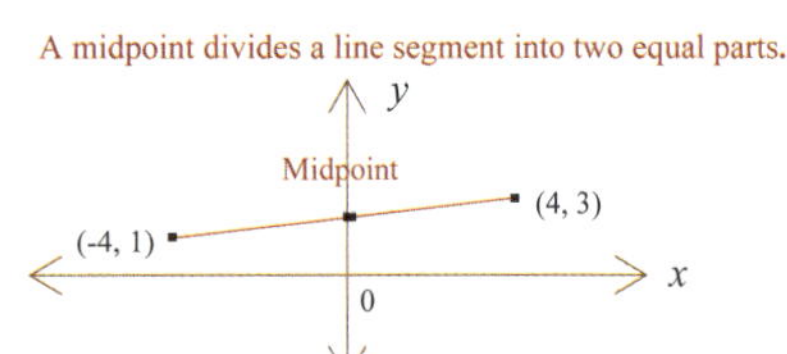

The Circle

- **Circle:** every point on the curve is equally distant from the center.

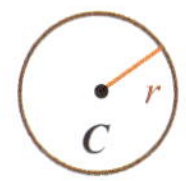

C – center
r – radius

- **Circles in the real world**

Ring	Pizza	Clock	Smiley face

- **Equation of circles**

Center of a Circle	The Standard Form Equation	Example
center at origin (0, 0)	$x^2 + y^2 = r^2$	$x^2 + y^2 = 3^2$ $r = 3$
center at (h, k)	$(x - h)^2 + (y - k)^2 = r^2$	$(x - 2)^2 + (y - 1)^2 = 2^2$ $(h, k) = (2, 1)$, $r = 2$

r – radius

Example: Identify the center and radius of the following circles.

Equation	Center	Radius	Graph
$x^2 + y^2 = 1$ $x^2 + y^2 = 1^2$	(0, 0)	1	$r = 1$
$x^2 + y^2 = 4$ $x^2 + y^2 = 2^2$	(0, 0)	2	$r = 2$
$(x - 3)^2 + (y + 2)^2 = 9$ $(x - 3)^2 + [y - (-2)]^2 = 3^2$	(3, -2)	3	(3, -2) $r = 3$

- **General form equation for a circle**

The General Form	Example
$x^2 + y^2 + Cx + Dy + E = 0$	$x^2 + y^2 - 2x + 4y - 20 = 0$

Example: Identify the center and the radius of the following circle.

$\mathbf{x^2 + y^2 - 2x + 4y - 20 = 0}$ — Add 20 to both sides.

$x^2 + y^2 - 2x + 4y = 20$ — Regroup x and y terms together.

$(x^2 - 2x \quad) + (y^2 + 4y \quad) = 20$ — Complete the square.

$\left(\frac{-2}{2}\right)^2 = 1$ $\left(\frac{4}{2}\right)^2 = 4$ — $x^2 + bx + c = 0$; $\left(\frac{-b}{2}\right)^2$

$(x^2 - 2x + 1) + (y^2 + 4y + 4) = 20 + 1 + 4$ — Add 1 and 4 to both sides.

$(x - 1)^2 + (y + 2)^2 = 5^2$ — Factor.

Center: (1, -2) , radius $r = 5$ — $(x - h)^2 + (y - k)^2 = r^2$; center: (h, k).

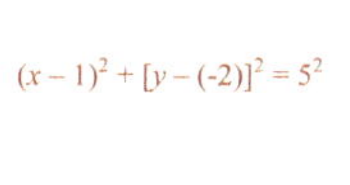

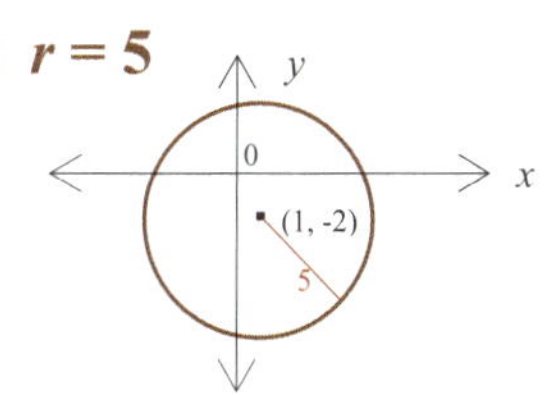

9-2 PARABOLAS

Introduction to Parabolas

- **Parabola:** a curve ('U' shaped curve) where every point is the same distance from a **fixed point** (the focus ***F***) and a **fixed line** (the **directrix**).

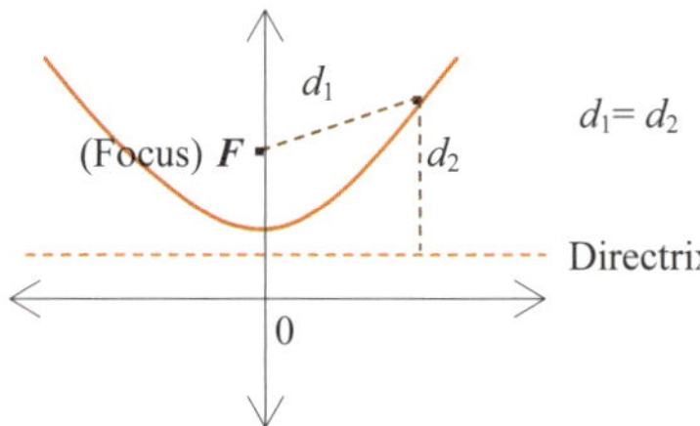

- **Parabolas in the real world**

Dome	Rainbow	Suspension Bridge	Arch

- **Parabola terminology**

Term	Definition	Diagram
focus	A fixed point whose relationship with a directrix defines a parabola.	F (focus), Vertex, Directrix, Axis of symmetry
directrix	A fixed straight line perpendicular to the axis of symmetry.	
axis of symmetry	A line segment that is perpendicular to the directrix and passes through the vertex and focus of a parabola.	
vertex	The point where a parabola makes its sharpest turn as it crosses its axis of symmetry. It is where the distance from the focus and directrix is shortest.	

- **Recall: equations of parabolas**

Equations of Parabolas	
$y = Ax^2 + Bx + C$	$x = Ay^2 + By + C$
$y = Ax^2$	$x = Ay^2$
$y = Ax^2 + C$	$x = Ay^2 + C$
$y = A(x - h)^2$	$x = A(y - k)^2$
$y = A(x - h)^2 + k$	$x = A(y - k)^2 + h$

Function: $f(x) = Ax^2 + Bx^2 + C$　　　$f(y) = Ay^2 + By^2 + C$

- **The graph of a quadratic function or equation is a parabola.**

Graphing a Parabola

An easy method for graphing parabolas: make a table of x and y values for the equation and plot the points.

Example: Sketch the graph of $y = 3x^2$.

- Make a table of x values for the equation.
- Pick some values of x and solve for each corresponding y to get the ordered pairs (points)
  Tip: Pick points on both sides of the axis.
- Plot the points and connect them with a smooth curve.

x	$y = 3x^2$	(x, y)
0	$y = 3 \cdot 0^2 = 0$	(0, 0)
1	$y = 3 \cdot 1^2 = 3$	(1, 3)
-1	$y = 3 \cdot (-1)^2 = 3$	(-1, 3)
2	$y = 3 \cdot 2^2 = 12$	(2, 12)
-2	$y = 3 \cdot (-2)^2 = 12$	(-2, 12)

Choose. Calculate.

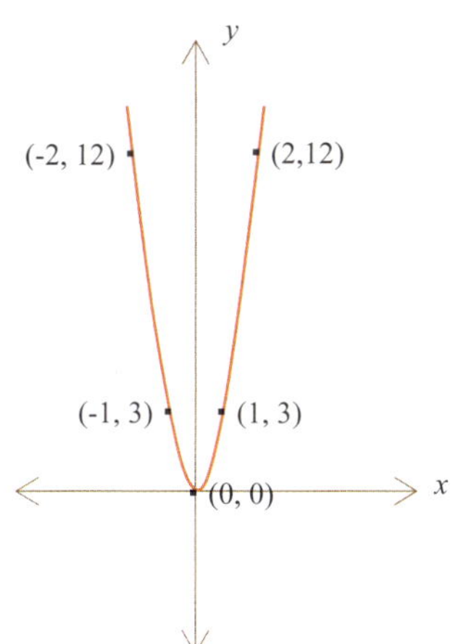

Parabola in the Form $f(x) = Ax^2$ and $f(y) = Ay^2$

- **General information for a parabola of the form $f(x) = Ax^2$ and $f(y) = Ay^2$**

Equation	Vertex	Axis of Symmetry	Equation for the Axis of Symmetry
$f(x) = Ax^2$	(0, 0)	symmetry about the y – axis	$x = 0$
$f(y) = Ay^2$	(0, 0)	symmetry about the x – axis	$y = 0$

Equation	General	Shape	Example	Table	Graph
$f(x) = Ax^2$	$A > 0$ Opens up		$y = 2x^2$ ($A = 2 > 0$)	x: 0 1 -1 2 -2; y: 0 2 2 8 8	(-2, 8) (2, 8) (-1, 2) (1, 2)
	$A < 0$ Opens down		$y = -2x^2$ ($A = -2 < 0$)	x: 0 1 -1 2 -2; y: 0 -2 -2 -8 -8	(-1, -2) (1,-2) (-2, -8) (2, -8)
$f(y) = Ay^2$	$A > 0$ Opens to the right		$x = 2y^2$ ($A = 2 > 0$)	(Pick y values) y: 0 1 -1 2 -2; x: 0 2 2 8 8 (Calculate x values)	(2, 1) (2,-1) (8, 2) (8,-2)
	$A < 0$ Opens to the left		$x = -2y^2$ ($A = -2 < 0$)	y: 0 1 -1 2 -2; x: 0 -2 -2 -8 -8	(-8, 2) (-8,-2) (-2, 1) (-2,-1)

- **The line of symmetry** divides the parabola into two equal halves.
- **The coefficient A in $f(x) = Ax^2$ can shrink or stretch the parabola**

The Coefficient A in $y = Ax^2$ & $x = Ay^2$			Example
- The larger the $\|A\|$, the narrower the curve.	$f(x) = Ax^2$	$A > 0$	$y = x^2$, $y = \frac{1}{2}x^2$, $y = 3x^2$
- The smaller the $\|A\|$, the wider the curve.		$A < 0$	$y = -\frac{1}{2}x^2$, $y = -x^2$, $y = -3x^2$

Parabola in the Form $y = Ax^2 + C$ & $x = Ay^2 + C$

- The graph of $y = Ax^2 + C$ or $x = Ay^2 + C$ is a parabola that has the same shape as $y = Ax^2$ or $x = Ay^2$, but is shifted C units vertically or horizontally.

- **General information for a parabola of the form $y = Ax^2 + C$ and $x = Ay^2 + C$**

Parabola Equation	Vertex	Axis of Symmetry	Shifting
$y = Ax^2 + C$	$(0, C)$	symmetry about the y - axis	The same shape as $y = Ax^2$, but is shifted C units vertically.
$x = Ay^2 + C$	$(C, 0)$	symmetry about the x - axis	The same shape as $y = Ax^2$, but is shifted C units horizontally.

Equation	C	Shifting	Vertex	Graph	Example	Graph
$y = Ax^2 + C$ $A > 0$: opens up $A < 0$: opens down	$C > 0$	$y = Ax^2$ is shifted C units **up**.	$(0, C)$	$(0, C)$	$y = 2x^2 + 1$ $(C = 1 > 0)$	$(0, 1)$
	$C < 0$	$y = Ax^2$ is shifted C units **down**.		$(0, C)$	$y = 2x^2 - 3$ $(C = -3 < 0)$	$(0, -3)$
$x = Ay^2 + C$ $A > 0$: opens to the right $A < 0$: opens to the left	$C > 0$	$x = Ay^2$ is shifted C units to the **right**.	$(C, 0)$	$(C, 0)$	$x = 2y^2 + 4$ $(C = 4 > 0)$	$(4, 0)$
	$C < 0$	$x = Ay^2$ is shifted C units to the **left**.		$(C, 0)$	$x = 2y^2 - \frac{1}{3}$ $(C = -\frac{1}{3} < 0)$	$(\frac{-1}{3}, 0)$

Tips: - C indicates how far the parabola has been shifted vertically or horizontally.

- If $A > 0$, the parabola opens up or to the right. If $A < 0$, the parabola opens down or to the left.

Example: Sketch the graph of $y = -3x^2 - 2$. $(A = -3 < 0,$ opens down$)$

- Make a table for $y = -3x^2$

x	0	1	-1
$y = -3x^2$	0	-3	-3

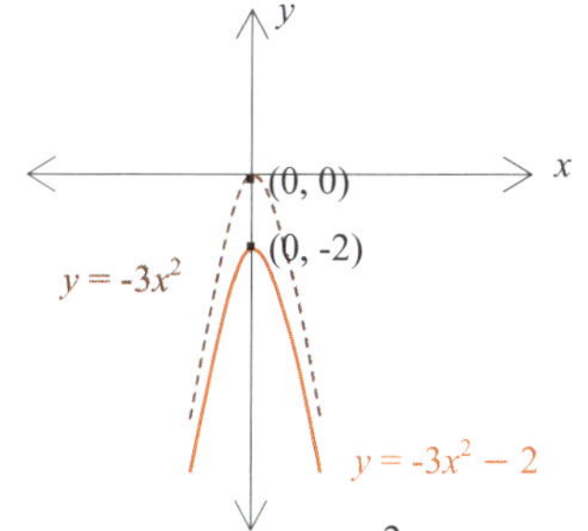

- Plot $y = -3x^2$: $A = -3 < 0$, opens down.

- Plot $x = -3y^2 - 2$: $C = -2 < 0$, shift 2 units down from $y = -3x^2$.

Parabola in the Form $y = A(x - h)^2$ & $x = A(y - h)^2$

- The graph of $y = A(x - h)^2$ or $x = A(y - h)^2$ is a parabola that has the same shape as $y = Ax^2$ or $x = Ay^2$, but is shifted h units horizontally or vertically.

- **General information for a parabola of the form $y = A(x - h)^2$ and $x = A(y - h)^2$**

Equation	Vertex	Axis of Symmetry	Shifting
$y = A(x - h)^2$	$(h, 0)$	symmetry about the line $x = h$	The same shape as $y = Ax^2$, but is shifted h units horizontally.
$x = A(y - h)^2$	$(0, h)$	symmetry about the line $y = h$	The same shape as $y = Ax^2$, but is shifted h units vertically.

Equation	h	Shifting	Vertex	Graph	Example	Graph
$y = A(x - h)^2$ $A > 0$: opens up $A < 0$: opens down	$h > 0$	$y = Ax^2$ is shifted h units to the **right**.	$(h, 0)$	$(h, 0)$	$y = 2(x - 3)^2$ $(h = 3 > 0)$	$(3, 0)$
	$h < 0$	$y = Ax^2$ is shifted h units to the **left.**		$(h, 0)$	$y = 2(x + 3)^2$ $(h = -3 < 0)$ $y = 2[x - (-3)]^2$	$(-3, 0)$
$x = A(y - h)^2$ $A > 0$: opens to the right $A < 0$: opens to the left	$h > 0$	$x = Ay^2$ is shifted h units **up.**	$(0, h)$	$(0, h)$	$x = 2(y - 3)^2$ $(h = 3 > 0)$	$(0, 3)$
	$h < 0$	$x = Ay^2$ is shifted h units **down.**		$(0, h)$	$x = 2(y + 3)^2$ $(h = -3 < 0)$ $x = 2[y - (-3)]^2$	$(0, -3)$

Tip: h shows how far the parabola has been shifted vertically or horizontally.

Example: Sketch the graph of $x = -3(y - 4)^2$.

- Make a table for $x = -3y^2$

y	0	1	-1	(Pick y values.)
$x = -3y^2$	0	-3	-3	(Calculate x values.)
(x, y)	(0, 0)	(-3, 1)	(-3, -1)	

- Plot $x = -3y^2$ $A = -3 > 0$, opens left.

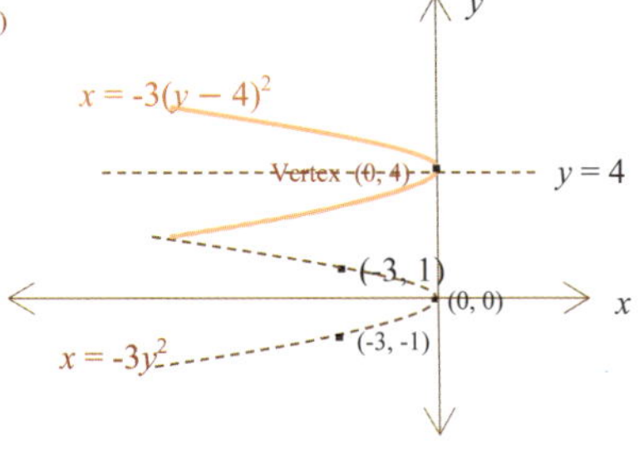

- Plot $x = -3(y - 4)^2$: $h = 4 > 0$, $x = -3y^2$ is shifted 4 units up.
- Vertex: (0, 4)
- Axis of symmetry: $y = 4$

Parabola in the Form $y = A(x - h)^2 + k$ & $x = A(y - k)^2 + h$

General information for a parabola of the form $y = A(x - h)^2 + k$ and $x = A(y - k)^2 + h$

Equation	Vertex	Axis of Symmetry
$y = A(x-h)^2 + k$	(h, k)	symmetry about the line $x = h$
$x = A(y-k)^2 + h$		symmetry about the line $y = h$

Equation	Graph	Example	Graph
$y = A(x - h)^2 + k$ $A > 0$: opens up $A < 0$: opens down	(h, k), 0	$y = 2(x-3)^2 + 4$ $(h = 3,\ k = 4)$	(3, 4), 0
$x = A(y - k)^2 + h$ $A > 0$: opens to the right $A < 0$: opens to the left	(h, k), 0	$x = 2(y-3)^2 + 4$ $(h = 4,\ k = 3)$	(4, 3), 0

Example: Sketch the graph of $y = -2x^2 - 4x - 5$.

- Convert to $y = A(x-h)^2 + k$ by completing the square. $\left(\frac{b}{2}\right)^2$

$$y = -2x^2 - 4x - 5$$
$$= -2(x^2 + 2x \qquad) - 5 \qquad \text{Factor out -2.}$$
$$= -2(x^2 + 2x + 1 - 1) - 5 \qquad \left(\frac{b}{2}\right)^2 = \left(\frac{2}{2}\right)^2 = 1$$
$$= -2(x^2 + 2x + 1) + (-2)(-1) - 5$$
$$= -2(x^2 + 2x + 1) - 3$$
$$\mathbf{y = -2(x + 1)^2 - 3} \qquad y = -2[x - (-1)]^2 + (-3)$$

- Identify the vertex: (h, k)　　**$(h, k) = (-1, -3)$**　　$y = A(x-h)^2 + k$
- Determine the axis of symmetry: $x = h$　　$x = h = -1$
- Check A $\begin{cases} A > 0: \text{ opens up} \\ A < 0: \text{ opens down} \end{cases}$　　$A = -2 < 0$: opens down　　$y = -2(x+1)^2 - 3$
- Plot the vertex and the axis of symmetry.
- Make a table and find a few points.

x	$y = -2x^2 - 4x - 5$	(x, y)
0	$y = -2 \cdot 0^2 - 4 \cdot 0 - 5 = -5$	(0, -5)
-2	$y = -2\,(-2)^2 - 4\,(-2) - 5 = -5$	(-2, -5)
1	$y = -2 \cdot 1^2 - 4 \cdot 1 - 5 = -11$	(1, -11)
-3	$y = -2\,(-3)^2 - 4\,(-3) - 5 = -11$	(-3, -11)

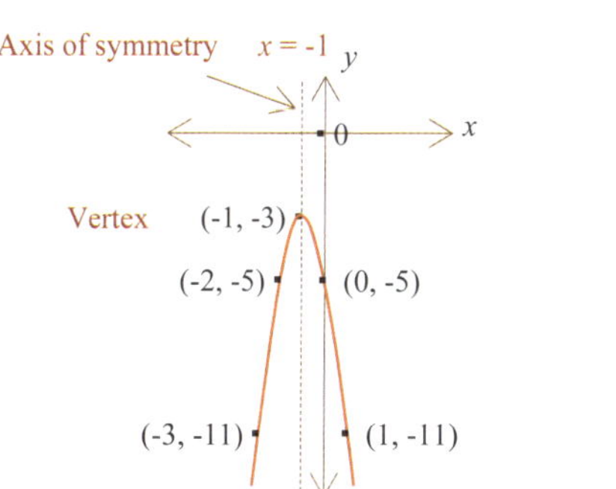

Parabola in the Form $f(x) = Ax^2 + Bx + C$ & $f(y) = Ay^2 + By + C$

Equation	General Shape	Axis of Symmetry	Vertex (h, k)
$f(x) = Ax^2 + Bx + C$ or $y = Ax^2 + Bx + C$	$A > 0$: opens up; $A < 0$: opens down	$x = -\frac{B}{2A}$	$(h, k) = (-\frac{B}{2A}, f\left(\frac{-B}{2A}\right))$
$f(y) = Ay^2 + By + C$ or $x = Ay^2 + By + C$	$A > 0$: opens to the right; $A < 0$: opens to the left	$y = -\frac{B}{2A}$	$(h, k) = (f\left(\frac{-B}{2A}\right), -\frac{B}{2A})$

Example: Sketch the graph of $f(x) = x^2 - 4x + 6$.

Steps

- Determine the axis of symmetry: $x = \frac{-B}{2A}$
- Identify the vertex: $(h, k) = (-\frac{B}{2A}, f\left(\frac{-B}{2A}\right))$
- Check A $\begin{cases} A > 0: \text{opens up} \\ A < 0: \text{opens down} \end{cases}$
- Plot the vertex and the axis of symmetry.
- Find a few more points.

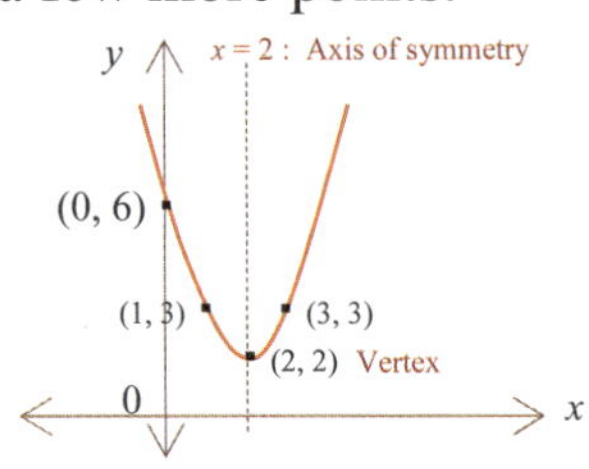

Solution

$x = \frac{-B}{2A} = \frac{-(-4)}{2(1)} = 2$ $y = Ax^2 + Bx + C$

$h = \frac{-B}{2A} = 2$

$k = f\left(\frac{-B}{2A}\right) = 2^2 - 4(2) + 6 = 2$ $f(x) = 1 \cdot x^2 - 4x + 6$

$(h, k) = (2, 2)$

$A = 1 > 0$: opens up $A = 1$

x	$y = x^2 - 4x + 6$	(x, y)
0	$y = 0^2 - 4 \cdot 0 + 6 = 6$	(0, 6)
1	$y = 1^2 - 4 \cdot 1 + 6 = 3$	(1, 3)
3	$y = 3^2 - 4 \cdot 3 + 6 = 3$	(3, 3)

Example: Sketch the graph of $f(y) = y^2 - 2y - 8$.

- The axis of symmetry: $y = \frac{-B}{2A} = \frac{-(-2)}{2 \cdot 1} = 1$ $x = Ay^2 + By + C$
- Vertex: $k = \frac{-B}{2A} = 1$, $h = f\left(\frac{-B}{2A}\right) = 1^2 - 2(1) - 8 = -9$ $(h, k) = \left(f\left(\frac{-B}{2A}\right), \frac{-B}{2A}\right)$, $(h, k) = (-9, 1)$
- Check A: $A = 1 > 0$, opens to the right.
- Plot the vertex and the axis of symmetry.
- Make a table and find a few points.

y	$x = y^2 - 2y - 8$	(x, y)
0	$x = 0^2 - 2 \cdot 0 - 8 = -8$	(-8, 0)
2	$x = 2^2 - 2 \cdot 2 - 8 = -8$	(-8, 2)
4	$x = 4^2 - 2 \cdot 4 - 8 = 0$	(0, 4)
-2	$x = (-2)^2 - 2(-2) - 8 = 0$	(0, -2)

Pick y. Calculate x.

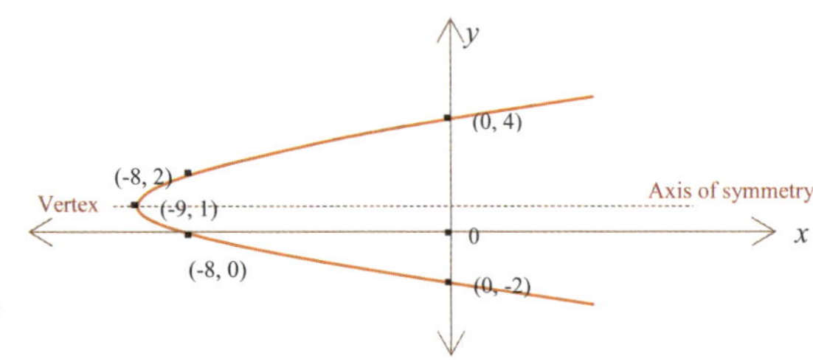

Summary of the Parabola

Equation of Parabolas (Standard Form)	Axis of Symmetry	Vertex	Shape	Graph
$y = Ax^2$	y - axis	(0, 0)	$A > 0$: opens up $A < 0$: opens down	
$x = Ay^2$	x - axis		$A > 0$, opens right $A < 0$, opens left	
$y = Ax^2 + C$	y - axis	$(0, C)$	The same shape as $y = Ax^2$ $C > 0$, C units up $C < 0$, C units down	(0, C) (0, -C)
$x = Ay^2 + C$	x - axis	$(C, 0)$	The same shape as $x = Ay^2$ $C > 0$: C units to the right $C < 0$: C units to the left	(C, 0) (C, 0)
$y = A(x - h)^2$	$x = h$	$(h, 0)$	The same shape as $y = Ax^2$ $h > 0$: h units to the right $h < 0$: h units to the left	(h, 0) (h, 0)
$x = A(y - h)^2$	$y = h$	$(0, h)$	The same shape as $x = Ay^2$ $h > 0$: h units up $h < 0$: h units down	(0, h) (0, h)
$y = A(x - h)^2 + k$	$x = h$	(h, k)	Symmetry about the $x = h$	(h, k)
$x = A(y - k)^2 + h$	$y = k$	(h, k)	Symmetry about the $y = h$	(h, k)
$y = Ax^2 + Bx + C$	$x = \frac{-B}{2A}$	$\left(\frac{-B}{2A}, f\left(\frac{-B}{2A}\right)\right)$	$A > 0$: opens up $A < 0$: opens down	
$x = Ay^2 + By + C$	$y = \frac{-B}{2A}$	$\left(f\left(\frac{-B}{2A}\right), \frac{-B}{2A}\right)$	$A > 0$: opens right $A < 0$: opens left	

9-3 ELLIPSES

Introduction to Ellipse

- **Ellipse:** a curve (oval) where every point on it whose sum of the distances from two fixed points (foci) is a constant.

Graph

$x_1 + x_2 = x_3 + x_4 = \text{constant}$

Example

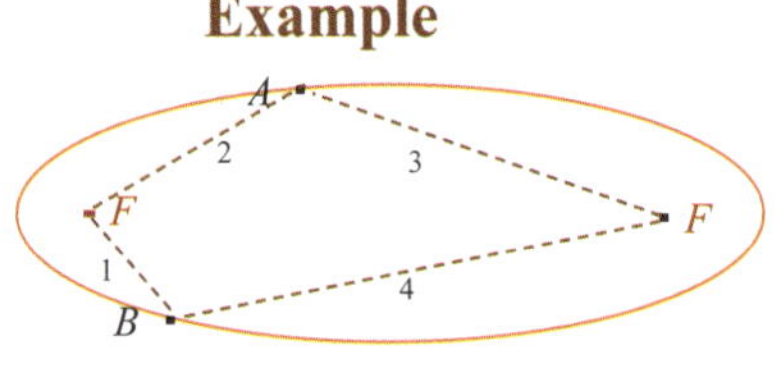

$2 + 3 = 1 + 4 = 5$

- **Ellipse in the real world**

Ellipse	Diagram
football	
orbits of the planets (Earth, Mars, etc.)	
oval mirror	

- **Ellipse terminology**

Term	Definition	Diagram
foci	Two fixed points (F) inside of an ellipse that define the curve.	
major axis	The longest diameter of the ellipse. (The longer axis and passes through both foci)	
minor axis	The shortest diameter of the ellipse. (The shorter axis)	
vertex	The point where an ellipse makes its sharpest turn. (On the major axis)	

- **Equations of ellipse**

Standard Form
$\frac{x^2}{a^2} + \frac{y^2}{b^2} = 1$
$\frac{(x-h)^2}{a^2} + \frac{(y-k)^2}{b^2} = 1$

Ellipse in the Form $\frac{x^2}{a^2} + \frac{y^2}{b^2} = 1$

General information for an ellipse in the form $\frac{x^2}{a^2} + \frac{y^2}{b^2} = 1$

Equation	Shape	Center	Axis of Ellipse	Graph	Example
$\frac{x^2}{a^2} + \frac{y^2}{b^2} = 1$	$a > b$: horizontal ellipse	(0, 0)	major axis: x-axis minor axis: y-axis		$\frac{x^2}{2^2} + \frac{y^2}{1^2} = 1$
	$b > a$: vertical ellipse		major axis: y-axis minor axis: x-axis		$\frac{x^2}{2^2} + \frac{y^2}{3^2} = 1$

Note: If $a = b$, then the ellipse is a circle.

Equation	Vertex	Co-Vertex	Focus
$\frac{x^2}{a^2} + \frac{y^2}{b^2} = 1$ $a > b$	$(-a, 0)$, $(a, 0)$	$(0, b)$, $(0, -b)$	$(F, 0)$, $(-F, 0)$ $F = \sqrt{a^2 - b^2}$
$\frac{x^2}{a^2} + \frac{y^2}{b^2} = 1$ $b > a$	$(0, b)$, $(0, -b)$	$(-a, 0)$, $(a, 0)$	$(0, F)$, $(0, -F)$ $F = \sqrt{b^2 - a^2}$

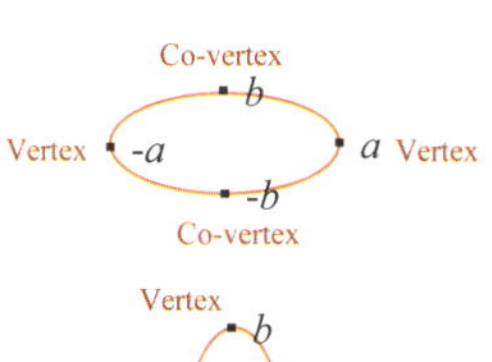

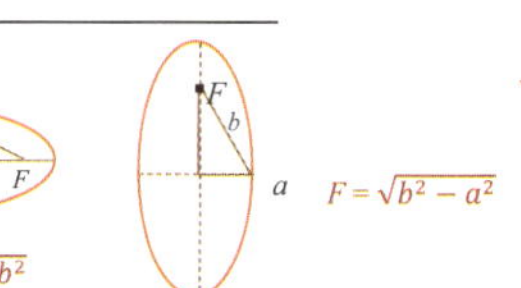

Example: Sketch the graph of $\frac{x^2}{2^2} + \frac{y^2}{3^2} = \mathbf{1}$.

$\frac{x^2}{a^2} + \frac{y^2}{b^2} = 1, \quad b > a$

- Vertices: $(0, 3)$, $(0, -3)$ — $(0, b)$, $(0, -b)$

  Co-vertex: $(-2, 0)$, $(2, 0)$ — $(-a, 0)$, $(a, 0)$

- Foci: $F = \sqrt{b^2 - a^2} = \sqrt{3^2 - 2^2} = \sqrt{5}$

  $(0, F) = (0, \sqrt{5})$, $(0, -F) = (0, -\sqrt{5})$ — $(0, F)$, $(0, -F)$

- The major axis: y-axis
- The minor axis: x-axis

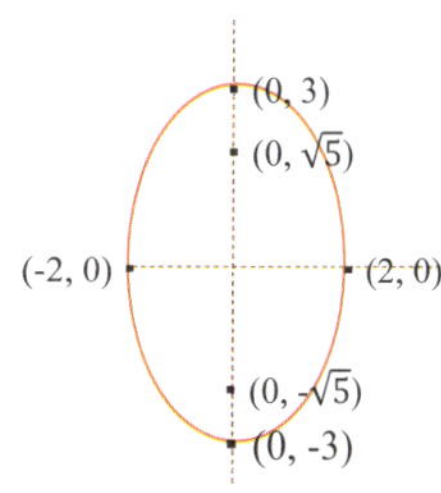

Graph the Ellipse $\frac{x^2}{a^2}+\frac{y^2}{b^2}=1$

Procedure to graph the ellipse: $\frac{x^2}{a^2}+\frac{y^2}{b^2}=1$

Steps	Example: Graph $\frac{x^2}{16}+\frac{y^2}{4}=1.$
- Rewrite in standard form: $\frac{x^2}{a^2}+\frac{y^2}{b^2}=1$ and determine a and b.	$\frac{x^2}{4^2}+\frac{y^2}{2^2}=1$ $a=4,\quad b=2$
- Check a and b $\begin{cases} a>b\text{: horizontal ellipse} \\ b>a\text{: vertical ellipse}\end{cases}$	$a>b$: $4>2$ Horizontal ellipse
- Find the vertices: $(-a, 0)$, $(a, 0)$	Vertices: $(-4, 0)$, $(4, 0)$
Find the co-vertices: $(0, b)$, $(0, -b)$	Co-vertices: $(0, 2)$, $(0, -2)$

- Sketch the ellipse (passes through the vertices and co-vertices).

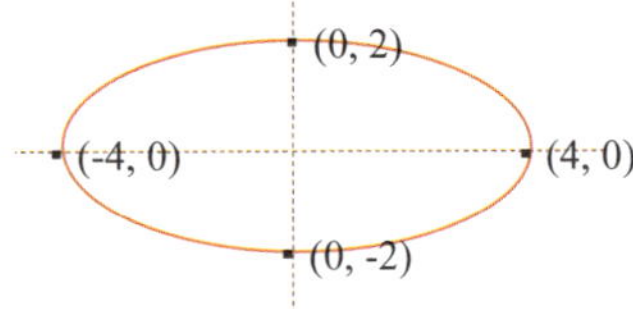
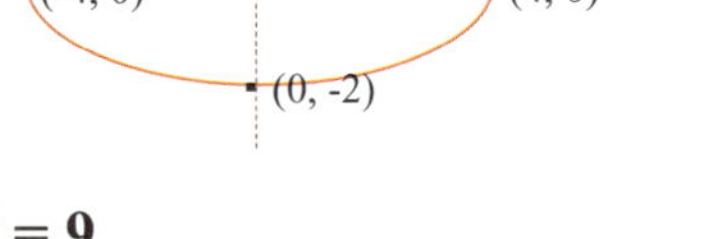

Example: Sketch the graph of $\mathbf{9x^2+y^2=9}$.

- Standard form: $\frac{x^2}{1^2}+\frac{y^2}{3^2}=1$ — Divide 9 by each term.
- $a=1,\ b=3$ — $\frac{x^2}{a^2}+\frac{y^2}{b^2}=1$
- $3>1$: vertical ellipse — $b>a$
- Vertices: $(0, 3)$, $(0, -3)$ — $(0,\ b)$, $(0, -b)$

  Co-vertices: $(-1, 0)$, $(1, 0)$ — $(-a,\ 0)$, $(a,\ 0)$
- Sketch.

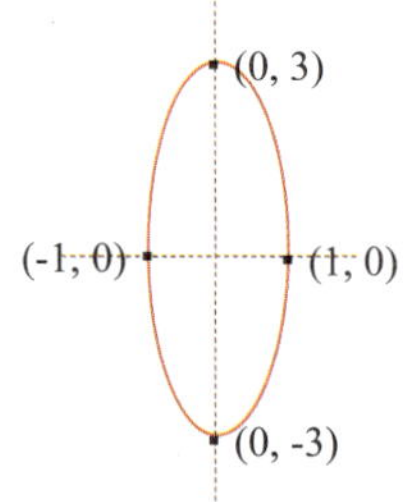

Ellipse in the Form $\frac{(x-h)^2}{a^2}+\frac{(y-k)^2}{b^2}=1$

- **General information for an ellipse of the form $\frac{(x-h)^2}{a^2}+\frac{(y-k)^2}{b^2}=1$**

Equation	Shape	Center	Graph	Example	Graph
$\frac{(x-h)^2}{a^2}+\frac{(y-k)^2}{b^2}=1$	$a>b$: horizontal ellipse	(h, k)	(h, k), 0	$\frac{(x-3)^2}{4^2}+\frac{(y-5)^2}{2^2}=1$ $(h, k)=(3, 5)$ $a=4$, $b=2$	(3, 5), 2, -4, 4, -2
	$b>a$: vertical ellipse		(h, k)	$\frac{(x-3)^2}{2^2}+\frac{(y-5)^2}{4^2}=1$ $(h, k)=(3, 5)$ $a=2$, $b=4$	(3, 5), 4, -2, 2, -4

a and b	Vertex	Co-Vertex	Focus	Graph
$a>b$	$(h+a, k), (h-a, k)$	$(h, k+b), (h, k-b)$	$(h+F, k), (h-F, k)$ $F=\sqrt{a^2-b^2}$	$(h, k+b)$, $(h-a, k)$, (h, k), $(h+a, k)$, $(h, k-b)$, 0
$b>a$	$(h, k+b), (h, k-b)$	$(h+a, k), (h-a, k)$	$(h+F, k), (h-F, k)$ $F=\sqrt{b^2-a^2}$	$(h, k+b)$, $(h-a, k)$, $(h+a, k)$, (h, k), $(h, k-b)$, 0

- **Procedure to graph the ellipse $\frac{(x-h)^2}{a^2}+\frac{(y-k)^2}{b^2}=1$**

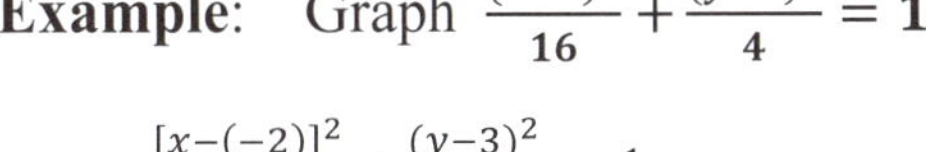

Steps	**Example**: Graph $\frac{(x+2)^2}{16}+\frac{(y-3)^2}{4}=1$
- Write in standard form: $\frac{(x-h)^2}{a^2}+\frac{(y-k)^2}{b^2}=1$	$\frac{[x-(-2)]^2}{4^2}+\frac{(y-3)^2}{2^2}=1$
- Determine the center (h, k).	$(h, k)=(-2, 3)$
- Determine a and b.	$a=4$, $b=2$
- Check a and b $\begin{cases} a>b: \text{ horizontal ellipse} \\ b>a: \text{ vertical ellipse}\end{cases}$	$a>b$: $4>2$ horizontal ellipse
- Determine the vertices: $(h+a, k), (h-a, k)$ Determine the co-vertices: $(h, k+b), (h, k-b)$	Vertices: (2, 3), (-6, 3) [-2 + 4, -2 – 4] Co-vertices: (-2, 5), (-2, 1) [3 + 2, 3 – 2]

- Sketch the ellipse.

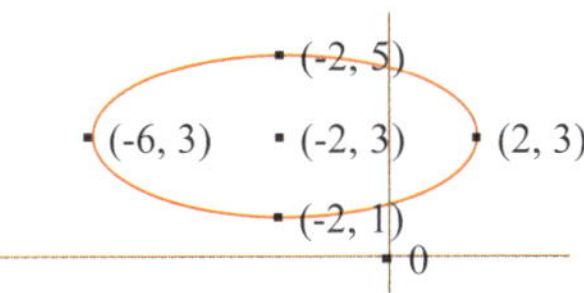

9-4 HYPERBOLAS

Introduction to Hyperbolas

- **Hyperbola:** a curve (arch) with two branches in which difference of distances of all the points from two fixed points (foci) is a constant.

A hyperbola has two arches — each one is a mirror image of the other.

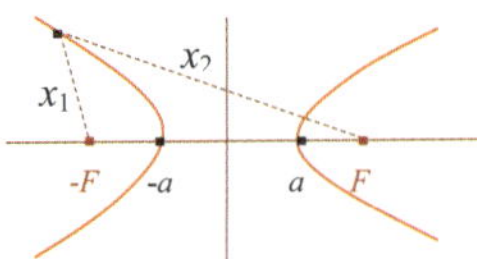

$|x_2 - x_1| = \text{constant} = 2a$

Example

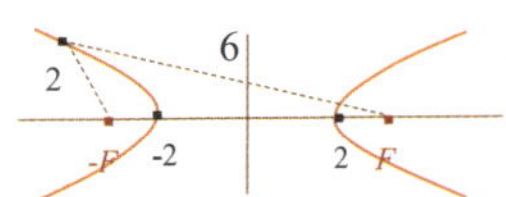

$|6 - 2| = 4 \quad (2a = 2 \cdot 2 = 4)$

- **Hyperbola in the real world**

Ellipse	Diagram
hourglass	
nuclear cooling tower	

- **Hyperbola terminology**

Term	Definition	Diagram
foci	Two fixed points (F) inside each branch of a hyperbola that define the curve.	
axis of symmetry	The line segment on which a hyperbola is reflected onto itself. Each hyperbola has two axes of symmetry that intersect at the center.	
vertex	The points (V) where a hyperbola makes its sharpest turns.	
asymptote	Line segment that is approaching but never touching or crossing the hyperbola. Each hyperbola has two asymptotes.	
transverse axis	The line segment that passes through the vertices and foci.	

Note: An asymptote is a line segment whose distance to a given curve approaches zero and shows where the curve would go.

- **Equations of hyperbolas**

Standard Form	
$\frac{x^2}{a^2} - \frac{y^2}{b^2} = 1$	$\frac{y^2}{a^2} - \frac{x^2}{b^2} = 1$
$\frac{(x-h)^2}{a^2} - \frac{(y-k)^2}{b^2} = 1$	$\frac{(y-k)^2}{a^2} - \frac{(x-h)^2}{b^2} = 1$

Hyperbolas in the Form $\frac{x^2}{a^2} - \frac{y^2}{b^2} = 1$ & $\frac{y^2}{a^2} - \frac{x^2}{b^2} = 1$

- **General information for hyperbolas of the form** $\frac{x^2}{a^2} - \frac{y^2}{b^2} = 1$ & $\frac{y^2}{a^2} - \frac{x^2}{b^2} = 1$

Equation	Shape	Center	Axis of Symmetry	Graph	Example
$\frac{x^2}{a^2} - \frac{y^2}{b^2} = 1$ Horizontal (x is first)	▪ horizontal transverse axis ▪ opens left and right	(0, 0)	y - axis	(-a, 0) (a, 0)	$\frac{x^2}{2^2} - \frac{y^2}{3^2} = 1$
$\frac{y^2}{a^2} - \frac{x^2}{b^2} = 1$ Vertical (y is first)	▪ vertical transverse axis ▪ opens up and down		x - axis	(0, a) (0, -a)	$\frac{y^2}{2^2} - \frac{x^2}{3^2} = 1$

Recall: The transverse axis is the line that passes through the vertices and foci.

Equation	Vertices	Foci	Asymptotes	Graph	Example	Graph
$\frac{x^2}{a^2} - \frac{y^2}{b^2} = 1$	(-a, 0), (a, 0)	(F, 0) , (-F, 0) $F = \sqrt{a^2 + b^2}$	$y = \pm\frac{b}{a}x$	$y = \frac{b}{a}x$ $y = \frac{-b}{a}x$	$\frac{x^2}{2^2} - \frac{y^2}{3^2} = 1$	(0, 3) (-2, 0) (2, 0) (0, -3)
$\frac{y^2}{a^2} - \frac{x^2}{b^2} = 1$	(0, a), (0, -a)	(0, F) , (0, -F) $F = \sqrt{a^2 + b^2}$	$y = \pm\frac{a}{b}x$	$y = \frac{a}{b}x$ $y = \frac{-a}{b}x$	$\frac{y^2}{2^2} - \frac{x^2}{3^2} = 1$	(0, 2) (-3, 0) (3, 0) (0, -2)

Tips:
- The equation of the ellipse is $\frac{x^2}{a^2} + \frac{y^2}{b^2} = 1$ (sum).
- The equation of the hyperbola is $\frac{x^2}{a^2} - \frac{y^2}{b^2} = 1$ (difference).

- **Procedure to graph**

Steps	Example: $\frac{x^2}{16} - \frac{y^2}{4} = 1$
- Write in standard form: $\frac{x^2}{a^2} - \frac{y^2}{b^2} = 1$	$\frac{x^2}{4^2} - \frac{y^2}{2^2} = 1$
- Determine a and b.	$a = 4, \quad b = 2$
- Locate the points (-a, 0) , (a, 0) , (0, b), (0, -b).	(-4, 0) , (4, 0) , (0, 2) , (0, -2)
- Sketch a reference rectangle intersecting at above four points.	(0, 2) (-4, 0) (4, 0) (0, -2)
- Sketch the asymptotes by extending the diagonals of the rectangle.	
- Determine the vertices: (-a, 0) , (a, 0).	(-4, 0) , (4, 0)
- Sketch the hyperbola. Using the vertices and asymptotes as guides to sketch.	$\frac{x^2}{a^2} - \frac{y^2}{b^2} = 1$: opens left and right (x is first).

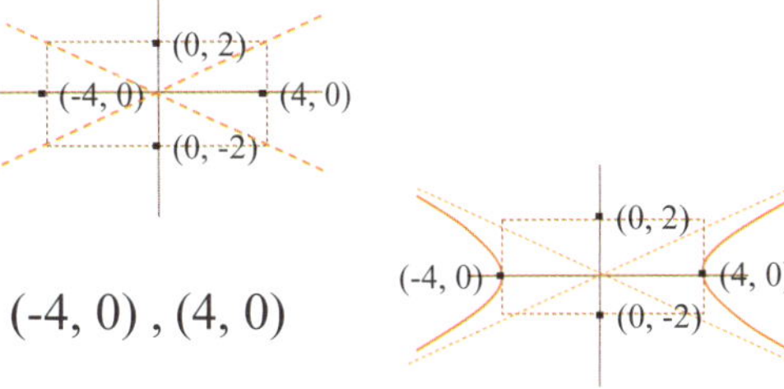

Graph the Hyperbola: $\frac{x^2}{a^2} - \frac{y^2}{b^2} = 1$ & $\frac{y^2}{a^2} - \frac{x^2}{b^2} = 1$

Example: Graph $\frac{y^2}{25} - \frac{x^2}{9} = 1$ and identify the vertices, foci and the asymptotic lines.

- Write in standard form: $\frac{y^2}{5^2} - \frac{x^2}{3^2} = 1$ Standard form: $\frac{y^2}{a^2} - \frac{x^2}{b^2} = 1$
- $a = 5, \quad b = 3$
- Locate 4 points: (0, 5), (0, -5), (-3, 0), (3, 0) $(0, a)$, $(0, -a)$, $(-b, 0)$, $(b, 0)$
- Sketch a reference rectangle intersecting at the four points from above.

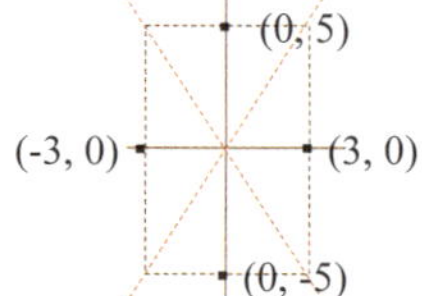

- Sketch the asymptotes.
- Determine the vertices: (0, 5), (0, -5) $(0, a)$, $(0, -a)$
- Sketch the curve:

It opens up and down. $\frac{y^2}{a^2} - \frac{x^2}{b^2} = 1$ (y is first).

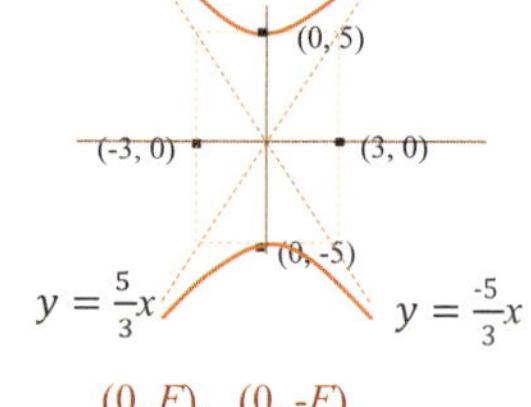

- Calculate the asymptote: $y = \pm\frac{a}{b}x = \pm\frac{5}{3}x$
- Calculate the foci: $F = \sqrt{a^2 + b^2} = \sqrt{5^2 + 3^2} \approx 5.83$

  (0, 5.83), (0, -5.83) $(0, F)$, $(0, -F)$

Example: Sketch the graph of $y^2 - 4x^2 = 4$.

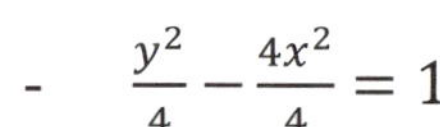

- $\frac{y^2}{4} - \frac{4x^2}{4} = 1$ Divide both sides by 4.
- $\frac{y^2}{2^2} - \frac{x^2}{1^2} = 1$ Write in standard form.
- $a = 2, \; b = 1$ $\frac{y^2}{a^2} - \frac{x^2}{b^2} = 1$
- 4 Points: (0, 2), (0, -2), (-1, 0), (1, 0) $(0, a)$, $(0, -a)$, $(-b, 0)$, $(b, 0)$
- Vertices: (0, 2) (0, -2) $(0, a)$, $(0, -a)$
- Sketch: It opens up and down. $\frac{y^2}{a^2} - \frac{x^2}{b^2} = 1$

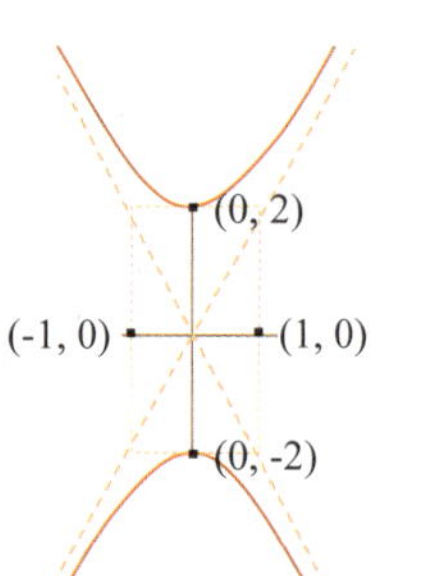

Hyperbolas in the Form $\frac{(x-h)^2}{a^2} - \frac{(y-k)^2}{b^2} = 1$ & $\frac{(y-k)^2}{a^2} - \frac{(x-h)^2}{b^2} = 1$

- **General information for a hyperbola of the form $\frac{(x-h)^2}{a^2} - \frac{(y-k)^2}{b^2} = 1$ & $\frac{(y-k)^2}{a^2} - \frac{(x-h)^2}{b^2} = 1$**

Equation	Shape	Center	Axis of Symmetry	Graph	Example
$\frac{(x-h)^2}{a^2} - \frac{(y-k)^2}{b^2} = 1$	▪ horizontal transverse axis ▪ opens left and right (x is first)	(h, k)	$x = h$	k, -a, a, b, -b, 0, h	$\frac{(x-5)^2}{3^2} - \frac{(y-3)^2}{2^2} = 1$
$\frac{(y-k)^2}{a^2} - \frac{(x-h)^2}{b^2} = 1$	▪ vertical transverse axis ▪ opens left and right (y is first)		$y = k$	k, -a, a, b, -b, h	$\frac{(y-3)^2}{3^2} - \frac{(x-5)^2}{2^2} = 1$

The transverse axis: the line that passes through the vertices and foci.

Equation	Vertices	Foci	Asymptotes
$\frac{(x-h)^2}{a^2} - \frac{(y-k)^2}{b^2} = 1$	$(h-a, k)$ $(h+a, k)$	$(h-F, k)$ $(h+F, k)$ $F = \sqrt{a^2+b^2}$	$y - k = \pm\frac{b}{a}(x-h)$
$\frac{(y-k)^2}{a^2} - \frac{(x-h)^2}{b^2} = 1$	$(h, k-a)$ $(h, k+a)$	$(h, k-F)$ $(h, k+F)$ $F = \sqrt{a^2+b^2}$	$y - k = \pm\frac{a}{b}(x-h)$

- **Procedure to graph hyperbola**

Steps

- Write in standard form: $\frac{(x-h)^2}{a^2} - \frac{(y-k)^2}{b^2} = 1$
- Determine the center (h, k).
- Identify a and b.
- Determine and plot the vertices: $(h-a, k)$, $(h+a, k)$
- Determine the up/down midpoints of a reference rectangle by moving 'b' units up and down from the center (h, k).
- Sketch the reference rectangle crossing at the 4 points from above.
- Sketch the asymptotes by extending the diagonals of the rectangle.
- Sketch the hyperbola.

Determine if the curve is opening to the left and right (x is first) or up and down (y is first).

Example: $\frac{(x+1)^2}{9} - \frac{(y-2)^2}{16} = 1$

$\frac{[(x-(-1)]^2}{3^2} - \frac{(y-2)^2}{4^2} = 1$

$(h, k) = (-1, 2)$

$a = 3, \quad b = 4$

$(-4, 2), \quad (2, 2)$

-1-3 -1+3

Move 4 units up and down from (-1, 2).

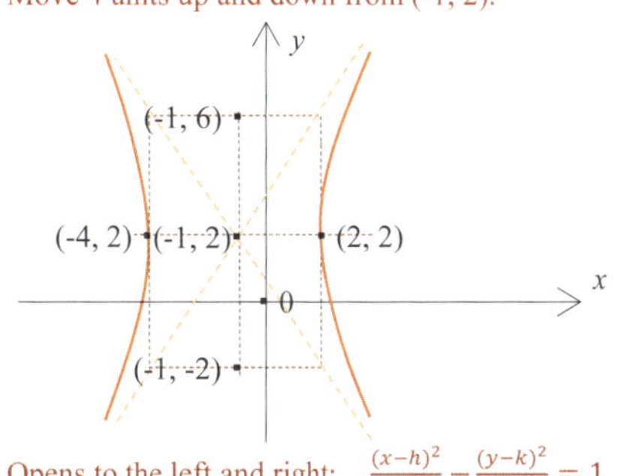

Opens to the left and right: $\frac{(x-h)^2}{a^2} - \frac{(y-k)^2}{b^2} = 1$

x is first

9-5 THE GENERAL CONIC FORM

Function Transformations

- **Conic Sections - summary:** **center at (0, 0)**

Conics	Standard Form	Shape	Graph
circle	$x^2 + y^2 = r^2$		
parabola	$y = Ax^2$	$A > 0$: opens up $A < 0$: opens down	
	$x = Ay^2$	$A > 0$, opens right $A < 0$, opens left	
ellipse	$\frac{x^2}{a^2} + \frac{y^2}{b^2} = 1$	$a > b$: horizontal ellipse $b > a$: vertical ellipse	
hyperbola	$\frac{x^2}{a^2} - \frac{y^2}{b^2} = 1$	opens left and right	
	$\frac{y^2}{a^2} - \frac{x^2}{b^2} = 1$	opens up and down	

- **Function transformations**: change the position of the graph of the function.

  It includes shifting, stretching / shrinking, or reflecting graphs.

- **Shifting**

Function	Shifting	Example	Diagram
$y = f(x) + C$ $y = f(x) - C$	Shift the graph of $f(x)$ C units up. Shift the graph of $f(x)$ C units down.	$y = x^2 + 2$ Shift $f(x) = x^2$ 2 units up. $y = x^2 - 2$ Shift $f(x) = x^2$ 2 units down.	$y = x^2 + 2$ $y = x^2$ $y = x^2 - 2$ 2 0 -2
$y = f(x + C)$ $y = f(x - C)$	Shift the graph of $f(x)$ C units to the left. Shift the graph of $f(x)$ C units to the right.	$y = (x + 2)^2$ Shift x^2 2 units to the left $y = (x - 2)^2$ Shift x^2 2 units to the right	$y = x^2$ $y = (x + 2)^2$ $y = (x - 2)^2$ -2 0 2

- **Reflection**

Function	Reflection	Example	Graph
$y = -f(x)$	Reflect the graph of $y = f(x)$ about the x-axis.	$y = x^2$ and $y = -(x^2)$	y $y = x^2$ x $y = -(x^2)$
$y = f(-x)$	Reflect the graph of $y = f(x)$ about the y-axis.	$y = 2x+1$ and $y = 2(-x)+1$ $= -2x+1$	y $y = 2x + 1$ x $y = -2x + 1$

General-Form Conic Equation

- A general-form conic equation (a second-degree equation)

Equation
$Ax^2 + Bxy + Cy^2 + Dx + Ey + F = 0$

- The type of conic sections can be determined from the discriminant $B^2 - 4AC$.
- **Identify the type of conic section from the sign of $B^2 - 4AC$**

$B^2 - 4AC$	The Graph is a:
$B^2 - 4AC = 0$	parabola
$B^2 - 4AC < 0$	ellipse
$B^2 - 4AC > 0$	hyperbola

Example: Sketch the graph of $\mathbf{9y^2 - 4x^2 = 36}$.

Steps	Example
- Write in general conic form. $Ax^2 + Bxy + Cy^2 + Dx + Ey + F = 0$	A B C D E F: $-4x^2 + 0xy + 9y^2 + 0 \cdot x + 0 \cdot y - 36 = 0$
- Calculate $B^2 - 4AC$.	$0^2 - 4(-4) \cdot 9 - 144 > 0$: Hyperbola
- Convert to standard form.	$9y^2 - 4x^2 = 36$ ÷ 36 both sides.
The standard equation of a hyperbola: $\frac{y^2}{a^2} - \frac{x^2}{b^2} = 1$	$\frac{y^2}{4} - \frac{x^2}{9} = \frac{36}{36}$
- Graph. Opens up and down (*y* is first). Vertices: $(0, a), (0, -a) = (0, 2), (0, -2)$	$\frac{y^2}{2^2} - \frac{x^2}{3^2} = 1$

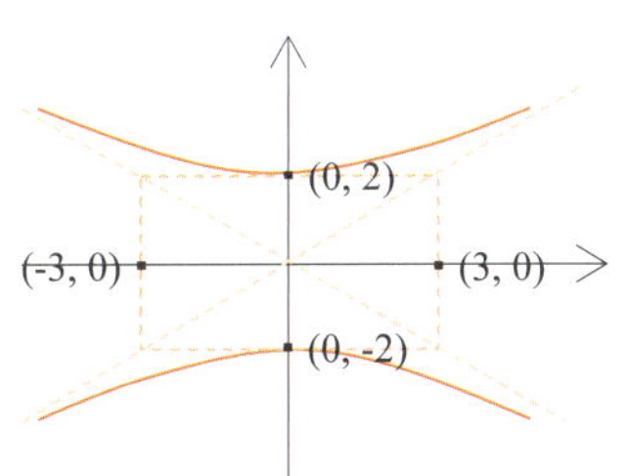

Example: Convert $\mathbf{x + 3y^2 + 6y + 1 = 0}$ to standard form and graph it.

Steps	Example
- Write in general conic form. $Ax^2 + Bxy + Cy^2 + Dx + Ey + F = 0$	A B C D E F: $0x^2 + 0xy + 3y^2 + 1 \cdot x + 6y + 1 = 0$
- Calculate $B^2 - 4AC$.	$B^2 - 4AC = 0^2 - 4 \cdot 0 \cdot 3 = 0$ Parabola
- Convert to standard form.	$3y^2 + 6y + x + 1 = 0$
○ Collect *y* terms on the left-hand side; collect *x* terms & constants on the right-hand side.	$3y^2 + 6y = -x - 1$ $3(y^2 + 2y + \square) = -x - 1 + 3\square$ Factor out 3; Add 3 $\square$

- Completing the square.

  $\square = \left(\frac{b}{2}\right)^2$

  $3(y^2 + 2y + 1) = -x - 1 + 3 \cdot 1$ $\left(\frac{b}{2}\right)^2 = \left(\frac{2}{2}\right)^2 = 1$

  1 should be multiplied by 3 on the right-hand side.

  $3(y + 1)^2 = 2 - x$ Isolate x.

  Standard form of a parabola: $x = A(y - k)^2 + h$

  $x = -3(y + 1)^2 + 2 = -3[y - (-1)^2] + 2$

  ($A = -3$, $k = -1$, $h = 2$)

- Graph. $A = -3 < 0$: opens left
  Vertex: $(h, k) = (2, -1)$
  Symmetry: $y = k = -1$

  (Find a few more points.)

y	$x = -3(y + 1)^2 + 2$	(x, y)
0	$x = -3(0 + 1)^2 + 2 = -1$	(-1, 0)
-2	$x = -3(-2 + 1)^2 + 2 = -1$	(-1, -2)

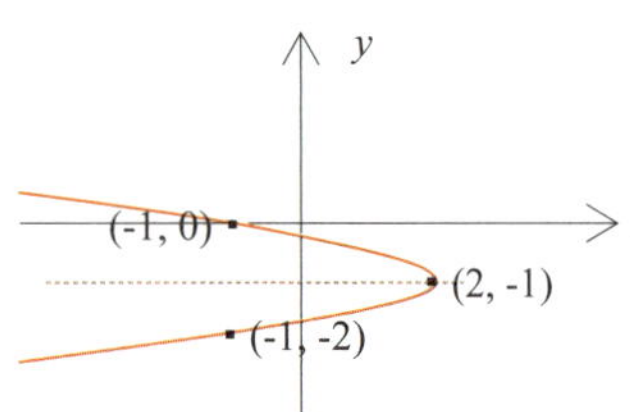

Example: Convert $\mathbf{16x^2 + 9y^2 - 64x - 18y - 71 = 0}$ to standard form and graph it.

Steps	Example
- Write in general conic form. $Ax^2 + Bxy + Cy^2 + Dx + Ey + F = 0$	A, B, C, D, E, F: $16x^2 + 0xy + 9y^2 - 64x - 18y - 71 = 0$
- Calculate $B^2 - 4AC$.	$B^2 - 4AC = 0^2 - 4 \cdot 16 \cdot 9 = -576 < 0$ Ellipse
- Convert to standard form by completing the square. $\square = \left(\frac{b}{2}\right)^2$	$(16x^2 - 64x \quad) + (9y^2 - 18y \quad) - 71 = 0$ Regroup.
	$16(x^2 - 4x + \square) + 9(y^2 - 2y + \square) = 71 + 16\square + 9\square$ Factor out 16 and 9. Add 71 ; add $16\square$, $9\square$
	$16(x^2 - 4x + 4) + 9(y^2 - 2y + 1) = 71 + 16 \cdot 4 + 9 \cdot 1$ $\left(\frac{-4}{2}\right)^2 = 4$, $\left(\frac{-2}{2}\right)^2 = 1$ 4 and 1 should be multiplied by 16 and 9 on the right-hand side.
	$16(x - 2)^2 + 9(y - 1)^2 = 144$ ÷ 144 both sides.
	$\frac{(x-2)^2}{9} + \frac{(y-1)^2}{16} = \frac{144}{144}$ $\frac{16}{144} = \frac{1}{9}$; $\frac{9}{144} = \frac{1}{16}$
Standard form of an ellipse: $\frac{(x-h)^2}{a^2} + \frac{(y-k)^2}{b^2} = 1$	$\mathbf{\frac{(x-2)^2}{3^2} + \frac{(y-1)^2}{4^2} = 1}$ $b > a$
- Graph.	- Center: $(h, k) = (2, 1)$ - Vertices: $(h, k \pm b) = (2, 5)$, $(2, -3)$ (1+4, 1-4) - Co-vertices: $(h \pm a, k) = (5, 1)$, $(-1, 1)$ (2+3, 2-3)

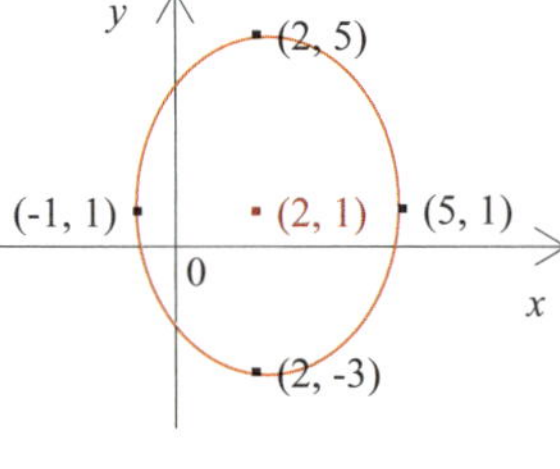

9-6 NONLINEAR SYSTEMS OF EQUATIONS

Nonlinear Systems

- **Nonlinear equation:** the highest power of the variable is higher than one (an equation whose graph is not a straight line).

  Example $2x^2 + y = 3$

- **Nonlinear system of equations:** a system in which the highest power of the variable is higher than one.
- **Solutions of the systems of equations:** the particular values of the variables in the system that make the system true.

Example: Solve the system.

$\mathbf{x^2 + y^2 = 25}$ (1)
$\mathbf{x - y + 1 = 0}$ (2)

Solution: $x = y - 1$ (3) — Solve for x in (2).

$(y-1)^2 + y^2 = 25$ — (3) ⟶ (1) — Substitute $y-1$ for x in (1).

$y^2 - 2y + 1 + y^2 = 25$ — $(a-b)^2 = a^2 - 2ab + b^2$

$2y^2 - 2y - 24 = 0$

$2(y^2 - y - 12) = 0$ — Factor out 2.

$2(y-4)(y+3) = 0$ — Factor.

$(y-4) = 0$ | $(y+3) = 0$ — Zero-product property

$\mathbf{y = 4}$ | $\mathbf{y = -3}$

$\mathbf{x} = y - 1 = 4 - 1 = \mathbf{3}$ | $\mathbf{x} = y - 1 = -3 - 1 = \mathbf{-4}$ — Substitute 4 & -3 for y in (3).

Solution sets: **(3, 4)** | **(-4, -3)**

Check:

(x, y)	$x^2 + y^2 = 25$	$x - y + 1 = 0$
(3, 4)	$3^2 + 4^2 \stackrel{?}{=} 25$ $9 + 16 = 25$ √	$3 - 4 + 1 \stackrel{?}{=} 0$ $0 = 0$ √
(-4, -3)	$(-4)^2 + (-3)^2 \stackrel{?}{=} 25$ $16 + 9 = 25$ √	$-4 - (-3) + 1 \stackrel{?}{=} 0$ $0 = 0$ √

Correct!

- **Check by graphing:** Graph the equations in the system. The point(s) of intersection in the graph are the solutions to the system.

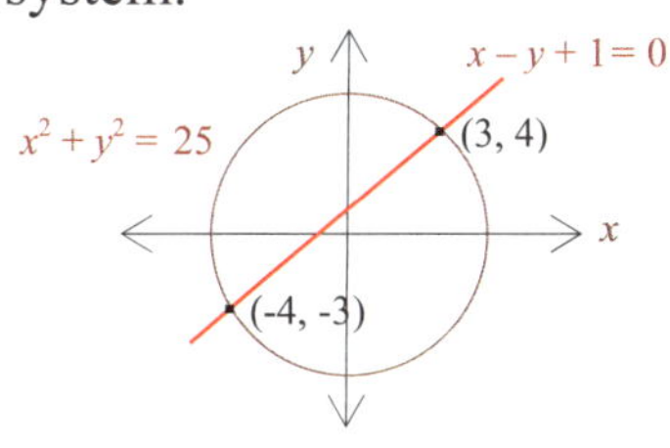

The graphs intersect at the points (3, 4) and (-4, -3), correct!

Solving Nonlinear Systems

Example: Solve the system.

$$\mathbf{9x^2 + 4y^2 = 9} \quad (1)$$
$$\mathbf{y - x = 2} \quad (2)$$

Solution:

$y = x + 2$ (3) — Solve for y in (2).

$9x^2 + 4(x+2)^2 = 9$ (3) → (1) — Substitute $x + 2$ for y in (1).

$9x^2 + 4(x^2 + 4x + 4) = 9$ — $(a+b)^2 = a^2 + 2ab + b^2$

$9x^2 + 4x^2 + 16x + 16 = 9$

$13x^2 + 16x + 7 = 0$

$$x = \frac{-16 \pm \sqrt{16^2 - 4(13)(7)}}{2 \cdot 13}$$ — $x = \frac{-b \pm \sqrt{b^2 - 4ac}}{2a}$

$$= \frac{-16 \pm \sqrt{-108}}{26}$$

$$= \frac{-16 \pm \sqrt{(-1)27 \cdot 4}}{26}$$

$$= \frac{-16 \pm 2\sqrt{27}\,i}{26}$$

$$\mathbf{x = \frac{-8}{13} \pm \frac{\sqrt{27}}{13} i}$$ — $i = \sqrt{-1}$

$x = \frac{-8}{13} + \frac{\sqrt{27}}{13} i$	$x = \frac{-8}{13} - \frac{\sqrt{27}}{13} i$
$y = \frac{-8}{13} + \frac{\sqrt{27}}{13} i + 2$	$y = \frac{-8}{13} - \frac{\sqrt{27}}{13} i + 2$
$= \frac{-8}{13} + \frac{\sqrt{27}}{13} i + \frac{26}{13}$	$= \frac{-8}{13} - \frac{\sqrt{27}}{13} i + \frac{26}{13}$
$\mathbf{y = \frac{18}{13} + \frac{\sqrt{27}}{13} i}$	$\mathbf{y = \frac{18}{13} - \frac{\sqrt{27}}{13} i}$

Substitute x in (3): $y = x + 2$.

Solution sets:

$$\left(\frac{-8}{13} + \frac{\sqrt{27}}{13} i\ ,\ \frac{18}{13} + \frac{\sqrt{27}}{13} i\right)$$
$$\left(\frac{-8}{13} - \frac{\sqrt{27}}{13} i\ ,\ \frac{18}{13} - \frac{\sqrt{27}}{13} i\right)$$

These are imaginary solutions.
The two graphs do not intersect.

Unit 9 Summary

- **Distance and midpoint formulas**

Distance Formula	Example
$d = \sqrt{(x_2 - x_1)^2 + (y_2 - y_1)^2}$	$(x_1, y_1) = (1, 2)$, $(x_2, y_2) = (3, 3)$ $d = \sqrt{(3-1)^2 + (3-2)^2} = \sqrt{4+1} = \sqrt{5}$

Midpoint Formula	Example
$\left(\frac{x_1 + x_2}{2}, \frac{y_1 + y_2}{2}\right)$	$(x_1, y_1) = (4, 3)$, $(x_2, y_2) = (-4, 1)$ Midpoint $= \left(\frac{4+(-4)}{2}, \frac{3+1}{2}\right) = (0, 2)$

- **Equation of circles**

Center of a Circle	The Standard Form Equation	Example
center at origin $(0, 0)$	$x^2 + y^2 = r^2$	$x^2 + y^2 = 3^2$ $r = 3$
center at (h, k)	$(x-h)^2 + (y-k)^2 = r^2$	$(x-2)^2 + (y-1)^2 = 2^2$ $(h, k) = (2, 1)$, $r = 2$

r – radius

- **The general form equation for a circle**

The General Form	Example
$x^2 + y^2 + Cx + Dy + E = 0$	$x^2 + y^2 - 2x + 4y - 20 = 0$

- **Parabola terminology**

Term	Definition	Diagram
focus	A fixed point whose relationship with a directrix defines a parabola.	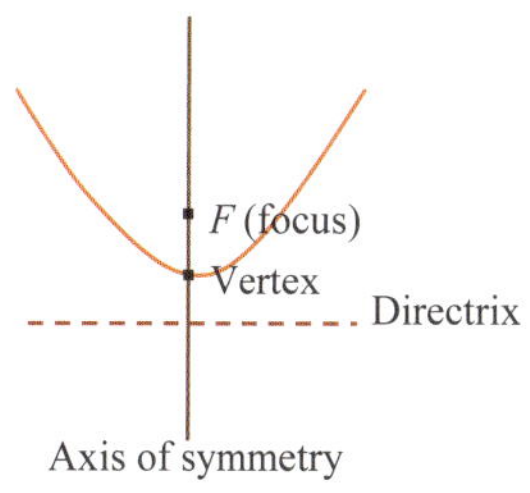 F (focus) Vertex Directrix Axis of symmetry
directrix	A fixed straight line perpendicular to the axis of symmetry.	
axis of symmetry	A line segment that is perpendicular to the directrix and passes through the vertex and focus of a parabola.	
vertex	The point where a parabola makes its sharpest turn as it crosses its axis of symmetry. It is where the distance from the focus and directrix is shortest.	

- **The graph of a quadratic function or equation is a parabola.**

- **The coefficient A in $f(x) = Ax^2$ can shrink or stretch the parabola**

The Coefficient A in $y = Ax^2$ & $x = Ay^2$			Example
▪ The larger the $\lvert A \rvert$, the narrower the curve.	$f(x) = Ax^2$	$A > 0$	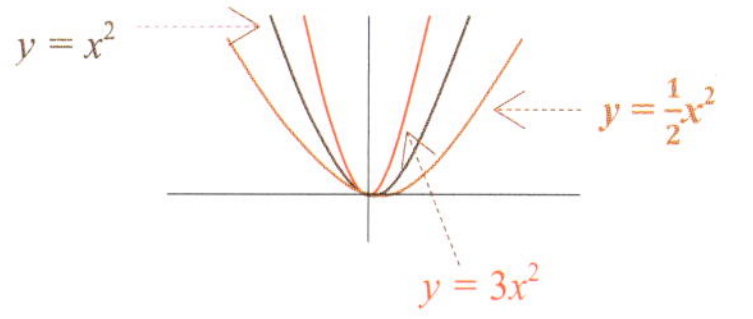 $y = x^2$ $y = \frac{1}{2}x^2$ $y = 3x^2$
▪ The smaller the $\lvert A \rvert$, the wider the curve.		$A < 0$	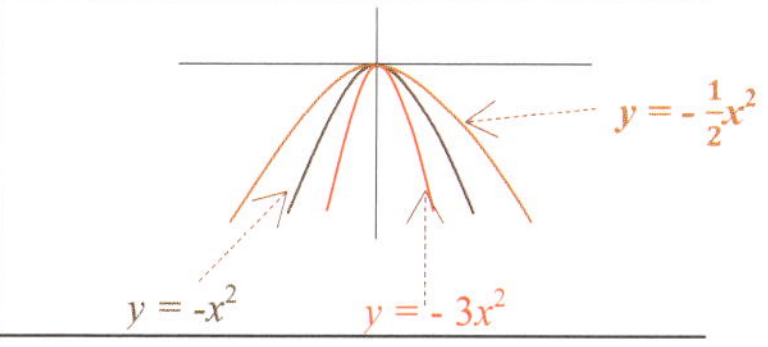 $y = -\frac{1}{2}x^2$ $y = -x^2$ $y = -3x^2$

- **Equations of parabolas**

Equation of Parabolas (Standard Form)	Axis of Symmetry	Vertex	Shape	Graph
$y = Ax^2$	y - axis	(0, 0)	$A > 0$: opens up $A < 0$: opens down	
$x = Ay^2$	x - axis	(0, 0)	$A > 0$, opens right $A < 0$, opens left	
$y = Ax^2 + C$	y - axis	$(0, C)$	The same shape as $y = Ax^2$ $C > 0$, C units up $C < 0$, C units down	(0, C) (0, -C)
$x = Ay^2 + C$	x - axis	$(C, 0)$	The same shape as $x = Ay^2$ $C > 0$: C units to the right $C < 0$: C units to the left	(C, 0) (C, 0)
$y = A(x - h)^2$	$x = h$	$(h, 0)$	The same shape as $y = Ax^2$ $h > 0$: h units to the right $h < 0$: h units to the left	(h, 0) (h, 0)
$x = A(y - h)^2$	$y = h$	$(0, h)$	The same shape as $x = Ay^2$ $h > 0$: h units up $h < 0$: h units down	(0, h) (0, h)
$y = A(x - h)^2 + k$	$x = h$	(h, k)	Symmetry about the $x = h$	(h, k)
$x = A(y - k)^2 + h$	$y = k$	(h, k)	Symmetry about the $y = h$	(h, k)
$y = Ax^2 + Bx + C$	$x = \frac{-B}{2A}$	$\left(\frac{-B}{2A}, f\left(\frac{-B}{2A}\right)\right)$	$A > 0$: opens up $A < 0$: opens down	
$x = Ay^2 + By + C$	$y = \frac{-B}{2A}$	$\left(f\left(\frac{-B}{2A}\right), \frac{-B}{2A}\right)$	$A > 0$: opens right $A < 0$: opens left	

- **Ellipse terminology**

Term	Definition	Diagram
foci	Two fixed points (F) inside of an ellipse that define the curve.	Minor axis, b, $-a$, F, F, a, Major axis, $-b$
major axis	The longest diameter of the ellipse. (The longer axis and passes through both foci)	
minor axis	The shortest diameter of the ellipse. (The shorter axis)	
vertex	The point where an ellipse makes its sharpest turn. (On the major axis)	

- General information for an ellipse in the form $\frac{x^2}{a^2} + \frac{y^2}{b^2} = 1$

Equation	Shape	Center	Axis of Ellipse	Graph	Example
$\frac{x^2}{a^2} + \frac{y^2}{b^2} = 1$	$a > b$: horizontal ellipse	(0, 0)	major axis: x-axis minor axis: y-axis		$\frac{x^2}{2^2} + \frac{y^2}{1^2} = 1$
	$b > a$: vertical ellipse		major axis: y-axis minor axis: x-axis		$\frac{x^2}{2^2} + \frac{y^2}{3^2} = 1$

Equation	Vertex	Co-Vertex	Focus
$\frac{x^2}{a^2} + \frac{y^2}{b^2} = 1$, $a > b$	$(-a, 0)$, $(a, 0)$	$(0, b)$, $(0, -b)$	$(F, 0)$, $(-F, 0)$ $F = \sqrt{a^2 - b^2}$
$\frac{x^2}{a^2} + \frac{y^2}{b^2} = 1$, $b > a$	$(0, b)$, $(0, -b)$	$(-a, 0)$, $(a, 0)$	$(0, F)$, $(0, -F)$ $F = \sqrt{b^2 - a^2}$

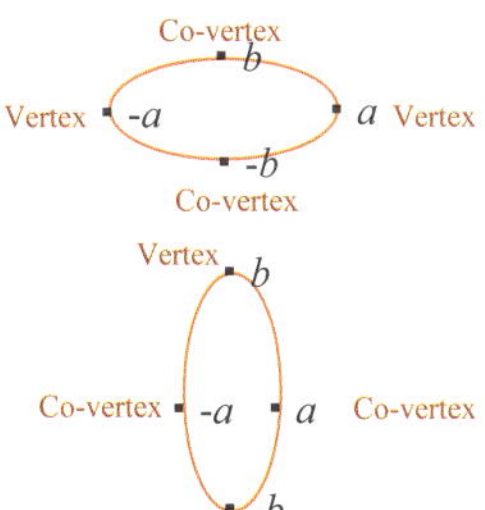

- **General information for an ellipse of the form** $\frac{(x-h)^2}{a^2} + \frac{(y-k)^2}{b^2} = 1$

Equation	Shape	Center	Graph	Example	Graph
$\frac{(x-h)^2}{a^2} + \frac{(y-k)^2}{b^2} = 1$	$a > b$: horizontal ellipse	(h, k)		$\frac{(x-3)^2}{4^2} + \frac{(y-5)^2}{2^2} = 1$ $(h, k) = (3, 5)$ $a = 4$, $b = 2$	
	$b > a$: vertical ellipse			$\frac{(x-3)^2}{2^2} + \frac{(y-5)^2}{4^2} = 1$ $(h, k) = (3, 5)$ $a = 2$, $b = 4$	

a and b	Vertex	Co-Vertex	Focus	Graph
$a > b$	$(h + a, k)$, $(h - a, k)$	$(h, k+b)$, $(h, k-b)$	$(h + F, k)$, $(h - F, k)$ $F = \sqrt{a^2 - b^2}$	
$b > a$	$(h, k+b)$, $(h, k-b)$	$(h + a, k)$, $(h - a, k)$	$(h, k + F)$, $(h, k - F)$ $F = \sqrt{b^2 - a^2}$	

- **Hyperbola terminology**

Term	Definition	Diagram
foci	Two fixed points (F) inside each branch of a hyperbola that define the curve.	
axis of symmetry	The line segment on which a hyperbola is reflected onto itself. Each hyperbola has two axes of symmetry that intersect at the center.	
vertex	The points (V) where a hyperbola makes its sharpest turns.	
asymptote	Line segment that is approaching but never touching or crossing the hyperbola. Each hyperbola has two asymptotes.	
transverse axis	The line segment that passes through the vertices and foci.	

- **General information for hyperbolas of the form** $\frac{x^2}{a^2} - \frac{y^2}{b^2} = 1$ **&** $\frac{y^2}{a^2} - \frac{x^2}{b^2} = 1$

Equation	Shape	Center	Axis of Symmetry	Graph	Example
$\frac{x^2}{a^2} - \frac{y^2}{b^2} = 1$ Horizontal (x is first)	▪ horizontal transverse axis ▪ opens left and right	(0, 0)	y - axis	(-a, 0) (a, 0)	$\frac{x^2}{2^2} - \frac{y^2}{3^2} = 1$
$\frac{y^2}{a^2} - \frac{x^2}{b^2} = 1$ Vertical (y is first)	▪ vertical transverse axis ▪ opens up and down		x - axis	(0, a) (0, -a)	$\frac{y^2}{2^2} - \frac{x^2}{3^2} = 1$

Equation	Vertices	Foci	Asymptotes	Graph	Example	Graph
$\frac{x^2}{a^2} - \frac{y^2}{b^2} = 1$	(-a, 0), (a, 0)	(F, 0) , (-F, 0) $F = \sqrt{a^2 + b^2}$	$y = \pm\frac{b}{a}x$	$y = \frac{b}{a}x$ $y = \frac{-b}{a}x$	$\frac{x^2}{2^2} - \frac{y^2}{3^2} = 1$	(0, 3) (-2, 0) (2, 0) (0, -3)
$\frac{y^2}{a^2} - \frac{x^2}{b^2} = 1$	(0, a), (0, -a)	(0, F) , (0, -F) $F = \sqrt{a^2 + b^2}$	$y = \pm\frac{a}{b}x$	$y = \frac{a}{b}x$ $y = \frac{-a}{b}x$	$\frac{y^2}{2^2} - \frac{x^2}{3^2} = 1$	(0, 2) (-3, 0) (3, 0) (0, -2)

- **General information for a hyperbola of the form** $\frac{(x-h)^2}{a^2} - \frac{(y-k)^2}{b^2} = 1$ **&** $\frac{(y-k)^2}{a^2} - \frac{(x-h)^2}{b^2} = 1$

Equation	Shape	Center	Axis of Symmetry	Graph	Example
$\frac{(x-h)^2}{a^2} - \frac{(y-k)^2}{b^2} = 1$	▪ horizontal transverse axis ▪ opens left and right (x is first)	(h, k)	$x = h$	k b -a a -b 0 h	$\frac{(x-5)^2}{3^2} - \frac{(y-3)^2}{2^2} = 1$
$\frac{(y-k)^2}{a^2} - \frac{(x-h)^2}{b^2} = 1$	▪ vertical transverse axis ▪ opens left and right (y is first)		$y = k$	k b -a a -b h	$\frac{(y-3)^2}{3^2} - \frac{(x-5)^2}{2^2} = 1$

Equation	Vertices	Foci	Asymptotes
$\frac{(x-h)^2}{a^2} - \frac{(y-k)^2}{b^2} = 1$	$(h-a, k)$ $(h+a, k)$	$(h-F, k)$ $(h+F, k)$ $F = \sqrt{a^2 + b^2}$	$y - k = \pm\frac{b}{a}(x-h)$
$\frac{(y-k)^2}{a^2} - \frac{(x-h)^2}{b^2} = 1$	$(h, k-a)$ $(h, k+a)$	$(h, k-F)$ $(h, k+F)$ $F = \sqrt{a^2 + b^2}$	$y - k = \pm\frac{a}{b}(x-h)$

- **Summary of conic sections:** **center at (0, 0)**

Conics	Standard Form	Shape	Graph
circle	$x^2 + y^2 = r^2$		
parabola	$y = Ax^2$	$A > 0$: opens up $A < 0$: opens down	
	$x = Ay^2$	$A > 0$, opens right $A < 0$, opens left	
ellipse	$\frac{x^2}{a^2} + \frac{y^2}{b^2} = 1$	$a > b$: horizontal ellipse $b > a$: vertical ellipse	
hyperbola	$\frac{x^2}{a^2} - \frac{y^2}{b^2} = 1$	opens left and right	
	$\frac{y^2}{a^2} - \frac{x^2}{b^2} = 1$	opens up and down	

- **Function transformations**: change the position of the graph of the function. It includes shifting, stretching / shrinking, or reflecting graphs.

- **Shifting**

Function	Shifting	Example	Diagram
$y = f(x) + C$ $y = f(x) - C$	Shift the graph of $f(x)$ C units up. Shift the graph of $f(x)$ C units down.	$y = x^2 + 2$ Shift $f(x) = x^2$ 2 units up. $y = x^2 - 2$ Shift $f(x) = x^2$ 2 units down.	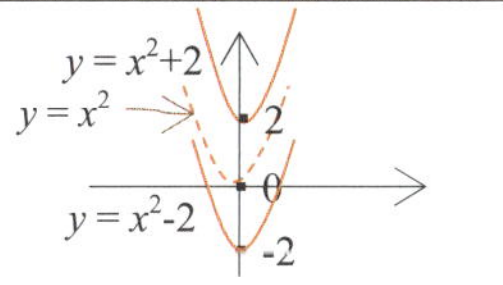 $y = x^2+2$, $y = x^2$, $y = x^2-2$, 2, 0, -2
$y = f(x + C)$ $y = f(x - C)$	Shift the graph of $f(x)$ C units to the left. Shift the graph of $f(x)$ C units to the right.	$y = (x + 2)^2$ Shift x^2 2 units to the left $y = (x - 2)^2$ Shift x^2 2 units to the right	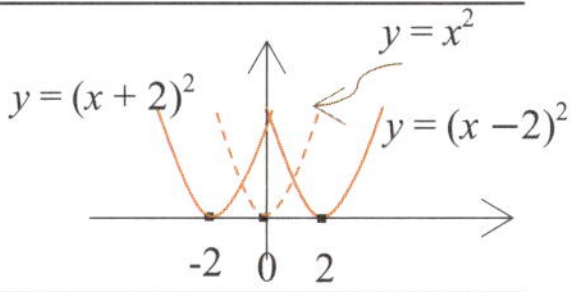 $y = x^2$, $y = (x + 2)^2$, $y = (x - 2)^2$, -2, 0, 2

- **Reflection**

Function	Reflection	Example	Graph
$y = -f(x)$	Reflect the graph of $y = f(x)$ about the x-axis.	$y = x^2$ and $y = -(x^2)$	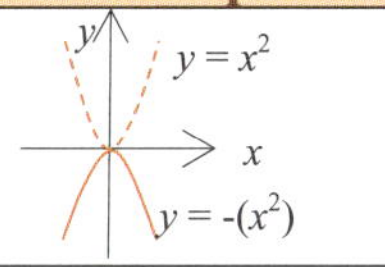 y, $y = x^2$, x, $y = -(x^2)$
$y = f(-x)$	Reflect the graph of $y = f(x)$ about the y-axis.	$y = 2x+1$ and $y = 2(-x)+1$ $= -2x+1$	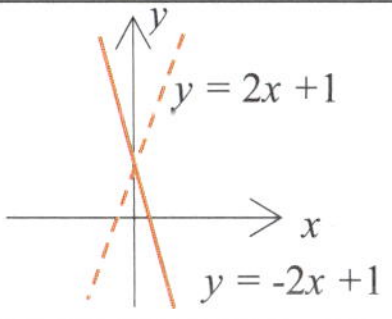 y, $y = 2x + 1$, x, $y = -2x + 1$

- A general-form conic equation (a second - degree equation)

Equation
$Ax^2 + Bxy + Cy^2 + Dx + Ey + F = 0$

- **Identify the type of conic section from the sign of $B^2 - 4AC$**

$B^2 - 4AC$	The Graph is a:
$B^2 - 4AC = 0$	parabola
$B^2 - 4AC < 0$	ellipse
$B^2 - 4AC > 0$	hyperbola

- Nonlinear system of equations: a system in which the highest power of the variable is higher than one.

- Solutions of the systems of equations: the particular values of the variables in the system that make the system true.

PRACTICE QUIZ

Unit 9 Conics

1. Identify the center and radius of the following circle.

   $x^2 + y^2 - 4x + 10y + 20 = 0$

2. Sketch the graph of $f(x) = x^2 - 8x + 12$.

3. Sketch the graph of $\frac{(x+1)^2}{25} + \frac{(y-2)^2}{9} = 1$.

4. Sketch the graph of $y^2 - 9x^2 = 9$.

5. Convert $4x^2 + 25y^2 + 24x - 50y - 39 = 0$ to standard form and graph it.

6. Solve the system.

   $x^2 + y^2 = 10$
   $2x + y = 1$

UNIT 10 EXPONENTIAL & LOGARITHMIC FUNCTIONS

10-1 EXPONENTIAL FUNCTIONS

Introduction to Exponential Functions

- **An exponential function:** a function in which the independent variable appears as an exponent.

Exponential Function			Example
$f(x) = a^x$	a – base	$a > 0,\ \ a \neq 1$	$f(x) = 5^x$
	x – independent variable	any real number	
	$f(x)$ – function		

Note:
- If $a = 1$: $f(x) = 1^x = 1$
- If $a < 0$: example: $f(x) = (-3)^x = (-3)^{\frac{1}{2}} = \sqrt{-3}$ This is not a real number.

- **Graph $f(x) = a^x$**

Steps

- Make a table.

Example: Graph $y = 3^x$ and $y = 3^{-x}$

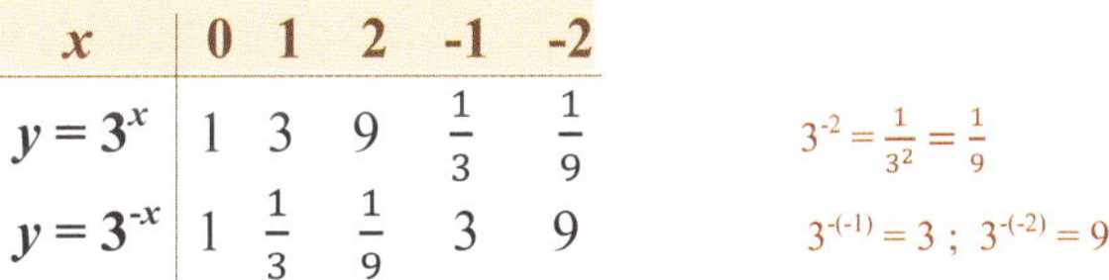

x	0	1	2	-1	-2
$y = 3^x$	1	3	9	$\frac{1}{3}$	$\frac{1}{9}$
$y = 3^{-x}$	1	$\frac{1}{3}$	$\frac{1}{9}$	3	9

$3^{-2} = \frac{1}{3^2} = \frac{1}{9}$

$3^{-(-1)} = 3\ ;\ 3^{-(-2)} = 9$

- Plot points.
- Connect points with a smooth curve.

Tip: The x-axis is the asymptote.

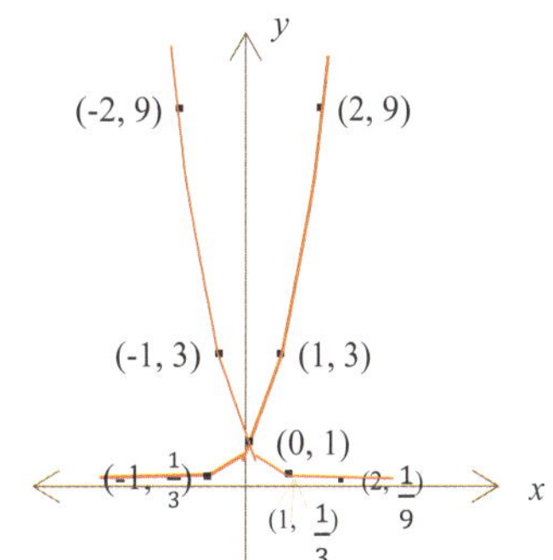

Note: The graph of $f(x) = 3^{-x}$ is a mirror image or reflection of $f(x) = 3^x$ about the y-axis.

- **Calculator tip:** Use [^] or [y^x] key.

Example: **1.** $3^{\pi} \approx 31.54$ 3 [y^x] [π] [=] or 3 [^] [2nd] [π] [ENTER]

2. $(\sqrt{5})^{\sqrt{2}} \approx 3.12$ $\sqrt{\ }$ 5 [y^x] $\sqrt{\ }$ 2 [=] or [2nd] $\sqrt{\ }$ 5 [^] [2nd] [$\sqrt{\ }$] 2 [ENTER]

Characteristics of Exponential Functions

- **The graph of a typical exponential function**

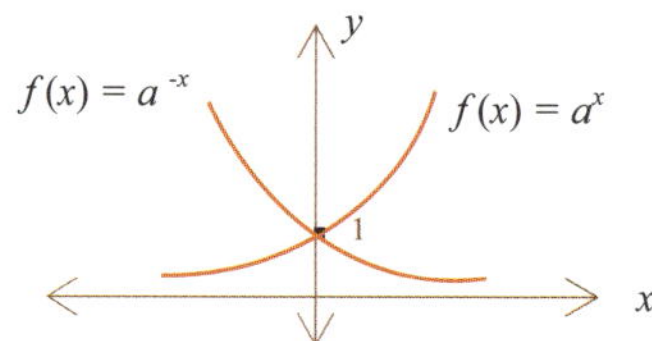

The graph is asymptotic to the x-axis as x approaches $\pm\infty$.

- **Characteristics of exponential functions**

Characteristic	$f(x) = a^x$	$f(x) = a^{-x}$
growth / decay	The graph increases (grows) from left to right.	The graph falls (decays) from left to right.
example	$f(x) = 3^x$ (0, 1) Exponential growth	$f(x) = 3^{-x}$ (0, 1) Exponential decay
asymptote	x-axis $(y = 0)$ The curve is very close but never touches the x-axis as x approaches $-\infty$.	x-axis $(y = 0)$ The curve is very close but never touches the x-axis as x approaches $+\infty$.
y - intercept	$y = 1$ Curve always passes through (0,1).	
domain x values	$x =$ All real numbers or $x = (-\infty, \infty)$	
range y values	$y = (0, \infty)$ or $\{y \mid y > 0\}$ All positive real numbers (graph is always above the x – axis).	

- **Stretching or shifting**

Function	Stretch or Shrink	Example	Graph
$f(x) = a^x$	The larger the a, the narrower the curve. The smaller the a, the wider the curve.	$f(x) = 4^x$ and $f(x) = 2^x$	$f(x) = 4^x$ $f(x) = 2^x$ 1

- **Reflecting (mirror image)**

Function	Reflection	Example	Graph
$f(x) = a^{-x}$	Reflect the graph of $f(x) = a^x$ about the y – axis.	$f(x) = 2^x$ and $f(x) = 2^{-x}$	$f(x) = 2^{-x}$ $f(x) = 2^x$ 1 0
$f(x) = -a^x$	Reflect the graph of $f(x) = a^x$ about the x – axis.	$f(x) = 2^x$ and $f(x) = -2^x$	$f(x) = 2^x$ 1 $f(x) = -2^x$

Transformations of Exponential Functions

- **Transformations of exponential functions:** change the position of the graph of the exponential function. It includes shifting, stretching / shrinking, or reflecting for exponential functions.

- **Shifting**

Exponential Function	Shifting	Example	Graph
$f(x) = a^x + C$ $f(x) = a^x - C$	Shift the graph of $y = a^x$ C units up. Shift the graph of $y = a^x$ C units down.	$f(x) = 2^x + 1$ $f(x) = 2^x - 1$	$f(x) = 2^x$ $f(x) = 2^x + 1$ $f(x) = 2^x - 1$ 0
$f(x) = a^{x+C}$ $f(x) = a^{x-C}$	Shift the graph of $y = a^x$ C units to the left. Shift the graph of $y = a^x$ C units to the right.	$f(x) = 2^{x+1}$ $f(x) = 2^{x-1}$	$f(x) = 2^x$ $f(x) = 2^{x+1}$ $f(x) = 2^{x-1}$ 0

Example: Sketch the graph of $f(x) = 3^x + 2$.

- Make a table.

x	0	1	2	-1	-2
$y = 3^x + 2$	$3^0 + 2 = 3$	$3^1 + 2 = 5$	$3^2 + 2 = 11$	$3^{-1} + 2 = \frac{1}{3} + 2$ ≈ 2.33	$3^{-2} + 2 = \frac{1}{3^2} + 2$ ≈ 2.11
(x, y)	(0, 3)	(1, 5)	(2, 11)	(-1, 2.33)	(-2, 2.11)

- Plot the points and connect them with a smooth curve.

Note: The graph of $f(x) = 3^x + 2$ has the same shape as of $f(x) = 3^x$ but is shifted 2 units up. The asymptote is $y = 2$.

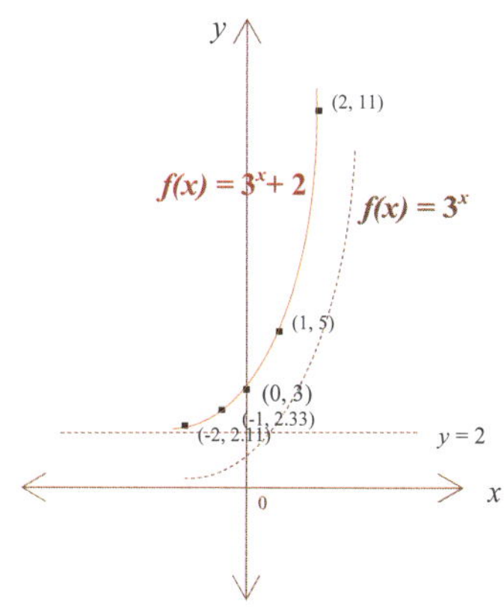

Graphing Exponential Functions

Example: Sketch the graph of $\boldsymbol{f(x) = 4^x}$ amd $\boldsymbol{f(x) = 4^{-x}}$.

- Make a table.

x	0	1	2	-1	-2
$y = 4^x$	$4^0 = 1$	$4^1 = 4$	$4^2 = 16$	$4^{-1} = \frac{1}{4}$	$4^{-2} = \frac{1}{4^2} = \frac{1}{16}$
(x, y)	(0, 1)	(1, 4)	(2, 16)	$(-1, \frac{1}{4})$	$(-2, \frac{1}{16})$

- Plot $f(x) = 4^x$.
- Reflect the graph of $f(x) = 4^x$ about the y – axis for $f(x) = 4^{-x}$.

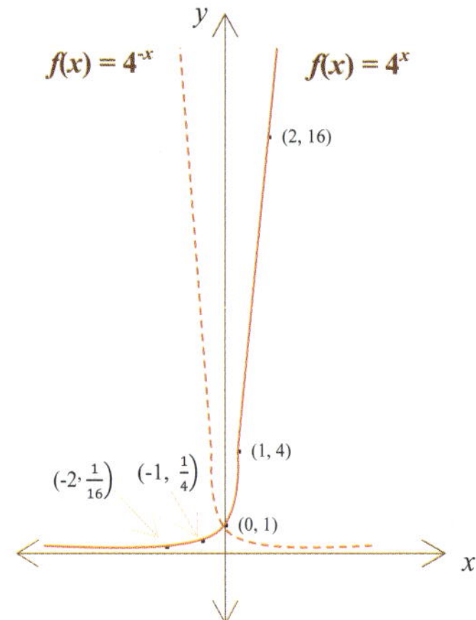

X and Y interchanging

Function	Shape	Example	Graph
$\boldsymbol{y = a^x}$ and $\boldsymbol{x = a^y}$	Reflect the graph of $y = a^x$ about the line $y = x$ to get $x = a^y$	$y = 2^x$ and $x = 2^y$	$y = 2^x$, $x = 2^y$, $y = x$, 0

Example: Sketch the graph of $\boldsymbol{x = 4^y}$.

- Sketch $y = 4^x$.
- Plot the line $y = x$.
- Reflect the graph of $y = 4^x$ about the line $y = x$ to get the graph of $x = 4^y$.

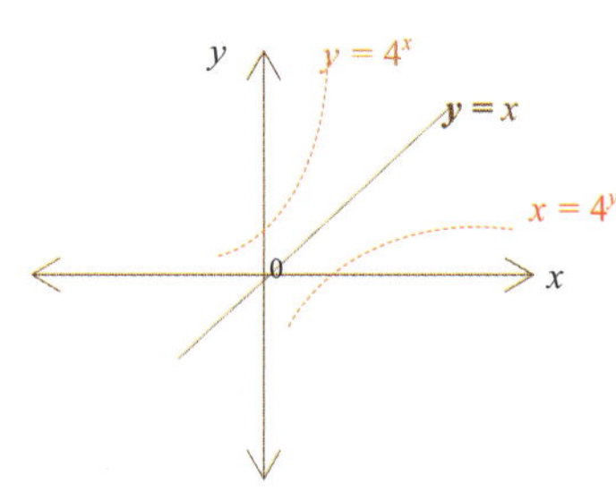

10-2 INVERSE AND COMPOSITE FUNCTIONS

Inverse Relation

- **Recall – relation:** a set of ordered pairs (x, y)
- **Inverse relation:** a relation formed when the order of the elements in a given relation is switched.

Domain (x)	Range (y)	Relation (x, y)
2	-1	(2,-1)
-3	1	(-3, 1)

Relation: $x \to y$; Inverse relation: $y \to x$

Example:
- Relation: {(2, -1) , (-3, 1) , (-4, 0)}
- Inverse relation: {(-1, 2) , (1, -3) , (0, -4)}
- Graph:

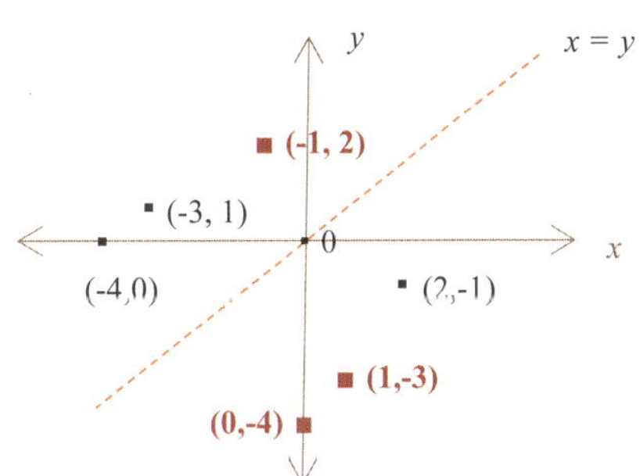

- **The graph of inverse relation** is a reflection (mirror image) of the relation about the line $y = x$.
- **Inverse equation:** switching x and y in the original equation produces an inverse equation.

Example:
- Equation: $y = 2x - 3$
- Inverse equation: $x = 2y - 3$ (Switch x and y.)
- Graph:

Equation

x	$y = 2x - 3$
0	-3
1	-1

Inverse equation (solve for y from $x = 2y - 3$).

x	$y = \frac{x+3}{2}$
-3	0
-1	1

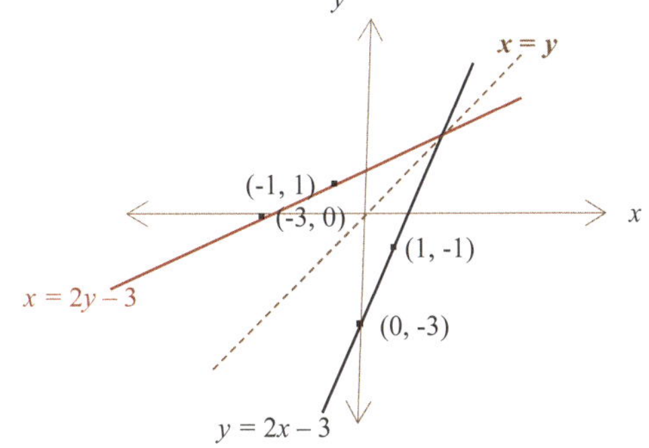

One-to-One Function & Its Inverse

- **One-to-one function:** a function for which every element of the range (y-value) corresponds to a unique domain (x-value).

Example: 1. {(1, 2), (3, -4), (5, 3)} — **One-to-one function**

2. {(1, 2), (3, -4), (5, 2)} — **Not one-to-one**
∵ $y = 2$ is assigned with two x (1 and 5).

- **The horizontal-line test:** If a horizontal line cuts the graph of a function only once, then the function is one-to-one and its inverse is a function.

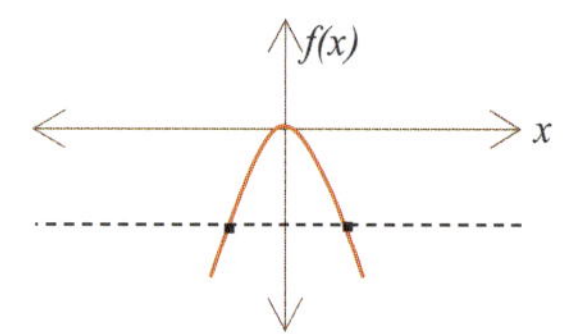

Not one-to-one
(A horizontal line cuts the graph more than once.)

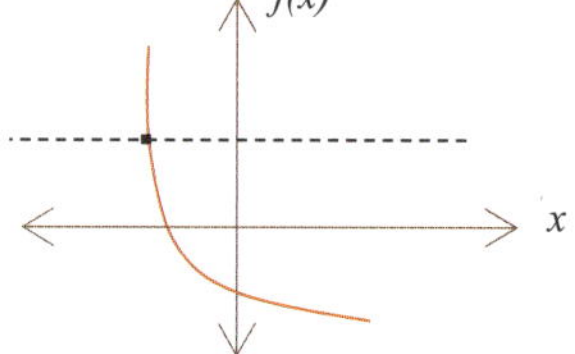

One-to-one
(There is no horizontal line that cut the graph more than once.)

Example: Determine whether each function is one-to-one.

1. $f(x) = 3x^2 + 2$

x	$f(x) = 3x^2 + 2$
0	2
1	5
-1	5

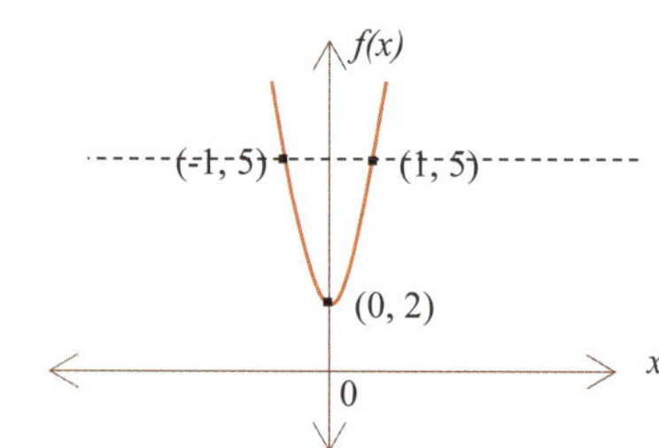

Not one-to-one

2. $f(x) = 2^x$

x	$f(x) = 2^x$
0	1
1	2
2	4

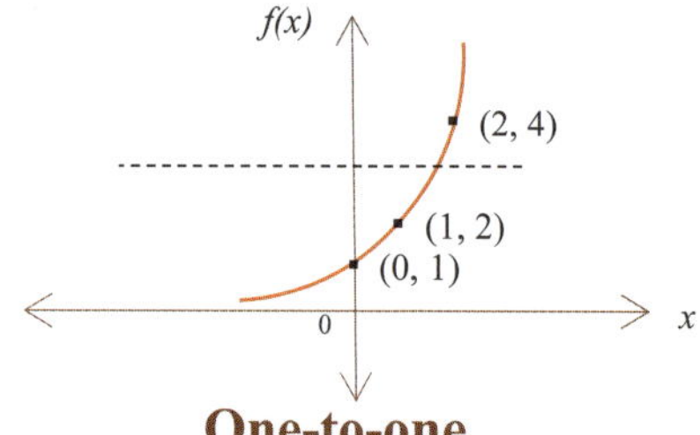

One-to-one

Inverse Function

- **Inverse function $f^{-1}(x)$:** the function formed when the order of the elements in a given function is switched.

$$x \xrightarrow{\text{Function } f(x)} y \qquad y \xrightarrow{\text{Inverse function } f^{-1}(x)} x$$

- **The graph of inverse function $f^{-1}(x)$** is a reflection the original function $f(x)$ about the line $y = x$.

- **If a function $f(x)$ is one-to-one,** its inverse function $f^{-1}(x)$ can be found as follows:

Steps | **Example: $f(x) = 2x + 3$**

- Confirm that the function is 1-to-1.

Graph $f(x)$:

x	$f(x) = 2x + 3$
0	3
1	5

Yes, 1-to-1

$f(x)$　$y = x$　$f^{-1}(x)$　0

- Rewrite $f(x)$ as y.

$y = 2x + 3$

- Switch x and y.

$x = 2y + 3$

- Solve for y.

$y = \frac{x-3}{2}$　　Subtract 3; divide by 2.

- Replace y with $f^{-1}(x)$.

$f^{-1}(x) = \frac{x-3}{2}$

- Graph $f^{-1}(x)$: reflect the graph of $f(x)$ across the line $y = x$.

Note: A function has an inverse function $f^{-1}(x)$ only if the function is a one-to-one function.

Graph the Function and Its Inverse

Example: Determine whether the function is one-to-one. If it is, find its inverse function.

$f(x) = \frac{4}{x}$

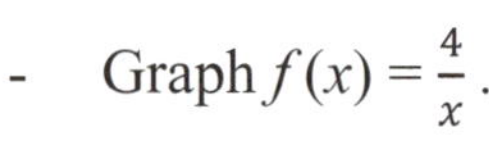

- Graph $f(x) = \frac{4}{x}$.

x	$y = 4/x$
1	4
2	2
4	1
-1	-4
-2	-2
-4	-1

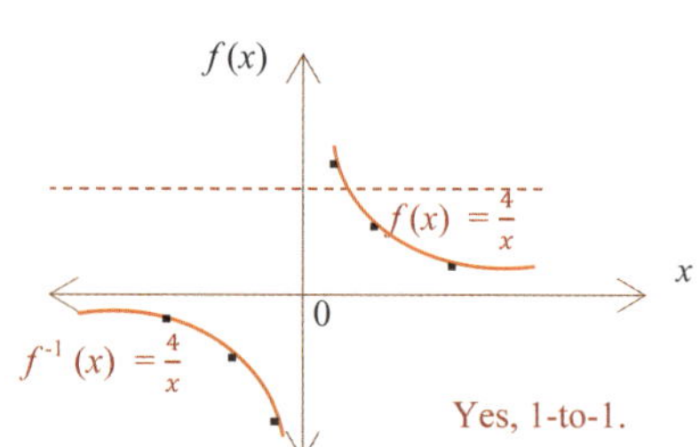

- Let $y = f(x)$. $\quad y = \frac{4}{x}$
- Switch x and y. $\quad x = \frac{4}{y}$
- Solve with y. $\quad y = \frac{4}{x}$ $\quad$ Divide by x; multiply by y.
- Replace y with $f^{-1}(x)$. $\quad \boldsymbol{f^{-1}(x) = \frac{4}{x}}$

Example: Sketch the graph of the function $h(x) = \frac{2}{3}x + 1$ and its inverse.

- Graph $h(x) = \frac{2}{3}x + 1$.

x	$h(x) = \frac{2}{3}x + 1$
0	1
3	3

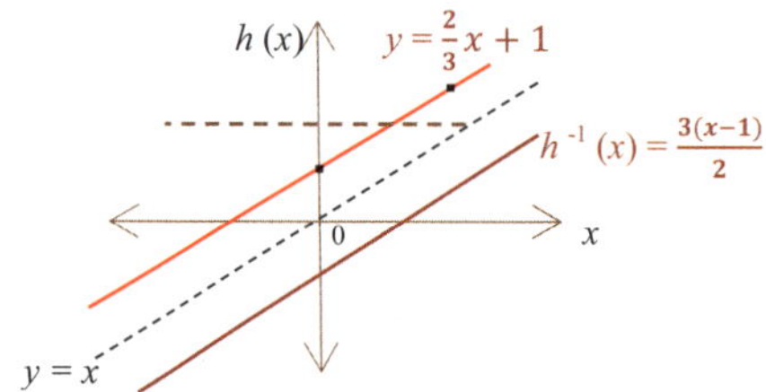

Yes, 1-to-1

- Replace $h(x)$ with y. $\quad y = \frac{2}{3}x + 1$ $\quad$ Rewrite $h(x)$ as y.
- Switch x and y. $\quad x = \frac{2}{3}y + 1$
- Solve for y. $\quad x - 1 = \frac{2}{3}y \quad , \quad 3(x - 1) = 2y$

$$y = = \frac{3(x-1)}{2}$$

- Replace y with $h^{-1}(x)$. $\quad \boldsymbol{h^{-1}(x) = \frac{3(x-1)}{2}}$
- Graph $h^{-1}(x)$: $\quad$ reflect the graph of $h(x)$ across the line $y = x$.

Composition of Functions

Composite function $f \circ g(x)$: a combination of two or more functions in which the result of one function is applied to another function (substitute a function into another function).

Composite Function	Formula	Comments
$f \circ g(x)$	$f \circ g(x) = f[g(x)]$	$g(x)$ (inner function) → $f(\ )$ (outer function). The result of $g(\ )$ is applying to $f(\ )$.
$g \circ f(x)$	$g \circ f(x) = g[f(x)]$	$f(x)$ (inner function) → $g(\ )$ (outer function). The result of $f(\ )$ is applying to $g(\ )$.

Tips
- Composite function: a function within another function.
- Read: $f \circ g(x)$: "f of g of x"; $g \circ f(x)$: "g of f of x"

Example: Find $f \circ g(x)$ and $g \circ f(x)$.

If $f(x) = 3 - 2x$,

and $g(x) = x - 4$

- $f \circ g(x) = f[g(x)]$ — $g(x) = x - 4$

  $= f[x - 4]$ — $f(\ )$ — Replace $g(x)$ with $(x - 4)$.

  $= 3 - 2(x - 4)$ — $3 - 2(\ )$ — Replace $(x - 4)$ with x in $f(x)$. $f(x) = 3 - 2x$

  $= 3 - 2x + 8$

  $f \circ g(x) = 11 - 2x$

- $g \circ f(x) = g[f(x)]$ — $f(x) = 3 - 2x$

  $= g(3 - 2x)$ — $g(\ )$ — Replace $f(x)$ with $(3-2x)$.

  $= (3 - 2x) - 4$ — $(\ ) - 4$ — Replace $(3 - 2x)$ with x in $g(x)$. $g(x) = x - 4$

  $= 3 - 2x - 4$

  $g \circ f(x) = -2x - 1$

Example: Find $f \circ g(x)$ and $g \circ f(x)$.

If $f(x) = \frac{1}{x}$,

and $g(x) = 2 - 3x^2$

- $f \circ g(x) = f[g(x)]$

$= f[2 - 3x^2]$

$= \frac{1}{2-3x^2}$

$g(x) = 2 - 3x^2$; $f(\ )$ = $\frac{1}{(\ )}$

Replace $g(x)$ with $(2 - 3x^2)$.

Replace $(2 - 3x^2)$ with x in $f(x)$. $f(x) = \frac{1}{x}$

- $g \circ f(x) = g[f(x)]$

$= g\left[\frac{1}{x}\right]$

$= 2 - 3\left(\frac{1}{x}\right)^2$

$= 2 - \frac{3}{x^2}$

$f(x) = \frac{1}{x}$; $g(\ )$ = $2 - 3(\ )^2$

Replace $f(x)$ with $\frac{1}{x}$.

Replace $\frac{1}{x}$ with x in $g(x)$. $g(x) = 2 - 3x^2$

Example: Determine $f(x)$ and $g(x)$ such that $h(x) = f \circ g(x)$, $h(x) = (3 - 2x)^2$.

Solution: $\because \ h(x) = f \circ g(x) = f[g(x)]$

$h(x) = (3 - 2x)^2$; $g(x) = 3 - 2x$; $f(\ ) = (\ )^2$

$\therefore \ f(x) = x^2$

$g(x) = 3 - 2x$

$h(x) = (3 - 2x)^2$ ↑ $g(x)$

Check: $h(x) = f \circ g(x) = f[g(x)]$

$= f(3 - 2x)$

$= (3 - 2x)^2$

$g(x) = 3 - 2x$; $f(\ )$ = $(\ )^2 = h(x)$

Replace $g(x)$ with $(3 - 2x)$.

$f(x) = x^2$

√

$\therefore \ h(x) = (3 - 2x)^2$

Correct!

Inverse Functions and Composition

Inverse Function
If a function is one-to-one, then $f^{-1} \circ f(x) = x$ and $f \circ f^{-1}(x) = x.$

Example: Use composition to show that the inverse is correct.

$f(x) = \frac{2}{3}x$,

$f^{-1}(x) = \frac{3}{2}x$

- $f^{-1} \circ f(x) = f^{-1}[f(x)]$ $\quad f(x) = \frac{2}{3}x$ $\quad \because f \circ g(x) = f[g(x)]$ $\quad \therefore f^{-1} \circ f(x) = f^{-1}[f(x)]$

$= f^{-1}[\frac{2}{3}x]$

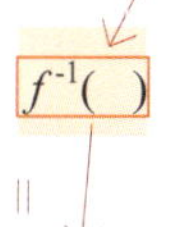

$= \frac{3}{2}(\frac{2}{3}x)$ $\quad \frac{3}{2}(\ )$ $\quad f^{-1}(x) = \frac{3}{2}x$

$= \frac{6}{6}x$

$= x$

- $f \circ f^{-1}(x) = f[f^{-1}(x)]$ $\quad f^{-1}(x) = \frac{3}{2}x$ $\quad \because f \circ g(x) = f[g(x)]$ $\quad \therefore f \circ f^{-1}(x) = f[f^{-1}(x)]$

$= f[\frac{3}{2}x]$

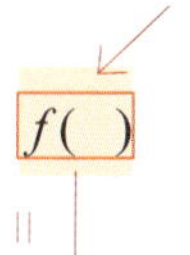

$= \frac{2}{3}(\frac{3}{2}x)$ $\quad \frac{2}{3}(\ )$ $\quad f(x) = \frac{2}{x}x$

$= \frac{6}{6}x$

$= x$

$f^{-1} \circ f(x) = f \circ f^{-1}(x) = x$ $\quad$ Correct!

Example: Determine the inverse of the given function. Then use composition to show whether the inverse is correct.

$$\boldsymbol{f(x) = -2x}$$

- Find the inverse function $f^{-1}(x)$.
  - Rewrite $f(x)$ with y. $\quad y = -2x \qquad f(x) = -2x$
  - Switch x and y. $\quad x = -2y$
  - Solve for y. $\quad y = -\frac{x}{2}$
  - Replace y with $f^{-1}(x)$. $\quad \boldsymbol{f^{-1}(x) = -\frac{x}{2}}$

- Determine $f^{-1} \circ f(x)$ and $f \circ f^{-1}(x)$

$f^{-1}(x) \circ f(x) = f^{-1}[f(x)]$ $\qquad \boxed{f(x)} = -2x$

$= f^{-1}[-2x]$ $\qquad \boxed{f^{-1}(\ )}$

$= -\frac{(-2x)}{2}$ $\qquad -\frac{(\ )}{2}$

$= x$

$f \circ f^{-1}(x) = f[f^{-1}(x)]$ $\qquad \boxed{f^{-1}(x)} = -\frac{x}{2}$

$= f[-\frac{x}{2}]$ $\qquad \boxed{f(\ )}$

$= -2(-\frac{x}{2})$ $\qquad \boxed{-2(\ )}$

$= x$

- Check: $\quad f^{-1} \circ f(x) = f \circ f^{-1}(x) \stackrel{?}{=} x \qquad$ Definition

$$x \stackrel{\surd}{=} x \qquad \text{Correct!}$$

10-3 LOGARITHMIC FUNCTIONS

Introduction to Logarithms

- **The logarithmic function $f(x) = \log_a x$:** a function that is the inverse of an exponential function ($y = a^x$).

Exponent question:

$3^2 = ?$

Logarithmic question:

$3^? = 9$ 3 to what power gives 9?

$3^2 = 9$ Two multiples of 3s are required to get 9.

$\log_3 9 = 2$

- **Definition of logarithm**

Logarithmic Function	Definition of Logarithm	Example
$f(x) = \log_a x$ ($x > 0$, $a > 0$, $a \neq 1$)	if $y = a^x$, then $\log_a y = x$. Or if $x = a^y$, then $\log_a x = y$.	If $9 = 3^2$, then $\log_3 9 = 2$. Read: "the log, base 3 of 9, is 2" or "log of 9, base 3, equals 2."

- **Logarithm of zero $\log_a(0)$:** the logarithm of 0 is undefined.
  $\because$ if $a^x = 0$, x does not exist.

  Example
  $3^x = 0$ is undefined.
  x does not exist for $3^x = 0$.

- **Logarithm of negative number $\log_a(-y)$:** the logarithm of negative numbers is undefined.
  $\because$ base $a > 0$, $y = a^x > 0$, y must be positive for any real x.

  $\log_3(-9)$ is undefined.
  $\because$ $3 > 0$, $3^2 > 0$

- **Converting between exponential and logarithmic forms**

  Example

  - Exponential to log form: $a^x = y$ → $\log_a y = x$ Example: $3^2 = 9$ → $\log_3 9 = 2$
  - Log to exponential form: $\log_a y = x$ → $a^x = y$ Example: $\log_3 9 = 2$ → $3^2 = 9$

Evaluating Logarithms

Example: Write in logarithmic form.

1. $2^3 = 8$

$\log_2(8) = (3)$ **$\log_2 8 = 3$**

2. $10^5 = 100{,}000$

$\log_{10}(100{,}000) = (5)$ **$\log_{10} 100{,}000 = 5$**

3. $a^t = b$

$\log_a(b) = (t)$ **$\log_a b = t$**

Example: Write in exponential form.

1. $\log_3 81 = 4$

$3^{(4)} = (81)$ **$3^4 = 81$**

2. $\log_{10} 0.0001 = -4$

$10^{(-4)} = (0.0001)$ **$10^{-4} = 0.0001$**

Note: The exponent can be negative, but the base must be positive $(x = a^y,\ a > 0)$.

3. $\log_5 \frac{1}{25} = -2$

$5^{(-2)} = \left(\frac{1}{25}\right)$ **$5^{-2} = \frac{1}{25}$**

Evaluating Logarithms

Steps

- Let $\log_a y = x$.
- Convert to exponential form.
- Write x in an exponent.

Example: $\log_4 16 = ?$

Let $\log_4 16 = x$

$4^{(x)} = (16)$ $4^x = 16$

$4^x = 4^2$

$\boldsymbol{x = 2}$

If $a^x = a^y$, then $x = y$. The exponents are the same.

Example: Find the value of **$\log_5 125$**.

Let $\log_5 125 = x$ Let $\log_a y = x$

$5^{(x)} = (125)$ $5^x = 125$ Convert to exponential form.

$5^x = 5^3$ $125 = 5^3$

$\boldsymbol{x = 3}$ If $a^x = a^y$, then $x = y$.

Solving Logarithmic Equations

- **Logarithmic equation:** an equation that contains a logarithmic expression.
- **The key to solve a logarithmic equation** is to convert log into exponential form.

Steps

- Convert to an exponential equation.
- Take the square root of both sides and solve for x.
- Check.

Example: Solve $\log_x 25 = 2$.

$\log_x 25 = 2$

$x^{(2)} = (25)$, $x^2 = 25$

$\sqrt{x^2} = \pm\sqrt{25}$

$\boldsymbol{x = \pm 5}$

$x = 5$: $\log_5 25 \overset{?}{=} 2$, $5^2 = 25$ Correct! **$x = 5$ is a solution**

$x = -5$: $\log_{(-5)} 25 \overset{?}{=} 2$ It is not defined. $y = \log_a x$, $a > 0$

Example: Solve each of the following equations.

1. $\log_3 x = -4$:

$\log_3 x = -4$

$3^{-4} = x$ — Log $\longrightarrow$ exponent.

$\frac{1}{3^4} = x$ — $a^{-x} = \frac{1}{a^x}$

$\boldsymbol{x = \frac{1}{81}}$ — $3^4 = 81$

Check: $\log_3 \frac{1}{81} \overset{?}{=} -4$

$3^{-4} = \frac{1}{81}$, $\frac{1}{3^4} \overset{\surd}{=} \frac{1}{81}$ — Correct!

2. $\log_2 16 = x$:

$\log_2 16 = x$

$2^x = 16$ — Log $\longrightarrow$ exponent.

$2^x = 2^4$ — Write 16 in an exponent: $16 = 2^4$

$\boldsymbol{x = 4}$ — If $a^x = a^y$, then $x = y$.

3. $\log_{16} \frac{1}{4} = x$:

$\log_{16} \frac{1}{4} = x$ — Log $\longrightarrow$ exponent.

$16^x = \frac{1}{4}$

$(4^2)^x = 4^{-1}$, $4^{2x} = 4^{-1}$ — $16 = 4^2$

$2x = -1$, $x = \frac{-1}{2}$ — If $a^x = a^y$, then $x = y$.

4. $\log_x 27 = 3$:

$\log_x 27 = 3$ — Log $\longrightarrow$ exponent.

$x^3 = 27$

$\sqrt[3]{x^3} = \sqrt[3]{27}$ — Take the cube root of both sides.

$\sqrt[3]{x^3} = \sqrt[3]{3^3}$, $\boldsymbol{x = 3}$ — $27 = 3^3$

Graphing Logarithmic Functions

- **The graph of a function** is the reflection of its inverse about the $y = x$ line.
- **Logarithmic functions and exponential functions are inverse functions.**
- **The graph of the logarithmic function** is the reflection of the graph of the exponential function about the $y = x$ line.
- **Graphing a logarithmic function using its inverse**

Steps

- Convert to exponential form.
- Switch x and y.
- Make a table for $y = a^x$.

Example: Graph $f(x) = \log_2 x$.

$\log_2 x = y$

$2^y = x$

$2^x = y$ or $y = 2^x$

Choose x. Calculate y.

x	0	1	2	-1	-2
$y = 2^x$	$2^0 = 1$	$2^1 = 2$	$2^2 = 4$	$2^{-1} = \frac{1}{2}$	$2^{-2} = \frac{1}{4}$
(x, y)	(0, 1)	(1, 2)	(2, 4)	$(-1, \frac{1}{2})$	$(-2, \frac{1}{4})$

- Graph $y = a^x$.

Graph $y = 2^x$

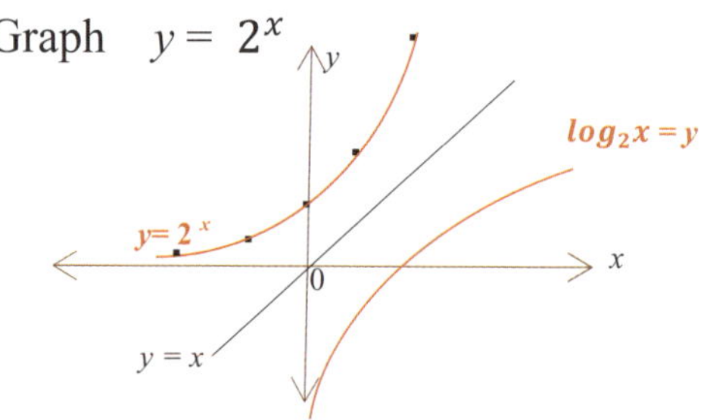

- Graph $f(x) = \log_a x$ by reflecting the curve of $y = a^x$ about the $y = x$ line.
- Or switch the x and y values in the table, then graph $y = \log_a x$.

Graph $f(x) = \log_2 x$ by reflecting $y = 2^x$ about the $y = x$ line.

Switch the x and y values in the table, then graph $y = \log_2 x$.

$y = 2^x$	(0, 1)	(1, 2)	(2, 4)	$(-1, \frac{1}{2})$	$(-2, \frac{1}{4})$
$\log_2 x = y$	(1, 0)	(2, 1)	(4, 2)	$(\frac{1}{2}, -1)$	$(\frac{1}{4}, -2)$

Tip: Switch the x and y values to get $\log_2 x = y$

Properties of Logarithms

- **Comparing properties of logarithmic and exponential functions**

Exponential Function $y = f(x) = a^x$		Logarithmic Function $\log_a x$	Example $y = 2^x$	$\log_2 x$
Domain (x-values)	$(-\infty, \infty)$ All real numbers.	$(0, \infty)$ or $x > 0$	$(-\infty, \infty)$	$(0, \infty)$
Range (y-values)	$(0, \infty)$ or $y > 0$	$(-\infty, \infty)$ All real numbers.	$y > 0$	$(-\infty, \infty)$
Intercept	y-intercept = 1	x-intercept = 1	1	1
Asymptote	x - axis	y - axis		

- **Basic properties of logarithms**

Property	Example	Proof
$\log_a 1 = 0$	$\log_4 1 = 0$	$\log_4 1 = 0$ → $4^0 = 1$
$\log_a a = 1$	$\log_7 7 = 1$	$\log_7 7 = 1$ → $7^1 = 7$
$\log_a a^x = x$	$\log_2 2^3 = 3$	$\log_2 2^3 = 3$ → $2^3 = 2^3$
$a^{\log_a x} = x$	$3^{\log_3 4} = 4$	$3^{\log_3 4} = 4$ → $\log_3 4 = \log_3 4$

Example: Evaluate each of the following.

1. $\log_9 1$ $\qquad \log_9 1 = 0$ $\qquad \log_a 1 = 0$
2. $\log_{21} 21$ $\qquad \log_{21} 21 = 1$ $\qquad \log_a a = 1$
3. $\log_5 5^7$ $\qquad \log_5 5^7 = 7$ $\qquad \log_a a^x = x$
4. $6^{\log_6 5}$ $\qquad 6^{\log_6 5} = 5$ $\qquad a^{\log_a x} = x$
5. $\log_7 49$ $\qquad \log_7 49 = \log_7 7^2 = 2$ $\qquad \log_a a^x = x$
6. $\log_{10} 0.001$ $\qquad \log_{10} 0.001 = \log_{10} 10^{-3} = -3$ $\qquad \log_a a^x = x$

10-4 RULES OF LOGARITHMS

Rules

- **Recall rules of exponents**

Name	Rule	Example
product rule	$a^m a^n = a^{m+n}$	$2^3 \cdot 2^4 = 2^{3+4}$
quotient rule	$\frac{a^m}{a^n} = a^{m-n}$	$\frac{3^5}{3^2} = 3^{5-2}$
power of a power	$(a^m)^n = a^{mn}$	$(4^3)^2 = 4^{3 \cdot 2}$

- **The rules of logarithms are very similar to the rules of exponents,** because the log function is the inverse of the exponential function.
- **Rules of logarithms**

Name	Rule	Example
product rule	$\log_a(A \cdot B) = \log_a A + \log_a B$ The log of a product is the sum of the logs.	$\log_5(3 \cdot 4) = \log_5 3 + \log_5 4$
quotient rule	$\log_a\left(\frac{A}{B}\right) = \log_a A - \log_a B$ The log of a quotient is the difference of the logs.	$\log_3\left(\frac{7}{2}\right) = \log_3 7 - \log_3 2$
power rule	$\log_a A^n = n \log_a A$ The log of a power is equal to the product of the exponent of the power and the log of its base.	$\log_2 3^4 = 4 \log_2 3$

Where $a > 0$, $A > 0$, $B > 0$, $\log a \neq 1$

Example: Write each of the following as simpler logarithms.

1. $\mathbf{\log_4(3y^3)} = \log_4 3 + \log_4 y^3$ — $\log_a(AB) = \log_a A + \log_a B$

   $= \log_4 3 + 3\log_4 y$ — $\log_a A^n = n\log_a A$

2. $\mathbf{\log_5\left(\frac{3x}{y^2}\right)} = \log_5 3 \cdot x - \log_5 y^2$ — $\log_a\left(\frac{A}{B}\right) = \log_a A - \log_a B$

   $= \log_5 3 + \log_5 x - \log_5 y^2$ — $\log_a(AB) = \log_a A + \log_a B$

   $= \log_5 3 + \log_5 x - 2\log_5 y$ — $\log_a A^n = n\log_a A$

3. $\mathbf{4\log_2 x + 2\log_2 y - 3\log_2 z}$

   $= \log_2 x^4 + \log_2 y^2 - \log_2 z^3$ — $n\log_a A = \log_a A^n$

   $= \log_2(x^4 \cdot y^2) - \log_2 z^3$ — $\log_a A + \log_a B = \log_a(AB)$

   $= \log_2\left(\frac{x^4y^2}{z^3}\right)$ — $\log_a\left(\frac{A}{B}\right) = \log_a A - \log_a B$

Proof of the Logarithms Rules

- **Proof: $\log_a(AB) = \log_a A + \log_a B$**
  - Let $\log_a A = x$ and $\log_a B = y$.
  - Convert to exponential form. $a^x = A$ $a^y = B$
  - Multiply A and B. $A \cdot B = a^x \cdot a^y = a^{x+y}$
  - Convert to logarithmic form. $a^{x+y} = AB$ $\log_a(AB) = x + y$
  - Replace x and y by $\log_a A$ and $\log_a B$. $\mathbf{\log_a(AB) = \log_a A + \log_a B}$

- **Proof: $\log_a\left(\frac{A}{B}\right) = \log_a A - \log_a B$**
  - Let $\log_a A = x$ and $\log_a B = y$.
  - Convert to exponential form. $a^x = A$ $a^y = B$
  - Divide A and B. $\frac{A}{B} = \frac{a^x}{a^y} = a^{x-y}$
  - Convert to logarithmic form. $a^{x-y} = \frac{A}{B}$ $\log_a\left(\frac{A}{B}\right) = x - y$
  - Replace x and y by $\log_a A$ and $\log_a B$. $\mathbf{\log_a\left(\frac{A}{B}\right) = \log_a A - \log_a B}$

- **Proof: $\log_a A^n = n \log_a A$**
  - Let $\log_a A = x$.
  - Convert to exponential form. $a^x = A$
  - Raise both sides to nth power. $(a^x)^n = A^n$ or $a^{xn} = A^n$
  - Convert to logarithmic form. $\log_a A^n = xn$
  - Replace x by $\log_a A$. $\log_a A^n = (\log_a A)n$

$$\mathbf{\log_a A^n = n \log_a A}$$

Applying Rules of Logarithm

Example: Expand $\boldsymbol{log_4\sqrt[3]{\frac{x^3y}{z}}}$.

$log_4\sqrt[3]{\frac{x^3y}{z}} = log_4\left(\frac{x^3y}{z}\right)^{\frac{1}{3}}$ $\qquad \sqrt[n]{a} = a^{\frac{1}{n}}$

$= \frac{1}{3}log_4\frac{x^3y}{z}$ $\qquad log_a A^n = n\,log_a A$

$= \frac{1}{3}\,[log_4(x^3\cdot y) - log_4 z]$ $\qquad log_a\left(\frac{A}{B}\right) = log_a A - log_a B$

$= \frac{1}{3}\,(log_4 x^3 + log_4 y - log_4 z)$ $\qquad log_a(AB) = log_a A + log_a B$

$= \frac{1}{3}\,(3log_4 x + log_4 y - log_4 z)$ $\qquad log_a A^n = n\,log_a A$

$\boldsymbol{= log_4 x + \frac{1}{3}log_4 y - \frac{1}{3}log_4 z}$

Example: Given $\boldsymbol{log_a 4 = 0.6}$ and $\boldsymbol{log_a 5 = 0.7}$, find the following.

1. $\boldsymbol{log_a 20} = log_a(4\cdot 5)$

$= log_a 4 + log_a 5$ $\qquad log_a(AB) = log_a A + log_a B$

$\approx 0.6 + 0.7 = \mathbf{0.13}$ $\qquad$ Given $log_a 4 = 0.6$, $log_a 5 = 0.7$

2. $\boldsymbol{log_a\frac{25}{4}} = log_a 25 - log_a 4$ $\qquad log_a\left(\frac{A}{B}\right) = log_a A - log_a B$

$= log_a 5^2 - log_a 4$

$= 2\,log_a 5 - log_a 4$ $\qquad log_a A^n = n\,log_a A$

$= 2(0.7) - 0.6 = \mathbf{0.8}$ $\qquad$ Given $log_a 4 = 0.6$, $log_a 5 = 0.7$

3. $\boldsymbol{log_a\sqrt{5}} = log_a 5^{\frac{1}{2}}$ $\qquad \sqrt[n]{a} = a^{\frac{1}{n}}$

$= \frac{1}{2}log_a 5$ $\qquad log_a A^n = n\,log_a A$

$= \frac{1}{2}(0.7) = \mathbf{0.35}$ $\qquad$ Given $log_a 5 = 0.7$

10-5 COMMON AND NATURAL LOGARITHMS

Common Logarithm

- **The common logarithm** is a logarithm with base 10, i.e. $log_{10}x$. It is usually denoted as $log\ x$ (without writing the base 10).

Notation for Common Log	Example
$log_{10}x = log\ x$ Base 10 (↑ under 10) No base means base 10. (↑ under log)	$log_{10}3 = log\ 3$

Example: $log10000 = log_{10}10000$

$= log_{10}10^4 = \mathbf{4}$ $log_a a^x = x$

$log\ 0.0001 = log_{10}0.0001$

$= log_{10}10^{-4} = \mathbf{-4}$ $log_a a^x = x$

- **The log of a negative number has no real number answers.**

Example: $log_{10}(-3) = x$

$10^x = -3$

No matter what the value of x may be, 10^x will never be negative.

$\therefore$ $log\ (-3)$ is undefined.

- **Calculator tip:** for the common logarithm, use the [LOG] key.

Example: **1.** $log\ 312 \approx 2.494$ [LOG] 312 [ENTER]   [ENTER] or [=]

2. $log\ 0.146 \approx -0.836$ [LOG] 0.146 [=]   [=] or [ENTER]

3. $10^{3.1532} \approx 1423$ [2nd] [10^x] 3.1532 [ENTER]   [2nd] or [INV]

Natural Logarithm

- **The natural logarithm:** the logarithm with base e, i.e. $\log_e x$. It is usually denoted as $\ln x$.
- **The number e:** e is not a whole number (an irrational number).

  $e \approx 2.718281828 \ldots$ The decimal expansion of e never ends nor repeats.

Notation for natural log	Example
$log_e x = ln\,x$ (↑ Base e)	$log_e 3 = ln\,3$

- **Calculator tip:** for the natural logarithm, use the [LN] key.

Example

1. $ln\,3 \approx 1.099$ — [LN] 3 [=] or [ENTER]
2. $ln\,0.03 \approx -3.51$ — [LN] 0.03 [ENTER] or [=]
3. $ln\,(-7)$ is undefined
4. $e^{2.153} \approx 8.61$ — [2nd] [e^x] 2.153 [=] — [2nd] or [INV]

- **Graphing of $f(x) = ln\,x$, e^x and e^{-x}**
  - The graph of the exponential function (e^x) is a reflection of the graph of (e^{-x}) about the y-axis.

    Recall: The graph of a^{-x} is the reflection of graph of a^x about the y-axis.
  - The graph of the natural logarithmic function $ln\,x$ is the reflection of the graph of the exponential function e^x about the $y = x$ line.

Example: Sketch the graphs of $y = e^x$, $y = e^{-x}$ and $y = ln\,x$.

- Make a table for $y = e^x$ — Calculator tip: [2nd] [e^x] …

x	0	1	-1	-2
$y = e^x$	$e^0 = 1$	$e^1 \approx 2.72$	$e^{-1} \approx 0.37$	$e^{-2} \approx 0.14$
Pair (x, y)	(0, 1)	(1, 2.72)	(-1, 0.37)	(-2, 0.14)

- Graph $y = e^x$.
- Graph $y = e^{-x}$: reflect the curve of $y = e^x$ about the y-axis.
- Graph $y = ln\,x$: reflect the curve of $y = e^x$ about the $y = x$ line.

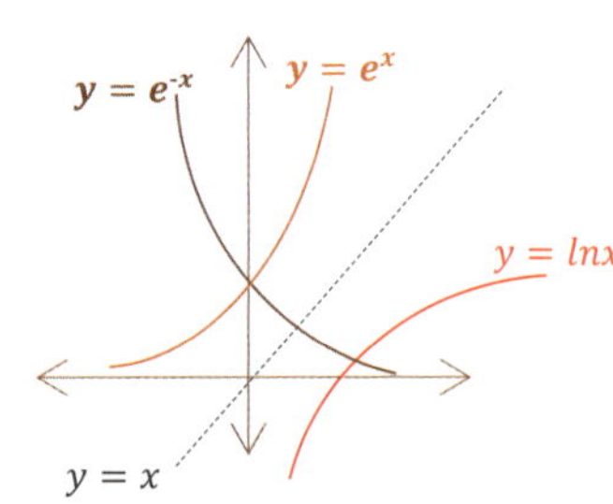

Changing the Base of a Logarithm

- Most scientific calculators have keys for only base 10 (the common log LOG) and base e (the natural log LN).
- **Change of base formula** evaluates logarithms with different bases other than 10 or e.

Such as $log_{23}128 = ?$

Change of Base Formula	$log_b x = \frac{log_a x}{log_a b}$	Example	
change to base 10	$log_b x = \frac{log\ x}{log\ b}$	$log_3 5 = \frac{log\ 5}{log 3} \approx 1.465$	LOG 5) ÷ LOG 3
change to base *e*	$log_b x = \frac{ln\ x}{ln\ b}$	$log_3 5 = \frac{ln\ 5}{ln\ 3} \approx 1.465$	LN 5) ÷ LN 3

Note: x, a, and b are positive, $a \neq 1, b \neq 1$.

Tip: The same answer will result regardless of the logarithm (log or ln) that we use in the change of base.

Example: Derivative of $log_b x = \frac{log_a x}{log_a b}$.

Let $log\ _b x = u$

$b^u = x$ — Convert log to exponential form.

$log_a b^u = log\ _a x$ — Take log both sides.

$u\ log_a b = log_a x$ — $log_a\ A^n = n\ log_a A$

$u = \frac{log_a x}{log_a b}$ — Divide both sides by $log_a b$.

$log_b x = \frac{log_a x}{log_a b}$ — Replace u with $log_b x$.

Example: Evaluate each of the following.

1. $log_6 17 = \frac{log 17}{log 6} \approx 1.581$ — $log_b x = \frac{log\ x}{log\ b}$
2. $log_{0.4} 9 = \frac{ln 9}{ln 0.4} \approx -2.398$ — $log_b x = \frac{ln\ x}{ln\ b}$
3. $log_\pi 3.2 = \frac{log 3.2}{log \pi} \approx 1.016$ — $log_b x = \frac{ln\ x}{ln\ b}$

10-6 EXPONENTIAL AND LOGARITHMIC EQUATIONS

Exponential Equations

- Exponential equation: an equation that contains variable(s) in the exponent.

Example

$3^x = 5$, $8^y = 5^{4x}$, $4^{x+5} = 2$

- The key to solve an exponential equation: take the logarithm of both sides.
- Procedure to solve an exponential equation

Steps	Example: Solve $3^x = 9$. Common Log Method	Natural Log Method
- Take the log or ln of both sides.	$\log 3^x = \log 9$	$\ln 3^x = \ln 9$
- Use the power rule. ($\log_a A^n = n\log_a A$)	$x\log 3 = \log 9$	$x\ln 3 = \ln 9$
- Isolate the variable.	$\frac{x\log 3}{\log 3} = \frac{\log 9}{\log 3}$ Divide both sides by $\log 3$.	$\frac{x\ln 3}{\ln 3} = \frac{\ln 9}{\ln 3}$ Divide both sides by $\ln 3$.
- Use a calculator to evaluate the log.	$x = \frac{\log 9}{\log 3} = \mathbf{2}$	$x = \frac{\ln 9}{\ln 3} = \mathbf{2}$
- Check.	$3^2 \overset{?}{=} 9$, $9 \overset{\surd}{=} 9$ Correct!	

Example: Solve the given equation.

$5^{3x} = 4$

$\log 5^{3x} = \log 4$ — Take the log of both sides.

$3x\log 5 = \log 4$ — $\log_a A^n = n\log_a A$

$x = \frac{\log 4}{3\log 5}$ — Divide both sides by $3\log 5$.

$\mathbf{x \approx 0.287}$ — LOG 4) ÷ (3 × LOG 5)

Check: $5^{3(0.287)} \overset{?}{=} 4$, $5^{0.861} \overset{\surd}{\approx} 4$ Correct! — 5 yˣ 0.861 = (yˣ or ^)

Solving Exponential Equations

Example: Solve each of the following equations.

1. $\mathbf{3^{2x+5} = 7}$

$ln3^{2x+5} = ln7$ — Take the ln of both sides.

$(2x + 5)\, ln3 = ln7$ — $log_a A^n = n\, log_a A$

$2x + 5 = \frac{ln7}{ln3}$ — Divide both sides by $ln3$.

$2x = \frac{ln7}{ln3} - 5$ — Subtract 5.

$x = \frac{ln2}{2ln3} - 2.5$ — Divide by 2.

$\mathbf{x \approx -2.185}$

2. $\mathbf{3(2^{x+1}) = 5^x}$

$log3(2^{x+1}) = log5^x$ — Take the log of both sides.

$log3 + log2^{x+1} = log5^x$ — $log_a(AB) = log_a A + log_a B$

$log3 + (x + 1)log2 = xlog5$ — $log_a A^n = n\, log_a A$

$log3 + xlog2 + log2 = xlog5$ — Distribute.

$x\, log2 - xlog5 = -log2 - log3$ — Isolate x terms.

$x\,(log2 - log5) = -log2 - log3$ — Factor out x.

$x = \frac{-log2 - log3}{log2 - log5}$ — Divide by $(log2 - log5)$

$x \approx \frac{-0.778}{-0.3979}$

$\mathbf{x \approx 1.96}$

Logarithmic Equations

- **Logarithmic equation**: an equation that contains logarithms of the expression (s).
- **The key to solve a log equation**: convert the logarithmic form into exponential form.

Example

$log_3(x+5) = 7$

$log_a x = y$

$a^y = x$

- **Procedure to solve a logarithmic equation**

Steps	Example: Solve $\boldsymbol{log_3(3+4x) = 2}$
	$log_3(3+4x) = 2$
- Convert the log equation to an exponential equation.	$3^2 = 3 + 4x$
- Isolate x term.	$3^2 - 3 = 4x$
- Solve for x.	$6 = 4x$, $\boldsymbol{x = 1.5}$
- Check.	$log_3[3 + 4(1.5)] \stackrel{?}{=} 2$
	$log_3 9 \stackrel{?}{=} 2$
	$\frac{log9}{log3} \stackrel{?}{=} 2$ $\quad log_b x = \frac{logx}{logb}$
	$2 \stackrel{\surd}{=} 2$ $\quad$ Correct!

Example: Solve the given equation.

$\boldsymbol{log_2 x = log_2(3x-2) + 3}$

$log_2 x - log_2(3x-2) = 3$ — Collect log terms on one side.

$log_2 \frac{x}{3x-2} = 3$ — $log_a\left(\frac{A}{B}\right) = log_a A - log_a B$

$2^3 = \frac{x}{3x-2}$ — log equation ⟶ exponential equation

$8 = \frac{x}{3x-2}$

$8(3x-2) = x$ — Solve for x.

$24x - 16 = x$

$\boldsymbol{x \approx 0.7}$

Example: Solve the given equation.

$\mathbf{\log (x+9) = 1 - \log x}$	Collect log terms on one side.
$\log (x+9) + \log x = 1$	$\log_u A + \log_u B = \log_u (AB)$
$\log [(x+9) \cdot x] = 1$	log equation ⟶ exponential equation
$\log_{10} x(x+9) = 1$	$\log (x+9)x = \log_{10} x(x+9)$
$10^1 = x(x+9)$	Distributive property.
$x^2 + 9x - 10 = 0$	Solve for x.
$(x-1)(x+10) = 0$	Factor.
$x - 1 = 0$ ⁞ $x + 10 = 0$	Zero-product property
$\mathbf{x = 1}$ ⁞ $\mathbf{x = -10}$	

Check: $\log (x+9) = 1 - \log x$

$x = 1$	$x = -10$
$\log (1+9) \overset{?}{=} 1 - \log 1$	$\log (-10+9) \overset{?}{=} 1 - \log(-10)$
$\log 10 \overset{?}{=} 1 - 0$	$\log (-1) \overset{?}{=} 1 - \log(-10)$ (↑ Undefined)
$1 \overset{\surd}{=} 1$ Correct!	$x = -10$ is not a solution.

Solution: $\mathbf{x = 1}$

Unit 10 Summary

- **Characteristics of exponential functions**

Characteristic	$f(x) = a^x$	$f(x) = a^{-x}$
growth / decay	The graph increases (grows) from left to right.	The graph falls (decays) from left to right.
example	$f(x) = 3^x$ 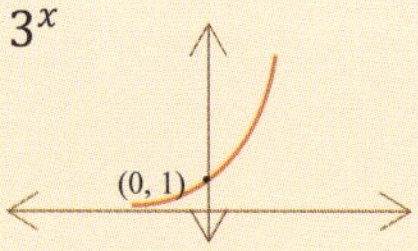 (0, 1) Exponential growth	$f(x) = 3^{-x}$ 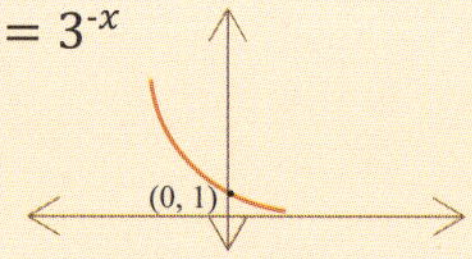 (0, 1) Exponential decay
asymptote	x-axis $(y = 0)$	x-axis $(y = 0)$
y - intercept	$y = 1$	
domain x values	$x =$ all real numbers or $x = (-\infty, \infty)$	
range y values	$y = (0, \infty)$ or $\{ y \mid y > 0 \}$	

- **Stretching or shifting**

Function	Stretch or Shrink	Example	Graph
$f(x) = a^x$	The larger the a, the narrower the curve. The smaller the a, the wider the curve.	$f(x) = 4^x$ and $f(x) = 2^x$	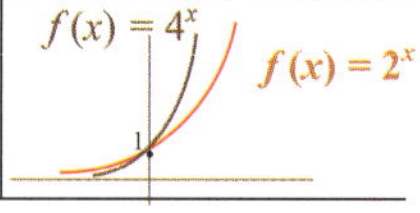 $f(x) = 4^x$ $f(x) = 2^x$

- **Reflecting (mirror image)**

Function	Reflection	Example	Graph
$f(x) = a^{-x}$	Reflect the graph of $f(x) = a^x$ about the y-axis.	$f(x) = 2^x$ and $f(x) = 2^{-x}$	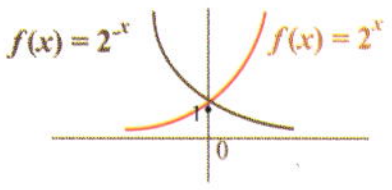 $f(x) = 2^{-x}$ $f(x) = 2^x$
$f(x) = -a^x$	Reflect the graph of $f(x) = a^x$ about the x-axis.	$f(x) = 2^x$ and $f(x) = -2^x$	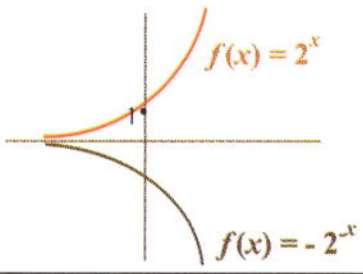 $f(x) = 2^x$ $f(x) = -2^x$

- **Shifting**

Exponential Function	Shifting	Example	Graph
$f(x) = a^x + C$ $f(x) = a^x - C$	Shift the graph of $y = a^x$ C units up. Shift the graph of $y = a^x$ C units down.	$f(x) = 2^x + 1$ $f(x) = 2^x - 1$	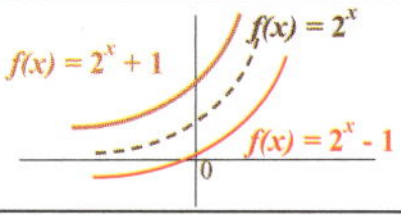 $f(x) = 2^x + 1$ $f(x) = 2^x$ $f(x) = 2^x - 1$
$f(x) = a^{x+C}$ $f(x) = a^{x-C}$	Shift the graph of $y = a^x$ C units to the left. Shift the graph of $y = a^x$ C units to the right.	$f(x) = 2^{x+1}$ $f(x) = 2^{x-1}$	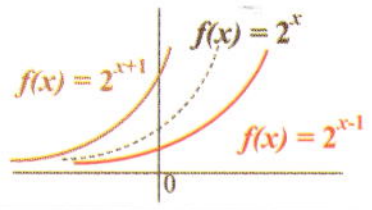 $f(x) = 2^{x+1}$ $f(x) = 2^x$ $f(x) = 2^{x-1}$

- ***X* and *Y* interchanging**

Function	Shape	Example	Graph
$y = a^x$ and $x = a^y$	Reflect the graph of $y = a^x$ about the line $y = x$ to get $x = a^y$	$y = 2^x$ and $x = 2^y$	$y = 2^x$, $x = 2^y$, $y = x$, 0

- One-to-one function: a function for which every element of the range (*y*-value) corresponds to a unique domain (*x*-value).
- The horizontal-line test: if a horizontal line cuts the graph of a function only once, then the function is one-to-one and its inverse is a function.
- Inverse function $f^{-1}(x)$: the function formed when the order of the elements in a given function is switched.
- The graph of inverse function $f^{-1}(x)$ is a reflection the original function $f(x)$ about the line $y = x$.
- If a function $f(x)$ is one-to-one, its inverse function $f^{-1}(x)$ can be found as follows:
  - Confirm that the function is 1-to-1.
  - Rewrite $f(x)$ as y.
  - Switch x and y.
  - Solve for y.
  - Replace y with $f^{-1}(x)$.
  - Graph $f^{-1}(x)$: reflect the graph of $f(x)$ across the line $y = x$.
- Composite function $f \circ g(x)$: a combination of two or more functions in which the result of one function is applied to another function (substitute a function into another function).

Composite Function	Formula	Comments
$f \circ g(x)$	$f \circ g(x) = f[g(x)]$	$g(x)$ (inner function) ↓ $f(\ )$ (outer function). The result of $g(\ )$ is applying to $f(\ )$.
$g \circ f(x)$	$g \circ f(x) = g[f(x)]$	$f(x)$ (inner function) ↓ $g(\ )$ (outer function). The result of $f(\ )$ is applying to $g(\ )$.

Inverse Function
If a function is one-to-one, then $f^{-1} \circ f(x) = x$ and $f \circ f^{-1}(x) = x$.

- The logarithmic function $f(x) = \log_a x$: a function that is the inverse of an exponential function ($y = a^x$).

- **Definition of logarithm**

Logarithmic Function	Definition of Logarithm	Example
$f(x) = \log_a x$ $(x > 0,\ a > 0,\ a \neq 1)$	if $y = a^x$, then $\log_a y = x$. Or if $x = a^y$, then $\log_a x = y$.	If $9 = 3^2$, then $2 = \log_3 9$. Read: "the log base 3 of 9 is 2" or "log of 9, base 3, equals 2".

- Logarithm of zero $\log_a(0)$: the logarithm of 0 is undefined.
- Logarithm of negative number $\log_a(-x)$: the logarithm of negative numbers is undefined.
- Converting between exponential and logarithmic forms
  - Exponential to log form: $a^x = y$ → $\log_a y = x$
  - Log to exponential form: $\log_a y = x$ → $a^x = y$
- Logarithmic equation: an equation that contains a logarithmic expression.
- The key to solve a logarithmic equation: convert log into exponential form.
- Logarithmic functions and exponential functions are inverse functions.
- The graph of the logarithmic function is the reflection of the graph of the exponential function about the $y = x$ line.
- **Comparing properties of logarithmic and exponential functions**

	Exponential Function $y = f(x) = a^x$	Logarithmic Function $\log_a x$	Example $y = 2^x$	Example $\log_2 x$
Domain (x-values)	$(-\infty, \infty)$ All real numbers.	$(0, \infty)$ or $x > 0$	$(-\infty, \infty)$	$(0, \infty)$
Range (y-values)	$(0, \infty)$ or $y > 0$	$(-\infty, \infty)$ All real numbers.	$y > 0$	$(-\infty, \infty)$
Intercept	y-intercept = 1	x-intercept = 1	1	1
Asymptote	x - axis	y - axis		

- **Basic properties of logarithms**

Property	Example
$\log_a 1 = 0$	$\log_4 1 = 0$
$\log_a a = 1$	$\log_7 7 = 1$
$\log_a a^x = x$	$\log_2 2^3 = 3$
$a^{\log_a x} = x$	$3^{\log_3 4} = 4$

- **Rules of logarithms**

Name	Rule	Example
product rule	$\log_a(A \cdot B) = \log_a A + \log_a B$	$\log_5(3 \cdot 4) = \log_5 3 + \log_5 4$
quotient rule	$\log_a \left(\frac{A}{B}\right) = \log_a A - \log_a B$	$\log_3 \left(\frac{7}{2}\right) = \log_3 7 - \log_3 2$
power rule	$\log_a A^n = n \log_a A$	$\log_2 3^4 = 4 \log_2 3$

- **The common logarithm**

Notation for Common Log	Example
$log_{10}x = log\ x$ (Base 10; No base means base 10)	$log_{10}3 = log\ 3$

- **The natural logarithm**

Notation for Natural Log	Example
$log_e x = ln\ x$ (Base e)	$log_e 3 = ln\ 3$

- **Graphing of $f(x) = ln\ x$, e^x and e^{-x}**
  - The graph of the exponential function (e^x) is a reflection of the graph of (e^{-x}) about the y-axis.
  - The graph of the natural logarithmic function $ln\ x$ is the reflection of the graph of the exponential function e^x about the $y = x$ line.

- **Change of base formula**

Change of Base Formula	$log_b x = \dfrac{log_a x}{log_a b}$	Example	
change to base 10	$log_b x = \dfrac{log\ x}{log\ b}$	$log_3 5 = \dfrac{log\ 5}{log 3} \approx 1.465$	LOG 5) ÷ LOG 3
change to base e	$log_b x = \dfrac{ln\ x}{ln\ b}$	$log_3 5 = \dfrac{ln\ 5}{ln\ 3} \approx 1.465$	LN 5) ÷ LN 3

- Exponential equation: an equation that contains variable(s) in the exponent.

- The key to solve an exponential equation: take the logarithm of both sides.

PRACTICE QUIZ

Unit 10 Exponential & Logarithmic Functions

1. Sketch the graph of $f(x) = 2^x$ amd $f(x) = 2^{-x}$.

2. Determine $f(x)$ and $g(x)$ such that $h(x) = f \circ g(x)$, $h(x) = (4 - 3x)^3$

3. Determine the inverse of the given function $f(x) = -5x$.

4. Solve each of the following equations.

a. $\log_3 81 = x$

b. $\log_{27} \frac{1}{3} = x$

5. Find the value of $8^{\log_8 3}$.

6. Write each of the following as simpler logarithms.

a. $\log_4 \left(\frac{6x}{y^5}\right)$

b. $\log_5 \sqrt[4]{\frac{a^2 b}{c}}$

7. Evaluate each of the following.

a. $\log_{0.3} 12$

b. $\log_{\pi} 4.7$

8. Solve each of the following equations.

a. $4(2^{x+1}) = 6^x$

b. $log_3 x = log_3(4x - 1) + 2$

UNIT 11 DETERMINANTS AND MATRICES

11-1 DETERMINANTS

Second-Order Determinants

- **Determinant** $|\ \ |$: a square set of numbers (called elements) enclosed in two lines that represents the sum of the products of numbers, and is useful for solving systems of linear equations.
- **Dimensions of a determinant:** a determinant has m rows and n columns $(m \times n)$

  Rows Columns

- **A second-order determinant (2 × 2):**

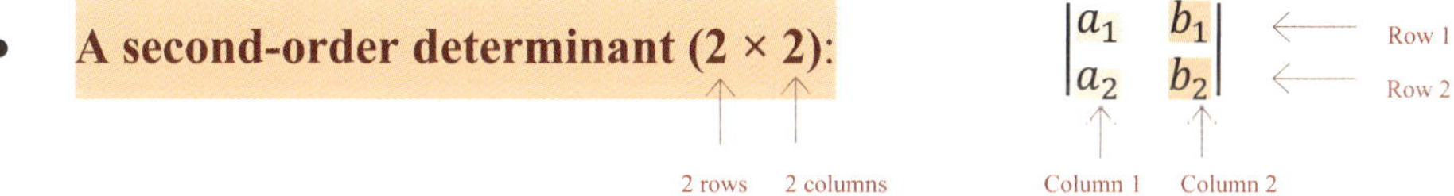

$$\begin{vmatrix} a_1 & b_1 \\ a_2 & b_2 \end{vmatrix}$$

- **Evaluate a 2 × 2 determinant**

Determinant	Evaluation	Example
$\begin{vmatrix} a_1 & b_1 \\ a_2 & b_2 \end{vmatrix}$	$\begin{vmatrix} a_1 & b_1 \\ a_2 & b_2 \end{vmatrix} = a_1b_2 - b_1a_2$	$\begin{vmatrix} 2 & 1 \\ 3 & 4 \end{vmatrix} = 2 \cdot 4 - 1 \cdot 3 = 5$

- Draw a diagonal from the first element of the top row downward to the right.
- Draw a diagonal from the second element of the top row downward to the left.
- Multiply the elements on the diagonals, and subtract the products.

  descending from left to right is positive → **is +**

  descending from right to left is negative → **is –**

Example: Evaluate the following determinants.

1. $\begin{vmatrix} 2 & 4 \\ -2 & -3 \end{vmatrix} = 2(-3) - 4(-2) = -6 + 8 = \mathbf{2}$

2. $\begin{vmatrix} 2 & x \\ -3 & 5 \end{vmatrix} = 2 \cdot 5 - x(-3) = \mathbf{10 + 3x}$

Third-Order Determinants
Expansion by Diagonals

- **A third-order determinant (3 × 3):** $\begin{vmatrix} a_1 & b_1 & c_1 \\ a_2 & b_2 & c_2 \\ a_3 & b_3 & c_3 \end{vmatrix}$ ← Row 1, Row 2, Row 3; ↑ Column 1, Column 2, Column 3

- **Evaluate a 3 × 3 Determinant – Method I: Using Diagonals**

Steps

- Copy the first two columns of the determinant to its right. $\begin{vmatrix} a_1 & b_1 & c_1 \\ a_2 & b_2 & c_2 \\ a_3 & b_3 & c_3 \end{vmatrix} \Rightarrow \begin{vmatrix} a_1 & b_1 & c_1 \\ a_2 & b_2 & c_2 \\ a_3 & b_3 & c_3 \end{vmatrix} \begin{matrix} a_1 & b_1 \\ a_2 & b_2 \\ a_3 & b_3 \end{matrix}$
- Draw three diagonals from each element of the top row downward to the right.
- Draw three diagonals from each element of the top row downward to the left.
- Multiply the elements on the diagonals, and sum the products.

{descending from left to right is positive. ↘ is +
{descending from right to left is negative. ↙ is −

$a_1b_2c_3+b_1c_2a_3+c_1a_2b_3$

$-c_1b_2a_3-a_1c_2b_3-b_1a_2c_3$

3 × 3 Determinant	Expansion by Diagonals	Example
$\begin{vmatrix} a_1 & b_1 & c_1 \\ a_2 & b_2 & c_2 \\ a_3 & b_3 & c_3 \end{vmatrix}$	$\begin{vmatrix} a_1 & b_1 & c_1 \\ a_2 & b_2 & c_2 \\ a_3 & b_3 & c_3 \end{vmatrix} \begin{matrix} a_1 & b_1 \\ a_2 & b_2 \\ a_3 & b_3 \end{matrix}$ $= a_1b_2c_3+b_1c_2a_3+c_1a_2b_3$ $-c_1b_2a_3-a_1c_2b_3-b_1a_2c_3$	$\begin{vmatrix} 1 & 1 & 3 \\ 4 & 3 & 2 \\ 3 & 1 & 2 \end{vmatrix} \begin{matrix} 1 & 1 \\ 4 & 3 \\ 3 & 1 \end{matrix}$ = 1·3·2 + 1·2·3 + 3·4·1 −3·3·3 − 1·2·1 − 1·4·2 = 6 + 6 + 12 – 27 – 2 – 8 = **-13**

Note: 'Expansion by diagonals' does not work with 4 × 4 or higher-order determinants.

Example: Evaluate the determinant. $\begin{vmatrix} 3 & 2 & 0 \\ -1 & 0 & 1 \\ 4 & 1 & 5 \end{vmatrix}$

$\begin{vmatrix} 3 & 2 & 0 \\ -1 & 0 & 1 \\ 4 & 1 & 5 \end{vmatrix} \begin{matrix} 3 & 2 \\ -1 & 0 \\ 4 & 1 \end{matrix} = 3\cdot0\cdot5 + 2\cdot1\cdot4 + 0\cdot(-1)\cdot1 - 0\cdot0\cdot4 - 3\cdot1\cdot1 - 2\cdot(-1)\cdot5$

$= 0 + 8 + 0 - 0 - 3 + 10 = \mathbf{15}$

Third-Order Determinants
Expansion by Minors

- **The minor of an element in a determinant** is a determinant of the next lower order. It is the determinant that results from crossing out the row and the column that contain that element.

  Example: Find the minor of element a_1 and b_2.

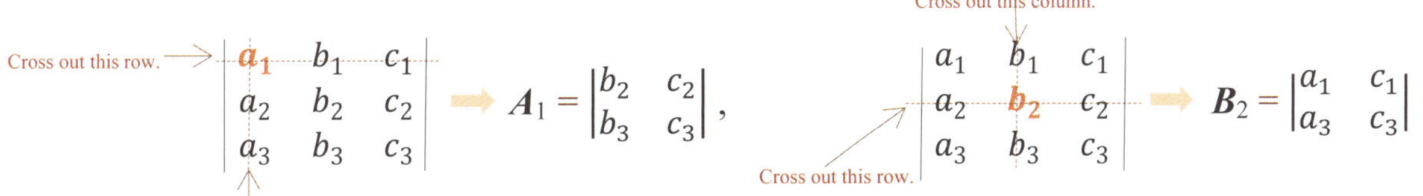

$$\begin{vmatrix} a_1 & b_1 & c_1 \\ a_2 & b_2 & c_2 \\ a_3 & b_3 & c_3 \end{vmatrix} \Rightarrow A_1 = \begin{vmatrix} b_2 & c_2 \\ b_3 & c_3 \end{vmatrix}, \quad \begin{vmatrix} a_1 & b_1 & c_1 \\ a_2 & b_2 & c_2 \\ a_3 & b_3 & c_3 \end{vmatrix} \Rightarrow B_2 = \begin{vmatrix} a_1 & c_1 \\ a_3 & c_3 \end{vmatrix}$$

- **Placing signs for minor:** the sign of a minor is determined by its position in the determinant.
  - A 3×3 determinant: $\begin{vmatrix} + & - & + \\ - & + & - \\ + & - & + \end{vmatrix}$
  - A 4×4 determinant: $\begin{vmatrix} + & - & + & - \\ - & + & - & + \\ + & - & + & - \\ - & + & - & + \end{vmatrix}$

- **Cofactors**: minors + place signs = cofactors

$$\begin{vmatrix} A_1 & B_1 & C_1 \\ A_2 & B_2 & C_2 \\ A_3 & B_3 & C_3 \end{vmatrix} + \begin{vmatrix} + & - & + \\ - & + & - \\ + & - & + \end{vmatrix} \Rightarrow \begin{vmatrix} A_1 & -B_1 & C_1 \\ -A_2 & B_2 & -C_2 \\ A_3 & -B_3 & C_3 \end{vmatrix}$$

minors   place signs   cofactors

- **Evaluate a 3 × 3 determinant – Method II: expansion by minors**

  Steps

  - Choose any row or column in the determinant.

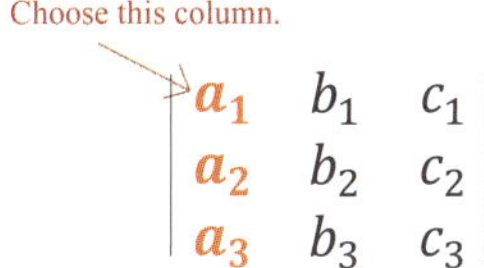

$$\begin{vmatrix} a_1 & b_1 & c_1 \\ a_2 & b_2 & c_2 \\ a_3 & b_3 & c_3 \end{vmatrix}$$

  - Multiply each element in the chosen row/column by its cofactor.

$$\begin{vmatrix} a_1 & b_1 & c_1 \\ a_2 & b_2 & c_2 \\ a_3 & b_3 & c_3 \end{vmatrix} = a_1 \begin{vmatrix} b_2 & c_2 \\ b_3 & c_3 \end{vmatrix} - a_2 \begin{vmatrix} b_1 & c_1 \\ b_3 & c_3 \end{vmatrix} + a_3 \begin{vmatrix} b_1 & c_1 \\ b_2 & c_2 \end{vmatrix}$$

$$\begin{vmatrix} + & - & + \\ - & + & - \\ + & - & + \end{vmatrix}$$

a_1	a_2	a_3
$\begin{vmatrix} a_1 & b_1 & c_1 \\ a_2 & b_2 & c_2 \\ a_3 & b_3 & c_3 \end{vmatrix}$	$\begin{vmatrix} a_1 & b_1 & c_1 \\ a_2 & b_2 & c_2 \\ a_3 & b_3 & c_3 \end{vmatrix}$	$\begin{vmatrix} a_1 & b_1 & c_1 \\ a_2 & b_2 & c_2 \\ a_3 & b_3 & c_3 \end{vmatrix}$

Tip: Multiply a_1, a_2, and a_3 by a minor that is not in its row or column.

Expansion by Minors
Expansion by any Row / Column

Evaluate a determinant that can be expanded by any row or column

- **Expanding along column 1**

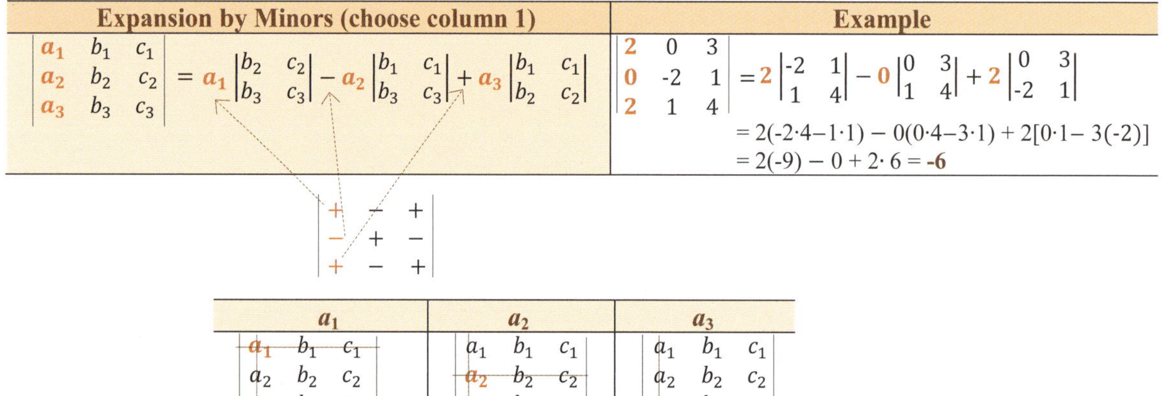

Expansion by Minors (choose column 1)	Example
$\begin{vmatrix} a_1 & b_1 & c_1 \\ a_2 & b_2 & c_2 \\ a_3 & b_3 & c_3 \end{vmatrix} = a_1\begin{vmatrix} b_2 & c_2 \\ b_3 & c_3 \end{vmatrix} - a_2\begin{vmatrix} b_1 & c_1 \\ b_3 & c_3 \end{vmatrix} + a_3\begin{vmatrix} b_1 & c_1 \\ b_2 & c_2 \end{vmatrix}$	$\begin{vmatrix} 2 & 0 & 3 \\ 0 & -2 & 1 \\ 2 & 1 & 4 \end{vmatrix} = 2\begin{vmatrix} -2 & 1 \\ 1 & 4 \end{vmatrix} - 0\begin{vmatrix} 0 & 3 \\ 1 & 4 \end{vmatrix} + 2\begin{vmatrix} 0 & 3 \\ -2 & 1 \end{vmatrix}$ $= 2(-2\cdot4-1\cdot1) - 0(0\cdot4-3\cdot1) + 2[0\cdot1 - 3(-2)]$ $= 2(-9) - 0 + 2\cdot6 = \mathbf{-6}$

$$\begin{vmatrix} + & - & + \\ - & + & - \\ + & - & + \end{vmatrix}$$

a_1	a_2	a_3
$\begin{vmatrix} a_1 & b_1 & c_1 \\ a_2 & b_2 & c_2 \\ a_3 & b_3 & c_3 \end{vmatrix}$	$\begin{vmatrix} a_1 & b_1 & c_1 \\ a_2 & b_2 & c_2 \\ a_3 & b_3 & c_3 \end{vmatrix}$	$\begin{vmatrix} a_1 & b_1 & c_1 \\ a_2 & b_2 & c_2 \\ a_3 & b_3 & c_3 \end{vmatrix}$

- **Expanding along row 1**

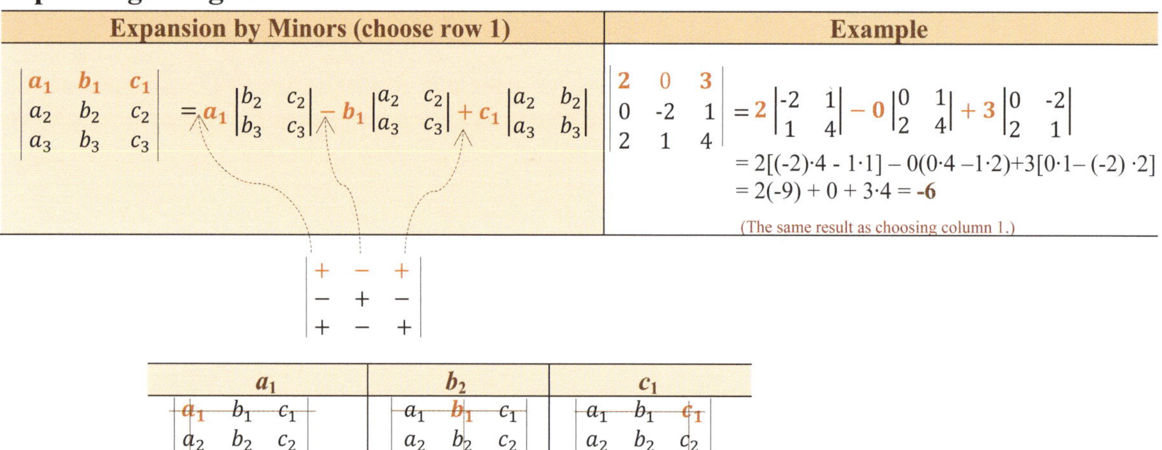

Expansion by Minors (choose row 1)	Example
$\begin{vmatrix} a_1 & b_1 & c_1 \\ a_2 & b_2 & c_2 \\ a_3 & b_3 & c_3 \end{vmatrix} = a_1\begin{vmatrix} b_2 & c_2 \\ b_3 & c_3 \end{vmatrix} - b_1\begin{vmatrix} a_2 & c_2 \\ a_3 & c_3 \end{vmatrix} + c_1\begin{vmatrix} a_2 & b_2 \\ a_3 & b_3 \end{vmatrix}$	$\begin{vmatrix} 2 & 0 & 3 \\ 0 & -2 & 1 \\ 2 & 1 & 4 \end{vmatrix} = 2\begin{vmatrix} -2 & 1 \\ 1 & 4 \end{vmatrix} - 0\begin{vmatrix} 0 & 1 \\ 2 & 4 \end{vmatrix} + 3\begin{vmatrix} 0 & -2 \\ 2 & 1 \end{vmatrix}$ $= 2[(-2)\cdot4 - 1\cdot1] - 0(0\cdot4 - 1\cdot2) + 3[0\cdot1 - (-2)\cdot2]$ $= 2(-9) + 0 + 3\cdot4 = \mathbf{-6}$ (The same result as choosing column 1.)

$$\begin{vmatrix} + & - & + \\ - & + & - \\ + & - & + \end{vmatrix}$$

a_1	b_2	c_1
$\begin{vmatrix} a_1 & b_1 & c_1 \\ a_2 & b_2 & c_2 \\ a_3 & b_3 & c_3 \end{vmatrix}$	$\begin{vmatrix} a_1 & b_1 & c_1 \\ a_2 & b_2 & c_2 \\ a_3 & b_3 & c_3 \end{vmatrix}$	$\begin{vmatrix} a_1 & b_1 & c_1 \\ a_2 & b_2 & c_2 \\ a_3 & b_3 & c_3 \end{vmatrix}$

- **Expanding along column 2**

Expansion by Minors (choose column 2)	Example
$\begin{vmatrix} a_1 & b_1 & c_1 \\ a_2 & b_2 & c_2 \\ a_3 & b_3 & c_3 \end{vmatrix} = -b_1\begin{vmatrix} a_2 & c_2 \\ a_3 & c_3 \end{vmatrix} + b_2\begin{vmatrix} a_1 & c_1 \\ a_3 & c_3 \end{vmatrix} - b_3\begin{vmatrix} a_1 & c_1 \\ a_2 & c_2 \end{vmatrix}$	$\begin{vmatrix} 2 & 0 & 3 \\ 0 & -2 & 1 \\ 2 & 1 & 4 \end{vmatrix} = -0\begin{vmatrix} 0 & 1 \\ 2 & 4 \end{vmatrix} + (-2)\begin{vmatrix} 2 & 3 \\ 2 & 4 \end{vmatrix} - 1\begin{vmatrix} 2 & 3 \\ 0 & 1 \end{vmatrix}$ $= -0(0\cdot4 - 1\cdot2) - 2(2\cdot4 - 2\cdot3) - 1(2\cdot1 - 3\cdot0)$ $= 0 - 4 - 2 = \mathbf{-6}$ (The same result as choosing column 1 or row 1.)

$$\begin{vmatrix} + & - & + \\ - & + & - \\ + & - & + \end{vmatrix}$$

b_1	b_2	b_3
$\begin{vmatrix} a_1 & b_1 & c_1 \\ a_2 & b_2 & c_2 \\ a_3 & b_3 & c_3 \end{vmatrix}$	$\begin{vmatrix} a_1 & b_1 & c_1 \\ a_2 & b_2 & c_2 \\ a_3 & b_3 & c_3 \end{vmatrix}$	$\begin{vmatrix} a_1 & b_1 & c_1 \\ a_2 & b_2 & c_2 \\ a_3 & b_3 & c_3 \end{vmatrix}$

11-2 CRAMER'S RULE

Cramer's Rule to Solve a 2 × 2 System

- **Cramer's rule:** Use the determinant method to solve the system of linear equations.
- **Using Cramer's rule to solve a 2×2 system**

A 2×2 System	Cramer's Rule
$\begin{cases} a_1x + b_1y = k_1 \\ a_2x + b_2y = k_2 \end{cases}$	The solution of the system: $x = \frac{D_x}{D}$, $y = \frac{D_y}{D}$ $(D \neq 0)$ $D = \begin{vmatrix} a_1 & b_1 \\ a_2 & b_2 \end{vmatrix}$, $D_x = \begin{vmatrix} k_1 & b_1 \\ k_2 & b_2 \end{vmatrix}$, $D_y = \begin{vmatrix} a_1 & k_1 \\ a_2 & k_2 \end{vmatrix}$

coefficients of x; coefficients of y; constant

Replace the column a in D with k. Replace the column b in D with k.

Example	Using Cramer's Rule to Solve a 2×2 System
$\begin{cases} 3x + y = 1 \\ 2x - 3y = 4 \end{cases}$	$D = \begin{vmatrix} 3 & 1 \\ 2 & -3 \end{vmatrix} = 3(-3) - 1 \cdot 2 = \mathbf{-11}$, $D_x = \begin{vmatrix} 1 & 1 \\ 4 & -3 \end{vmatrix} = 1 \cdot (-3) - 1 \cdot 4 = \mathbf{-7}$, $D_y = \begin{vmatrix} 3 & 1 \\ 2 & 4 \end{vmatrix} = 3 \cdot 4 - 1 \cdot 2 = \mathbf{10}$ $x = \frac{D_x}{D} = \frac{-7}{-11} = \frac{7}{11}$, $y = \frac{D_y}{D} = \frac{10}{-11} = -\frac{10}{11}$, Solution: $\left(\frac{7}{11}, -\frac{10}{11}\right)$

Two equations in two unknowns (x & y).

Steps	Example: Solve. $\begin{cases} 2x = 2 - 3y \\ y = -3 - 4x \end{cases}$
- Write equations in standard form. $\begin{cases} a_1x + b_1y = k_1 \\ a_2x + b_2y = k_2 \end{cases}$	$\begin{cases} 2x + 3y = 2 \\ 4x + y = -3 \end{cases}$
- Determine the determinants D, D_x and D_y.	(the coefficients of the system)
$D = \begin{vmatrix} a_1 & b_1 \\ a_2 & b_2 \end{vmatrix} = a_1b_2 - b_1a_2$	$D = \begin{vmatrix} 2 & 3 \\ 4 & 1 \end{vmatrix} = 2 \cdot 1 - 3 \cdot 4 = -10$
$D_x = \begin{vmatrix} k_1 & b_1 \\ k_2 & b_2 \end{vmatrix} = k_1b_2 - b_1k_2$ Replace the column a in D with the column k.	$D_x = \begin{vmatrix} 2 & 3 \\ -3 & 1 \end{vmatrix} = 2 \cdot 1 - 3(-3) = 11$
$D_y = \begin{vmatrix} a_1 & k_1 \\ a_2 & k_2 \end{vmatrix} = a_1k_2 - k_1a_2$ Replace the column b in D with the column k.	$D_y = \begin{vmatrix} 2 & 2 \\ 4 & -3 \end{vmatrix} = 2(-3) - 2 \cdot 4 = -14$
- Solve for x and y. $x = \frac{D_x}{D}$	$x = \frac{D_x}{D} = \frac{11}{-10} = -\frac{11}{10}$
$y = \frac{D_y}{D}$	$y = \frac{D_y}{D} = \frac{-14}{-10} = \frac{7}{5}$

Cramer's Rule to Solve a 3 × 3 System
Expansion by Diagonals

- **Using Cramer's rule to solve a 3×3 system**

A 3×3 System	Cramer's Rule	D	D_x , D_y and D_z
$\begin{cases} a_1x + b_1y + c_1z = k_1 \\ a_2x + b_2\,y + c_2y = k_2 \\ a_3x + b_3\,y + c_3y = k_3 \end{cases}$	$x = \frac{D_x}{D}$ $y = \frac{D_y}{D}$ $z = \frac{D_z}{D}$	$D = \begin{vmatrix} a_1 & b_1 & c_1 \\ a_2 & b_2 & c_2 \\ a_3 & b_3 & c_3 \end{vmatrix}$ $D \neq 0$	$D_x = \begin{vmatrix} k_1 & b_1 & c_1 \\ k_1 & b_2 & c_2 \\ k_1 & b_3 & c_3 \end{vmatrix}$ $D_y = \begin{vmatrix} a_1 & k_1 & c_1 \\ a_2 & k_2 & c_2 \\ a_3 & k_3 & c_3 \end{vmatrix}$ $D_z = \begin{vmatrix} a_1 & b_1 & k_1 \\ a_2 & b_2 & k_2 \\ a_3 & b_3 & k_3 \end{vmatrix}$

Tip: Use either the 'expansion by minors' or 'expansion by diagonals' to solve the determinants D, D_x, D_y and D_z.

D	The determinant of the coefficient of variables x , y and z.
D_x	Replacing the coefficients of x in D with the column of constants k.
D_y	Replacing the coefficients of y in D with the column of constants k.
D_z	Replacing the coefficients of z in D with the column of constants k.

- **Using Cramer's rule to solve a 3×3 system (use expansion by diagonals)**

A 3×3 System	Determinants & Solutions	Example
$\begin{cases} a_1x + b_1y + c_1z = k_1 \\ a_2x + b_2\,y + c_2y = k_2 \\ a_3x + b_3\,y + c_3y = k_3 \end{cases}$	$D = \begin{vmatrix} a_1 & b_1 & c_1 \\ a_2 & b_2 & c_2 \\ a_3 & b_3 & c_3 \end{vmatrix} \begin{matrix} a_1 & b_1 \\ a_2 & b_2 \\ a_3 & b_3 \end{matrix}$	$D = \begin{vmatrix} 2 & -1 & 3 \\ 3 & 2 & 0 \\ 0 & 2 & -3 \end{vmatrix} \begin{matrix} 2 & -1 \\ 3 & 2 \\ 0 & 2 \end{matrix}$ $= 2{\cdot}2(-3) + (-1){\cdot}0{\cdot}0 + 3{\cdot}3{\cdot}2 - 3{\cdot}2{\cdot}0 - 2{\cdot}0{\cdot}2 - (-1){\cdot}3(-3)$ $= -12 + 0 + 18 - 0 - 0 - 9 = \mathbf{-3}$
	$D_x = \begin{vmatrix} k_1 & b_1 & c_1 \\ k_2 & b_2 & c_2 \\ k_3 & b_3 & c_3 \end{vmatrix} \begin{matrix} k_1 & b_1 \\ k_2 & b_2 \\ k_3 & b_3 \end{matrix}$	$D_x = \begin{vmatrix} 1 & -1 & 3 \\ -4 & 2 & 0 \\ 2 & 2 & -3 \end{vmatrix} \begin{matrix} 1 & -1 \\ -4 & 2 \\ 2 & 2 \end{matrix}$ $= 1{\cdot}2(-3) + (-1){\cdot}0{\cdot}2 + 3(-4){\cdot}2 - 3{\cdot}2{\cdot}2 - 1{\cdot}0{\cdot}2 - (-1)(-4)(-3)$ $= -6 + 0 - 24 - 12 - 0 + 12 = \mathbf{-30}$
Example: $\begin{cases} 2x - y + 3z = 1 \\ 3x + 2y + 0z = -4 \\ 0x + 2y - 3z = 2 \end{cases}$	$D_y = \begin{vmatrix} a_1 & k_1 & c_1 \\ a_2 & k_2 & c_2 \\ a_3 & k_3 & c_3 \end{vmatrix} \begin{matrix} a_1 & k_1 \\ a_2 & k_2 \\ a_3 & k_3 \end{matrix}$	$D_y = \begin{vmatrix} 2 & 1 & 3 \\ 3 & -4 & 0 \\ 0 & 2 & -3 \end{vmatrix} \begin{matrix} 2 & 1 \\ 3 & -4 \\ 0 & 2 \end{matrix}$ $= 2(-4)(-3) + 1{\cdot}0{\cdot}0 + 3{\cdot}3{\cdot}2 - 3(-4){\cdot}0 - 2{\cdot}0{\cdot}2 - 1{\cdot}3(-3)$ $= 24 + 0 + 18 + 0 - 0 + 9 = \mathbf{51}$
	$D_z = \begin{vmatrix} a_1 & b_1 & k_1 \\ a_2 & b_2 & k_2 \\ a_3 & b_3 & k_3 \end{vmatrix} \begin{matrix} a_1 & b_1 \\ a_2 & b_2 \\ a_3 & b_3 \end{matrix}$	$D_z = \begin{vmatrix} 2 & -1 & 1 \\ 3 & 2 & -4 \\ 0 & 2 & 2 \end{vmatrix} \begin{matrix} 2 & -1 \\ 3 & 2 \\ 0 & 2 \end{matrix}$ $= 2{\cdot}2{\cdot}2 + (-1)(-4){\cdot}0 + 1{\cdot}3{\cdot}2 - 1{\cdot}2{\cdot}0 - 2(-4)2 - (-1){\cdot}3{\cdot}2$ $= 8 + 0 + 6 - 0 + 16 + 6 = \mathbf{36}$
	Solutions: $x = \frac{D_x}{D}$, $y = \frac{D_y}{D}$, $z = \frac{D_z}{D}$	Solutions: $x = \frac{D_x}{D} = \frac{-30}{-3} = \mathbf{10}$, $y = \frac{D_y}{D} = \frac{51}{-3} = \mathbf{-17}$ $z = \frac{D_z}{D} = \frac{36}{-3} = \mathbf{-12}$

Cramer's Rule to Solve a 3 × 3 System
Expansion by Minors

Steps

- Write equations in standard form.

$$\begin{cases} a_1x + b_1y + c_1z = k_1 \\ a_2x + b_2y + c_2z = k_2 \\ a_3x + b_3y + c_3z = k_3 \end{cases}$$

- Determine D, D_x, D_y and D_z.

$$D = \begin{vmatrix} a_1 & b_1 & c_1 \\ a_2 & b_2 & c_2 \\ a_3 & b_3 & c_3 \end{vmatrix}$$

$$D_x = \begin{vmatrix} k_1 & b_1 & c_1 \\ k_2 & b_2 & c_2 \\ k_3 & b_3 & c_3 \end{vmatrix}$$

$$Dy = \begin{vmatrix} a_1 & k_1 & c_1 \\ a_2 & k_2 & c_2 \\ a_3 & k_3 & c_3 \end{vmatrix}$$

$$Dz = \begin{vmatrix} a_1 & b_1 & k_1 \\ a_2 & b_2 & k_2 \\ a_3 & b_3 & k_3 \end{vmatrix}$$

- Solve for x, y and z.

$$x = \frac{D_x}{D}$$

$$y = \frac{D_y}{D}$$

$$z = \frac{D_z}{D}$$

Example: Solve. $\begin{cases} \mathbf{2x = y - 3z + 1} \\ \mathbf{3x + 4 + 2y = 0} \\ \mathbf{2y - 3z = 2} \end{cases}$

$$\begin{cases} 2x - y + 3z = 1 \\ 3x + 2y + 0z = -4 \\ 0x + 2y - 3z = 2 \end{cases}$$

Tip: Add a coefficient for the missing variable.

Use 'expansion by minors.'

$$\begin{vmatrix} + & - & + \\ - & + & - \\ + & - & + \end{vmatrix}$$

$$D = \begin{vmatrix} 2 & -1 & 3 \\ 3 & 2 & 0 \\ 0 & 2 & -3 \end{vmatrix} = 2\begin{vmatrix} 2 & 0 \\ 2 & -3 \end{vmatrix} - 3\begin{vmatrix} -1 & 3 \\ 2 & -3 \end{vmatrix} + 0\begin{vmatrix} -1 & 3 \\ 2 & 0 \end{vmatrix}$$

$= 2[2(-3) - 0(2)] - 3[(-1)(-3) - 2\cdot3] + 0[(-1)\cdot0 - 3\cdot2]$

Choose column 1. $= 2(-6) - 3(3 - 6) + 0 = -12 + 9 = \mathbf{-3}$

$$D_x = \begin{vmatrix} 1 & -1 & 3 \\ -4 & 2 & 0 \\ 2 & 2 & -3 \end{vmatrix} = 1\begin{vmatrix} 2 & 0 \\ 2 & -3 \end{vmatrix} - (-4)\begin{vmatrix} -1 & 3 \\ 2 & -3 \end{vmatrix} + 2\begin{vmatrix} -1 & 3 \\ 2 & 0 \end{vmatrix}$$

$= 1[2(-3) - 0\cdot2] - (-4)[(-1)(-3) - 3\cdot2] + 2[(-1)\cdot0 - 3\cdot2]$

$= -6 + 4(3-6) + 2(-6) = -6 - 12 - 12 = \mathbf{-30}$

$$\begin{vmatrix} + & - & + \\ - & + & - \\ + & - & + \end{vmatrix}$$

$$D_y = \begin{vmatrix} 2 & 1 & 3 \\ 3 & -4 & 0 \\ 0 & 2 & -3 \end{vmatrix} = 3\begin{vmatrix} 3 & -4 \\ 0 & 2 \end{vmatrix} - 0\begin{vmatrix} 2 & 1 \\ 0 & 2 \end{vmatrix} + (-3)\begin{vmatrix} 2 & 1 \\ 3 & -4 \end{vmatrix}$$

Choose column 3. $= 3[3\cdot2 - (-4)\cdot0] - 0 + (-3)[2(-4) - 1\cdot3]$

$= 3\cdot6 - 3(-8 - 3) = 18 + 33 = \mathbf{51}$

$$\begin{vmatrix} + & - & + \\ - & + & - \\ + & - & + \end{vmatrix}$$

$$D_Z = \begin{vmatrix} 2 & -1 & 1 \\ 3 & 2 & -4 \\ 0 & 2 & 2 \end{vmatrix} = 0\begin{vmatrix} -1 & 1 \\ 2 & -4 \end{vmatrix} - 2\begin{vmatrix} 2 & 1 \\ 3 & -4 \end{vmatrix} + 2\begin{vmatrix} 2 & -1 \\ 3 & 2 \end{vmatrix}$$

Choose row 3. $= 0 - 2[2(-4) - 1\cdot3] + 2[2\cdot2 - (-1)3]$

$= -2(-8 - 3) + 2(4 + 3) = 22 + 14 = \mathbf{36}$

$$x = \frac{D_x}{D} = \frac{-30}{-3} = \mathbf{10}$$

$$y = \frac{D_y}{D} = \frac{51}{-3} = \mathbf{-17}$$

$$z = \frac{36}{-3} = \mathbf{-12}$$

Note: It gives the same answers as expansion by diagonals.

11-3 MATRICES

Introduction to Matrices

- **Array:** a set of elements arranged in rows and columns.

Example:

$$\begin{matrix} a_1 & b_1 \\ a_2 & b_2 \\ a_3 & b_3 \end{matrix}, \quad \begin{matrix} 2 & 3 \\ 4 & 5 \end{matrix}$$

- **Matrix:** a rectangular array of elements enclosed in brackets.

$$\begin{bmatrix} 3 & 5 & 1 \\ 2 & 4 & 7 \end{bmatrix}, \quad \begin{bmatrix} a_1 & b_1 & c_1 \\ a_2 & b_2 & c_2 \\ a_3 & b_3 & c_3 \end{bmatrix}$$

- **Columns and rows:**

$$\begin{bmatrix} a_{11} & b_{12} & c_{13} \\ a_{21} & b_{22} & c_{23} \\ a_{31} & b_{32} & c_{33} \end{bmatrix} \begin{matrix} \leftarrow \text{Row 1} \\ \leftarrow \text{Row 2} \\ \leftarrow \text{Row 3} \end{matrix}$$

Column 1 Column 2 Column 3

$$\begin{bmatrix} 2 & 1 & 5 \\ 4 & 2 & 4 \\ 5 & 3 & 2 \end{bmatrix}$$

- **Dimensions:** A matrix has $\begin{cases} m \text{ rows} \\ n \text{ columns} \end{cases}$ $\boxed{m \times n}$ ← dimensions

Rows Columns

$$\begin{bmatrix} 2 & 3 \\ 4 & 5 \end{bmatrix}_{2\times2}, \quad \begin{bmatrix} 3 & 5 & 1 \\ 2 & 4 & 7 \end{bmatrix}_{2\times3}$$

$$\begin{bmatrix} 3 \\ 5 \\ 2 \end{bmatrix}_{3\times1}, \quad \begin{bmatrix} 2 & 1 & 3 \end{bmatrix}_{1\times3}$$

- **A 3×3 system:**

Linear System

$$\begin{cases} a_1x + b_1y + c_1z = k_1 \\ a_2x + b_2y + c_2z = k_2 \\ a_3x + b_3y + c_3z = k_3 \end{cases}$$

Example

$$\begin{cases} 2x + 3y + 4z = 1 \\ x + 2y + 3z = 4 \\ 3x + y + 5z = 2 \end{cases}$$

- **Coefficient matrix:** the matrix obtained from the coefficients in a linear system.

Coefficient Matrix

$$\begin{bmatrix} a_1 & b_1 & c_1 \\ a_2 & b_2 & c_2 \\ a_3 & b_3 & c_3 \end{bmatrix}$$

Example

$$\begin{bmatrix} 2 & 3 & 4 \\ 1 & 2 & 3 \\ 3 & 1 & 5 \end{bmatrix}$$

- **Augmented matrix:** the matrix obtained from the coefficients and constant terms in a linear system.

Augmented Matrix

$$\left[\begin{array}{ccc|c} a_1 & b_1 & c_1 & k_1 \\ a_2 & b_2 & c_2 & k_2 \\ a_3 & b_3 & c_3 & k_3 \end{array}\right]$$

coefficients of x; coefficients of y; coefficients of z; constants (with a vertical line)

Example

$$\left[\begin{array}{ccc|c} 2 & 3 & 4 & 1 \\ 1 & 2 & 3 & 4 \\ 3 & 1 & 5 & 2 \end{array}\right]$$

Tip: augmented matrix = constants & coefficients

Matrix Addition & Subtraction

- **Naming a matrix with a single letter (bold face)**

Example: $\boldsymbol{A} = \begin{bmatrix} a_1 & b_1 \\ a_2 & b_2 \end{bmatrix}$ $\boldsymbol{B} = \begin{bmatrix} a_3 & b_3 \\ a_4 & b_4 \end{bmatrix}$ 2×2

or $\boldsymbol{A} = \begin{bmatrix} a_1 & b_1 \\ a_2 & b_2 \\ a_3 & b_3 \end{bmatrix}$ $\boldsymbol{B} = \begin{bmatrix} a_4 & b_4 \\ a_5 & b_5 \\ a_6 & b_6 \end{bmatrix}$ 3×2

- **Matrix equality:** two equal matrices have the same dimensions (or size) and the equal corresponding elements.

Example

  - The same dimensions: $\boldsymbol{A} = 2\times2$ & $\boldsymbol{B} = 2\times2$ or $\boldsymbol{A} = 3\times2$ & $\boldsymbol{B} = 3\times2$
  - The equal corresponding elements: $\boldsymbol{A} = \begin{bmatrix} x & 4 & y \\ 2 & 5 & 3 \end{bmatrix}$ (2×3), $\boldsymbol{B} = \begin{bmatrix} 6 & 4 & 3 \\ 2 & 5 & \sqrt{9} \end{bmatrix}$ (2×3)

$\boldsymbol{A} = \boldsymbol{B}$ only if $x = 6$ and $y = 3$

- **Requirements for adding/subtracting matrices:** only matrices of the same dimensions can be added or subtracted.

- **Add/subtract two matrices of the same dimensions:** combine the elements in the corresponding (or matching) positions.

	Matrix Operations	Example
matrix addition $\boldsymbol{A}+\boldsymbol{B}$	$\begin{bmatrix} a_1 & b_1 \\ a_2 & b_2 \end{bmatrix} + \begin{bmatrix} a_3 & b_3 \\ a_4 & b_4 \end{bmatrix} = \begin{bmatrix} a_1 + a_3 & b_1 + b_3 \\ a_2 + a_4 & b_2 + b_4 \end{bmatrix}$ 2×2 2×2 The same dimensions	$\begin{bmatrix} 1 & 3 \\ 2 & 4 \end{bmatrix} + \begin{bmatrix} 3 & 5 \\ 2 & 1 \end{bmatrix} = \begin{bmatrix} 1+3 & 3+5 \\ 2+2 & 4+1 \end{bmatrix}$ $= \begin{bmatrix} 4 & 8 \\ 4 & 5 \end{bmatrix}$
matrix subtraction $\boldsymbol{A}-\boldsymbol{B}$	$\begin{bmatrix} a_1 & b_1 \\ a_2 & b_2 \\ a_3 & b_3 \end{bmatrix} - \begin{bmatrix} a_4 & b_4 \\ a_5 & b_5 \\ a_6 & b_6 \end{bmatrix} = \begin{bmatrix} a_1-a_4 & b_1-b_4 \\ a_2-a_5 & b_2-b_5 \\ a_3-a_6 & b_3-b_6 \end{bmatrix}$ 3×2 3×2	$\begin{bmatrix} 3 & 8 \\ 5 & 7 \\ 6 & -9 \end{bmatrix} - \begin{bmatrix} 2 & 2 \\ 3 & -3 \\ 6 & 4 \end{bmatrix} = \begin{bmatrix} 3-2 & 8-2 \\ 5-3 & 7-(-3) \\ 6-6 & -9-4 \end{bmatrix}$ $= \begin{bmatrix} 1 & 6 \\ 2 & 10 \\ 0 & -13 \end{bmatrix}$

Matrix Multiplication

- **Scalar matrix multiplication:** the product of a scalar (a real number) and a matrix.

	Scalar Matrix Multiplication	Example
$k \cdot A$ k – scalar A – matrix	$k\begin{bmatrix} a_1 & b_1 \\ a_2 & b_2 \\ a_3 & b_3 \end{bmatrix} = \begin{bmatrix} ka_1 & kb_1 \\ ka_2 & kb_2 \\ ka_3 & kb_3 \end{bmatrix}$	$2\begin{bmatrix} 4 & -2 & y \\ 3 & 5 & 0 \end{bmatrix} = \begin{bmatrix} 2\cdot 4 & 2(-2) & 2\cdot y \\ 2\cdot 3 & 2\cdot 5 & 2\cdot 0 \end{bmatrix} = \begin{bmatrix} 8 & -4 & 2y \\ 6 & 10 & 0 \end{bmatrix}$

Tip: Multiply each element by the scalar.

Example: Find the following.

$$3\begin{bmatrix} 2 & 4 \\ 1 & 0 \\ 3 & -2 \end{bmatrix} - \frac{1}{2}\begin{bmatrix} 8 & 4 \\ 0 & -2 \\ 2 & 6 \end{bmatrix} = \begin{bmatrix} 3\cdot 2 & 3\cdot 4 \\ 3\cdot 1 & 3\cdot 0 \\ 3\cdot 3 & 3(-2) \end{bmatrix} - \begin{bmatrix} \frac{1}{2}\cdot 8 & \frac{1}{2}\cdot 4 \\ \frac{1}{2}\cdot 0 & \frac{1}{2}\cdot(-2) \\ \frac{1}{2}\cdot 2 & \frac{1}{2}\cdot 6 \end{bmatrix} = \begin{bmatrix} 6 & 12 \\ 3 & 0 \\ 9 & -6 \end{bmatrix} - \begin{bmatrix} 4 & 2 \\ 0 & -1 \\ 1 & 3 \end{bmatrix}$$

$$= \begin{bmatrix} 6-4 & 12-2 \\ 3-0 & 0-(-1) \\ 9-1 & -6-3 \end{bmatrix} = \begin{bmatrix} 2 & 10 \\ 3 & 1 \\ 8 & -9 \end{bmatrix}$$

- **Matrix multiplication:** the product of two matrices.

- **Requirements for matrix multiplication:** the product of two matrices A and B is defined only when the number of columns of A (1st matrix) is equal to the number of rows of B (2nd matrix). **Recall:** $m \times n$ (Rows, Columns)

Requirements for Matrix Multiplication	If $A = m_1 \times n_1$, $B = m_2 \times n_2$ then $A\cdot B$ is defined only when $n_1 = m_2$. (column for A, row for B)

Example

Matrix A	Matrix B	$A \cdot B$
$A = \begin{bmatrix} 2 & 3 & -2 & 1 \\ 1 & 4 & 6 & 4 \end{bmatrix}$ 2×4, $n_1 = 4$	$B = \begin{bmatrix} 1 & 4 \\ 2 & 5 \\ 2 & 3 \\ -5 & 4 \end{bmatrix}$ 4×2, $m_2 = 4$	$n_1 = m_2$, $4 = 4$ $A\cdot B$ is defined
$A = \begin{bmatrix} 2 \\ 4 \\ 1 \\ 6 \end{bmatrix}$ 4×1, $n_1 = 1$	$B = \begin{bmatrix} 3 & 4 & 5 & 7 \end{bmatrix}$ 1×4, $m_2 = 1$	$n_1 = m_2$, $1 = 1$ $A\cdot B$ is defined
$A = \begin{bmatrix} 3 & 2 & 1 \end{bmatrix}$ 1×3, $n_1 = 3$	$B = \begin{bmatrix} 4 & 3 \\ 1 & -5 \end{bmatrix}$ 2×2, $m_2 = 2$	$n_1 \neq m_2$, $3 \neq 2$ $A\cdot B$ is not defined

- **Dimensions of the product** for matrix multiplication

Dimensions of the Product	If $A = (m_1 \times n_1)$ and $B = (m_2 \times n_2)$, then $A \cdot B = (m_1 \times n_1)(m_2 \times n_2) = (m_1 \times n_2)$.	**Example:** If $A = (3 \times 2)$ and $B = (2 \times 4)$, Then $A \cdot B = (3 \times 2)(2 \times 4) = (3 \times 4)$.

Tip: (Rows of A) × (Columns of B)

- **Product of $1 \times n$ and $n \times 1$ matrices**

Matrix Multiplication	Example	Dimension
If $A = [a_1 \quad a_2 \quad \dots \quad a_n]$	$A = [2 \quad 3 \quad 1]$	1×3
$B = \begin{bmatrix} b_1 \\ b_2 \\ \dots \\ b_n \end{bmatrix}$	$B = \begin{bmatrix} 3 \\ -1 \\ 4 \end{bmatrix}$	3×1
then $AB = a_1b_1 + a_2b_2 + \dots a_nb_n$	$AB = [2 \quad 3 \quad 1] \begin{bmatrix} 3 \\ -1 \\ 4 \end{bmatrix} = 2 \cdot 3 + 3(-1) + 1 \cdot 4 = 7$	1×1

Tip: Multiply each element of the row of the first matrix by the corresponding elements of the column in the second matrix, and then add the products.

- **Product of $1 \times n$ and $n \times 2$ matrices**

Matrix Multiplication	Example	Dimension
If $A = [a_1, a_2, \dots, a_n]$	$A = [4 \quad -1 \quad 2]$	1×3
$B = \begin{bmatrix} b_{11} & b_{12} \\ b_{21} & b_{22} \\ \dots & \dots \\ b_{n1} & b_{n2} \end{bmatrix}$	$B = \begin{bmatrix} 1 & -1 \\ 3 & 2 \\ 2 & 0 \end{bmatrix}$	3×2
then $AB = [a_1, a_2, \dots, a_n] \begin{bmatrix} b_{11} & b_{12} \\ b_{21} & b_{22} \\ \dots & \dots \\ b_{n1} & b_{n2} \end{bmatrix}$	$AB = [4 \quad -1 \quad 2] \begin{bmatrix} 1 & -1 \\ 3 & 2 \\ 2 & 0 \end{bmatrix}$	
$= [a_1b_{11} + a_2b_{21} + \dots + a_nb_{n1} \quad a_1b_{12} + a_2b_{22} + \dots + a_nb_{n2}]$ (row of A) × (1st column of B) (row of A) × (2nd column of B)	$= [4 \cdot 1 + (-1)3 + 2 \cdot 2 \quad 4(-1) + (-1)2 + 2 \cdot 0]$ $= [4-3+4 \quad -4-2] = [5 \quad -6]$	1×2

Tips: - Multiply each element of the row of the first matrix by the corresponding elements of each column in the second matrix, and then add the products.
- Double-digit subscripts: Example: b_{21} - the element in matrix B that is in row 2 and column 1.
b_{n2} - the element in matrix B that is in row n and column 2.

- **The general case**

Matrix Multiplication	Example
$AB = \begin{bmatrix} a_{11} & a_{12} & a_{13} \\ a_{21} & a_{22} & a_{23} \end{bmatrix} \begin{bmatrix} b_{11} & b_{12} \\ b_{21} & b_{22} \\ b_{31} & b_{32} \end{bmatrix}$ $A = 2 \times 3$, $B = 3 \times 2$	$\begin{bmatrix} 1 & 2 & 3 \\ 2 & 0 & 1 \end{bmatrix} \begin{bmatrix} 2 & 1 \\ 0 & 2 \\ 3 & -1 \end{bmatrix}$ 2×3, 3×2
(1st row of A) × (1st column of B) (1st row of A) × (2nd column of B) $= \begin{bmatrix} a_{11}b_{11} + a_{12}b_{21} + a_{13}b_{31} & a_{11}b_{12} + a_{12}b_{22} + a_{13}b_{32} \\ a_{21}b_{11} + a_{22}b_{21} + a_{23}b_{31} & a_{21}b_{12} + a_{22}b_{22} + a_{23}b_{32} \end{bmatrix}$ (2nd row of A) × (1st column of B) (2nd row of A) × (2nd column of B) 2×2	$= \begin{bmatrix} 1 \cdot 2 + 2 \cdot 0 + 3 \cdot 3 & 1 \cdot 1 + 2 \cdot 2 + 3(-1) \\ 2 \cdot 2 + 0 \cdot 0 + 1 \cdot 3 & 2 \cdot 1 + 0 \cdot 2 + 1(-1) \end{bmatrix}$ $= \begin{bmatrix} 11 & 2 \\ 7 & 1 \end{bmatrix}$ 2×2

Example: Find the products.

1. $\begin{bmatrix} 2 & 3 \\ 1 & -2 \end{bmatrix} \begin{bmatrix} 3 & 0 \\ -4 & 4 \end{bmatrix} = \begin{bmatrix} 2 \cdot 3 + 3(-4) & 2 \cdot 0 + 3 \cdot 4 \\ 1 \cdot 3 + (-2)(-4) & 1 \cdot 0 + (-2) \cdot 4 \end{bmatrix} = \begin{bmatrix} -6 & 12 \\ 11 & -8 \end{bmatrix}$

$2 \times 2 \qquad 2 \times 2 \qquad\qquad 2 \times 2$

2. $\begin{bmatrix} 1 & -1 & 2 \\ 0 & 3 & 0 \\ 2 & 1 & 2 \end{bmatrix} \begin{bmatrix} 2 & 0 & 1 \\ 3 & -2 & 0 \\ -2 & 1 & 2 \end{bmatrix}$

$3 \times 3 \qquad 3 \times 3$

(1st row of A) × (1st column of B) (1std row of A) × (2nd column of B) 1std row of A) × (3rd column of B)

$$= \begin{bmatrix} 1 \cdot 2 + (-1)3 + 2(-2) & 1 \cdot 0 + (-1)(-2) + 2 \cdot 1 & 1 \cdot 1 + (-1) \cdot 0 + 2 \cdot 2 \\ 0 \cdot 2 + 3 \cdot 3 + 0(-2) & 0 \cdot 0 + 3(-2) + 0 \cdot 1 & 0 \cdot 1 + 3 \cdot 0 + 0 \cdot 2 \\ 2 \cdot 2 + 1 \cdot 3 + 2(-2) & 2 \cdot 0 + 1(-2) + 2 \cdot 1 & 2 \cdot 1 + 1 \cdot 0 + 2 \cdot 2 \end{bmatrix}$$

(2nd row of A) × (1st column of B) (2nd row of A) × (2nd column of B) (2nd row of A) × (3rd column of B)

(3rd row of A) × (1st column of B) (3rd row of A) × (2nd column of B) (3rd row of A) × (3rd column of B)

$$= \begin{bmatrix} -5 & 4 & 5 \\ 9 & -6 & 0 \\ 3 & 0 & 6 \end{bmatrix}$$

3×3

Summary – Matrix Multiplication

- Multiply the elements of the first row of the first matrix by the corresponding elements of each column in the second matrix and add the products.

$$\begin{bmatrix} a_{11} & a_{12} & a_{13} \\ a_{21} & a_{22} & a_{23} \\ a_{31} & a_{32} & a_{33} \end{bmatrix} \begin{bmatrix} b_{11} & b_{12} & b_{13} \\ b_{21} & b_{22} & b_{23} \\ b_{31} & b_{32} & b_{33} \end{bmatrix} = \begin{bmatrix} c_{11} & c_{12} & c_{13} \\ c_{21} & c_{22} & c_{23} \\ c_{31} & c_{32} & c_{33} \end{bmatrix} \qquad c_{11} = a_{11}b_{11} + a_{12}b_{21} + a_{13}b_{31}$$

$$\begin{bmatrix} a_{11} & a_{12} & a_{13} \\ a_{21} & a_{22} & a_{23} \\ a_{31} & a_{32} & a_{33} \end{bmatrix} \begin{bmatrix} b_{11} & b_{12} & b_{13} \\ b_{21} & b_{22} & b_{23} \\ b_{31} & b_{32} & b_{33} \end{bmatrix} = \begin{bmatrix} c_{11} & c_{12} & c_{13} \\ c_{21} & c_{22} & c_{23} \\ c_{31} & c_{32} & c_{33} \end{bmatrix} \qquad c_{12} = a_{11}b_{12} + a_{12}b_{22} + a_{13}b_{32}$$

$$\begin{bmatrix} a_{11} & a_{12} & a_{13} \\ a_{21} & a_{22} & a_{23} \\ a_{31} & a_{32} & a_{33} \end{bmatrix} \begin{bmatrix} b_{11} & b_{12} & b_{13} \\ b_{21} & b_{22} & b_{23} \\ b_{31} & b_{32} & b_{33} \end{bmatrix} = \begin{bmatrix} c_{11} & c_{12} & c_{13} \\ c_{21} & c_{22} & c_{23} \\ c_{31} & c_{32} & c_{33} \end{bmatrix} \qquad c_{13} = a_{11}b_{13} + a_{12}b_{23} + a_{13}b_{33}$$

- Multiply the elements of the second row of the first matrix by the corresponding elements of cach column in thc sccond matrix and add thc products.

$$\begin{bmatrix} a_{11} & a_{12} & a_{13} \\ a_{21} & a_{22} & a_{23} \\ a_{31} & a_{32} & a_{33} \end{bmatrix} \begin{bmatrix} b_{11} & b_{12} & b_{13} \\ b_{21} & b_{22} & b_{23} \\ b_{31} & b_{32} & b_{33} \end{bmatrix} = \begin{bmatrix} c_{11} & c_{12} & c_{13} \\ c_{21} & c_{22} & c_{23} \\ c_{31} & c_{32} & c_{33} \end{bmatrix} \qquad c_{21} = a_{21}b_{11} + a_{22}b_{21} + a_{23}b_{31}$$

$$\begin{bmatrix} a_{11} & a_{12} & a_{13} \\ a_{21} & a_{22} & a_{23} \\ a_{31} & a_{32} & a_{33} \end{bmatrix} \begin{bmatrix} b_{11} & b_{12} & b_{13} \\ b_{21} & b_{22} & b_{23} \\ b_{31} & b_{32} & b_{33} \end{bmatrix} = \begin{bmatrix} c_{11} & c_{12} & c_{13} \\ c_{21} & c_{22} & c_{23} \\ c_{31} & c_{32} & c_{33} \end{bmatrix} \qquad c_{22} = a_{21}b_{12} + a_{22}b_{22} + a_{23}b_{32}$$

$$\begin{bmatrix} a_{11} & a_{12} & a_{13} \\ a_{21} & a_{22} & a_{23} \\ a_{31} & a_{32} & a_{33} \end{bmatrix} \begin{bmatrix} b_{11} & b_{12} & b_{13} \\ b_{21} & b_{22} & b_{23} \\ b_{31} & b_{32} & b_{33} \end{bmatrix} = \begin{bmatrix} c_{11} & c_{12} & c_{13} \\ c_{21} & c_{22} & c_{23} \\ c_{31} & c_{32} & c_{33} \end{bmatrix} \qquad c_{23} = a_{21}b_{13} + a_{22}b_{23} + a_{23}b_{33}$$

- Multiply the elements of the third row of the first matrix by the corresponding elements of each column in the second matrix and add the products.

$$\begin{bmatrix} a_{11} & a_{12} & a_{13} \\ a_{21} & a_{22} & a_{23} \\ a_{31} & a_{32} & a_{33} \end{bmatrix} \begin{bmatrix} b_{11} & b_{12} & b_{13} \\ b_{21} & b_{22} & b_{23} \\ b_{31} & b_{32} & b_{33} \end{bmatrix} = \begin{bmatrix} c_{11} & c_{12} & c_{13} \\ c_{21} & c_{22} & c_{23} \\ c_{31} & c_{32} & c_{33} \end{bmatrix} \qquad c_{31} = a_{31}b_{11} + a_{32}b_{21} + a_{33}b_{31}$$

$$\begin{bmatrix} a_{11} & a_{12} & a_{13} \\ a_{21} & a_{22} & a_{23} \\ a_{31} & a_{32} & a_{33} \end{bmatrix} \begin{bmatrix} b_{11} & b_{12} & b_{13} \\ b_{21} & b_{22} & b_{23} \\ b_{31} & b_{32} & b_{33} \end{bmatrix} = \begin{bmatrix} c_{11} & c_{12} & c_{13} \\ c_{21} & c_{22} & c_{23} \\ c_{31} & c_{32} & c_{33} \end{bmatrix} \qquad c_{32} = a_{31}b_{12} + a_{32}b_{22} + a_{33}b_{32}$$

$$\underset{3 \times 3}{\begin{bmatrix} a_{11} & a_{12} & a_{13} \\ a_{21} & a_{22} & a_{23} \\ a_{31} & a_{32} & a_{33} \end{bmatrix}} \underset{3 \times 3}{\begin{bmatrix} b_{11} & b_{12} & b_{13} \\ b_{21} & b_{22} & b_{23} \\ b_{31} & b_{32} & b_{33} \end{bmatrix}} = \underset{3 \times 3}{\begin{bmatrix} c_{11} & c_{12} & c_{13} \\ c_{21} & c_{22} & c_{23} \\ c_{31} & c_{32} & c_{33} \end{bmatrix}} \qquad c_{33} = a_{31}b_{13} + a_{32}b_{23} + a_{33}b_{33}$$

11-4 MATRIX INVERSE

Identity Matrix

- **Identity matrix I:** a square matrix in which all the elements are 0 except the main diagonal from the top left to the bottom right corner with 1s.

I	2×2	3×3	n×n
identity matrix I	$I=\begin{bmatrix}1 & 0\\0 & 1\end{bmatrix}$	$I=\begin{bmatrix}1 & 0 & 0\\0 & 1 & 0\\0 & 0 & 1\end{bmatrix}$	$I=\begin{bmatrix}1 & \cdots & 0\\\vdots & 1 & \vdots\\0 & \cdots & 1\end{bmatrix}$ main diagonal

- **Identity property:** When a square matrix A is multiplied by an identity matrix I, the result is A.

Identity Property for Matrices	$AI = IA = A$

Tip: Identity property for matrices is same as the identity property for real numbers.

$a \cdot 1 = 1 \cdot a = a$ **Example**: $3 \cdot 1 = 1 \cdot 3 = 3$

Example: $A=\begin{bmatrix}1 & 3\\-2 & 4\end{bmatrix}$, $I=\begin{bmatrix}1 & 0\\0 & 1\end{bmatrix}$

$$AI=\begin{bmatrix}1 & 3\\-2 & 4\end{bmatrix}\begin{bmatrix}1 & 0\\0 & 1\end{bmatrix}=\begin{bmatrix}1\cdot1+3\cdot0 & 1\cdot0+3\cdot1\\-2\cdot1+4\cdot0 & -2\cdot0+4\cdot1\end{bmatrix}=\begin{bmatrix}\mathbf{1} & \mathbf{3}\\\mathbf{-2} & \mathbf{4}\end{bmatrix}$$

$$IA=\begin{bmatrix}1 & 0\\0 & 1\end{bmatrix}\begin{bmatrix}1 & 3\\-2 & 4\end{bmatrix}=\begin{bmatrix}1\cdot1+0(-2) & 1\cdot3+0\cdot4\\0\cdot1+1(-2) & 0\cdot3+1\cdot4\end{bmatrix}=\begin{bmatrix}\mathbf{1} & \mathbf{3}\\\mathbf{-2} & \mathbf{4}\end{bmatrix}$$

The same result for AI and IA.

- **Properties of matrix**

Property of Multiplication	Property of Addition
A, B, and C are matrices	
associative property: $A(BC) = (AB)C$	associative property: $A + (B + C) = (A + B) + C$
distributive property: $A(B + C) = AB + AC$ $(B + C)A = BA + CA$	commutative property: $A + B = B + A$
scalar multiplication (k is a constant): $k(AB) = (kA)B$ or $A(kB)$	additive inverse: $A + (-A) = 0$
multiplicative identity: $IA = AI = A$	additive identity: $A + 0 = A$

Note: The zero matrix "**0**" is a matrix that has the same dimension as matrix A but has a "0" for each element.

Inverse of a Matrix

- **An inverse matrix (A^{-1}):** A^{-1} is the inverse of a matrix A.

$$A\,A^{-1} = A^{-1}\,A = I \qquad I \text{ - identity matrix}$$

Tip: ordinary algebra: $a \cdot \frac{1}{a} = aa^{-1} = 1 \qquad a^{-1} = \frac{1}{a}$

matrix algebra: $A\,A^{-1} = I \qquad A^{-1} \neq \frac{1}{A}$

Example: $A = \begin{bmatrix} 2 & 1 \\ 6 & 4 \end{bmatrix}$, $A^{-1} = \begin{bmatrix} 2 & \frac{-1}{2} \\ -3 & 1 \end{bmatrix}$

$$A\,A^{-1} = \begin{bmatrix} 2 & 1 \\ 6 & 4 \end{bmatrix}\begin{bmatrix} 2 & \frac{-1}{2} \\ -3 & 1 \end{bmatrix} = \begin{bmatrix} 2 \cdot 2 + 1 \cdot (-3) & 2 \cdot \frac{-1}{2} + 1 \cdot 1 \\ 6 \cdot 2 + 4 \cdot (-3) & 6 \cdot \left(\frac{-1}{2}\right) + 4 \cdot 1 \end{bmatrix}$$

$$= \begin{bmatrix} 4 - 3 & -1 + 1 \\ 12 - 12 & -3 + 4 \end{bmatrix} = \begin{bmatrix} 1 & 0 \\ 0 & 1 \end{bmatrix} = I, \quad A\,A^{-1} = I$$

- **Finding the inverse of a 2×2 matrix A^{-1}**

Steps	Example: $A = \begin{bmatrix} 2 & 1 \\ 6 & 4 \end{bmatrix}$
- Switch the main diagonal elements. $A = \begin{bmatrix} a_1 & b_1 \\ a_2 & b_2 \end{bmatrix} \Rightarrow \begin{bmatrix} b_2 & b_1 \\ a_2 & a_1 \end{bmatrix}$	$\begin{bmatrix} 4 & 1 \\ 6 & 2 \end{bmatrix}$
- Change signs for the remaining elements. $\begin{bmatrix} b_2 & -b_1 \\ -a_2 & a_1 \end{bmatrix}$	$\begin{bmatrix} 4 & -1 \\ -6 & 2 \end{bmatrix}$
- Divide the result of the last step by the determinant $\lvert A \rvert$. $A^{-1} = \dfrac{\begin{bmatrix} b_2 & -b_1 \\ -a_2 & a_1 \end{bmatrix}}{\begin{vmatrix} a_1 & b_1 \\ a_2 & b_2 \end{vmatrix}}$	$A^{-1} = \dfrac{\begin{bmatrix} 4 & -1 \\ -6 & 2 \end{bmatrix}}{\begin{vmatrix} 2 & 1 \\ 6 & 4 \end{vmatrix}} = \dfrac{\begin{bmatrix} 4 & -1 \\ -6 & 2 \end{bmatrix}}{8-6}$ $= \frac{1}{2}\begin{bmatrix} 4 & -1 \\ -6 & 2 \end{bmatrix} = \begin{bmatrix} \frac{4}{2} & \frac{-1}{2} \\ \frac{-6}{2} & \frac{2}{2} \end{bmatrix} = \begin{bmatrix} 2 & \frac{-1}{2} \\ -3 & 1 \end{bmatrix}$

- Check: $A\,A^{-1} \stackrel{?}{=} I$

$$A\,A^{-1} = \begin{bmatrix} 2 & 1 \\ 6 & 4 \end{bmatrix}\begin{bmatrix} 2 & \frac{-1}{2} \\ -3 & 1 \end{bmatrix} = \begin{bmatrix} 2 \cdot 2 + 1 \cdot (-3) & 2 \cdot \frac{-1}{2} + 1 \cdot 1 \\ 6 \cdot 2 + 4 \cdot (-3) & 6 \cdot \left(\frac{-1}{2}\right) + 4 \cdot 1 \end{bmatrix}$$

$$= \begin{bmatrix} 4 - 3 & -1 + 1 \\ 12 - 12 & -3 + 4 \end{bmatrix} = \begin{bmatrix} 1 & 0 \\ 0 & 1 \end{bmatrix} = I \qquad \text{Correct!}$$

Note: This method can only be used for finding the inverse of a **2 × 2** matrix.

Gauss-Jordan Elimination Method to Find A^{-1}

Gauss-Jordan Method to Find A^{-1}	- Transform matrix A into the identity matrix I. - Transform the identity matrix I into inverse matrix A^{-1}.	$A \; I$ $\downarrow \; \downarrow$ $I \; A^{-1}$

Procedure to use Gaussian-elimination method to find A^{-1}

Steps

Example: $A = \begin{bmatrix} 1 & 0 \\ 2 & 3 \end{bmatrix}$

- Write the augmented matrix $[A \mid I]$ by appending an identity matrix I on the right of matrix A.

$$\left[\begin{array}{cc|cc} 1 & 0 & 1 & 0 \\ 2 & 3 & 0 & 1 \end{array}\right]$$

(A on the left, I on the right; Row 1, Row 2; Column 1, Column 2)

- Use row operations to transform $[A \mid I]$ to $[I \mid A^{-1}]$. $I = \begin{bmatrix} 1 & 0 \\ 0 & 1 \end{bmatrix}$

  You can:
  - Switch any two rows.
  - Multiply or divide a row by a constant.
  - Add or subtract a row to another row.
  - Multiply a constant to a row.

$$\left[\begin{array}{cc|cc} 1 & 0 & 1 & 0 \\ 0 & 3 & -2 & 1 \end{array}\right]$$

-2 × row 1, add to row 2
Get a "0" in the row 2 column 1.

$$\left[\begin{array}{cc|cc} 1 & 0 & 1 & 0 \\ 0 & 1 & \frac{-2}{3} & \frac{1}{3} \end{array}\right]$$

$\frac{1}{3}$ × row 2
Get a "1" in the row 2 column 2.

Tip: This (row operations) is similar to the elimination method for solving a system of linear equations.

- Determine A^{-1}.

$$A^{-1} = \begin{bmatrix} \mathbf{1} & \mathbf{0} \\ \mathbf{\frac{-2}{3}} & \mathbf{\frac{1}{3}} \end{bmatrix}$$

- Check. $A A^{-1} \stackrel{?}{=} I$

$$\begin{bmatrix} 1 & 0 \\ 2 & 3 \end{bmatrix} \begin{bmatrix} 1 & 0 \\ \frac{-2}{3} & \frac{1}{3} \end{bmatrix} \stackrel{?}{=} \begin{bmatrix} 1 & 0 \\ 0 & 1 \end{bmatrix}$$

$$\begin{bmatrix} 1 \cdot 1 + 0\left(\frac{-2}{3}\right) & 1 \cdot 0 + 0\left(\frac{1}{3}\right) \\ 2 \cdot 1 + 3\left(\frac{-2}{3}\right) & 2 \cdot 0 + 3\left(\frac{1}{3}\right) \end{bmatrix} \stackrel{?}{=} \begin{bmatrix} 1 & 0 \\ 0 & 1 \end{bmatrix}$$

$$\begin{bmatrix} 1 & 0 \\ 0 & 1 \end{bmatrix} \stackrel{\surd}{=} \begin{bmatrix} 1 & 0 \\ 0 & 1 \end{bmatrix}$$

Correct!

Note: This method can be used for any $n \times n$ matrices.

Example: Using the Gauss-Jordan method to find A^{-1} of the following 3×3 matrix.

$$A = \begin{bmatrix} \mathbf{3} & \mathbf{2} & \mathbf{0} \\ \mathbf{1} & \mathbf{-1} & \mathbf{0} \\ \mathbf{0} & \mathbf{5} & \mathbf{1} \end{bmatrix}, \qquad A^{-1} = ?$$

- Write $[A \mid I]$. $\left[\begin{array}{ccc|ccc} 3 & 2 & 0 & 1 & 0 & 0 \\ 1 & -1 & 0 & 0 & 1 & 0 \\ 0 & 5 & 1 & 0 & 0 & 1 \end{array}\right]$

- Transform $[A \mid I]$ into $[I \mid A^{-1}]$.

$$\left[\begin{array}{ccc|ccc} 3 & 2 & 0 & 1 & 0 & 0 \\ 1 & -1 & 0 & 0 & 1 & 0 \\ 0 & 5 & 1 & 0 & 0 & 1 \end{array}\right] \Rightarrow \left[\begin{array}{ccc|ccc} 1 & -1 & 0 & 0 & 1 & 0 \\ 3 & 2 & 0 & 1 & 0 & 0 \\ 0 & 5 & 1 & 0 & 0 & 1 \end{array}\right] \Rightarrow \left[\begin{array}{ccc|ccc} 1 & -1 & 0 & 0 & 1 & 0 \\ 0 & 5 & 0 & 1 & -3 & 0 \\ 0 & 5 & 1 & 0 & 0 & 1 \end{array}\right]$$

Switch row 1 & row 2
Get a "1" in the row 1 column 1.

$-3 \times$ row 1 add to row 2
Get a "0" in the row 2 column 1.

$$\Rightarrow \left[\begin{array}{ccc|ccc} 1 & -1 & 0 & 0 & 1 & 0 \\ 0 & 5 & 0 & 1 & -3 & 0 \\ 5 & 0 & 1 & 0 & 5 & 1 \end{array}\right] \Rightarrow \left[\begin{array}{ccc|ccc} 1 & -1 & 0 & 0 & 1 & 0 \\ 0 & 1 & 0 & \frac{1}{5} & \frac{-3}{5} & 0 \\ 5 & 0 & 1 & 0 & 5 & 1 \end{array}\right]$$

$5 \times$ row 1 add to row 3
Get a "0" in the row 3 column 2.

Row 2 $\div$ 5
Get a "1" in the row 2 column 2.

$$\Rightarrow \left[\begin{array}{ccc|ccc} 1 & 0 & 0 & \frac{1}{5} & \frac{2}{5} & 0 \\ 0 & 1 & 0 & \frac{1}{5} & \frac{-3}{5} & 0 \\ 5 & 0 & 1 & 0 & 5 & 1 \end{array}\right] \Rightarrow \left[\begin{array}{ccc|ccc} 1 & 0 & 0 & \frac{1}{5} & \frac{2}{5} & \mathbf{0} \\ 0 & 1 & 0 & \frac{1}{5} & \frac{-3}{5} & \mathbf{0} \\ 0 & 0 & 1 & \mathbf{-1} & \mathbf{3} & \mathbf{1} \end{array}\right]$$

Row 2 add to row 1
Get a "0" in the row 1 column 2.

$-5\times$ row 1 add to row 3
Get a "0" in the row 3 column 1.

- Determine A^{-1}. $A^{-1} = \begin{bmatrix} \frac{1}{5} & \frac{2}{5} & \mathbf{0} \\ \frac{1}{5} & \frac{-3}{5} & \mathbf{0} \\ \mathbf{-1} & \mathbf{3} & \mathbf{1} \end{bmatrix}$

Find Inverse Matrix A^{-1} – Method II

- **Find the inverse of a 3 × 3 matrix – Method II**

Example: Find A^{-1} of the following 3 × 3 matrix.

$$A = \begin{bmatrix} 3 & 2 & 0 \\ 1 & -1 & 0 \\ 0 & 5 & 1 \end{bmatrix} \qquad A^{-1} = ?$$

Steps

- **Find the cofactor matrix:** determine the cofactor (minors + place signs) of each element.

$$\begin{bmatrix} 3 & 2 & 0 \\ 1 & -1 & 0 \\ 0 & 5 & 1 \end{bmatrix} \rightarrow \begin{bmatrix} \begin{vmatrix} -1 & 0 \\ 5 & 1 \end{vmatrix} & -\begin{vmatrix} 1 & 0 \\ 0 & 1 \end{vmatrix} & \begin{vmatrix} 1 & -1 \\ 0 & 5 \end{vmatrix} \\ -\begin{vmatrix} 2 & 0 \\ 5 & 1 \end{vmatrix} & \begin{vmatrix} 3 & 0 \\ 0 & 1 \end{vmatrix} & -\begin{vmatrix} 3 & 2 \\ 0 & 5 \end{vmatrix} \\ \begin{vmatrix} 2 & 0 \\ -1 & 0 \end{vmatrix} & -\begin{vmatrix} 3 & 0 \\ 1 & 0 \end{vmatrix} & \begin{vmatrix} 3 & 2 \\ 1 & -1 \end{vmatrix} \end{bmatrix} \qquad \begin{vmatrix} + & - & + \\ - & + & - \\ + & - & + \end{vmatrix}$$

$$\text{cofactor matrix} = \begin{bmatrix} -1 & -1 & 5 \\ -2 & 3 & -15 \\ 0 & 0 & -5 \end{bmatrix}$$

- **Determine the transpose of the cofactor matrix A^T:** exchange all the rows and columns.

$$A^T = \begin{bmatrix} -1 & -2 & 0 \\ -1 & 3 & 0 \\ 5 & -15 & -5 \end{bmatrix}$$

- **Calculate the determinant |A| of the matrix**

$$|A| = \begin{vmatrix} 3 & 2 & 0 \\ 1 & -1 & 0 \\ 0 & 5 & 1 \end{vmatrix} = 3\begin{vmatrix} -1 & 0 \\ 5 & 1 \end{vmatrix} - 2\begin{vmatrix} 1 & 0 \\ 0 & 1 \end{vmatrix} + 0\begin{vmatrix} 1 & -1 \\ 0 & 5 \end{vmatrix} = -3 - 2 = -5$$

Choose row 1.

- **Determine inverse matrix A^{-1}** $\quad A^{-1} = \frac{1}{|A|} A^T$

$$A^{-1} = \frac{1}{|A|} A^T = \frac{1}{-5}\begin{bmatrix} -1 & -2 & 0 \\ -1 & 3 & 0 \\ 5 & -15 & -5 \end{bmatrix} = \begin{bmatrix} \frac{1}{5} & \frac{2}{5} & 0 \\ \frac{1}{5} & \frac{-3}{5} & 0 \\ -1 & 3 & 1 \end{bmatrix}$$

It gives the same result as the Gauss-Jordan method.

Solving a Linear System Using the Inverse Matrix

- **Write systems of linear equations in matrix form**

	Linear System	Matrix Form	Example
2×2 system	$\begin{cases} a_{11}x + b_{12}y = c_1 \\ a_{21}x + b_{22}y = c_2 \end{cases}$	$\begin{bmatrix} a_{11} & b_{12} \\ a_{21} & b_{22} \end{bmatrix} \begin{bmatrix} x \\ y \end{bmatrix} = \begin{bmatrix} c_1 \\ c_2 \end{bmatrix}$ $A \cdot X = C$	$\begin{cases} 2x + 3y = 1 \\ 3x - 4y = 2 \end{cases}$ $\begin{bmatrix} 2 & 3 \\ 3 & -4 \end{bmatrix} \begin{bmatrix} x \\ y \end{bmatrix} = \begin{bmatrix} 1 \\ 2 \end{bmatrix}$
3×3 system	$\begin{cases} a_{11}x + a_{12}y + a_{13}z = c_1 \\ a_{21}x + a_{22}y + a_{23}z = c_2 \\ a_{31}x + a_{32}y + a_{33}z = c_3 \end{cases}$	$\begin{bmatrix} a_{11} & a_{12} & a_{13} \\ a_{21} & a_{22} & a_{23} \\ a_{31} & a_{32} & a_{33} \end{bmatrix} \begin{bmatrix} x \\ y \\ z \end{bmatrix} = \begin{bmatrix} c_1 \\ c_2 \\ c_3 \end{bmatrix}$ $A \cdot X = C$	$\begin{cases} 3x + 2y + z = 1 \\ 2x - 3y + 4z = 3 \\ 5x + 2y - z = 2 \end{cases}$ $\begin{bmatrix} 3 & 2 & 1 \\ 2 & -3 & 4 \\ 5 & 2 & -1 \end{bmatrix} \begin{bmatrix} x \\ y \\ z \end{bmatrix} = \begin{bmatrix} 1 \\ 3 \\ 2 \end{bmatrix}$

- **Solving a linear system using the inverse matrix**

The Matrix Equation of a Linear System	$AX = C$	$\begin{cases} A - \text{coefficient matrix} \\ C - \text{constant matrix} \\ X - \text{variable matrix} \end{cases}$
Solving Using A^{-1}	$X = A^{-1}C$	A^{-1} – inverse matrix

$AX = C$
$A^{-1}AX = A^{-1}C$
$IX = A^{-1}C$
$X = A^{-1}C$

Note: $X = A^{-1}C$, $X \neq CA^{-1}$ $\because AB \neq BA$ Multiplication of matrices is not commutative.

Example: Use matrices to solve a 2×2 system. $\begin{cases} \boldsymbol{x - y = 1} \\ \boldsymbol{2x + 3y = 2} \end{cases}$

Steps	Example
- Write the system in matrix form. $AX = C$	$\begin{bmatrix} 1 & -1 \\ 2 & 3 \end{bmatrix} \begin{bmatrix} x \\ y \end{bmatrix} = \begin{bmatrix} 1 \\ 2 \end{bmatrix}$ (A, X, C)
- Find A^{-1}. - Switch the main diagonal elements. - Change signs for the remaining elements. - Divide by the determinant. $A^{-1} = \dfrac{\begin{bmatrix} b_2 & -b_1 \\ -a_2 & a_1 \end{bmatrix}}{\begin{vmatrix} a_1 & b_1 \\ a_2 & b_2 \end{vmatrix}}$	$A^{-1} = \dfrac{\begin{bmatrix} 3 & 1 \\ -2 & 1 \end{bmatrix}}{\begin{vmatrix} 1 & -1 \\ 2 & 3 \end{vmatrix}} = \dfrac{\begin{bmatrix} 3 & 1 \\ -2 & 1 \end{bmatrix}}{3-(-1)2} = \dfrac{1}{5}\begin{bmatrix} 3 & 1 \\ -2 & 1 \end{bmatrix}$ $= \begin{bmatrix} \frac{3}{5} & \frac{1}{5} \\ \frac{-2}{5} & \frac{1}{5} \end{bmatrix}$
- Solve for X: $X = A^{-1}C$	$X = A^{-1}C = \begin{bmatrix} \frac{3}{5} & \frac{1}{5} \\ \frac{-2}{5} & \frac{1}{5} \end{bmatrix} \begin{bmatrix} 1 \\ 2 \end{bmatrix} = \begin{bmatrix} \frac{3}{5}\cdot 1 + \frac{1}{5}\cdot 2 \\ \frac{-2}{5}\cdot 1 + \frac{1}{5}\cdot 2 \end{bmatrix} = \begin{bmatrix} 1 \\ 0 \end{bmatrix}$
	i.e. $\begin{bmatrix} x \\ y \end{bmatrix} = \begin{bmatrix} 1 \\ 0 \end{bmatrix}$ or $\begin{cases} \boldsymbol{x = 1} \\ \boldsymbol{y = 0} \end{cases}$ or $\boldsymbol{(1, 0)}$

Example: Use matrices to solve a 3×3 system. $\begin{cases} \mathbf{2x = y - 3z + 1} \\ \mathbf{3x + 4 + 2y = 0} \\ \mathbf{2y - 3z = 2} \end{cases}$

Steps	**Example**
- Write the system in standard form.	$\begin{cases} 2x - y + 3z = 1 \\ 3x + 2y + 0z = -4 \\ 0x + 2y - 3z = 2 \end{cases}$
- Write the system in matrix form. $AX = C$	$\begin{bmatrix} 2 & -1 & 3 \\ 3 & 2 & 0 \\ 0 & 2 & -3 \end{bmatrix} \begin{bmatrix} x \\ y \\ z \end{bmatrix} = \begin{bmatrix} 1 \\ -4 \\ 2 \end{bmatrix}$

- Find A^{-1}.
  - Find the cofactor matrix.

$$\begin{bmatrix} 2 & -1 & 3 \\ 3 & 2 & 0 \\ 0 & 2 & -3 \end{bmatrix} \Rightarrow \begin{bmatrix} \begin{vmatrix} 2 & 0 \\ 2 & -3 \end{vmatrix} & -\begin{vmatrix} 3 & 0 \\ 0 & -3 \end{vmatrix} & \begin{vmatrix} 3 & 2 \\ 0 & 2 \end{vmatrix} \\ -\begin{vmatrix} -1 & 3 \\ 2 & -3 \end{vmatrix} & \begin{vmatrix} 2 & 3 \\ 0 & -3 \end{vmatrix} & -\begin{vmatrix} 2 & -1 \\ 0 & 2 \end{vmatrix} \\ \begin{vmatrix} -1 & 3 \\ 2 & 0 \end{vmatrix} & -\begin{vmatrix} 2 & 3 \\ 3 & 0 \end{vmatrix} & \begin{vmatrix} 2 & -1 \\ 3 & 2 \end{vmatrix} \end{bmatrix} \qquad \begin{vmatrix} + & - & + \\ - & + & - \\ + & - & + \end{vmatrix}$$

$$\text{cofactor matrix} = \begin{bmatrix} -6 & 9 & 6 \\ 3 & -6 & -4 \\ -6 & 9 & 7 \end{bmatrix}$$

  - Determine the transpose of the cofactor matrix A^T. $A^T = \begin{bmatrix} -6 & 3 & -6 \\ 9 & -6 & 9 \\ 6 & -4 & 7 \end{bmatrix}$ Exchange rows & columns.

  - Calculate the determinant $|A|$. $|A| = \begin{vmatrix} 2 & -1 & 3 \\ 3 & 2 & 0 \\ 0 & 2 & -3 \end{vmatrix} \begin{matrix} 2 & -1 \\ 3 & 2 \\ 0 & 2 \end{matrix}$ Expansion by diagonals.

$$= 2\cdot2(-3) + (-1)\cdot0\cdot0 + 3\cdot3\cdot2 - 3\cdot2\cdot0 - 2\cdot0\cdot2 - (-1)\cdot3(-3)$$
$$= -12 + 18 - 9 = \boxed{-3}$$

  - Determine the inverse matrix A^{-1}. $A^{-1} = \frac{1}{|A|} A^T = \frac{1}{-3}\begin{bmatrix} -6 & 3 & -6 \\ 9 & -6 & 9 \\ 6 & -4 & 7 \end{bmatrix} = \begin{bmatrix} 2 & -1 & 2 \\ -3 & 2 & -3 \\ -2 & \frac{4}{3} & \frac{-7}{3} \end{bmatrix}$

- Solve for $\boldsymbol{X}$. $X = A^{-1}C$

$$X = \begin{bmatrix} 2 & -1 & 2 \\ -3 & 2 & -3 \\ -2 & \frac{4}{3} & \frac{-7}{3} \end{bmatrix} \begin{bmatrix} 1 \\ -4 \\ 2 \end{bmatrix} = \begin{bmatrix} 2\cdot1 + (-1)(-4) + 2\cdot2 \\ (-3)\cdot1 + 2(-4) + (-3)\cdot2 \\ (-2)\cdot1 + \frac{4}{3}(-4) + \frac{-7}{3}\cdot2 \end{bmatrix}$$

$$= \begin{bmatrix} 2 + 4 + 4 \\ -3 - 8 - 6 \\ -2 - \frac{16}{3} - \frac{14}{3} \end{bmatrix} = \begin{bmatrix} 10 \\ -17 \\ -12 \end{bmatrix}$$

i.e. $\begin{bmatrix} x \\ y \\ z \end{bmatrix} = \begin{bmatrix} 10 \\ -17 \\ -12 \end{bmatrix}$ or $\begin{cases} \mathbf{x = 10} \\ \mathbf{y = -17} \\ \mathbf{z = -12} \end{cases}$ or **(10, -17,-12)**

It gives the same result as using Cramer's rule for a 3×3 system.

Matrix Inverse on a Graphing Calculator (TI-83 Plus)

- **Creating a matrix on a graphing calculator**

Example: $A = \begin{bmatrix} 2 & -1 & 3 \\ 3 & 2 & 0 \\ 0 & 2 & -3 \end{bmatrix}$

Keystrokes	Explanation
[2nd] [MATRX]	Enter the matrix screen.
	Select the 'Edit' command.
3 [ENTER] 3 [ENTER]	Define a 3×3 matrix.
2 [ENTER] -1 [ENTER] 3 [ENTER]	Enter the numbers of the matrix.
3 [ENTER] 2 [ENTER] 0 [ENTER]	
0 [ENTER] 2 [ENTER] -3 [ENTER]	

NAMES MATH **EDIT**
1: [A]
2: [B]

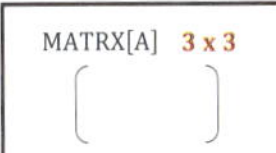

- **Finding an inverse matrix on a graphing calculator**

Example: $A = \begin{bmatrix} 2 & -1 & 3 \\ 3 & 2 & 0 \\ 0 & 2 & -3 \end{bmatrix}$ $\quad A^{-1} = ?$

Keystrokes	Explanation
[2nd] [MATRX]  [ENTER]	Enter the matrix screen; select the 'Edit' command.
3 [ENTER] 3 [ENTER]	Define a 3×3 matrix.
2 [ENTER] -1 [ENTER] 3 [ENTER]	Enter the numbers of the matrix.
3 [ENTER] 2 [ENTER] 0 [ENTER]	
0 [ENTER] 2 [ENTER] -3 [ENTER]	
[2nd] [QUIT]	Return to the home screen.
[2nd] [MATRX] [ENTER]	Re-enter the matrix screen.
[x^{-1}] [MATH] [ENTER] [ENTER]	Select the '1: ▶ Frac' command.

$[A]^{-1}$ > Frac

Display: $\begin{bmatrix} 2 & -1 & 2 \\ -3 & 2 & -3 \\ -2 & \frac{4}{3} & \frac{-7}{3} \end{bmatrix}$ — Display the inverse matrix A^{-1}.

It gives the same result as manual calculation.

Solving a System Using Matrices & Graphing Calculator (TI-83 Plus)

Example: Solve a 3×3 system. $\begin{cases} 2x = y - 3z + 1 \\ 3x + 4 + 2y = 0 \\ 2y - 3z = 2 \end{cases}$

Write the system in standard form. $\begin{cases} 2x - y + 3z = 1 \\ 3x + 2y + 0z = -4 \\ 0x + 2y - 3z = 2 \end{cases}$

[2nd] [MATRX] — Enter the matrix screen.

[▶] [▶] [ENTER] — Select the 'Edit' command.

3 [ENTER] 4 [ENTER] — Define a 3 × 4 matrix.

MATRX[A] 3 x 4

2 [ENTER] -1 [ENTER] 3 [ENTER] 1 [ENTER] — Enter the augmented matrix.

3 [ENTER] 2 [ENTER] 0 [ENTER] -4 [ENTER]

0 [ENTER] 2 [ENTER] -3 [ENTER] 2 [ENTER]

$$\begin{bmatrix} 2 & -1 & 3 & 1 \\ 3 & 2 & 0 & -4 \\ 0 & 2 & -3 & 2 \end{bmatrix}$$

[2nd] [QUIT] — Return to the home screen.

[2nd] [MATRX] — Re-enter the matrix screen.

[▶] — Select the 'MATH' command.

NAMES MATH EDIT
1: det (
2: T
… …

[▲] [▲] [▲] [▲] [▲] [ENTER] — Select the 'B:rref (' command.

NAMES MATH EDIT
0: cumSum (
A:ref (
B:rref (
C:rowSwap (
D: row+ (
… …

[2nd] [MATRX] [ENTER] [ENTER]

rref (

Display: $\begin{bmatrix} 1 & 0 & 0 & 10 \\ 0 & 1 & 0 & -17 \\ 0 & 0 & 1 & -12 \end{bmatrix}$

i.e. $\begin{bmatrix} x \\ y \\ z \end{bmatrix} = \begin{bmatrix} 10 \\ -17 \\ -12 \end{bmatrix}$ or $\begin{cases} x = 10 \\ y = -17 \\ z = -12 \end{cases}$

It gives the same result as manual calculation.

Unit 11 Summary

- **Evaluate a 2×2 determinant**

Determinant	Evaluation	Example
$\begin{vmatrix} a_1 & b_1 \\ a_2 & b_2 \end{vmatrix}$	$\begin{vmatrix} a_1 & b_1 \\ a_2 & b_2 \end{vmatrix} = a_1 b_2 - b_1 a_2$	$\begin{vmatrix} 2 & 1 \\ 3 & 4 \end{vmatrix} = 2 \cdot 4 - 1 \cdot 3 = 5$

- **Evaluate a 3×3 Determinant – Method I: Using Diagonals**

3×3 Determinant	Expansion by Diagonals	Example
$\begin{vmatrix} a_1 & b_1 & c_1 \\ a_2 & b_2 & c_2 \\ a_3 & b_3 & c_3 \end{vmatrix}$	$\begin{vmatrix} a_1 & b_1 & c_1 \\ a_2 & b_2 & c_2 \\ a_3 & b_3 & c_3 \end{vmatrix} \begin{matrix} a_1 & b_1 \\ a_2 & b_2 \\ a_3 & b_3 \end{matrix}$ $= a_1 b_2 c_3 + b_1 c_2 a_3 + c_1 a_2 b_3$ $- c_1 b_2 a_3 - a_1 c_2 b_3 - b_1 a_2 c_3$	$\begin{vmatrix} 1 & 1 & 3 \\ 4 & 3 & 2 \\ 3 & 1 & 2 \end{vmatrix} \begin{matrix} 1 & 1 \\ 4 & 3 \\ 3 & 1 \end{matrix}$ $= 1 \cdot 3 \cdot 2 + 1 \cdot 2 \cdot 3 + 3 \cdot 4 \cdot 1$ $-3 \cdot 3 \cdot 3 - 1 \cdot 2 \cdot 1 - 1 \cdot 4 \cdot 2$ $= 6 + 6 + 12 - 27 - 2 - 8 =$ **-13**

Note: 'Expansion by diagonals' does not work with 4×4 or higher-order determinants.

- **Cofactors:** minors + place signs = cofactors

$$\begin{vmatrix} A_1 & B_1 & C_1 \\ A_2 & B_2 & C_2 \\ A_3 & B_3 & C_3 \end{vmatrix} + \begin{vmatrix} + & - & + \\ - & + & - \\ + & - & + \end{vmatrix} \Rightarrow \begin{vmatrix} A_1 & -D_1 & C_1 \\ -A_2 & B_2 & -C_2 \\ A_3 & -B_3 & C_3 \end{vmatrix}$$

minors place signs cofactors

- **Evaluate a 3×3 determinant – Method II: expansion by minors**
  - Choose any row or column in the determinant.
  - Multiply each element in the chosen row/column by its cofactor.

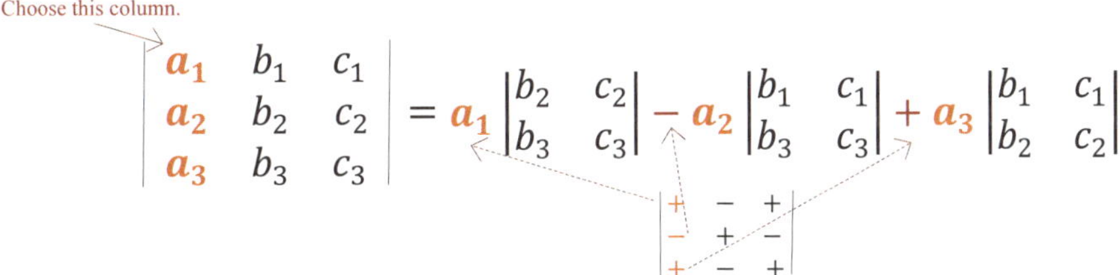

$$\begin{vmatrix} a_1 & b_1 & c_1 \\ a_2 & b_2 & c_2 \\ a_3 & b_3 & c_3 \end{vmatrix} = a_1 \begin{vmatrix} b_2 & c_2 \\ b_3 & c_3 \end{vmatrix} - a_2 \begin{vmatrix} b_1 & c_1 \\ b_3 & c_3 \end{vmatrix} + a_3 \begin{vmatrix} b_1 & c_1 \\ b_2 & c_2 \end{vmatrix}$$

$$\begin{vmatrix} + & - & + \\ - & + & - \\ + & - & + \end{vmatrix}$$

- **Evaluate a determinant that can be expanded by any row or column**
- **Using Cramer's rule to solve a 2×2 system**

A 2×2 System	Cramer's Rule
$\begin{cases} a_1 x + b_1 y = k_1 \\ a_2 x + b_2 y = k_2 \end{cases}$	The solution of the system: $x = \frac{D_x}{D}$, $y = \frac{D_y}{D}$ $(D \neq 0)$ $D = \begin{vmatrix} a_1 & b_1 \\ a_2 & b_2 \end{vmatrix}$, $D_x = \begin{vmatrix} k_1 & b_1 \\ k_2 & b_2 \end{vmatrix}$, $D_y = \begin{vmatrix} a_1 & k_1 \\ a_2 & k_2 \end{vmatrix}$

coefficients of x

coefficients of y

constant

Replace the column a in D with k.

Replace the column b in D with k.

- **Using Cramer's rule to solve a 3×3 system**

A 3×3 System	Cramer's Rule	D	D_x , D_y and D_z
$\begin{cases} a_1x+b_1y+c_1z=k_1 \\ a_2x+b_2\,y+c_2y=k_2 \\ a_3x+b_3\,y+c_3y=k_3 \end{cases}$	$x=\frac{D_x}{D}$ $y=\frac{D_y}{D}$ $z=\frac{D_z}{D}$	$D=\begin{vmatrix} a_1 & b_1 & c_1 \\ a_2 & b_2 & c_2 \\ a_3 & b_3 & c_3 \end{vmatrix}$ $D\neq 0$	$D_x=\begin{vmatrix} k_1 & b_1 & c_1 \\ k_1 & b_2 & c_2 \\ k_1 & b_3 & c_3 \end{vmatrix}$ $D_y=\begin{vmatrix} a_1 & k_1 & c_1 \\ a_2 & k_2 & c_2 \\ a_3 & k_3 & c_3 \end{vmatrix}$ $D_z=\begin{vmatrix} a_1 & b_1 & k_1 \\ a_2 & b_2 & k_2 \\ a_3 & b_3 & k_3 \end{vmatrix}$

- **Matrix:** a rectangular array of elements enclosed in brackets.

- **Dimensions:** A matrix has $\begin{cases} m \text{ rows} \\ n \text{ columns} \end{cases}$

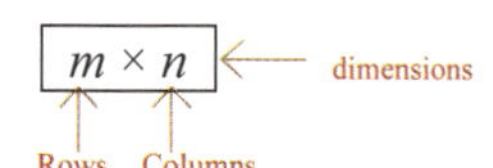

- **A 3×3 system:**

Linear System	Example
$\begin{cases} a_1x+b_1y+c_1z=k_1 \\ a_2x+b_2\,y+c_2y=k_2 \\ a_3x+b_3\,y+c_3y=k_3 \end{cases}$	$\begin{cases} 2x+3y+4z=1 \\ x+2y+3z=4 \\ 3x+\ y+5z=2 \end{cases}$

- **Coefficient matrix:**

$$\begin{bmatrix} a_1 & b_1 & c_1 \\ a_2 & b_2 & c_2 \\ a_3 & b_3 & c_3 \end{bmatrix} \qquad \begin{bmatrix} 2 & 3 & 4 \\ 1 & 2 & 3 \\ 3 & 1 & 5 \end{bmatrix}$$

- **Augmented matrix:**

$$\left[\begin{array}{ccc|c} a_1 & b_1 & c_1 & k_1 \\ a_2 & b_2 & c_2 & k_2 \\ a_3 & b_3 & c_3 & k_3 \end{array}\right] \qquad \left[\begin{array}{ccc|c} 2 & 3 & 4 & 1 \\ 1 & 2 & 3 & 4 \\ 3 & 1 & 5 & 2 \end{array}\right]$$

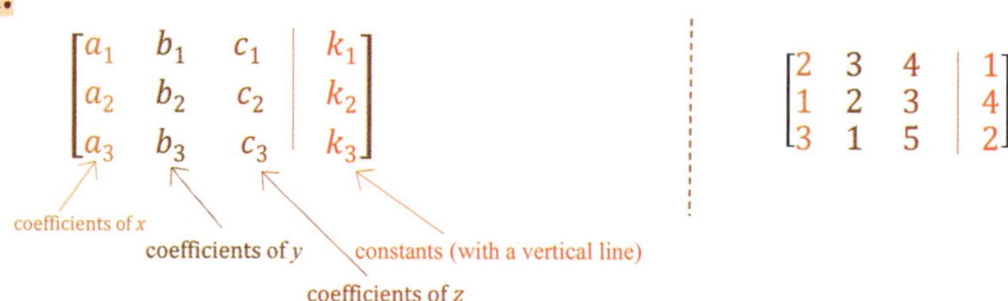

- **Matrix equality:** two equal matrices have the same dimensions (or size) and the equal corresponding elements.

- **Add/subtract two matrices of the same dimensions**

	Matrix Operations	Example
matrix addition $A+B$	$\begin{bmatrix} a_1 & b_1 \\ a_2 & b_2 \end{bmatrix}+\begin{bmatrix} a_3 & b_3 \\ a_4 & b_4 \end{bmatrix}=\begin{bmatrix} a_1+a_3 & b_1+b_3 \\ a_2+a_4 & b_2+b_4 \end{bmatrix}$ 2×2, 2×2: The same dimensions	$\begin{bmatrix} 1 & 3 \\ 2 & 4 \end{bmatrix}+\begin{bmatrix} 3 & 5 \\ 2 & 1 \end{bmatrix}=\begin{bmatrix} 1+3 & 3+5 \\ 2+2 & 4+1 \end{bmatrix}$ $=\begin{bmatrix} 4 & 8 \\ 4 & 5 \end{bmatrix}$
matrix subtraction $A-B$	$\begin{bmatrix} a_1 & b_1 \\ a_2 & b_2 \\ a_3 & b_3 \end{bmatrix}-\begin{bmatrix} a_4 & b_4 \\ a_5 & b_5 \\ a_6 & b_6 \end{bmatrix}=\begin{bmatrix} a_1-a_4 & b_1-b_4 \\ a_2-a_5 & b_2-b_5 \\ a_3-a_6 & b_3-b_6 \end{bmatrix}$ 3×2, 3×2	$\begin{bmatrix} 3 & 8 \\ 5 & 7 \\ 6 & -9 \end{bmatrix}-\begin{bmatrix} 2 & 2 \\ 3 & -3 \\ 6 & 4 \end{bmatrix}=\begin{bmatrix} 3-2 & 8-2 \\ 5-3 & 7-(-3) \\ 6-6 & -9-4 \end{bmatrix}$ $=\begin{bmatrix} 1 & 6 \\ 2 & 10 \\ 0 & -13 \end{bmatrix}$

- **Scalar matrix multiplication**

	Scalar Matrix Multiplication	Example
$k \cdot A$ k – scalar A – matrix	$k\begin{bmatrix} a_1 & b_1 \\ a_2 & b_2 \\ a_3 & b_3 \end{bmatrix} = \begin{bmatrix} ka_1 & kb_1 \\ ka_2 & kb_2 \\ ka_3 & kb_3 \end{bmatrix}$	$2\begin{bmatrix} 4 & -2 & y \\ 3 & 5 & 0 \end{bmatrix} = \begin{bmatrix} 2\cdot 4 & 2(-2) & 2\cdot y \\ 2\cdot 3 & 2\cdot 5 & 2\cdot 0 \end{bmatrix}$ $= \begin{bmatrix} 8 & -4 & 2y \\ 6 & 10 & 0 \end{bmatrix}$

- **Requirements for matrix multiplication**

Requirements for Matrix Multiplication	If $A = m_1 \times n_1$, $B = m_2 \times n_2$ then $A \cdot B$ is defined only when $n_1 = m_2$. column for A　row for B

- **Dimensions of the product for matrix multiplication**

Dimensions of the Product	If $A = (m_1 \times n_1)$ and $B = (m_2 \times n_2)$, then $A \cdot B = (m_1 \times n_1)(m_2 \times n_2) = (m_1 \times n_2)$.	**Example:** If $A = (3 \times 2)$ and $B = (2 \times 4)$, Then $A \cdot B = (3 \times 2)(2 \times 4) = (3 \times 4)$.

- **Matrix multiplication**

Matrix Multiplication	Example
$AB = \begin{bmatrix} a_{11} & a_{12} & a_{13} \\ a_{21} & a_{22} & a_{23} \end{bmatrix}\begin{bmatrix} b_{11} & b_{12} \\ b_{21} & b_{22} \\ b_{31} & b_{32} \end{bmatrix}$　$A = 2\times 3$, $B = 3\times 2$ (1st row of A) × (1st column of B)　(1st row of A) × (2nd column of B) $= \begin{bmatrix} a_{11}b_{11} + a_{12}b_{21} + a_{13}b_{31} & a_{11}b_{12} + a_{12}b_{22} + a_{13}b_{32} \\ a_{21}b_{11} + a_{22}b_{21} + a_{23}b_{31} & a_{21}b_{12} + a_{22}b_{22} + a_{23}b_{32} \end{bmatrix}$ (2nd row of A) × (1st column of B)　(2nd row of A) × (2nd column of B) 2×2	$\begin{bmatrix} 1 & 2 & 3 \\ 2 & 0 & 1 \end{bmatrix}\begin{bmatrix} 2 & 1 \\ 0 & 2 \\ 3 & -1 \end{bmatrix}$　2×3, 3×2 $= \begin{bmatrix} 1\cdot 2 + 2\cdot 0 + 3\cdot 3 & 1\cdot 1 + 2\cdot 2 + 3(-1) \\ 2\cdot 2 + 0\cdot 0 + 1\cdot 3 & 2\cdot 1 + 0\cdot 2 + 1(-1) \end{bmatrix}$ $= \begin{bmatrix} 11 & 2 \\ 7 & 1 \end{bmatrix}$　2×2

- **Identity matrix *I***

I	2×2	3×3	$n\times n$
identity matrix *I*	$I = \begin{bmatrix} 1 & 0 \\ 0 & 1 \end{bmatrix}$	$I = \begin{bmatrix} 1 & 0 & 0 \\ 0 & 1 & 0 \\ 0 & 0 & 1 \end{bmatrix}$	$I = \begin{bmatrix} 1 & \cdots & 0 \\ \vdots & 1 & \vdots \\ 0 & \cdots & 1 \end{bmatrix}$ main diagonal

- **Identity property**

Identity Property for Matrices	$AI = IA = A$

- **Properties of matrix**

Property of Multiplication	Property of Addition
A, B, and C are matrices	
associative property: $A(BC) = (AB)C$	associative property: $A + (B + C) = (A + B) + C$
distributive property: $A(B + C) = AB + AC$ $(B + C)A = BA + CA$	commutative property: $A + B = B + A$
scalar multiplication (k is a constant): $k(AB) = (kA)B$ or $A(kB)$	additive inverse: $A + (-A) = 0$
multiplicative identity: $IA = AI = A$	additive identity: $A + 0 = A$

- **An inverse matrix (A^{-1}):** A^{-1} is the inverse of a matrix A.

  $A A^{-1} = A^{-1} A = I$ I - identity matrix

- **Finding the inverse of a 2×2 matrix A^{-1}**
  - Switch the main diagonal elements. $A = \begin{bmatrix} a_1 & b_1 \\ a_2 & b_2 \end{bmatrix} \rightarrow \begin{bmatrix} b_2 & b_1 \\ a_2 & a_1 \end{bmatrix}$
  - Change signs for the remaining elements. $\begin{bmatrix} b_2 & -b_1 \\ -a_2 & a_1 \end{bmatrix}$
  - Divide the result of the last step by the determinant $|A|$.

  $$A^{-1} = \frac{\begin{bmatrix} b_2 & -b_1 \\ -a_2 & a_1 \end{bmatrix}}{\begin{vmatrix} a_1 & b_1 \\ a_2 & b_2 \end{vmatrix}}$$

  - Check: $A A^{-1} \overset{?}{=} I$

- **Gauss-Jordan Method to Find A^{-1}**

Gauss-Jordan Method to Find A^{-1}	- Transform matrix A into the identity matrix I. - Transform identity matrix I into inverse matrix A^{-1}.	A I ↓ ↓ I A^{-1}

- **Find the inverse of a 3 × 3 matrix – Method II**
  - Find the cofactor matrix (minors + place signs).
  - Determine the transpose of the cofactor matrix A^T: exchange all the rows and columns.
  - Calculate the determinant $|A|$ of the matrix.
  - Determine inverse matrix A^{-1}. $A^{-1} = \frac{1}{|A|} A^T$

- **Write systems of linear equations in matrix form**

	Linear System	Matrix Form	Example
2×2 system	$\begin{cases} a_{11}x + b_{12}y = c_1 \\ a_{21}x + b_{22}y = c_2 \end{cases}$	$\begin{bmatrix} a_{11} & b_{12} \\ a_{21} & b_{22} \end{bmatrix} \begin{bmatrix} x \\ y \end{bmatrix} = \begin{bmatrix} c_1 \\ c_2 \end{bmatrix}$ $A \cdot X = C$	$\begin{cases} 2x + 3y = 1 \\ 3x - 4y = 2 \end{cases}$ $\begin{bmatrix} 2 & 3 \\ 3 & -4 \end{bmatrix} \begin{bmatrix} x \\ y \end{bmatrix} = \begin{bmatrix} 1 \\ 2 \end{bmatrix}$
3×3 system	$\begin{cases} a_{11}x + a_{12}y + a_{13}z = c_1 \\ a_{21}x + a_{22}y + a_{23}z = c_2 \\ a_{31}x + b_{32}y + a_{33}z = c_3 \end{cases}$	$\begin{bmatrix} a_{11} & a_{12} & a_{13} \\ a_{21} & a_{22} & a_{23} \\ a_{31} & a_{32} & a_{33} \end{bmatrix} \begin{bmatrix} x \\ y \\ z \end{bmatrix} = \begin{bmatrix} c_1 \\ c_2 \\ c_3 \end{bmatrix}$ $A \cdot X = C$	$\begin{cases} 3x + 2y + z = 1 \\ 2x - 3y + 4z = 3 \\ 5x + 2y - z = 2 \end{cases}$ $\begin{bmatrix} 3 & 2 & 1 \\ 2 & -3 & 4 \\ 5 & 2 & -1 \end{bmatrix} \begin{bmatrix} x \\ y \\ z \end{bmatrix} = \begin{bmatrix} 1 \\ 3 \\ 2 \end{bmatrix}$

- **Solving a linear system using the inverse matrix**

The Matrix Equation of a Linear System	$A X = C$	$\begin{cases} A - \text{coefficient matrix} \\ C - \text{constant matrix} \\ X - \text{variable matrix} \end{cases}$
Solving Using A^{-1}	$X = A^{-1} C$	A^{-1} – inverse matrix

PRACTICE QUIZ

Unit 11 Determinants and Matrices

1. Evaluate the determinant: $\begin{vmatrix} 2 & -1 & 0 \\ 0 & 3 & -2 \\ 2 & 4 & -1 \end{vmatrix}$

2. Solve the system using Cramer's rule: $\begin{cases} 3x - 2y = -5z + 2 \\ 4x - 7y - z = 19 \\ 5x = 6y - 4z + 13 \end{cases}$

3. Find the products: $\begin{bmatrix} 3 & 1 \\ 1 & -1 \end{bmatrix}\begin{bmatrix} 2 & -3 \\ 0 & 1 \end{bmatrix}$

4. Solve a 2×2 system using matrices: $\begin{cases} 5x + 4y = 1 \\ 4x + 3y = -1 \end{cases}$

5. Solve a 3×3 system using matrices: $\begin{cases} 3x - 2y + 5z = 2 \\ 4x - 7y - z = 19 \\ 5x - 6y + 4z = 13 \end{cases}$

Answers for Practice Quizzes

Unit 1

Reference Page Number

1. $A = \{ x \mid x$ is a number between -5 and 2$\}$
$A = \{-4, -3, -2, -1, 0, 1\}$ (1-1: page 2)

2. **a.** $\{-9\}$
b. $\{7\pi, \sqrt{5}\}$ (1-1: page 3)

3. a
b.

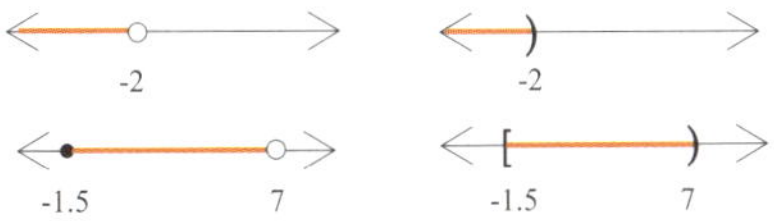

(1-1: page 4)

4. **a.** -3.3
b. 19
c. -1.5
d. -3 (1-2: page 6)

5. **a.** - 0.008
b. m^3
c. 1
d. -6 (1-3: page 9)

6. 8 (1-4: page 10)

7. **a.** $7y - 3$
b. $2(t + 9)$ (1-4: page 11)

8. **a.** Inverse property of addition
b. Associative property of multiplication (1-4: page 12)

9. **a.** $5c\,(ab - 5b + 7)$
b. $-6pq + 3pr$
c. $2x^2 + y$
d. $-x^2 + 8x - 19$ (1-5: page 13)

10. **a.** $\frac{-8x^6}{y^{12}}$
b. $\frac{y^6}{8x^3}$ (1-6: page 16)

11. **a.** 1.3975×10^5
b. 5.75×10^{-8} (1-6: page 17)

Unit 2

1. **a.** $x = 2.8$
b. $y \approx 0.06$
c. $y \approx 3.67$ (2-1: pages 26-27)

2. $4x - 5 = 9 + \frac{x}{2}$, $x = 4$ (2-2: page 30)

3. $4x = (x + 2) + (x + 4) - 2$, 1st = 2, 2nd = 4, 3rd = 6 (2-2: page 32)

4. $2r + 2(r - 10) = 340$, $r = 90$ km/h , $r - 10 = 80$ km/h (2-2: page 36)

5. Downstream: $t = \frac{d}{r} = \frac{4}{26+12} \approx 0.11$ hr

Upstream: $t = \frac{d}{r} = \frac{3}{26-12} \approx 0.21$ hr (2-2: page 36)

6. $46x + 66(3+x) + 86\left(\frac{1}{2}x + 2\right) = 680$; 2, 5, 3 (2-2: page 37)

7. **a.**

$(-\infty, -2]$ or $\{x \mid x \le -2\}$

b.

$(-\infty, 1)$ or $\{x \mid x < 1\}$

c.

$\left[\frac{11}{9}, \infty\right)$ or $\left\{x \mid x \ge \frac{11}{9}\right\}$ (2-3: page 43)

8. $76 < \frac{x+78}{2} < 80$, $74 < x < 82$ (2-3: page 44)

9. **a.** True
b. False (2-3: page 45)

10. **a.** $A = \{11, 13, 17\}$
$B = \{13, 14, 15\}$
$A \cup B = \{11, 13, 14, 15, 17\}$, $A \cap B = \{13\}$

b. $A \cup B$ $\{1, 2, 3, 4, 5, 7\}$
$A \cap B$ $\{3, 5\}$
$A \cap C$ $\emptyset$ (2-4: page 46)

11. $\{x \mid -5 < x \le 1\}$ or $(-5, 1]$

(2-4: page 46)

12. **a.** $\{-8, 2\}$
b. $\left\{-1, \frac{3}{4}\right\}$ (2-5: pages 49-50)

13. **a.** $\left\{x \mid -1 \le x \le \frac{11}{3}\right\}$ or $\left[-1, \frac{11}{3}\right]$
b. $\left\{x \mid x < \frac{-1}{5} \text{ or } x > \frac{7}{5}\right\}$
or $\left(-\infty, \frac{-1}{5}\right) \cup \left(\frac{7}{5}, \infty\right)$ (2-5: pages 51-52)

Unit 3

1. **a.**

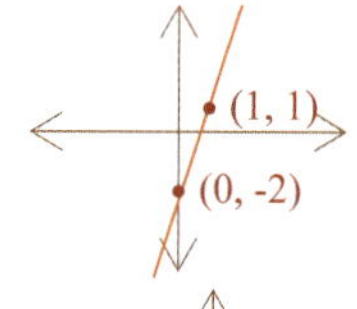

(3-1: page 60)

b.

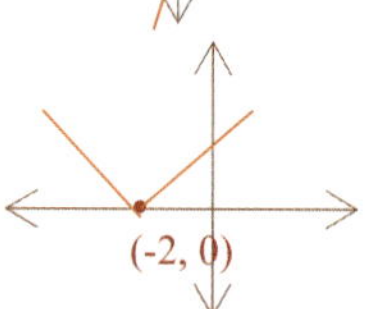

(3-1: page 61)

2. **a.** 52
b. -1 (3-2: page 63)

3. **a.** $5a - 13$
b. 18 (3-2: page 63)

4. $f(2012) \approx 85$ (3-2: page 64)

5. **a.** $\{3, -1, 6, -4\}$
b. $\{4, 6, 3\}$ (3-1: page 66)

6. $\{x \mid x \text{ is a real number and } x \neq 5\}$ or $(-\infty, 5) \cup (5, \infty)$
$\{x \mid x \text{ is a real number and } x \neq \frac{5}{7}\}$ or $(-\infty, \frac{5}{7}) \cup (\frac{5}{7}, \infty)$ (3-3: page 67)

7. **a.** $m = 6, \; b = -15$ (3-4: page 68)
b. $m = \frac{1}{2}$ (3-4: page 70)

8. -125 (3-4: page 70)

9.

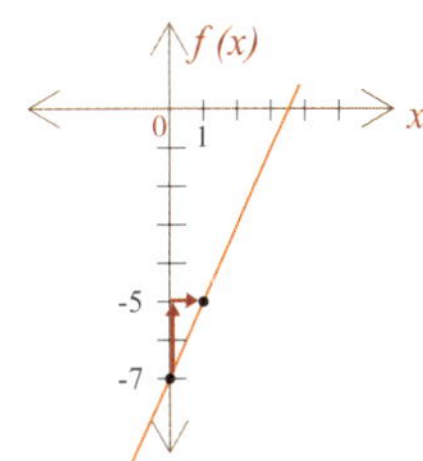

(3-5: page 72)

10. $m_1 = m_2 = \frac{-7}{2}, \quad L_1 \parallel L_2$ (3-5: page 74)

11. $y = -7x + 17$ (3-5: page 76)

12. **a.** $y = \frac{-1}{3}x - \frac{7}{3}, \quad L_1 \parallel L_2$
b. $y = 3x - 9, \quad L_1 \perp L_2$ (3-5: page 77)

13. $f(t) = 20{,}000 - 1{,}000t$, \$15,000

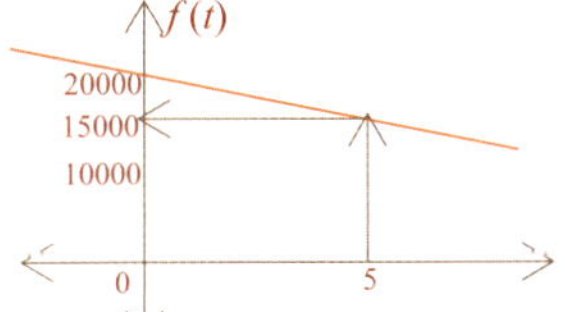

(3-6: page 78)

Unit 4

1. $(x, y) = (1, 1)$

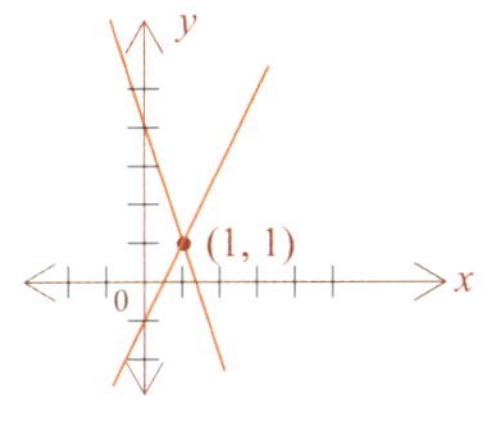

(4-1: page 84)

2. **a.** $x = 1, \; y = 1$ (4-1: page 86)
b. $x = 0, \; y = 6$ (4-1: pages 87-88)

3. $\begin{cases} 2l + 2w = 140 \\ l = 4w + 10 \end{cases}$
$w = 12\text{m}, \; l = 58\text{m}$ (4-2: page 89)

4. **a.**

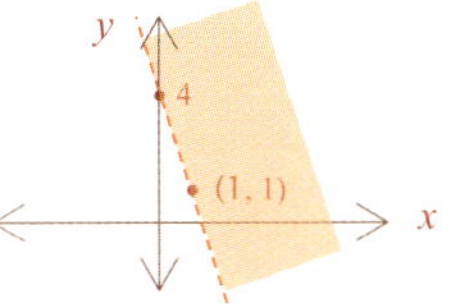

(4-3: page 91)

b.

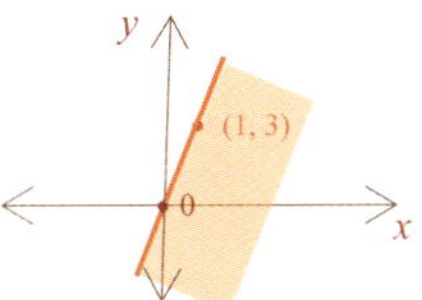

(4-3: page 92)

5.

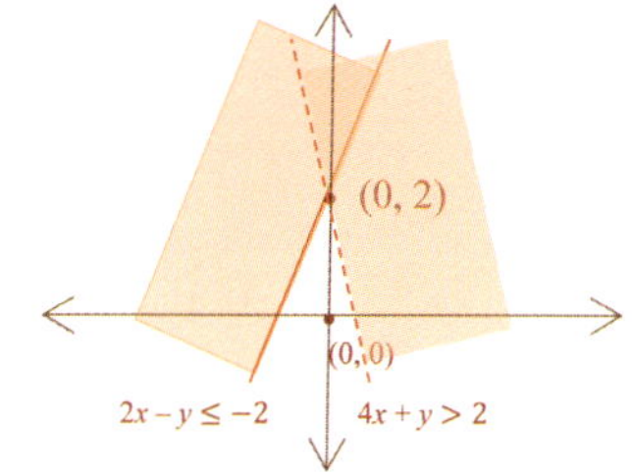

The solution set is the region where the shading overlaps. The vertex is (0, 2). (4-3: page 93)

Unit 5

1. a. $f(40) = 2{,}960$
   b. $f(30) \approx 2{,}500$ (5-1: page 99)

2. a. $7x^3 - 2x^2 - 5x + 6 = 0$
   b. $4x^3 + 7x^2 - x - 2 = 0$ (5-1: page 100)

3. a. $12t^2 - 16t - 3$
   b. $u^3 + 6u^2 + 12u + 8$ (5-2: page 103)

4. $-b(b + 2)$ (5-2: page 103)

5. a. $(2c - d)(2cd + 1)$
   b. $3xy(3x + y)(3x - y)$
   c. $(x + 1)(x - 3)$ (5-3: pages 105-106)
   d. $(x - 3)(3x - 8) = 0$
   e. $(t + \frac{1}{3})^2 = 0$ (5-4: pages 107-108)

6. a. $(2x + 3y)(2x - 3y)$
   b. $2\left[\left(\frac{u}{3} + \frac{v}{5}\right)\left(\frac{u}{3} - \frac{v}{5}\right)\right]$
   c. $(t^2 + 4)(t + 2)(t - 2)$
   d. $(x^2 - 2y^2)(x^4 + 2x^2y^2 + 4y^4)$ (5-5: pages 110-112)

Unit 6

1. a. $\frac{x}{12} - \frac{1}{3}$
   b. b (6-1: page 117)

2. a. $(x + 1)(x + 3)$
   b. $\frac{3(y-1)}{2}$ (6-1: pages 118-119)
   c. $\frac{8}{x}$ (6-2: page 120)

3. $12x^4y^2$ (6-2: page 122)

4. $\frac{2b^2+3b+5}{(b+2)(b-2)}$ (6-2: page 123)

5. $9y - 3 - \frac{12}{y}$ (6-3: page 124)

6. a. $(2y - 1) + \frac{4}{3y}$
   b. $(x^2 + 3x + 3) + \frac{6}{x-1}$ (6-3: pages 125-126)

7. $(2x^2 + x + 7) + \frac{7}{x-2}$ (6-3: page 127)

8. a. $\frac{1+5x}{1+x^2}$
   b. $\frac{y-7}{3y(y+3)(y-2)}$ (6-4: pages 128-129)

9. a. $y = \frac{5}{28}$ (6-5: page 130)
   b. $x = -2$ (6-5: page 131)

10. $t \approx 1.71$ hr (6-6: page 134)

11. \$42 (6-6: page 135)

12. $r = 5$ km/hr (6-6: page 136)

Unit 7

1. **a.** $\sqrt{17}$, $\sqrt{2}$

b. $\{x \mid x \geq -\frac{2}{5}\}$ or $[-\frac{2}{5}, \infty)$ (7-1: page 143)

2. **a.** $\frac{1}{3}$

b. $2u$ (7-1: page 145)

3. -3 (7-1: page 145)

4. **a.** $\frac{-3\,y^{3/4}}{x^{2/3}\,y^{1/5}}$

b. $\frac{v^{3/2}}{u^{9/4}}$

c. $x^9 y^{12}$

d. $\frac{b^4}{a^4}$

e. 1 (7-1: page 147)

5. **a.** $2x^2\sqrt[4]{y^3}$

b. $\sqrt[20]{b}$

c. $\sqrt[12]{u^8 v^6 w^9}$

d. $\sqrt[4]{\frac{a^3b^3}{cd}}$ (7-2: page 148)

6. **a.** $2x\sqrt[3]{7xy}$

b. $2ab\sqrt[4]{b}$ (7-3: page 150)

7. **a.** $y\sqrt{5y}\,(4\sqrt{3} - 3)$ (7-4: page 151)

b. $3a\,(b - 4)$ (7-4: page 152)

c. $\frac{\sqrt[3]{5yx^2}}{x}$ (7-5: page 154)

8. **a.** $\frac{3}{7}$ (7-6: page 156)

b. $x = 7$ (7-6: page 158)

9. $\frac{23}{29} - \frac{14}{29}i$ (7-7: page 163)

Unit 8

1. $y = -5 \pm \sqrt{3}$ or $y \approx \begin{cases} -3.268 \\ -6.732 \end{cases}$ (8-1: page 170)

2. $x = -2 \pm \sqrt{7}$ (8-2: page 171)

3. $A = P(1+r)^t$, $r \approx 5\%$ (8-2: page 173)

4. **a.** $x = 2 \pm \sqrt{3}$

b. $\frac{-3}{2} \pm \frac{1}{2}i$ (8-3: pages 175-176)

5. $w(w+30) = 4{,}000$
$w = 50$m, $l = 80$m (8-4: page 177)

6. $x^2 + x^2 = 10^2$, $x = \sqrt{50} = 5\sqrt{2}$ (8-4: page 178)

7. 11 & 12 (8-4: page 179)

8. $b^2 - 4ac = 91 > 0$: 2 real solutions (8-5: page 181)

9. Let $u = m^{-1}$, $m = \frac{1}{7}$, $m = -1$ (8-6: page 184)

10.

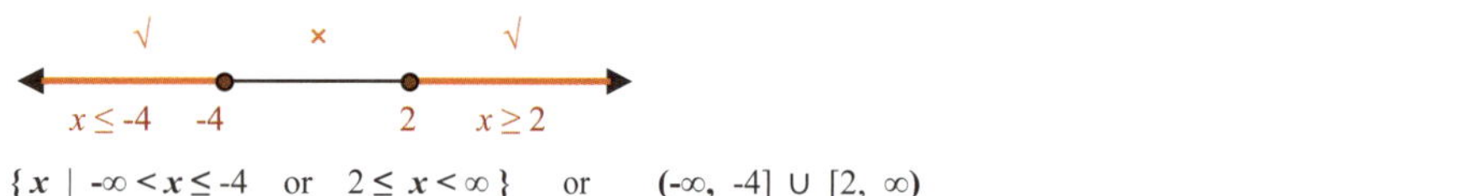

$\{x \mid -\infty < x \leq -4 \text{ or } 2 \leq x < \infty\}$ or $(-\infty, -4] \cup [2, \infty)$ (8-6: page 187)

Unit 9

1. Center: (2, -5), radius $r = 3$ (9-1: page 195)

2.

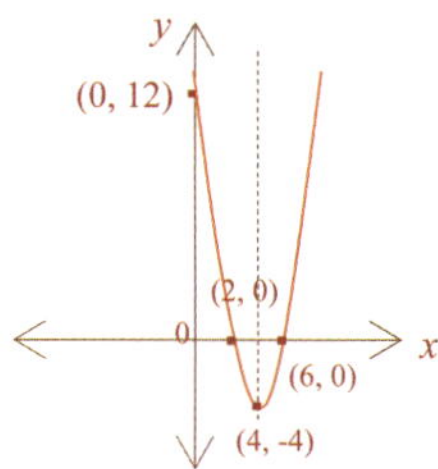

(9-2: page 202)

3.

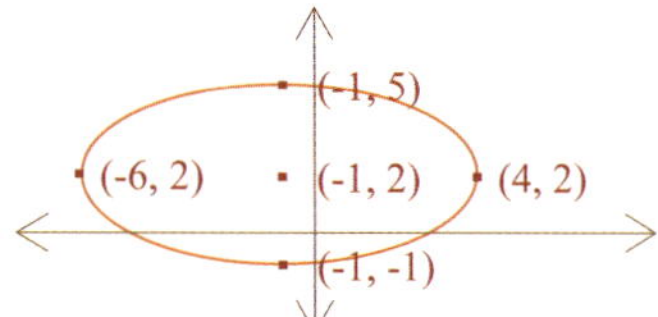

(9-3: page 207)

4. $\frac{y^2}{3^2} - \frac{x^2}{1^2} = 1$

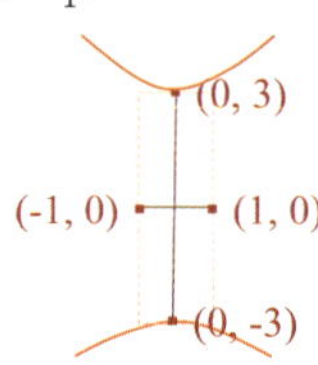

(9-4: page 210)

5. $\frac{(x+3)^2}{5^2} + \frac{(y-1)^2}{2^2} = 1$

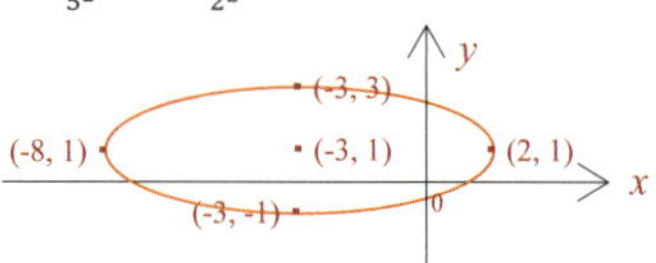

(9-5: pages 214, 207)

6. (-1, 3), $\left(\frac{9}{5}, \frac{-13}{5}\right)$ (9-6: page 216)

Unit 10

1.

$f(x) = 2^{-x}$ $f(x) = 2^x$

(0, 1)

(10-1: page 226)

2. $f(x) = x^3$, $g(x) = 4 - 3x$ (10-2: page 232)

3. $f^{-1}(x) = -\frac{x}{5}$ (10-2: page 234)

4. **a.** $x = 4$
b. $x = -\frac{1}{3}$ (10-3: page 237)

5. 3 (10-3: page 239)

6. **a.** $\log_4 6 + \log_4 x - 5\log_4 y$ (10-4: page 240)
b. $\frac{1}{2}\log_5 a + \frac{1}{4}\log_5 b - \frac{1}{4}\log_5 c$ (10-4: page 242)

7. **a.** ≈ -2.06
b. ≈ 1.35 (10-5: page 245)

8. **a.** $x = \frac{\log 8}{\log 3} \approx 1.89$ (10-5: pages 246-247)
b. $x = \frac{9}{35} \approx 0.26$ (10-6: page 248)

Unit 11

1. 14 (11-1: page 256)

2. $D = -5$, $D_x = -5$, $D_y = 10$, $D_z = 5$, (1, -2, -1) (11-2: pages 260-261)

3. $\begin{bmatrix} 6 & -8 \\ 2 & -4 \end{bmatrix}$ (11-4: page 266)

4. $\begin{bmatrix} -7 \\ 9 \end{bmatrix}$ (11-4: page 273)

5. (1, -2, -1) (11-4: page 274)

Index